The Tragedy
of Sir John French

The Tragedy
of Sir John French

George H. Cassar

Newark
University of Delaware Press
London and Toronto: Associated University Presses

940.54
F874 xc

Associated University Presses
440 Forsgate Drive
Cranbury, NJ 08512

Associated University Presses
25 Sicilian Avenue
London WC1A 2QH, England

Associated University Presses
2133 Royal Windsor Drive
Unit 1
Mississauga, Ontario
Canada L5J 1K5

Library of Congress Cataloging in Publication Data

Cassar, George H.
  The tragedy of Sir John French.

  Bibliography: p.
  Includes index.
  1. World War, 1914–1918—Campaigns—France.
2. French, John Denton Pinkstone, Earl of Ypres,
1852–1925.   3. France—History—German occupation, 1914–
1918.   I. Title.
D548.C28   1984   940.54′21   82-49302
ISBN 0-87413-241-X

86. 3184

For Dr. Alfred G. Bailey
mentor and friend

Contents

Illustrations

Maps

Preface

Given the nature of and the appalling slaughter during the First World War, it is hard even now to avoid emotional judgments. So strong is the sense of horror that it has become fashionable to depict the commanding generals as mindless automatons, unable to deal effectively with problems for which, in retrospect, the solution seemed self-evident. The popular conception is that more intelligent soldiers would have avoided the mistakes that consigned hundreds of thousands of young men to various forms of mutilation on the battlefield.

For unknown reasons British military leaders, notably French and Haig, have come under sharper attack than their counterparts across the Channel. Indeed, one critic entitled his study simply *The Donkeys*. In truth only the most blinkered could deny that the British generals showed a lack of tactical imagination. Whatever their limitations, it is essential to bear a few points in mind. These were the same men who built the BEF, which by all accounts was the best army Britain had ever put in the field. During the war the generals' freedom of action was restricted since the BEF was subordinated to and dependent on the French. They were handicapped by shortages of war material resulting from the nation's unpreparedness in 1914. Finally they had to confront an awesome military machine.

Recently Haig has had his share of defenders who have, at least partially, rehabilitated his reputation. On the other hand, French, although frequently discussed in books relating to the Great War, has not drawn anywhere near the biographical attention that Haig has. In fact there is not a single scholarly, independent assessment of the man. It was largely to fill a gap in the history of the First World War that I chose to write about French. I was also attracted by the disparity between his reputation as a cavalry officer and that as a commander-in-chief. This book, therefore, is not a full-dressed biography of French but a study of him as a soldier and in particular as a commander-in-chief.

A biographer inevitably comes to have personal feelings about his subject and the nature of those feelings should be stated so that the reader may take them into account. At the outset, as a student of the First World War, my attitude towards French was unfavorable but I was determined to be objective. However, I reget to say that before long I had, if anything, formed an even lower opinion of my subject. If I have appeared harsh at times I can only say that I have tried to present an honest appraisal of the historical record.

It would be fatuous to claim that the last word on French has been written. Certainly no single historian, however able and conscientious, can give the whole story. The life and career of a man who held such a position at such a crucial time in his nation's history will be a continuing subject of debate and controversy.

G.H.C.
Ypsilanti, Michigan

Acknowledgments

Many people and institutions through the years have helped in the preparation of this book and it is a pleasure to thank them. I should like at the outset to record my indebtedness to Her Majesty the Queen for her gracious permission to consult the papers of George V in the Royal Archives at Windsor Castle. In this context I am very grateful to Mr. Robert Mackworth-Young, the librarian, and to Miss Jane Langton, for their patience and diligence in pursuing the many requests made of them.

A number of individuals have assisted my attempts to locate documentary material or given me access to papers either that belong to them or are in their possession. My thanks go to Viscount Esher; Lord Haig; Professor Michael Howard; Mr. James Johnston; Lady Patricia Kingsbury; Major Eustace Robb; Mrs. Blair Sperber; Mr. William W. Sturm; and Major Cyril Wilson.

Grateful acknowledgment is also due to the following for the help they have given me in facilitating my researches: Mr. Gordon Phillips, archivist, *The Times* Library; Mr. J. F. Russell, research assistant, National Library of Scotland; Miss Julia Sheppard, former archivist at King's College Library; Mr. J. S. G. Simmons, librarian, All Souls College Library; Mr. R. Suddaby, keeper, Department of Documents, Imperial War Museum; the staff and librarians of the British Museum, Churchill College Library, Eastern Michigan University Library, the House of Lords Record Office, Michigan University Graduate Library, and the Public Record Office.

For permission to quote from documents for which they hold the copyright I am indebted to Mr. Mark Bonham-Carter; Churchill College Library; Viscount Esher; Mr. A. J. Fitzgerald; Lord Haig; Lord Hankey; Imperial War Museum; Mr. James Johnston; Lady Patricia Kingsbury; King's College Library; Major Cyril Wilson, and Mrs. Blair Sperber. Material from the Royal Archives is quoted by gracious permission of Her Majesty the Queen. All quotations from official records in the Public Record Office are reproduced by kind permission of the Controller of Her Majesty's Stationary Office.

Dr. Robert Ward and Mr. Steve Vanover rendered me an inestimable service by drawing nearly all the maps. I am also grateful to Dr. S. R. Williamson, Jr., for permission to reproduce Map 7 from his book *The Politics of Grand Strategy* (Cambridge, Mass: Harvard University Press, 1969) and to Eversley Belfield for permission to reproduce Maps 4 and 5 from his book, *The Boer War* (London: Leo Cooper, 1975).

The events recorded in these pages happened many years ago and in some cases I have not been able to trace the holders of copyright. I hope that anyone whose copyright has been unwittingly infringed will accept my apologies.

It has not been possible to list the names of everyone who has responded kindly to my inquiries but I would like particularly to thank Mr. F. H. P. Barker; Lady Patricia Kingsbury; Mrs. Joan Shivarg; Mr. A. J. P. Taylor, and Lord Waterpark.

I should like to express my appreciation to Eastern Michigan University for giving me release time in 1978–79 to complete my research abroad and also aid from the Faculty Research Fund to defray the cost of the trip.

No less a debt of appreciation is owed by me to Professor Richard Goff and Professor Ira Wheatley, who followed the progress of this work at every stage and contributed greatly to the clarification of many of its ideas. My thanks are likewise due to the following for advice and information of various kinds about my subject: Professor W. D. Briggs; Lieutenant-Colonel (retired) M. L. Chirio; Lieutenant-Colonel (retired) R. H. Cowan; Professor Gilbert Cross; Professor L. B. Gimelli; Professor Dominick Graham; Professor Michael Howard; Professor Roger King; Colonel (retired) K. T. Macek; Professor Walter Moss; Professor Lester Scherer; and Professor Trevor Wilson.

A special note of gratitude goes to Mrs. Margaret Blevins, who typed the entire manuscript and to Ms. Jane Spires, who typed the revisions. Both kept a keen eye towards content and style, correcting errors in grammar, spelling, and meaning.

I hardly need add that no one but the author is responsible for whatever mistakes in fact or judgment may be found in the text.

1

The Victorian Years

Legend has it that Sir John's forebears came over to England after the Norman conquest. If this is the case they subsequently moved to Ireland, where the earliest known document in which their name appears concerns one Walter French, who was Sovereign (Chief Magistrate) of Galway in 1444–45. Prior to the start of the seventeenth century, information on the family is sketchy at best. What little we do know comes chiefly from the Corporation Book of Galway, which recorded the activities of the mayors of the town, an office created in 1485 (sixteen members of the French family served as mayors of Galway). But beginning with Patrick French we can trace the succession through each generation leading to Sir John French.

Born in 1583, Patrick French left Galway to oversee property that he had acquired in Roscommon County. His son John, having been brought up a Protestant, fought in King William's Army and commanded a unit of Enniskillen Dragoons at the Battle of Aughrim. It was another John French who made the decision to quit Ireland. He married Eleonora, daughter of Colonel Pinkstan, and by her had two sons. The youngest, Fleming, came into an estate in Ripple Vale, Kent, when he married his second wife.

John Tracey William French, Fleming's grandson, entered the Royal Navy and reached the rank of commander in 1847. In 1842 he married Margaret Eccles, daughter of a prosperous Glasgow merchant.[1] The couple had six daughters in succession and then on September 28, 1852, a son was born, named John Denton Pinkstone French, the subject of this volume. The commander died in 1854 and his widow, left with the responsibility of bringing up their large family, suffered a mental breakdown, gradually lost her mind, and was committed to an insane asylum in 1860. Consequently, John's early education was superintended by his sisters, in particular by the eldest, Charlotte, who later as Mrs. Despard became well known in the feminist movement. The girls adored their baby brother and pandered to

19

his smallest needs and whims.[2] The absence of firm authority during his childhood marked John's character and in adult life it may have contributed to his sense of uncertainty and his inability to manage his finances and personal life.[3]

The first years of John's life present no remarkable picture. As a child he was headstrong, high-spirited, and full of mischief, though he was somewhat troubled with nervousness. He was fond of playing with toy soldiers and of wearing one of his sisters' nightdresses as a surplice and preaching to his relatives.[4] In short, he appeared to be a very normal and healthy boy with nothing to mark him off from his peers.

At an early age John was sent to a preparatory school at Harrow. He was outgoing and popular but showed no marked aptitude either as a scholar or athlete. Since it was his ambition to follow in his father's profession, he left at the age of thirteen for Eastman's Naval College in Portsmouth. There he went through a brief period of cramming and in his fourteenth year passed the entrance examination for entry into the navy. In 1866 French joined the training ship *Britannia* as a cadet and in due course became a midshipman. However, his inability to bear the great heights of the mastheads, on which midshipmen were expected to perform a large part of their training, settled his fate as a future naval officer.[5] At the age of eighteen French left the navy in order to seek a career in the army.

With that object in mind French tried to obtain a commission through the militia, popularly known as the "back-door," a loophole established for gentlemen unable to qualify for entrance into a military academy. By passing a qualifying test he earned the right to try for a direct commission in the regular army after two militia trainings. In 1870 he began the first of them with the Suffolk Artillery Militia. Four years later, having completed his second militia training, he went up for his direct commission. He failed the first competitive examination, but passed the second and on September 28 was gazetted lieutenant in the Eighth Hussars. The following month he transferred to the Nineteenth Hussars, a unit nicknamed "the Dumpies" because it admitted, and so attracted, shorter men than other cavalry regiments.[6]

History reveals as little on John French the subaltern as it does on John French the midshipman. Nearly all that survives of this period is what his fellow subalterns saw and reported in later years. French is described as being about five feet six inches in height, solidly built, with piercing blue eyes, black hair and a bushy moustache. He is said to have been sensitive, impulsive, hot-tempered, and fearless of personal danger. Records show that he was a good sportsman and excellent rider, adept at polo and steeplechasing.

The professional demands of a young cavalry officer of French's generation were not unduly burdensome. During the drill season, which lasted from April to late August or early September, there were frequent ceremonial parades plus brigade and divisional field days once or twice a month. At the regimental level there was only limited training or instruction and, of course, none during the September-to-March leave period. Reflecting on his early days at Aldershot with the Nineteenth Hussars, French wrote:

> The great idea was to have sleek fat horses and, with the limited allowance of forage, this was not consistent with too much work in the field. On most days in the year the horses were exercised in a "wattering order" parade under the command of the orderly officer. In fact, when I left Aldershot with my regiment in 1874, the permanent requirement in the cavalry was individual good horsemanship, a smart turn-out and good stable management. A highly proficient knowledge of the art of war was not deemed a necessary qualification for the cavalry soldier of that day.[7]

Burning with energy and ambition, French was determined to make a success of his career. He admitted that it was difficult for him to concentrate on his work since in those days the average cavalry subaltern was interested more in sport, women, and partying than in seeking to improve his professional skills. Although French occasionally indulged in such pleasures, his mind was actually never far removed from the problems of soldiering. He was an avid reader and contemporaries note that, while his brother officers were at polo or other afternoon amusements, he would remain in his room and pour over the works of such military writers as von Schmidt and Jomini. French does not appear to have been fond of theoretical works, preferring the less intellectual campaign histories, notably those of Napoleon. By his own admission he was heavily influenced by General Hamley's *The Operations of War,* a textbook that tries to draw lessons from past battles but displays little insight into the significance of modern tactical developments and, as Professor Luvaas has observed, was "better calculated to reaffirm established truths than to discover new ones."[8]

As a young officer who applied himself assiduously to his regimental duties, French caught the attention of his superiors and consequently his advancement proved rapid. In October 1880 he was promoted to captain and in April 1881 he was appointed adjutant to the Northumberland Yeomanry, attaining major's rank just two years later.

In the meantime French made a hasty and ill-advised marriage and within a year or so he was eager to shed his wife. It appears that the marriage was kept secret not only from his brother officers but from his second wife and children as well. French's brother-in-law, John Lydall, was a solicitor and was invaluable in arranging for the dissolution of the union without attracting publicity.[9] Victorian society did not take kindly to divorce and had it leaked out, French's career might have been ruined.

The experience did not sour him on the institution of marriage because in 1880, at the age of 28, he wed a second time. The bride, Eleanora Selby-

Lowndes, was a pretty, mature, level-headed woman whose father was a prosperous country squire. She was ideal for French and he became passionately devoted to her. The couple took a place called "High House" in Morpeth, near Newcastle. Of their five children only three survived, two sons and a daughter. The eldest, John Richard Lowndes, became a successful painter after a hunting accident ended his military career. Edward Gerald Fleming followed a normal career in the army, went out to France in 1915, and was severely wounded. Essex Eleanora devoted much of her efforts to charitable causes, serving as secretary of the Almeric Paget Message Corps during the First World War.

The feeling of contentment and happiness that French enjoyed in his personal life during the early years of his marriage did not carry over to his work with the Yeomanry Hussars. The task of administrating the regiment's personnel was a monotonous one, affording insufficient scope for the employment of his abilities. And yet his sense of frustration did not affect the quality of his work. In fact, the conscientiousness and assiduous care with which he went about his duties were duly acknowledged by the regiment historian.[10]

In 1882 the regular cavalry unit in which French was serving was ordered to embark for Egypt to take part in an expedition aimed at restoring Khedival authority. The previous year an Egyptian nationalist called Arabi had staged a coup d'état but he was unable to restore order and in June 1882 riots broke out in Alexandria in which fifty foreign residents were killed. The British reply was instant. A force under the command of General Wolseley was sent to Egypt. The Nineteenth Hussars were among those selected, embarking at Southampton on August 10.

French was not permitted to accompany his regiment because of his duties with the Northumberland Yeomanry. Since first-hand experience of war is worth months and often years of training, one can understand French's bitter disappointment at being left behind. It is doubtful that he gained much consolation when told that his work at home was of greater value to the army than any service he might perform abroad.

The invasion of Egypt was a model of military efficiency. British landings occurred in a number of places but the main ones were at Port Said at the northern end of the Suez Canal. At dawn on September 13, after a long night march, the British crossed the Egyptian lines and fell upon Arabi's forces from two sides. Although caught completely by surprise, the Egyptians fought back with reckless courage. The battle of Tel-el-Kebir lasted about thirty minutes. At the end Arabi's army was no more, some 10,000 lay dead or wounded, and the remnant streamed across the desert in every direction.

The Nineteenth Hussars played a conspicuous role in the battle that destroyed Arabi's power and brought the campaign to a close. Once affairs seemed to be settling down in Egypt the Hussars received orders to get

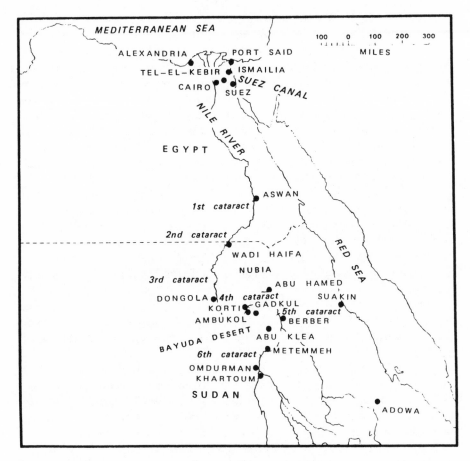

EGYPT AND NORTHERN SUDAN

ready to return to England.[11] But to the south extraordinary events were taking place that would alter all arrangements and provide French with an opportunity for active service.

For over half a century the Sudan had been under Egypt's oppressive rule and the collapse of Khedival authority in 1881–82 let loose a revolt that quickly assumed the strength of a tornado. The leader of the rebellion was Mohammed Ahmed, a former slave trader who proclaimed himself to be the Mahdi, or Moslem Messiah. On November 5, 1883, 10,000 Egyptian troops under the command of a British officer, Hicks Pasha, were trapped and butchered in the desert. The Khedive had not the means to reconquer the Sudan alone but the Gladstone government refused to be drawn into further adventures. To placate Egyptian feeling, however, the prime minister agreed to send a suitable British officer to organize the evacuation of the remaining Egyptian garrisons in the Sudan. The man chose for the mission was General Charles Gordon, a fearless evangelical who had gained wide popularity in England through his military exploits.

After arriving at Khartoum in February 1884, Gordon exceeded his orders and began formulating plans, not for withdrawal, but for the destruction of the Mahdi and the subjugation of the Sudan. While Gordon sent constant telegrams to Cairo urging an official change of policy, the Mahdi and his vast armies advanced, began to invest Khartoum, and cut the telegraph lines. By May Gordon was in grave danger but the government thought it unnecessary to send troops to his assistance. Finally in August public pressure compelled a change of mind and an expedition was authorized with General Wolseley in command.

By this time French, his term as adjutant of the Northumberland Yeomanry having expired, rejoined the Nineteenth Hussars in Egypt. During his absence many changes had taken place in the regiment. Under the inspired leadership of Colonel Percy Barrow the Nineteenth had been transformed into a first-class unit. The men had an average of seven years' service and most of them had seen action at Tel-el-Kebir and subsequently at Suakin.

The Nineteenth was to be included in the expeditionary force that was being assembled. On October 25, 1884, three squadrons of the regiment under Colonel Barrow left Cairo and, after a brief stay at Wadi Halfa, reached the forward base at Korti.

Wolseley's original intention had been to follow the longer but less hazardous route along the Nile river. On November 4, however, a message from Gordon revealed that Khartoum was completely surrounded and dangerously low on supplies. Wolseley was now faced with the necessity of having to speed up progress. Accordingly he made plans to take the bulk of his force by river to attack Berber and to send General Stewart with a flying column across the Bayuda Desert to Metemmeh, where Gordon's steamers would be waiting to carry them upstream to Khartoum. The Nineteenth Hussars furnished one squadron to the river column and two squadrons to the desert column. Both Barrow and French accompanied the latter force.

Between Korti and Metemmeh lay 186 miles of barren and hostile country. Since Stewart did not possess a sufficient number of camels to carry the supplies and the 1,600 officers and enlisted men in one rush he decided to form an intermediate depot at Gadkul. The main body of troops started out from Korti on December 30 and reach Gadkul three days later. Stewart returned to Korti for the remainder of his troops and stores and on January 14 the column was ready to resume the march to Metemmah. Early on the 16th the Hussars, who were ahead of the main force, ran into a band of dervishes in the hills near the Abu Klea wells. French with a small patrol pursued a number of the Arabs into the gorge leading to the wells and captured one of them. But he was compelled to release his prisoner when enemy horsemen appeared and threatened to cut him off. French rejoined

Barrow at the entrance of the gorge. Here the Hussars dismounted in order to keep the way open for the column. The Arabs made an attempt to overwhelm the Hussars' position but they were easily beaten back.[12]

The Hussars had come in touch with the scouting party of a large Arab army that was camped between the British column and the wells. As the news did not reach Stewart until late in the afternoon he decided to sit tight until the next morning. The men were set to work to build a *zeriba* (an enclosure made of stones and thorns) to resist a possible attack. But the enemy did nothing beyond occasional sniping from a distance.

On the morning of the 17th, after vainly waiting for the dervishes to take the initiative, Stewart ordered his men to form a square, preparatory to an advance. Simultaneously he sent the Nineteenth Hussars to the left to keep the enemy on the hills from working around to the rear of the *zeriba*. At about 10 A.M. the square began to move forward. The little band advanced slowly, pausing frequently to answer the fire from the hills and to permit the sluggish camels to close up. The terrain was rugged, marked by rocky hillocks and ravines that concealed the full strength of the enemy. Without warning, a horde of dervishes, estimated to be 5,000 strong, rose from a fold in the ground and rushed at the advancing column. The Arabs hurled themselves against the rear of the square with such force and ferocity that they penetrated it right up to the line of the camels. The troops on the right and front of the square turned around and directed a withering volley at the main body of the attackers, who were seeking to follow up the success gained by their comrades. This concentrated fire broke the momentum of the charge. The British soldiers, some fighting nearly back-to-back, rallied and closed the gap. All the Mahdists inside the square were killed after savage hand-to-hand combat. The assailants outside, their fanatical energy expended, turned and retreated.[13]

The Nineteenth Hussars, who had supported the beleaguered column with carbine fire, followed and cut off stragglers. Because their horses were exhausted from thirst and hard riding, they did not attempt to engage large bodies of the retreating enemy. When the dervishes disappeared behind the hills, Barrow and his men pushed on and occupied the wells.

In this brief battle, 1,100 Arab bodies, out of a force of some 10,000, were counted in close proximity to the square. British losses were 74 killed, including Colonel Burnaby, the second in command. After burying the dead and caring for the wounded the British force marched to the wells, where it slaked its great thirst with muddy water that would have been declared unfit under ordinary conditions.

The next day the advance on Metemmeh was continued with the Nineteenth in the vanguard. All night the column plodded through dense scrub and wild country that would have been difficult to traverse even in broad daylight. The men were exhausted, many falling asleep and dropping like logs or straying from the column. Stores fell off the camels and had to be haphazardly repacked. The sun finally came to the aid of the British and allowed them to see the way. At 7:30 A.M., from the top of a gravelly ridge, the Nile was sighted. But Stewart could not reach the river without further fighting, for another large force of Mahdists barred the route.

While a *zeriba* was hastily being constructed, the enemy opened a desultory fire and a stray bullet mortally wounded Stewart. The command devolved upon Sir Charles Wilson, an officer well known for his intelligence work but without experience in desert warfare. Wilson's first objective was to capture Metemmeh or establish a post on the Nile. To do so he felt it necessary to leave the wounded and bulk of the stores in the *zeriba*. The *zeriba* was in such obvious danger that a sizable portion of the force had to be left to protect it. The Nineteenth Hussars, their horses too spent for further work, were among the units left behind.

Wilson set off at 3:00 P.M. with about 900 men, advancing slowly in square formation. Ahead he could see the great clouds of Arabs who were gathering on a hill behind a line of green and white banners. As the column neared the ridge many men fell from the enemy's intensified fire. Suddenly, the firing ceased and a horde of 800 screaming tribesmen, led by emirs on magnificent horses, bore down on the British ranks. In the square the men waited, calmly and confidently, and when the Mahdists got to within 200 yards, the call "commence firing" was given. They fired in volleys at the order, one rank after another, never faltering and in perfect time. The target was one that even the most inexpert could hardly miss. And yet the dervishes came on, row upon row, crumbling into heaps in the face of the murderous fire, their successors trampling over their bodies to carry the standards a few painful yards closer to the infidels before they too were cut down. The slaughter was so great that the tribesmen in the rear of the charge turned and fled, leaving 300 of their dead on the field. Although British casualties during the day had been heavy (23 dead and 98 wounded), not a single soldier was killed or wounded in repelling the assault.[14]

During the remaining three miles Wilson encountered no further opposition, reaching the banks of the river at Gubat, a little to the south of Metemmeh, in the evening. The strain of the long march, the two battles, and the losses incurred were all forgotten when Gordon's streamers were sighted the next day. The men broke out in loud cheers and rushed down to the river to greet them. The captain of the small fleet had brought with him six volumes of Gordon's journals. From the final entry made on December 14 it was apparent that Khartoum was in desperate straits. The obvious urgency was cause for Wilson to proceed at once. Yet three days were spent in overhauling the steamers' engine and in reconnoitering the Nile both north and south of Metemmeh. Satisfied that all was well, Wilson started upstream for Khartoum on January 24, taking with him some 200 troops in two steamers.

The vessels surmounted all the difficulties of the river and as they came within sight of the city on January 28 they ran into a gauntlet of heavy fire from guns and rifles on both banks of the Nile. Jeering Arabs shouted from the shore that Khartoum had fallen and that Gordon was dead. Wilson turned his glass on the palace. There was no flag flying about it. On the sandspit close to the city swarms of tribesmen had collected, waving a battle flag of the Mahdi and capering and gesticulating in defiance. The help that Gordon had called for many months ago arrived belatedly. Two days earlier the Mahdists had stormed the city and killed Gordon. There was now no point in attempting a landing. Thus the two steamers turned about and headed downstream.

The Nineteenth Hussars were at Gubat with the main column when news of Gordon's death arrived. The effect on the men was devastating: some stood still with frozen expressions on their faces, others wept unashamedly, but all were bitter over the knowledge that their sacrifices and labors had been in vain. For the next several days the dispirited little force fortified its position, believing that hostile reinforcements were on their way from Khartoum and that an attack might be expected. The Nineteenth were employed to scout at short distances from the camp and occasionally they engaged in skirmishes with the outlying pickets of the enemy. On February 11 General Redvers Buller arrived to take command of the column with orders to retire to Abu Klea.

As the day broke on February 14 the British left Gubat, followed by the enemy, who kept up a harassing fire from long range. The men marched ten miles one day and sixteen the next before reaching Abu Klea, which was to have been occupied permanently with a view to a second advance on Khartoum in the autumn. But Buller found it impossible to carry out his instructions. His transport facilities were in a deplorable state and his position was threatened by the advance of a large dervish army. Buller was compelled to retire quickly rather than risk having his retreat cut off.

On February 16 the Nineteenth Hussars started out in the direction of Korti, leaving thirteen of their numbers under French with Buller at Abu Klea. A week later the last of the desert column left Abu Klea. During the withdrawal French displayed courage and resourcefulness in covering the rear of the column. Time and time again he and his small band surprised and scattered enemy scouting parties and employed ruses to misdirect the pursuit. All those who left records of the march have paid generous tribute to French and his men.[15] Buller himself wrote:

I wish expressly to remark on the excellent work done by the small detachment of the 19th Hussars, both during our occupation of Abu

Klea and during our retirement. Each man has done the work of ten, and it is not too much to say that the force owes much to Major French and his 13 troopers.[16]

Early in March the desert column straggled back to Korti, exhausted and in disorder. Once reunited, the army proceeded to summer quarters in the province of Dongola. Towards the end of April the British government announced that it no longer intended to advance on Khartoum or undertake any further offensive operations in the Sudan. Accordingly orders were issued for the withdrawal of the troops. On June 22 the headquarters of the Nineteenth evacuated Dongola, the last of the force to leave for Lower Egypt, and by August 14 the regiment was once again reunited in Cairo.[17]

French was one of a handful of officers to emerge from the ill-fated expedition with an enhanced military reputation. He was mentioned in the dispatches and given the Egyptian medal with clasps "Abu Klea" and "Nile 1884–85" and the Khedive's star. In addition he was promoted lieutenant colonel, so that he returned to England as second in command of the Nineteenth.

There followed five years of quiet routine at home, during which French, stimulated by his experiences in the Sudan and by the example of his late commander, the brilliant Colonel Barrow,[18] devoted much thought to the training of the cavalry. In February 1889 he succeeded Lieutenant-Colonel Combe as commander of the Nineteenth Hussars. As a practical officer French employed the newly instituted system of squadron training with the result that his regiment became famous for its efficiency in the army.

In 1891 the Nineteenth went to India where French became staff officer to General Sir George Luck, inspector-general of cavalry. In that capacity he participated in the introduction of many innovations in cavalry training associated with that officer's name. One way to increase the efficiency of the cavalry was to organize extensive maneuvres. French much impressed Luck by the manner in which he coordinated troops dispersed over a wide area, allotting particular objectives to the various units, and bringing the entire exercise to a brilliant conclusion.

But governments do not always recognize or compensate those who excel at their work. Upon expiration of his term as commander of the Nineteenth Hussars, French returned to England and was placed on half-pay.[19] The ensuing months must have been unbearable. Here was a highly ambitious man possessing enormous drive, devoted to his profession, and of proven ability, suddenly finding himself unemployed. French was neither wealthy nor comfortably off and the drop from full to half-pay also created financial difficulties. Worse still, unless he obtained a new appointment before the end of the half-pay period, he would face compulsory retirement.

French spent most of his time during this terribly irksome phase of his career in playing with the children, reading, and going for long walks in the nearby woods. In 1894 he commanded a brigade in the cavalry maneuvres in Berkshire. French deployed his force in numbers of lines that gave him considerably more flexibility in attack than the heavy angle line favored by his opponent. He was seen as the unofficial winner and emerged from the exercise with credit. At the conclusion he gave a lecture, stressing the importance of firepower in future cavalry warfare. The core of his remarks were recorded by a journalist who was present:

> There is no subject upon which more misconception exists than as regards the real role of the cavalry in warfare. My conception of the duties and functions of the mounted arm is not to cut and to hack and to thrust at your enemy wherever and however he may be found. The real business of cavalry is so to manoeuvre your enemy as to bring him within effective range of the corps artillery of your own side for which a position suitable for battle, and commanding a field for an infantry engagement if necessary, would previously have been selected.[20]

At long last, when the half-pay period was drawing to a close, French received a call to serve under his old chief, Sir George Luck, at the War Office. He was ecstatic over the appointment. His army career was again open to him. Forgotten were the past months of frustration and anxiety as he prepared to take up his new duties.

Through most of the nineteenth-century British military leaders essentially believed that the function of cavalry was, as Sir Baker Russell[21] tersely put it, "to look pretty in time of peace and to get killed in time of war." This meant that the cavalry was expected in quarters to act and look smart; and in the field, besides performing daring deeds at moments of crisis, to occupy the honorable and dangerous position of a protective screen for the army, whether advancing or retiring. Thus cavalry training was restricted to drill and parade movements with occasional field maneuvres. But the improvement in firearms, combined with the lessons learned from the Franco-Prussian War, brought about a recognition of the need for a more advanced system of training and for closer cooperation between the branches of the service. The task of reorganizing the cavalry arm fell to the lot of Sir George Luck, recently appointed inspector general of cavalry in Great Britain. Mindful of French's admirable work in India, Luck appointed him assistant adjutant-general at the Horse Guards and made him responsible for producing a new edition of the *Cavalry Drill Book*.

The manual, issued in two volumes in 1896, was a distinct improvement on its predecessors. It was more practical and more aware of modern developments, especially the effect of the improved firearms. Attention was given to the importance of scouting and dismounted duties of the cavalry, as well as the need for exercises to simulate wartime situations. However, some traditional ideas on the role of the cavalry still persisted. Above all, undue emphasis was placed on the importance of the cavalry charge.

French was then charged with putting into force many of the prescribed changes. Chief among these was the introduction of the squadron system that he had first established in his own regiment some years before. This involved grouping three regiments into a brigade under the command of a staff colonel who was entirely responsible for their administration and training.

French was unhappy at the Horse Guards, in spite of the important reforms that he had helped to inaugurate. He chafed at the sedentary nature of his duties and at the tedious, interminable disentangling of knots that is part and parcel of higher administration. He was a man who enjoyed open-air work and vigorous physical exercise. It was with a feeling of relief that French left London in 1897 to take up the command of the Second Cavalry Brigade at Canterbury.[22]

There is little of special interest to record in respect to his command during this period. One incident, however, deserves to be mentioned, for it enabled French to apply and demonstrate the superiority of theories he had long advocated. In the maneuvres of 1898 at Salisbury, French was chosen to lead Buller's force. His opponent in the simulated campaign was General Talbot, an older officer who adhered to traditional methods.

French dismayed observers by the amount of time that he took in laying out plans and doing reconnaissance work. But events proved that he was right. By the extreme mobility of his force he continually checked and out-maneuvred his adversary, appearing where he was least expected and of-fering opposition where it was least anticipated. Near the end of the exercise French surprised several batteries of the enemy's horse artillery. He forced them to dismount and claimed the entire body as his prisoners, a claim that was upheld by the umpires.[23]

There were many officers in the audience who concluded that French's success was due to good fortune rather than sound tactics. They believed that he had been rash and imprudent and that in actual warfare such recklessness was apt to lead to disaster. Some even spoke of French as being a dangerous person, to whom it would be unwise to entrust any important command. But evidently the higher authorities thought otherwise, because a few months later French was given command of the First Cavalry Brigade at Aldershot with the temporary rank of major-general.

By making him a general at the young age of forty-seven, fate had been kind to John French. Although his career had advanced rapidly, the qualities that had brought such distinction were known only in a restricted circle. There had been no limelight that, for a soldier, can be achieved only through distinguished service in periods of conflict. However, active duty is dangerous, not only to life but to professional reputation. Many excellent peacetime officers have come to abrupt and bitter ends under the strain of war. For French the hard test lay immediately ahead.

2

Winning Laurels in South Africa

At the time that French was posted to Aldershot, then commanded by General Sir Redvers Buller, it seemed likely that the British would be forced into some military action against the Boer republic of the Transvaal. In June when negotiations broke off, the British government decided that if armed action became necessary, a force of three infantry divisions and one cavalry division under Buller would be sent to South Africa. What the authorities did not consider then was the problem of time and distance. The mobilization of troops, their transportation and deployment overseas, would require at least three months and in the interval the colony of Natal was extremely vulnerable to invasion by the Boers. Thus in July Whitehall arranged to send a contingent of 10,000 men to reinforce the Natal garrison. These troops were drawn principally from India and Malta and were intended to supplement Buller's force, which still had not been mobilized.

In mid-September French, on Buller's recommendation,[1] was appointed to command the British cavalry in Natal. He boarded the Union Castle liner *Norman* at Southampton on September 23. He shared a cabin with his principal staff officer, Major Haig, on the top deck. French first met Haig in 1895 and over the next few years a very genuine feeling of amity and respect had developed between the two men. French's military career might have ended before the South African war had it not been for Haig's assistance. French, it appears, had suffered serious financial reverses through unwise speculation in the South Africa gold market. In May 1899 his creditors were so pressing that he would have been obliged to leave the service if Haig, who was a man of substance, had not provided him with a loan of £2,000. A grateful French subsequently presented Haig with a small gold flask bearing the inscription: "A very small memento, my dear dear Douglas, of our long and tried friendship proved 'in Sunshine and in Shadow,' J.F. 1902."[2]

French had no way of getting news at sea, for these were the days before wireless. When he reached Cape Town on October 10 he was anxious to know what had occurred in the meantime. On the previous day the Transvaal president, Paul Kruger, had issued an ultimatum demanding that the British withdraw their troops and stop interfering in his country's domestic affairs. French did not think that the British government would submit to Kruger's insolent demands. He was right and the war began after the ultimatum expired on October 11. The Orange Free State, no party to the quarrel, threw in its lot with the Transvaal.

Although the authorities in Whitehall had realized the possible consequences of their strained relations with the Transvaal, the outbreak of hostilities found the British Army woefully unprepared. There was no general staff like the Prussian model to plan and coordinate strategy. British training had severely neglected such fundamentals as tactics, marksmanship, and self-reliance. Emphasis was placed on courage and discipline, and indeed, at the beginning, volley fire was still standard practice. Troops in close order, shoulder to shoulder, might destroy spear-waving dervishes with volleys of rifle fire, but they presented a fixed target to an enemy that possessed modern arms and fought from cover.

On the other hand, the Boers were mainly mounted, tough, resourceful, and were fighting across country they knew intimately. They were experts in the use of ground and when natural protection was absent they were adept at providing themselves with artificial cover. Armed with the clip-loading German Mauser, which was superior to the single-shot English Lee-Metford, they had a high standard of marksmanship. Their senior commanders tended to lack initiative and imagination but some of their junior officers were magnificent leaders by any standard. Discipline, unlike the British Army, was lax. The Boers thought of themselves as civilians under arms and took leave or slipped off home whenever they chose. During a crisis they were apt to melt away, since dying was not part of their philosophy.[3]

Initially the Boers deployed 50,000 men against 15,000 British, many of whom were isolated in Ladysmith, Kimberley, and Mafeking. Their best course was to contain the immobilized British garrisons in these towns and invade Cape Colony in strength, raising the Dutch inhabitants as they went. Time was not on their side. They needed to win a series of early victories to dishearten the British and drive them to negotiate a settlement. As it happened they let the British off the hook. They were distracted by the unnecessary sieges of Kimberley and Mafeking and by an obsession to gain Durban (in Natal) as a seaport.

French was still in Cape Town when he received a cable from the War Office ordering him to proceed immediately to Natal. Reembarking on the liner *Norman* on October 14 and five days later landing at Durban, 830

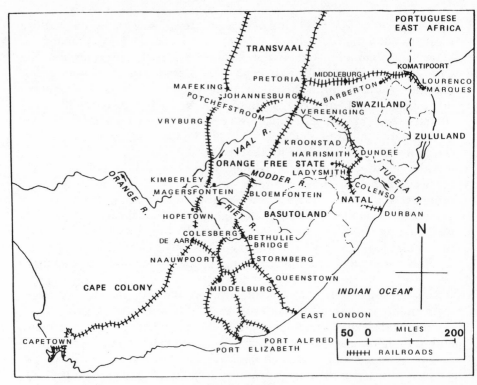

SOUTH AFRICA

miles farther east, French went on by night train to Ladysmith and arrived the next morning. He reported at once to Sir George White, commander of the British forces in Natal, and was placed in charge of the cavalry.

Earlier White, against his better judgment, had allowed Major-General Penn Symons' brigade to defend the rich coalfields in the vicinity of Dundee. Before dawn on October 20, a Boer unit under Luke Meyer surprised and routed a British battalion holding Talana Hill, two miles east of Dundee. Symons, who believed that his brigade could dispose of any numbers of burghers, launched an ill-advised counterattack. Courageously in the lead, Symons fell mortally wounded but his men fought their way to the summit of the hill. It was a pyrrhic victory. The British had not only suffered 500 casualties but were in danger of being out-flanked by superior forces. The new British commander, Brigadier-General J. H. Yule, decided to move the remnant of the brigade back to Ladysmith.[4] The Boers were slow to react but a raiding party led by General Kock did cut the railway line at Elandslaagte, half way betwen Dundee and Ladysmith. It was this incident that gave French his first opportunity to fight a Western enemy.

At 11:00 A.M. on October 20, French, having assembled a small mounted force, moved off to reconnoitre the area. French was warned not to go too far and after capturing several members of an enemy patrol, he returned in the evening. Information from the prisoners and other sources seemed to suggest that it would not be difficult to restore communications with Dundee. White therefore ordered French to clear the Boers from Elandslaagte.[5]

At 4:00 A.M. French's mounted column started, moving north along the Newcastle road until it drew up on the higher ground southwest of Elandslaagte station. French sent patrols ahead on either side of the line. A slight mist covered the ground and, as it lifted, parties of Boers could be seen about the station and colliery buildings and over the yellow veld. French turned the guns of his Natal Volunteer Field Battery against the town. A round from the seven-pounders inadvertently hit the Boer field hospital but another scored a direct hit on the tin outbuildings of the station, evicting the defenders. The latter leaped on their ponies and galloped away to join their compatriots, who had taken a defensive position on a horseshoe-shaped line of kopjes (small hills) some two miles to the south. The Imperial Light Horse then entered the station yard, ferreted out the remaining Boers, and released a trainload of British prisoners captured the previous day.[6]

Suddenly the Boers among the kopjes came to life. Shells from their Krupp guns dropped in rapid succession into the British battery and smashed an ammunition wagon. British gunners returned the fire but could not inflict any damage on the enemy since their pieces were outranged by over 500 yards. French considered his present force too inadequate to dislodge the Boers from the hills. Wisely he decided to withdraw his men and guns out of range and call for help.

White at once sent up two cavalry squadrons with two batteries of artillery as well as three infantry battalions under Colonel Ian Hamilton. By mid-afternoon the last of the reinforcements had reached French. French's force now consisted of 3,000 infantry (Manchesters, Devonshires, Gordon Highlanders) and mounted troops (Lancers, Dragoons, Imperial Light Horse), outnumbering the enemy by about three to one. Around 4:00 P.M., as the rain clouds gathered in the sky, White arrived from Ladysmith.[7] He left French in command and watched the progress of the battle from a hilltop behind the British lines.

The British plan of attack was remarkably simple. The Devonshires were to assault the line of kopjes frontally, while the Gordons and Manchesters worked around the curve of the horseshoe to roll up the enemy line from the south. The cavalry would protect both flanks and be ready when the moment came for the pursuit.

The light was fading rapidly owing to the approaching storm and so after a mere half-hour's artillery bombardment Hamilton received orders to send in the infantry. First to go were the Devonshires who advanced, not

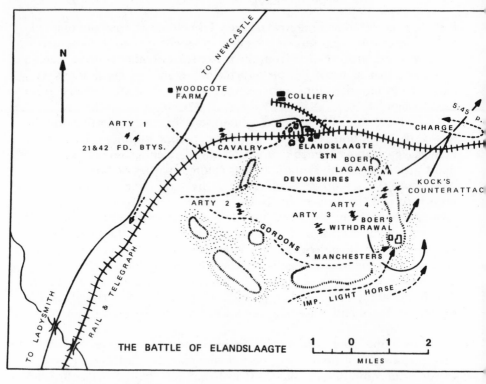

THE BATTLE OF ELANDSLAAGTE

shoulder-to-shoulder as was the current practice in the British Army, but in open formation. Enemy guns opened fire but most of their projectiles went high or burst in the spaces between the men. The Devonshires sustained light casualties until they came within 1,200 yards of the ridge and ran into a hail of bullets. They paused to return the fire, taking advantage of such cover as was provided by ant-hills and stones. Although the accuracy of the Boers increased, the Devonshires pressed on steadily and at length gained a shallow ravine some 800 yards from the crest of the ridge. Here they halted to await the development of the flank attack.

To the south the Manchesters and Gordons rounded the bend of the horseshoe where they were joined by the dismounted Imperial Light Horse. As the men entered into a depression the storm broke in a blinding torrent of rain. The shower lasted only about ten minutes but it gave the troops perfect cover until they reached the boulders at the base of the ridge. Then upon command wave after wave of men swept up to the skyline. The air whistled with Mauser bullets as the soldiers stumbled forward over the rocks and bodies of their comrades. Men stopped, fired from cover, and rose to rush another few yards. The line of advance was dotted with khaki-clad bodies, some still in death, others writhing in agony. As the British clustered to cut gaps in the wire fences they were mowed down in batches. However, the intensity of the Boer fire cleared a way and the British forces continued up the slope. The defenders appeared to be wavering when a handful of Germans[8] emerged from among the farm buildings and flung themselves recklessly against the British right. The Imperial Light Horse shot them down almost to a man. Still, this diversion put new life into the defenders and in the fading light the British drive was halted.

At this moment Hamilton, having directed the Devonshires to move forward again, scrambled towards the front of the line with many men who had held back. He shouted for a bugler and ordered the "charge" to be sounded. With fixed bayonets, shouting and cheering, the British infantry surged forward and cleared the crest, overrunning the still-smoking guns and killing the frock-coated burghers who had served them. As the British reached the laager (military encampment) a small group of Boers held up a white flag and Hamilton called for the "cease fire." The parties began to reform as if on maneuvres and, for a few minutes, there was a lull in the action. Suddenly there was a furious burst of musketry and forty or fifty Boers, who had lain hidden below the rear of the crest, dashed up the slope, emptying their magazines point blank into the unsuspecting British soldiers crowded on the top. The British reeled and fell back in confusion and it seemed that the ridge, won with such gallantry, was about to be lost. Hamilton sprang forward to rally his disconcerted men, shouting wildly that help was at hand. French himself rode up to the front and everywhere the officers tried to stem the panic. The retreat was stopped. The men charged forward as two companies of Devonshires came over the crest to the left. In a wild three minutes the combined assault cleared the summit for a second time.

Most of the Boer survivors (only a few surrendered) mounted their ponies and headed north. East of Elandslaagte station, the Dragoons and the Lancers waited and watched the Boers stream ragged across the veld, many within three hundred yards of their position. Lances leveled and sabers drawn, they walked their horses over the rise that had concealed them. On hearing the command "gallop," the troopers thundered down the slope and crashed into the panic-stricken burghers. Some of the Boers tried to defend themselves by bringing their rifles to bear; others threw themselves on the ground and begged for mercy. The majority of Boers sought to break away but their little ponies were no match for the big striding cavalry. Because the Boers had violated a flag of truce the British showed no mercy. In one instance two Boers riding on a pony were pierced by a single thrust of a lance; in another a young Boer prisoner was found to have received sixteen lance wounds. For a mile and a half the cavalry rode through the Boer fugitives, hacking and spearing. Then they rallied and galloped back to complete the havoc. During the second gallop the cavalry began to take groups of prisoners. Only the onset of darkness prevented the British from wiping out the entire retreating force.[9]

After the battle was over the British troops bivouacked on the position that they had won. The action had proved costly to both sides. British casualties were 55 killed and 205 wounded; Boer losses were 46 killed, 105 wounded, and 181 missing or taken prisoner. The Boer leader, General Kock, was found fatally wounded and carried into Ladysmith.

Elandslaagte, French believed, was the turning point in his career and its anniversary was frequently acknowledged in his diary and in letters to friends. It would not be unfair to say, as some critics have, that French had been favored by unusual good fortune:[10] the presence of an infantry commander, Ian Hamilton, who had not only deployed his men skillfully but whose courage on the battlefield at a crucial moment may have been decisive; the thunderstorm that had helped the infantry to advance; and the failing light, which shielded the cavalry charge. Still, French did contribute significantly to the success of the attack. His tactical plan was sound, he effectively coordinated the three arms (artillery, infantry, and cavalry), and he was on the scene when most needed. In short, Elandslaagte was won through a rare combination of admirable leadership and good luck. Had the British in the early months won several more victories like Elandslaagte, the war might never have assumed the proportions that it did.

When White returned to Ladysmith on the evening of the battle he was informed that Boer columns were approaching the city from the northwest. He therefore decided to abandon Elandslaagte. French's force withdrew early next morning. Lack of preparation and fear of a Boer attack turned the retreat into a rout. The British, having just won a battle, behaved as though they had lost it and in their haste to fall back on Ladysmith, they abandoned large quantities of captured stores, arms, and ammunition. What was even stranger was the abandonment of thirty or forty Boer prisoners, who were simply left to wander back to their units.

White was now faced with the problem of having to cover the return of Yule's brigade from Talana. At the height of the rainy season Yule had been forced to take an indirect route, going over nearly impassable roads and dangerously high rivers.[11] Before reaching Ladysmith he had to pass close to Rietfontein. There, on the morning of the 24th, White and a 5,000-man army held off the pursuing Boers. The cavalry played only a minor role in the action, which was essentially an artillery duel. At midday, having learned that Yule's column was safely through, White pulled back and returned to Ladysmith.[12]

During the next few days French's cavalry reconnaissances indicated the location of the enemy forces converging on Ladysmith. On the east side the Transvaalers were about to occupy Long Hill, five miles from the city, where they could join hands with the Orange Free State contingent advancing from the northwest. By the 28th White had made up his mind to launch a large-scale attack on the Boer forces before they could complete their investment of the city. His plan called for Colonel Grimwood, supported by French's cavalry, to swing north and attack the Boer flank on Long Hill and thence Pepworth. To cut off the Transvaalers' line of retreat White sent a column under Lieutenant Colonel Carleton to occupy a pass called Nicholson's Nek. The plan was complicated and White's instructions were so vague that at times it was difficult to understand what he wanted done.

The ensuing battle of Ladysmith, fought on October 30, was an unmitigated disaster. On the left flank Carleton, having started late, decided to spend the night on Tchrengula Mountain, two miles short of his goal. During the ascent of the hill the mules stampeded and ran off with the mountain guns and spare ammunition. The noise, increased by panic firing by some of the men, alerted the Boers in the area. When dawn broke

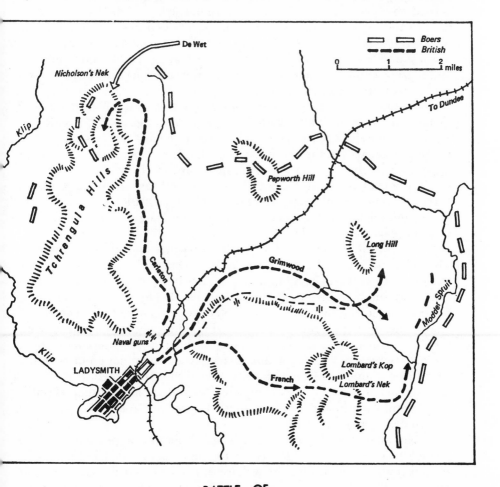

BATTLE OF LADYSMITH

Carleton faced an enemy not only superior in numbers but in a commanding position. Stalked on all sides, the British were driven back to the end of the plateau and ultimately forced to surrender.

The main attack also encountered difficulties. White had misjudged the extent of the Boer left, with the result that Grimwood's column was itself outflanked. French was supposed to protect the right of the infantry but he held his men back too far, ready to take up the pursuit should the tide of battle turn against the enemy. Told of Grimwood's predicament, French's cavalry rode forward, dismounted, and extended the British line. Together Grimwood and French, far from being able to advance, were pinned down in untenable positions, subjected to merciless rifle and artillery fire. By late morning White realized that the attack had failed, and, since he was concerned about reports that the Boers were massing and evidently intended to rush the city from the west, decided to recall Grimwood's forces. The withdrawal was carried out under fire so intense that all semblance of order was lost and the men dribbled back in a struggling crowd. Many men fell and more would have done so had not the Royal Artillery in the rear stood firm and drawn the Boer fire.[13]

The events of the day had a demoralizing effect on the British garrison in Ladysmith. Now White, with the option of withdrawing, decided to entrench himself in the city and await developments. French was not to remain to take part in the defensive battle. On November 2, after returning from a successful raid on a Boer laager, he found out that White had received a telegram from Buller, who had recently arrived in Cape Town. It read, "French should take command of Cavalry Division on its way from home, and it is my wish particularly that he and Haig should come here if you can spare them possibly."[14]

White placed no obstacles to their departure but it was uncertain whether a train would succeed in getting through the encircling enemy troops. At 1 P.M. French and his party left in what was to be the last train to leave Ladysmith before the Boer cordon closed. They were the only passengers abroad and they had been urged to keep out of sight for two hours. It was a harrowing journey. As bullets whistled through the compartment, the officers, in a rather undignified posture along the seats and floor, could not help but worry whether at any moment they might not go up with the train or be stopped and condemned to spend the rest of the war in captivity. Fortunately the trip was completed without serious mishap. French sailed from Durban and on November 8 arrived at Cape Town, where he reported to General Buller.

A man of great physical strength and imposing appearance, Buller seemed to have all the qualifications for high command. He was a good administrator, solicitous for the welfare of his men, as well as a brave and experienced battlefield officer—he had fought in five wars, winning the Victoria Cross twice. In reality it was difficult to conceive of a worse choice.

Buller lacked both imagination and resolution. It had been fifteen years since he had seen action and, in the interval, improvement in weaponry had brought about changes in tactics. During his desk assignments in Britain he had become addicted to a diet of rich foods and champagne. Soft living made him indolent and gave him a paunch and a double chin. Trusted completely by the public and politicians, his shortcomings were known only to a small and select circle in the army.

It had been Buller's intention to move his army corps inland by rail and then march northeast on the enemy capitals of Bloemfontein and Pretoria. But during his journey the situation had been altered. The Boer offensive in Natal had resulted in the encirclement of Ladysmith. On the extreme left Mafeking and Kimberley were holding out with difficulty against superior numbers. To add to this a Boer force was preparing to invade Cape Colony, where its advent would surely be welcomed by a large number of the Dutch inhabitants.

Buller was faced with a difficult strategic problem. The main line of advance was obvious but two urgent objectives had been imposed on him, namely the relief of Ladysmith and Kimberley. The capture of these two important centers by the Boers would have a disastrous effect on British prestige and would result in the loss of vital resources and thousands of troops. Buller decided to modify his plan and split his force. While he personally attempted to raise the siege of Ladysmith, Lord Methuen would cross the Orange River and relieve Kimberley. For the defense of the Cape he proposed to send General William Gatacre to Stormberg and French to operate towards Colesberg to harass the Boer commandos and to cover the concentration of Methuen's force.

After receiving his instructions, French, who now held the rank of local lieutenant-general, moved up to the rail junctions of De Aar and Naauwpoort.[15] The regular British cavalry regiments, augmented by mounted infantry units,[16] were soon in action against the Boers, who had crossed the border and occupied a ring of dominant kopjes before Colesberg. During the last days of November and throughout December, French conducted harassing operations with an enterprise that was unique among his fellow generals. These raids, supported by British propaganda stories of newly arrived reinforcements, unsettled the faint-hearted Boer leader, Commandant Schoeman, and caused him to fall back on Colesberg. French boldly pushed forward, occupying the hills west, south, and southeast of the town.

The tactics that French employed so successfully in the Colesberg area were essentially an adaptation of Boer methods. Day in and day out, for a duration of some ten weeks, French harried the Boers all along the front and gave them no rest. If it was not a night raid, then it was a miniature siege or flanking movement. His strategy was to demonstrate on the Boers' center while working around their flanks and to avoid a pitched battle. Whenever the Boers attempted to force a major encounter, French, by a series of simultaneous flank and rear movements, would render it impossible for their commanders to confer and cooperate in the planned general action. French's achievements are much more remarkable when one considers that he was up against forces two or three times the size of his.

French provided the only gleam of comfort to British pride at a period in which British forces encountered a succession of shattering setbacks. Between December 10 and December 15, in what was quickly christened "Black Week," Gatacre was repulsed at Stormberg, Methuen was defeated at Magersfontein, and Buller was trapped on the Tugela River and overcome at the battle of Colenso. French's nibbling operations did much to prevent the Boers from following up these successes. If the Boers had been able to move south through the disloyal territory of northern Cape Colony, where they would have gained recruits as they progressed, they might have won the war. Yet no one was under any illusion about the Cape's safety. At any moment the situation might be altered at Colesberg by the transferral of Boer forces from other fronts in order to deliver a paralyzing blow at the heart of British power.

To forestall that possibility French determined to take Colesberg. A frontal assault was out of the question since the town was occupied by a large force and enjoyed superb natural defenses. French believed that if he could seize Grassy Hill, a commanding kopje a mile north of Colesberg, he would render untenable all Boer positions on the western side, compelling an immediate evacuation of the town.

Colonel A. J. Watson of the Suffolks, thinking that the hill was barely guarded, if at all, persuaded French to allow him to lead a night assault. At midnight (January 6, 1900) Watson and his battalion crept noiselessly out of camp, wearing soft shoes in order to deaden the sound of their footsteps. Arriving at the base of the hill at 3 A.M., Watson warned his men to keep their rifles unloaded and to deal out silent death with the bayonet. They were scrambling breathlessly towards the summit when a deadly fire greeted them out of the darkness. Either reconnaissance had been faulty or the Boers had learned of the British plan and were prepared for it.

The British column was thrown into confusion, some men advancing and some retreating under blistering enemy fire. Watson, hoping to rally his men below the crest, gave the order to retire. In the panic half the men rushed blindly down the hill and eventually returned to camp. Watson gathered the rear units and with reckless gallantry led them up the slope. He was among the first to fall, his body riddled with bullets, and most of his officers perished with him as they pushed the men forward in repeated bayonet charges that failed to close with the enemy. The British artillery opened up at daybreak but was unable to convert failure into success, and around 5:30 A.M. the remnant of the attacking force surrendered. British losses in this unsuccessful affair were 11 officers and 150 men.

It was clear to French that he could make no progress against a position where the enemy was now strongly reinforced and on the alert. He decided instead to strike from the east and cut the railway line. Starting out from Slingersfontein on January 11, 1900, French attempted to turn the left flank of the enemy, who had taken a position on a long ridge running from near Slingersfontein towards the railway. French secured a good hold on the Boers' left wing and from there he hoped to push them westward and get across the railway. But timely reinforcements enabled the Boers to prolong their threatened flank and French, who had no intention of becoming seriously engaged, gradually retired to his base.

Now the newly arrived Boer commander on the left flank, General Koos de la Rey, with a force of 1,000 men, began to make his presence felt. An officer of exceptional ability, De la Rey was determined to render French's position at Slingersfontein untenable by capturing a high, steep hill immediately to the northwest. The hill, known afterwards as New Zealand Hill, was weakly guarded by a half company of Yorkshires and a company (60 men) of New Zealanders. At dawn about 30 Boers posted themselves on rock-covered hills to the north and east and began long-range sniping. Their fire, which grew imperceptibly in volume and accuracy, was directed chiefly at the New Zealanders on the east, giving the impression that an attack in that direction was imminent. Meanwhile a party of over 50 Boers climbed unperceived up the steep western side of the hill. They crawled right up to the forward sanger and then suddenly leaped up to their feet and opened fire on the Yorkshires, wounding the commanding officer and his color-sergeant. Deprived of their leaders the Yorkshires fell into confusion. The hill seemed lost when Captain W. N. Maddocks and a handful of New Zealanders, hurrying from the opposite side to assist, charged down on the Boers with fixed bayonets. After a brief struggle the Boers fled, leaving behind 21 dead.

While this skirmish was in progress, French turned once more to the west in an effort to drive the enemy from Colesberg. An opportunity seemed at hand when it was discovered that the Boers had left practically undefended an important pass known as Plessis Poort, through which ran the road leading north from Colesberg. If the British could gain control of this pass they could cut the Boers' line of retreat and northerly communications. French, determined to seize so valuable a point, sent units to occupy Bastard's Nek, five miles to the west. Covered by a cross fire of artillery the infantry was to move forward along the high ground towards Plessis Poort. In order to divert the Boers' attention a demonstration was ordered along the whole British line. The moved started too late and as a result the enemy was alerted. Advancing carefully towards the pass the column nearly fell into a trap. But French, who had grown suspicious because of the enemy's silence, abruptly ordered his men to retire. The moment they began to do so, a heavy burst of fire broke out from the enemy who were present in force on the ridges.

A Reconnaissance under Difficulty. General French's force in the Colesberg area, by R. Caton Woodville.
(Photo courtesy of The Mansell Collection)

Forward to Pretoria. Horse Artillery of French's division, by R. Caton Woodville.
(Photo courtesy of The Mansell Collection)

After this affair a stalemate set in on the whole front. It was a situation that was very much to the British advantage. The Boers depended on the progress of their invasion in order to encourage the Dutch population in the Cape to revolt. When they were checked, only 7,000 rebels of the expected 40,000 came forward.[17]

French's hope to turn the Boers out of Colesberg would remain unfulfilled. Changes had recently taken place in the British high command and French figured to play a major role in the upcoming war plans.

The humiliating disasters of Black Week had caused the British civil authorities to send out Lord Roberts to take over the supreme command although, strangely enough, they left Buller in northern Natal to continue the siege of Ladysmith. Roberts had secured the appointment of General Herbert Kitchener as his chief of staff. The two men, called to rescue the reputation of British arms, made a strange combination. Roberts, having spent nearly all his long career in India, was sixty-seven years old and on the verge of retirement. He was short in stature, outgoing, and secure in married life. His kindly nature, placing humanity above ambition, and his interest in th welfare of the common soldier earned him the nickname "Bobs" and the love of the army as a whole.

Only forty-nine years old and fresh from his conquest of the Sudan, Kitchener was in the process of a meteoric rise. He was tall, reserved, and made no attempt to cultivate the arts of popularity. Wedded to the army, he was filled with such intense desire to succeed that he never took personal feelings into account. Yet whatever their differences, Roberts and Kitchener worked well together, establishing strong bonds of sympathy and outlook.

Roberts and Kitchener had evolved a plan of operation during their voyage and only slight modification was required after they arrived in South Africa in January 1900. The idea was to concentrate the bulk of the British forces in the rear of Magersfontein at Modder River station and advance along the western railway line to relieve Kimberley. Rather than continue north along the railway, the army would strike eastward across the veld to capture Bloemfontein. If everything went well, the Boers now dominating northern Natal and pushing against French's cavalry screen to threaten Cape Colony would have to withdraw to defend their homeland.[18]

Roberts planned that French's cavalry division should ride in advance to relieve Kimberley by swinging in a great loop around Magersfontein. On January 29 he summoned French to Cape Town and spent a day discussing the part he intended the cavalry to play in his operations and the steps necessary to disengage these units from Colesberg without attracting the enemy's attention. Two days later French returned to his headquarters at Rensburg to break up his command, leaving Major-General R. A. P. Clements, with a mixed force, to cover the Colesberg area.

Roberts pushed forward the preparation for his flank march with speed

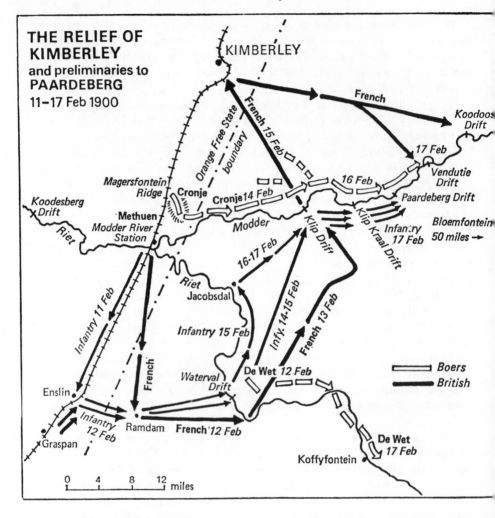

and secrecy. On February 8 he arrived at Modder River station, by then a wilderness of tents, railway sidings, transport wagons, and loose, burning sand. The total strength of the striking force was approximately 37,000 men. It was organized as follows:

Calvalry Division (Lieutenant-General J. French)

Sixth Infantry Division (Lieutenant-General T. Kelly-Kenny)

Seventh Infantry Division (Lieutenant-General C. Tucker)

Ninth Infantry Division (Lieutenant-General H. Colvile)

Roberts had revealed his plan only to a handful of key people since he was determined to achieve the advantage of surprise. He could not conceal the arrival of reinforcements but by sending many to nearby outposts, to be switched to the Modder River station at the last moment, and by making demonstrations on other fronts he was able to mislead the Boers as to his designs. The Boer Commander at Magersfontein, General A. P. Cronje, was under the impression that the British were planning a flank attack on him from the west. Roberts encouraged this belief by leaving Methuen's First Division in front of the lines at Magersfontein, while his main army, with French's cavalry leading, moved southwards towards Ramdam Farm. From there the striking force was to advance eastwards to seize Waterval Drift on the Riet River and, turning northwards, pass east of Jacobsdal and cross the Modder River at Klip Drift. This would cut off Cronje from his base and open a way for a dash on Kimberley by the cavalry.

The march was an ordeal for both man and horse. It was the peak of the summer season in South Africa and the temperatures on the veld, though comparatively cool at night, rose frequently to as high as 120 degrees Fahrenheit in the day. There was, moreover, little water to be found on the route selected except at the Riet and the Modder. Until these vital rivers could be reached, man and beast had to endure heat and thirst, aggravated by dust, over miles of desert waste.

The cavalry set out from the Modder River camp on February 11 at 1:30 A.M., leaving their tents standing to deceive the Boers. At Ramdam French completed the organization of his cavalry division and by the evening of the 12th he had crossed the Riet. The next phase of the campaign was a critical one. There was a twenty-five mile stretch of waterless veld between the Riet and Modder rivers and the direction of the march was bound to reveal the cavalry's true objective.

Around 2:00 P.M. on the 13th, as French neared the Modder, enemy parties brushed his right flank. French had no way of knowing whether he was dealing with their main army and afraid that they might try to wedge themselves between him and the river or, even worse, strike his flank while he was crossing, he decided to wheel his right and center brigades half right while allowing his left brigade to hold its course. This tactical maneuver, which dated back to the time of the Spartans, brought his left flank closer and closer to his real objective, Klip Drift, while giving the impression that he was making for Klip Kraal Drift to the east. When the green banks of the Modder could be seen, the whole force wheeled left and galloped for the crossing. The small detachment of Free Staters camped around Klip Drift were completely taken by surprise. Bewildered and frightened, they bolted precipitately, making little effort to dispute the crossing. By 5:00 P.M. French was able to report to Roberts that Klip Drift and the nearby hills were in his hands.

The Boers had left behind, in their haste to flee, forage and supplies of every kind. This was a godsend since the transport wagons, strung out over miles of dusty veld, were unlikely to arrive before the following day. The men wasted no time in quenching their thirst with the cool, muddy water, after which they threw themselves down to a well-earned rest. During the next few hours many stragglers made their way to camp, for about 500 horses were either dead or no longer fit to ride.

Although every moment was important, the cavalry could not advance until infantry supports came up to hold the drifts. The army had been delayed because of the difficulties in getting the supply wagons and guns over the Riet. On the evening of February 13 Roberts rode over to Waterval Drift and asked Kelly-Kenny if his men were capable of a forced march after their strenuous day. Told that they were, he assigned Kitchener to accompany them, so that all that relentless hustling could do to hurry them forward should be done. The division left at 1:00 A.M. on February 14 and despite fatigue, darkness, and a heavy rainstorm, it reached the Modder at 1:00 A.M. the following day, having covered twenty-seven miles, including detours, in twenty-four hours. With his lines of communications secured, French prepared to make a dash for Kimberley.

Thus far French had encountered only trifling resistance. However, during his enforced halt on the Modder, Cronje had realized that not only the cavalry but the infantry were marching around his flank. On the basis of his information the Boer leader concluded, erroneously once again, that the British were trying to draw him eastwards from his elaborately constructed defenses at Magersfontein so that they could attack from the south and southeast. Consequently he stayed where he was and ordered Commandants Froneman and de Beer with some 800 men to disperse the British cavalry. Instead of attacking French's exhausted forces, the two commanders took up a defensive position along a line of kopjes and ridges, barring any northward move on Kimberley.

At 9:30 A.M. on February 15 French and his column set out from Klip Drift on the last stage of their journey. They had advanced two miles when they came under fire from riflemen on the eastern ridge and artillery on the ridge to the northwest. French now summoned his brigadiers and explained the situation to them. The route to Kimberley ran straight ahead; any advance along it would be enfiladed from both flanks. Because he did not believe that the nek between the two ridges was strongly held he intended to take it at a gallop. The batteries were to maintain their fire on enemy positions until the last possible moment and then to limber up and follow the last brigade. The stage was now set for one of the last of the great cavalry charges.

With the Third Brigade leading, its four squadrons forming a double line extending to five-yard intervals between the files, wave after wave of horsemen thundered forward, pennants flying, lances and sabers at the ready. Boer riflemen occupying the heights on either flank, as well as those across the nek, poured a murderous fire into the great cloud of dust billowing up from the horses' hooves. A British officer who took part in the charge gave this account of his impressions: "The enterprise appeared to us at first as quite hopeless; we believed that only a few of us would come out of it alive, and, had we made a similar attack at Aldershot, we should certainly have all been put out of action, and have been looked upon as idiots." However, the heavy losses anticipated by almost everyone who took part in the charge did not occur. The speed and surprise of the charge, the open order, the cover produced by clouds of dust and the artillery support all contributed to rendering Boer fire ineffective. Here and there a horse went down or a trooper reeled and fell from the saddle but the lines swept on without any lessening of speed. The spectacle of a huge and fast moving cloud of dust from which came the continuous thunder of galloping hooves had a terrifying impact on the Boers in the valley. Before the cavalry approached to within effective rifle range most of the Boers took to flight. The few staunch men who remained behind were speared by the lancers or taken prisoner. Once their center was broken the Boers on the kopjes rode away, spreading panic like a contagion wherever they went. At the cost of 2 killed and 17 wounded the cavalry had taken a position that would have required the infantry or dismounted cavalry the better part of a day and probably would have entailed considerable losses.[19]

French waited only an hour for his division to recover wind and strength before moving on. Outnumbered and demoralized by the announcement that French had broken through with a great force, the Boers besieging Kimberley were melting away like mist. At 2:30 P.M. the cavalry came within distant view of the town and the men raised a tired cheer. French now got into heliographic communication with Kimberley but it required almost an hour to convince the operators there that they were not being misled by Boer signalers. Before French reached Kimberley some weak Boer detachments made a last effort to halt his advance. They were easily driven away. At 6:30 French, with his staff, rode into Kimberley and were welcomed by the mayor. An officer present observed: "The rejoicings were great, but what surprised everybody was the fat and sleek appearance of both horses and inhabitants of relieved Kimberley, as compared with that of the relievers."[20] French then went to the Sanatorium Hotel where he dined and passed the night.

Considering the heat, the absence of water, the weight of the equipment, and the nature of the opposition at Klip Drift, French and his men had succeeded in covering a distance of one hundred miles in four days. It was a feat of which they had every good reason to be proud.

When Cronje heard the news that French had broken through to Kimberley and, as a consequence, that he was in danger of being enveloped, he realized that his only remaining escape route was eastwards along the Modder River to Bloemfontein. Owing to the negligence of Methuen's First Division at the Modder River station, Cronje managed to slip through (on the night of February 15–16) the gap between the rear of the British cavalry and the vanguard of the Sixth Division under Kelly-Kenny. At dawn British patrols in the vicinity of Klip Drift sighted a long trail of dust to the northeast. Their reports excited Kitchener who, sensing that the Boers had broken out of the trap, swung the Sixth Division into hot pursuit. Simultaneously he telegraphed French to head off the convoy but Cronje had cut the telegraph wire on his way through and the message never arrived. Kitchener then handed a written order to a despatch rider who, setting out from Klip Drift at 6:00 P.M., reached French's headquarters late in the evening.[21]

A less determined man might have pleaded that his men and horses were too worn out to undertake the journey, but French, who seemed to thrive on adversity, responded magnificently to the call. The weary cavalrymen were roused from their sleep in the middle of the night and by 4:00 A.M. were drawn up in column, ready to start the grueling thirty-mile ride to Koodos Drift. Of the 5,000 men who had ridden with him to Kimberley, less than 1,200 were fit to move. French drove his exhausted men and horses hard and covered the distance in six and a half hours, arriving in the nick of time.

French went forward to reconnoitre in the direction where his patrols had sighted clouds of dust. He had scarcely ridden a thousand yards when he spotted the whole Boer force reposing below in the valley. He at once ordered the horse artillery to drag their guns to high ground and open fire.

Cronje had planned to cross the river at Vendutie Drift, about four miles west of the place predicted by Kitchener. He had with him some 5,000 men (of whom one-third were on foot), 400 wagons with their teams, numerous women and children, and a herd of cattle. He was confident that he had made good his escape. All that remained to be done was to cross over and take up suitable defensive positions so as to cover the road to Bloemfontein. He and his burghers were in no hurry. Most of the men were resting under the shade of their wagons or helping prepare the midday meal. The cattle were grazing in the open and some of the leading wagons began to descend the steep bank to enter the water. Suddenly guns boomed and seconds later shells were bursting in the midst of the camp. The cattle stampeded as men, women, and children rushed for the shelter of the bank. In the general confusion none of the Boer leaders thought about investigating the size of the attacking force. Outnumbered four to one and completely exhausted, French's men would have been hard pressed to withstand a determined assault.[22]

Throughout the day French's guns shelled the laager, making impossible any attempt to collect the cattle or to get the wagons across the river. Most of the Boer officers urged Cronje to break out during the night to avoid the risk of capture. Had he done so he could easily have crossed the river and escaped with most of his force. However, Cronje would not purchase safety at the cost of abandoning the wagons, which were the private property and formed a large part of the working capital of his burghers. Besides, too many of his men were without horses. He had already sent for reinforcements from Bloemfontein and he could count on friendly units operating in the area. He would stay where he was and fight it out.

The Boer laager lay in the middle of the open veld, the rim of which sloped gently down to the river. The Modder provided water and its banks, lined with a thick growth of mimosa, thorn, and other scrub, gave excellent cover. The plain across which the British would be obliged to attack was exposed and bare. Innumerable ravines on both sides of the river ran down to the ford, making natural trenches. For the remainder of February 17 and throughout the night the Boers labored with pick and shovel to improve and connect those trenches and to dig new ones where necessary. Faster than anyone believed possible, they constructed a defense system that gave them a clear field of fire over the surrounding veld.

From all directions British forces converged on the Boer position. Roberts, who was laid up at Jacobsdal with a feverish chill, had placed Kitchener in command even though he was junior to Kelly-Kenny. Kitchener, having inspected the enemy's defenses, decided to attack at once, overriding Kelly-Kenny, who favored investing the laager. Kitchener's plan was to engage the Boers from the south while simultaneous attacks were launched from east and west on both banks of the river. French's cavalry, too fatigued to participate in the assault, undertook to block the enemy's road of escape eastwards and to deal with any Boer commandos who might seek to intervene from the north.

There is no need to go into the battle beyond remarking that the various British attacks, owing to confusion, delay, and improper coordination, were all brought to a standstill.[23] The army's losses amounted to 324 killed and 924 wounded, roughly eight percent of the 15,000 men engaged and the highest of any day in the war. The next day Roberts, rising from his sick bed, journeyed to Paardeberg and took over control of the operation. Disinclined to risk additional casualties in bloody bayonet charges, he contented himself with keeping the Boers encircled and pounding them with his artillery. Cronje's position was hopeless and after suffering seven days of incessant bombardment he was forced to surrender unconditionally on February 27.

The surrender of Cronje was a severe blow to the morale of the Boers and led to the withdrawal of their forces from the Colesberg area. Buller relieved Ladysmith on February 28 and, except for the still-beleaguered Mafeking, the entire western front had collapsed. During the early days of March the Boer leadership struggled desperately to stem the sense of panic and prevent the breakup of their forces. At a conference the presidents of both the Transvaal and the Orange Free State, Kruger and Steyn, agreed to make every effort to stop Roberts' advance on Bloemfontein. Poplar Grove, ten miles east of Paardeberg and set among a line of hills astride the Modder, was selected as the first line of defense. Christiaan de Wet had 6,000 men entrenched there; De la Rey, with part of his commandos, was

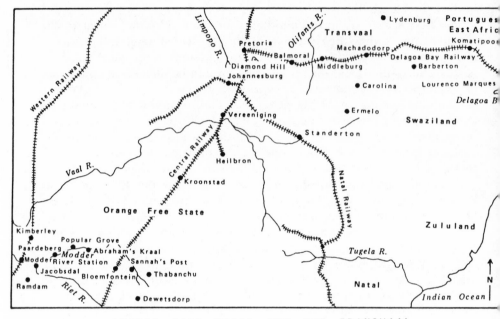

ORANGE   FREE   STATE   AND   THE   TRANSVAAL

near Bloemfontein and further reinforcements could be expected from
other fronts. In all, the presidents hoped to assemble upwards of 12,000
men.

On March 6 Roberts, having brought up reinforcements and fresh supplies, called his generals together to explain his plan of attack on de Wet at
Poplar Grove. The scheme called for two infantry divisions to move in
from the south and southwest while the cavalry swung around the Boers'
east (right) flank to cut off their line of retreat. The object was to drive the
Boers out of their fortifications into the river bed, where they would be
compelled to surrender.

The cavalry had to cover a distance of approximately seventeen miles
and French wanted to start that evening so that he would be well on his way
around the enemy's flank before daybreak. But Roberts, fearing that this
might betray his plan to the enemy, instructed the cavalry to move off at
2:00 A.M. French, who disliked long night marches, left camp an hour late.

He moved southeast at leisurely speed until he reached a depression at 5:00 A.M. Here he halted for forty-five minutes to wait for daylight. By doing so he held up the deployment of the Sixth Division, which closely followed the rear of the cavalry column. Pushing on at a somewhat better pace, French came upon a large dam and, as this seemed a good place to water his horses, he called another halt and another hour was lost. These delays, added to the late start, gave the Boers several hours of daylight in which to see the threat developing before them and to decide how to deal with it. Since de Wet and his men could not hope to hold their bastion against an enveloping attack by so overwhelming a force, the only course open to them was to escape with all speed while there was yet time. Accordingly at about 7:30 A.M. the Boers abandoned their positions and fled along the route Roberts had thought they would take.

At this hour French, having resumed the advance, was closer to the river than a great part of the mass of retreating Boers. Had he ridden hard he could still have attained his objective in time. But he hesitated. The Sixth Division, which should have been pushing on after the fleeing Boers, was nowhere in sight. The Boers were numerous, ably led, and had not been shaken by any attack. If trapped they were almost certain to attempt to break out. Finally the cavalry horses, not fully recovered from previous overwork and given inadequate fodder, were in very poor condition, some scarcely able to trot. French thus decided to close up his squadrons, lest the Boers try to break back through his extended lines, and swing north after their main body. This shortened the distance to be covered by his horses but it meant pushing against the Boers' rear instead of, as his instructions dictated, getting in front of them and barring their retreat. By departing from Roberts' plan French allowed the enemy to escape almost unscathed.[24]

Roberts was disgusted by the manner in which French had conducted the pursuit and accused him of wretched horsemanship.[25] What Roberts did not know until some time later was that both Kruger and Steyn were present during the action. With the two presidents and de Wet in British hands it is unlikely that the Boers could have continued the war. Given the significance of the event one can understand why it has aroused so much controversy.

The British Official History exonerated French on the ground that his horses were fatigued,[26] which they were, but as it turned out they covered considerably more ground during the day than was required for the execution of the original plan. Neither can the contention of the German Official Account that French should have been permitted to start the previous evening to have sufficient time to reach his appointed place be upheld by the facts.[27] The cavalry did have sufficient time despite the delays. J. G. Maydon, who served under French, admitted that his chief was "off his game";[28] and *The Times History* stated that French "never really seems to have had his heart in the business."[29] Indeed, French was not at his best. Recent military writers have contended that French lacked his habitual drive because he was in a huff, sulking over a wrong done him.

As the story goes, Roberts, owing to a great shortage of fodder, had issued strict orders to the cavalry not to exceed a daily ration of three pounds per horse. He was therefore annoyed when his chief supply officer, Colonel W. D. Richardson, informed him that the cavalry horses were receiving a larger ration than had been laid down. Roberts promptly summoned the brigade and division commanders and reprimanded them severely for disobeying his orders. Richardson had actually erred in his calculations. He had divided the issue of rations by the number of fit horses, forgetting that the animals unfit for duty also had to be fed. This was not known until later and French, who had to bear the brunt of the rebuke, rode out early on the morning of March 7 burning with a sense of injustice.[30]

Although French was a man of erratic moods, I cannot believe that the trivial nature of the incident would so upset the balance of his judgment as to practically cripple his initiative in battle. My own view is that French failed to act boldly at Poplar Grove because he was not prepared to see his division cut up in what he regarded was an impossible task.

For the next few days the army rested while supplies were brought up. On March 10 Roberts' force advanced in three columns, some ten miles apart, with the object of converging on the railway to the south of Bloemfontein. Troubled by rumors that Boer reinforcements were coming from the north, Roberts modified his plan on March 12, ordering French to ride full tilt for Brand Kop, a commanding hill four miles southeast of Bloemfontein. With two brigades French set out at 1:00 P.M. on a three-hour ride and in the waning light captured his objective after scaring away the defenders. The key to Bloemfontein had been won.[31]

News that the English commanded the approaches of the town and were within easy shelling distance broke the spirit of the burghers. Throughout the night of March 12 thousands of commandos and wagons trekked out north. President Steyn and other leaders departed by train, managing to get away just before one of French's patrols blew up the railway line. On March 13, one month after the beginning of the campaign, Roberts made his formal entry into Bloemfontein at the head of the cavalry division.

Being anxious to give the enemy no respite, Roberts intended to resume the march on Pretoria within two or three weeks. However, he remained six weeks in Bloemfontein, much longer than he or anyone else anticipated. The long delay was necessary in order to repair the railway lines, collect a reserve of supplies, and permit the horses to rest and recuperate. During that period French's cavalry units were sent into neighboring areas to distribute Roberts's proclamation allowing all burghers to return to their farms unmolested upon surrendering their arms and giving an oath to ab-

stain from further hostilities. They also occupied the new waterworks at
Sannah's Post, which was located twenty miles east of the town; and the
prominent hill of Thabanchu, twenty miles yet further east.[32]

In the first week of May Roberts opened his offensive against Pretoria
with a force of 120,000 men covering a 500-mile front. To stem the tide of
the British advance the Boers would have needed a well-conceived plan
and many more men than the 15,000 or so available to them. They tried to
make a stand at Sand River but, as the British columns threatened to
encircle them, broke off the engagement and fled. Keeping ahead of the
main British force, French turned out a party of Boers north of Kroonstad
and several days later crossed the Vaal and entered the Transvaal.[33] While
this was happening a British force ended the siege of Mafeking, to the
exuberant joy of the British people. On May 24, the Queen's official birth-
day, Roberts issued a proclamation annexing the Orange Free State and
changing its name to Orange River Colony.

Roberts continued marching along the railway while French on the left
raced up the main road towards Johannesburg. On approaching the Rand
gold mines Roberts learned that Louis Botha had concentrated a force on a
range of hills to the west and south of Johannesburg. Roberts's plan was to
send French to make a circuit around the city from the west and for
Hamilton's column to follow behind. On May 28 French found the flank at
Doornkop and, as he brought pressure to bear against it, drew off many
defenders from various sectors along the line. This enabled Hamilton's
Gordon Highlanders to carry the main Boer position at bayonet's point in
what was possibly the most violent and sustained charge of the war. Johannesburg, now at the mercy of Roberts, surrendered on the evening of the
30th.[34]

Leaving a garrison of 3,000 men behind, Roberts set out on June 3 to
cover the remaining forty miles to Pretoria. French rode ahead with orders
to sweep around Pretoria from the west and to sever the Central railway
line north of the city. In the capital large Boer forces, assembled from
various quarters, waited to deliver a united blow that they hoped would
send the British Army reeling back to the coast.[35] But when the time came
all thoughts of defending the city disappeared and there was a mass exodus
in whatever trains were still running (to the east), in carts and wagons, or
on foot. President Kruger, forced to leave his ailing wife behind, moved the
seat of his government to Middleburg.

On June 5 Roberts and his staff marched with all due ceremony into
Pretoria. They halted at Church Square, where the Union Jack was displayed again after an interval of nearly twenty years. There followed a
victory march past by the troops, Roberts savoring the triumphant climax
of his epic advance from Bloemfontein. In thirty-four days he had covered
three hundred miles, a distance that compares favorably with any in history
prior to the age of mechanization.[36]

Although the Boers had suffered only about 500 casualties during Roberts's advance to Pretoria they were in a desperate situation. They had lost almost all their principal towns, their railways, and their supply centers. Their political rulers were fugitives without a capital and their armies widely scattered. The demoralization was so deep that a group of their foremost generals arranged to meet with Roberts to discuss peace terms. But the conference did not take place because at this critical juncture it was learned that de Wet had staged a series of successful raids along the line north of Kroonstad, severing Roberts's link with Bloemfontein. While de Wet's exploits could not possibly force Roberts's retreat, much less lead to his defeat, they were sufficient to revive the flagging spirits of the Boers and provide an excuse to continue the struggle. Accordingly the conduct of the war was placed entirely in the hands of Botha, who, rallying 6,000 men, grouped them along a range of hills, twenty-five miles east of Pretoria.

Roberts was worried at the threat posed by the proximity of the Boers and so, when the peace talks failed, he decided to drive them out. For that purpose he could muster 14,000 men, owing to losses on the march and the necessity to guard places along the way. His aim was to turn both flanks with his cavalry and mounted infantry—French on the left and Hamilton on the right—while the Eleventh Division under Major-General Pole-Carew held the center. It was the familiar pattern of an outflanking movement, followed by a thrust against the Boer center which had then to give way for fear of being encircled.

Botha had anticipated Roberts's strategy and French's division was almost surrounded and forced to fight dismounted. French retained his poise and held on stubbornly, even though Roberts had granted him permission to withdraw. French's action permitted Hamilton on the other flank to storm and capture Diamond Hill, a steep-faced plateau that was the key to the Boer position. The Boers began retiring at 11:00 P.M. and carried out the movement so quietly that by the time Roberts discovered their departure they were beyond pursuit.[37]

There followed a six-week halt at Pretoria, a delay prolonged not as much by the need to bring up reinforcements and supplies as by de Wet's activities. On July 23 Roberts launched his army towards Komatipoort on the Portugese East African frontier, determined to dispossess the Boers of their last railway link with the outside world and so dispel their faint hopes of European intervention. The Boers, having responded to the exhortations of Botha, had established themselves (in front of Machadodorp) on a mountainous line extending on both sides of the Delagoa Bay railroad. Botha commanded no more than 5,000 burghers but his position was one of considerable natural strength. Buller, at last arriving from Natal after months of inexcusable delay, formed the right of Roberts's advance. Roberts planned a turning movement but Buller found a small gap in the enemy's center at Bergendal and drove his men through it.[38]

Once their center was broken, the Boers along the line lost heart and fled. The pursuit was not vigorously pressed and again the Boers escaped unscathed. Although the action at Bergendal was hardly a battle, as it has sometimes been termed, it did produce the effect of a major victory. On September 1 Roberts, anticipating an imminent end to the war, proclaimed the annexation of the Transvaal to the Queen's dominions.

The Boers, instead of retiring along the railway line as was their habit, fell back on the flanking towns of Lydenburg and Barberton. When Roberts learned of this development he made changes in the disposition of his columns. Leaving only Pole-Carew on the railway he sent Buller north to attack Lydenburg and French towards Barberton, thus fanning out his forces in an endeavor to enclose the enemy. Buller was the first to advance and without much happening along the way captured Lydenburg on September 6.

French undertook many difficult assignments during the whole course of the South African war but none required greater daring, courage, and physical exertion than the march on Barberton. Much of the country between him and Barberton resembled a miniature Alps. Together with men, horses, and guns he had to scale precipitous heights and negotiate passage along narrow ledges from which there was sometimes a fall of over a thousand feet. Apart from the difficult and dangerous route there was the problem of supply. When French started on his march he had only eight days' supplies left. These would prove insufficient if he encountered a serious check and without a chain of posts there was no possibility for convoys to reach him.

Before starting on September 9 French misled the Boers into believing that his objective was Ermelo, a town located thirty miles farther to the south. Sweeping eastward from Carolina, French fought his way to the summit of Nelhoogte Pass by September 12. It required nearly three days to bring up the baggage train. French, however did not wait. Leaving two brigades behind, he led the rest of his cavalry along a fifteen-mile goat track that twisted down to the Barberton valley. It was a risky ride. He could take no supplies except on horseback and no guns. The path was so narrow it was necessary for the men to advance in single file and in certain places the descent was so precipitous that the horses had to be led. The line of struggling horsemen would have presented a few well-posted skirmishers an easy target. But fortunately for French he reached the open ground without having to fire a shot or even seeing a Boer. Galloping into Barberton he surprised the garrison, which in its haste to flee left 80 British prisoners and a vast quantity of stores.[39] French had now cleared away the last major obstacle to Pole-Carew's avance on Komantipoort.

With British columns closing in from three directions and Boers were in danger of being pinned against the Portuguese frontier. Faced with what appeared to be certain defeat, the burghers split into small groups and dispersed. President Steyn, escorted by 250 men, set off north and gained the plateau beyond Buller's position as he tried to make his way back to the Orange River Colony. Several days later Botha made good his escape by following the same route. The aged Paul Kruger departed for Delagoa Bay to board a ship for Europe. Left at Komantipoort were some 3,000 men, nearly all of whom were unlikely to prove useful in the rough days ahead.

When leading elements of Pole-Carew's column entered Komantipoort they found it practically deserted. The defenders, rather than face the British, had crossed over into Portuguese territory and laid down their arms.

Roberts could see no more armies to fight, no other railroads or major cities to capture. There were 15,000 Boers behind barbed wire and an even great number had taken the oath of neutrality. Every military consideration encouraged Roberts to believe that the war was over except for some routine police action. On November 29, 1900, he handed over his command in South Africa to Kitchener and departed for England to take up his new duties as commander-in-chief of the British Army. Roberts had been premature in proclaiming the defeat of the Boers. The war of pitched battles was finished, but another of a wholly different character was about to begin.

The burghers still had a potential force of about 50,000 men and although their units were scattered, they were all in touch with each other. Conscious of their national identity and animated by a passionate belief in their cause, they were as determined as ever to maintain the struggle for independence. The Boer leaders recognized that if they were to go on fighting they would have to abandon orthodox warfare in favor of guerrilla tactics. A war conducted in guerrilla fashion suited the training and psychology of the Boers, who were superb horsemen, free, and independent-minded. Such informal fighting reduced the need for military discipline to a minimum and permitted individuals frequent if dangerous visits home. Most commandos lived off the country and operated in their home areas, snapping up convoys, ambushing small bodies of troops, destroying railways and bridges, and almost always inflicting many more casualties than they themselves suffered. They struck when and where they were least expected, melted back into the farming communities, or disappeared in the vastness of the veld and left the bewildered British wondering from which direction the next blow would descend. The Boers hoped that guerrilla activity would so exhaust and exasperate their foes that they would wring generous concessions from them; or that it might move one of the Great Powers to intervene on their behalf.

Kitchener adopted drastic measures to counter the raids. He divided much of the country into sections by building a network of blockhouses that were garrisoned and joined together by barbed wire. Mounted columns swept each compartmentalized area, destroying farms and livestock and herding noncombatants into concentration camps. By reducing the Boers' freedom of movement and their accessibility to food and shelter, Kitchener increasingly restricted their ability to wage guerrilla war.[40]

French returned to Pretoria on November 3, 1900, and while retaining his cavalry command, he assumed supreme control of the Johannesburg district. His movements during the remainder of the war are too wearisome to follow in detail and therefore will be treated only superficially. In June 1901 he was sent south and given command of all the mobile columns operating in Cape Colony. His object, essentially a defensive action, was to prevent Boer commandos from the Transvaal and River Colony from raising a rebellion in the Cape. With the Boers launching a new type of warfare, little theoretical or practical experience existed from which French could draw to formulate plans or counterplans. Inevitably there were errors in the conduct of this strange and desultory campaign.

French had the almost insuperable task of hunting down dozens of small guerrilla groups scattered over a large territory about the size of France. As his men grew in numbers and became smore experienced, French organized more frequent and elaborate drives. A successful drive depended on constant communication and on flawless coordination and timing, otherwise—as so often happened—gaps would form between both the parallel and converging columns, permitting the Boers to slip through the net. The work was wretched, backbreaking, and in time took its toll on French and his men.

To make matters worse there were occasions when outside Boer groups would slip into the Cape and render assistance. One such incursion, led by the Cambridge-educated lawyer Jan Smuts, deserves special mention. Smuts, with 500 mounted burghers, left the Transvaal in July 1901 and dashed southwards through the Orange River Colony. He then struck westward across the whole breadth of the Cape, covering a distance of some 1,800 miles in ten months, and destroying property and communications on his way. It was an amazing exploit. Smuts's success can be attributed partly to good fortune and the slowness of the British to react, but mostly to his ability to twist and turn and double back, throwing his pursuers off the scent for a few crucial hours. Although Smuts's prestige was further enhanced, his invasion foray was largely unproductive.[41]

French has sometimes been criticized for not destroying more of the Boer forces and for failing to capture more of their major leaders. But as the war progressed Boer ranks were substantially reduced until only the most dedicated and combat-hardened fighters remained. The rebellion in the Cape on which the Boers had fixed their last hopes did not materialize. Most of the Boer sympathizers and all the waverers required more than daring feats and an occasional spectacular coup before they were willing to show their hand. The commandos could do no better and so Botha and some of the other leaders, recognizing the futility of continuing the struggle, agreed to attend a conference with Kitchener at Vereeniging. On May 31, 1902, peace came at last.

French's part in the Boer war constitues the most successful chapter in his military career. He had won a valuable victory at Elandslaagte. His operations before Colesberg, generally regarded a minor classic, staved off an invasion of the Cape and materially influenced, if not absolutely determined, the entire future of the campaign. During Roberts's great flank march French relieved Kimberley, intercepted Cronje, frequently forced the enemy to abandon strongly defended positions, and was instrumental in the early surrender of Bloemfontein and Johannesburg. With one notable exception, Poplar Grove, French showed that he possessed the qualities of a first-rate commander. His courage and aggressiveness, his willingness to learn from the Boers, as well as his ability to anticipate their movements, the rapidity of his marches, his good sense in determining when and where to strike, and the skill with which he handled his men in battle all contributed to his success in the first and second phase of the war.

In the last or third phase it must be admitted that French did not impose the force of his personality upon the operations under his charge. He began well but as the months wore on his energies dwindled. Still he kept the war in the Cape within manageable limits, which was most important.

As compensation for his prominent role in the campaign his rank of lieutenant-general was made substantive and he was awarded the K.C.B. (1900) and K.C.M.G. (1902). While South Africa ruined many promising careers, French emerged a national hero with the reputation as the best cavalry officer in the British Army.

3
Between Two Wars

While still in South Africa Sir John, as we may now call him, learned that he had been chosen to succeed Sir Redvers Buller[1] in command at Aldershot. French's elation over the news was somewhat dampened by the knowledge that he would be replacing his old friend and chief. On November 23, 1901, he wrote to Buller, explaining that he had not been offered the post but had been appointed to it by the King, and concluded: "I can never hope to fill your place, but you may be sure I shall leave no stone unturned to profit by your lessons and follow in your footsteps."[2]

Roberts, although occasionally differing with French in the past, had been behind the appointment. His high regard for French was shared by Kitchener, who sent the following note to the Secretary of War: "I am very glad you have selected French [for the Aldershot Command]; you could not have picked a better man. French is the most thoroughly loyal, energetic soldier I have, and all under him are devoted to him—not because he is lenient, but because they admire his soldier-like qualities."[3]

In the first part of July 1902 Sir John and Kitchener returned home together, landing in Southampton, where they were greeted by a large crowd. In a brief speech French thanked the local dignitaries for their warm welcome, adding that whatever success he had enjoyed was due to the unbounded confidence inspired in him by the great chiefs he had served. The two soldiers were given another reception when they arrived in London later in the day. Wearing their khaki service dress they were driven through streets decorated with flags and bunting and lined with troops representing different parts of the Empire, amid a deafening roar of cheers from the inestimable thousands of onlookers. Kitchener, who disliked pomp and ceremony of any kind, was not in the best of humor and the only time he broke his silence was to utter the word "Colors" on passing the colors of one of the regiments along the route.[4] The procession ended at Buckingham Palace, where they were received by the new monarch, Edward VII.

French enjoyed the limelight and spared no pains to court the press. For weeks after his return he remained in the public eye, the recipient of an avalanche of honors, awards, congratulations, and banquets. Towns and cities competed for the distinction of making him an honorary freeman. Both Oxford and Cambridge conferred on him honorary degrees. A number of military organizations, including the Cavalry Club, claimed him as their guest. A group of staff officers closely associated with him during the campaign presented him with a fine oil painting entitled "To the Relief of Kimberley." Painted by a war correspondent, it shows French at the head of the cavalry, advancing under fire, with shells bursting on the ground and in the air.

French showed little sign of the hardships that he had endured almost without interruption during the three years of active service in South Africa. He was tanned, relaxed, and in excellent health, though he had put on a considerble amount of weight. Sensitive about his appearance, French took immediate steps to shed the excess weight. By means of regular physical exercises and a prescribed diet he attained his goal within a matter of weeks.

Sir John took over his duties at Aldershot in September 1902, residing at Government House in Farnsborough. The 30,000 troops in the Aldershot Command included two infantry divisions and a cavalry brigade and were expected to form the first echelon of a striking force. The prime responsibility of the commandant, therefore, was to organize and train his men so that they would be fit to take the field.

The Boer War had revealed glaring defects in almost every aspect of Britain's military system. One of the earliest tactical lessons of the conflict was the recognition that technological changes had greatly enhanced the power of the defensive side of war. The War Office concluded that it was extremely difficult, if not impossible, for a frontal bayonet assault to cross a fire-swept zone, and instead stressed flank attacks, envelopment, and fire superiority. Simultaneously, as a means to correct what it perceived was a spirit of hesitancy in attack among junior officers, the War Office underlined the importance of individuality, initiative, morale, character, and of "developing a resolutely offensive spirit."

The results of the Russo-Japanese War in which the Japanese had apparently won their battles through moral superiority, the spirit of the offensive, and frontal assaults with the bayonet, led to a reassessment in military thinking. The upshot was that the first conclusions were downgraded and undue emphasis placed on the second. That is not to say that fire power was ignored—indeed, the army stressed accurate and rapid musketry training and, as a precondition to the final assault, called for a combination of fire and movement—but that it was no longer the decisive element in battle.[5]

The lessons of Manchuria seemed so obvious that agreement in the

British army was widespread and quickly arrived at. On the other hand, the cavalry was judged to have played an inconclusive part in that conflict. This perhaps explains why efforts to develop a tactical doctrine for the British cavalry in the wake of the South African War were accompanied by lengthy, sometimes bitter, debate.[6] The basic issue was whether cavalry should persist in employing shock tactics, attempting to overwhelm an enemy by the sheer impact of a mass close order change, or whether it should adapt to new circumstances and learn to fight dismounted. Sir John, whose views represented a large portion of cavalrymen, took the lead in upholding the established methods of the *arme blanche*.[7]

French felt that there were occasions when cavalry would produce the greatest effect by dismounting to employ fire. But the rifle should be carried as a secondary weapon and it was upon the *arme blanche* that the trooper should rely. Shock action and steel weapons had served the cavalry well for centuries and he saw no reason why they should not continue to be effective. He was convinced that the quality of leadership affected cavalry performance more than changes in weaponry; in short, success was reserved to a cavalry force that was taught to believe it "can ride at anything or ride over anything."[8] He rejected any thought of increased dismount fighting for mounted troops on the ground that it would cramp their style and take the edge off their dash.

During the South African War, mobility, combined with accurate marksmanship, had been the key to many Boer victories against larger but slower-moving British forces. French himself had adopted such tactics with immense success during the first phase of the campaign, but he became a firm advocate of time-honored methods after his dash to relieve Kimberley. French saw Klip Drift as something that it was not and deduced from it erroneous conclusions. It was not a classical knee-to-knee charge, utilizing the factors of shock and surprise against formed bodies of troops, but a penetration through a thinly held part of the enemy's lines. In effect it was a skillful application of the Boers' use of the horse as a means to move riflemen rapidly from one place to another. Incidentally, had the Boers strung wire across the pass at Klip Drift, as they should have been expected to do, the outcome might have been different.

More conscious of the demands of modern war, the opponents of the *arme blanche,* which included Lord Roberts, Ian Hamilton, and Henry Wilson, reasoned that the cavalry could not survive without changing both its tactics and weapons. This group believed that the mounted soldier must be not only a trained horseman but able to fight dismounted and shoot as straight as an infantryman. With proper arms and training, the cavalry, in addition to reconnaissance and occasional pursuits, could be used to move quickly to a threatened point in the firing line or to occupy a position before the enemy could do so and hold it until the infantry arrived.

At first the army authorities took into account the experience of the Boer War. In March 1903 an army order directed that cavalry in the future would retain the sword but that the rifle or carbine would be considered the principal weapon. The *Cavalry Manual,* issued the following year under the watchful eye of Lord Roberts, continued to stress the importance of the rifle and dismounted action. But after Roberts left the War Office, French and his former lieutenant, Douglas Haig, gained control over cavalry doctrine and training. The previous emphasis on firepower and mounted infantry work was superseded by the charge, sword, and lance. The *Cavalry Manual* for 1907, known to embody the views of Sir John, stated, "It must be accepted as a principle that the rifle, effective as it is, cannot replace the effect produced by the speed of the horse, the magnetism of the charge and the terror of cold steel."[9]

French wanted to keep the cavalry as unchanged as possible and he lived for the day when his maneuvre at Klip Drift could be repeated on a still vaster scale and with more spectacular results. His belief in the *arme blanche* was a religious mystique, blinding him to its future war potential in the face of rapidly increasing development of firepower. Although the *Cavalry Manual* was reissued in 1912 and modified the emphasis on the *arme blanche,* the British cavalry entered the First World War still wedded to shock tactics.

If French erred when he rejected tactical innovations in his own arm, he made up for it in other ways. To begin he raised the quality of infantry training by applying progressive concepts. Officers were told to get to know their men, to look after them, and generally to identify themselves with those upon whom they would have to depend in war. In addition to squad drill, there was a growing emphasis on individual instruction and a soldier was taught to use his wits and act with initiative and responsibility. Finally, the command encouraged realism by improvising battle situations.

Because he understood the value of sea power, French was a strong advocate of close cooperation between the army and navy. The autumn maneuvres in 1904 were of special interest to him because they consisted in the landing of a hostile invasion force on the Essex coast and the defense of an area in the neighborhood of Clacton and Colchester. He endorsed the idea of large-scale operations in Syria following tensions with Turkey in 1906. He agreed with the Admiralty on combined operations in 1908 and again in 1912. All this was happening at a time when many high-ranking British officers were engaged in a campaign for an independent role for the army, a condition they felt would lead to their acceptance as professionals in the eyes of their counterparts abroad.[10]

Few generals cared as deeply for the well-being of the private soldier as did French. He mingled freely among the men, engaging in small talk or commenting about their work. He was frequently present to witness field exercises, regardless of the time of day or weather conditions. He improved the quality of the food and the comfort of barracks and made real provision for recreation. The men warmed to him as anyone warms to care and attention.

While at Aldershot Sir John was instrumental in modifying the rules for General Staff employment. A school represented by Henry Wilson and Brigadier-General Henry Rawlinson favored restricting General Staff appointments only to those officers with the army's main academic qualifications, the PSC certificate that marked successful completion of the Staff College course at Camberley. This group wanted the newly instituted General Staff to be a *corps d'elite* composed of the best brains in the army. French triggered a controversy when he requested that one of his aides-de-camp, Major Algeron Lawson, be appointed to the vacant office of brigade major of his First Cavalry Brigade. This was to be a General Staff post and Lawson had no PSC certificate. Sir John was adamant that there should be no hard and fast rule, that the chief of the General Staff should be free to select any officer, irrespective of whether or not he had passed through the Staff College. To do otherwise, French argued, would be to deprive the army of the services of many able and experienced officers. He encountered opposition, as was to be expected, but in the end, got his way.[11]

No sensational events so far as he and his command were concerned took place during this period. French was more than content with his work. He was surrounded by friends and a staff whom he trusted and liked. He found his setting as congenial as his work. Government House stood in country surroundings and, although sparsely furnished and poorly insulated against the cold, was on the whole comfortable and spacious. Happy in the reunion with his family after a period of foreign service, he combined, or liked to think that he did, the life of a serving officer with that of a country gentleman.

Since Aldershot was close to London and the showplace of the British army, it attracted an unending stream of visitors—royalty, politicians, journalists, as well as foreign and colonial officers. French, in carrying out his social responsibilities, was badly handicapped by lack of financial resources. In those days the commandant was expected to dip into his private means in order to entertain on the scale expected of a man in his position. French enjoyed the social side of his job and he and his wife were charming hosts, but as he had no money of his own, he was compelled to cut social engagements to the bone.

French hated to be tied down to his desk and delegated as much work as possible to his administrative aides. This left him more time to get to know the staff and watch the training of the men. He had enormous energy and to those around him appeared inexhaustible. He would return late from a long day's work, snatch a few hours' sleep, and be off again soon after daybreak. He had a good memory and there were few officers at the camp down to the company commanders whose name and abilities he did not know. When watching a unit at its training work he might occasionally exchange a few words with the officer in charge but he never interfered. If he had a criticism to offer he made it only to the commanders directly responsible to himself.

French set high standards but he was not nearly so unrelenting in his expectations as Kitchener. He was a strict disciplinarian and did not hesitate to dismiss subordinates whom he judged unsatisfactory or inefficient. On the other hand he was unfailingly kind and generous to those who were loyal and served him well and in some cases he made it a point to bring their qualities to the notice of the authorities and to ensure that they received due recognition.

Aldershot was not all hard work and entertaining, for French found time for physical activity, which kept him in the fit condition he enjoyed to the end of his life. He exercised conscientiously every morning, took daily walks, and rode as often as possible. French kept a scale in his bathroom to check his weight, which was apt to increase if not carefully watched.

It cannot be claimed that French was a well-rounded soldier or that he stood out as an intellectual giant in the military world. He lacked the factual grounding in administration and logistics common to staff officers who had attended the Staff College.[12] His military writings show that he was neither a clear nor profound thinker.[13] He might have remedied some of his shortcomings, or at the very least broadened and deepened his knowledge, if he had taken the trouble to read the literature in his field. But in mid-life he became mentally lazy, rarely picking up a book connected with his profession and, when he did, only glancing at it. Serious reading, he is supposed to have said, gave him "mental indigestion." He declined to think things out, relying on his experience and intuition to make the right move at the right time.

French had able subordinates from whom he extracted the maximum because he trusted them and was not afraid to use them. But he had no original outlook; he was not an innovator by nature and distrusted new theories. Although South Africa had taught him independence of thought and self-reliance, he emerged from that trial with many prejudices.

In short, French was a tough, physically courageous, no-nonsense soldier, popular with his aides, able to command obedience and respect, but limited in his grasp of his profession and in most ways conservative and conventional.

Apart from professional deficiencies French had serious personality flaws that became more pronounced as he grew older. He had a fearsome temper and anyone, including members of his own family, was apt to be at the receiving end of it without warning. His mercurial disposition alternated between extremes of exuberance at one moment and of depression the next. He craved publicity, was extremely sensitive to criticism, and lacked a sense of humor. While he was charming, warm, and kind with friends and casual acquaintances, he acted very differently towards those who challenged his views or threatened him in any way. At such times he was apt to be petty, hostile, and, if necessary, unscrupulous. This kind of behavior was at least partially related to his extreme insecurity. Indeed, there was much in his life to undermine his confidence—he came from a different background from that of his brother officers, most of whom were country gentlemen brought up in the tradition of imperial service; he was always in financial difficulties; he had little formal education; he was short in stature; he had obtained his commission through the militia; and he was not especially bright. Now, despite all odds, he had by hard work and dedication become a respected figure in the army and in the nation. Obsessed with the idea of fame and recognition and determined to continue the climb to the top of his profession, he struck out instinctively and harshly against anyone who threatened to stand in the way of his goal.

In February 1907 French was promoted to the rank of full general. It was now intended that he should take over the post of inspector-general of the forces in succession to the duke of Connaught. The change was not to take place until near the end of the year, and during part of the interim French stayed with King Edward at Balmoral and paid a visit to Russia. The closing days at Aldershot were painful ones to French. The determination of his officers to demonstrate how much they regretted his departure was in itself gratifying, but to someone like French it only served to make farewells all the more distressing. At a big dinner on November 28 French made his farewell speech and received extravagant praise from many of the senior officers assembled in his honor. He relinquished his command on November 30 and two days later assumed his new appointment at the Horse Guards.

The purpose of the inspector-general's office was to keep watch on the state of the army's training and report its findings to the Army Council.[14] Much of French's time was occupied in traveling, which kept him away from his family, and in delivering speeches, a task he disliked intensely. Still, his work was important and his new position brought him a step closer to the center of the stage.

In June 1909 French was honored by the king with the G.C.B. in the Order of the Bath. In recent years French's work had brought him into close contact with the king, who was keenly interested in the army and its training, and their acquaintance had ripened into a warm friendship. The death of Edward in May 1910 came as a sad bereavement to Sir John, who felt that he had lost a personal friend. French maintained cordial relations with the new king, George V, until the outbreak of the Great War, when his political activities caused him to lose favor at court.

As inspector-general French not only crisscrossed England many times, but he traveled extensively abroad. Late in 1909 he crossed over to France where he attended cavalry maneuvers near Chalons and saw an aerial

A group at Aldershot in 1909. The front row includes *center*, King Edward VII; *second from left*, Grierson; *fourth from left*, Smith-Dorrien; *third from right*, French; *extreme right*, Robertson.
(Photo courtesy of Lord Robertson)

At the French maneuvers. Guy Brooke and Henry Wilson are on the left of French.
(By permission of the Macmillan Publishing Co. Inc. for Cassell)

display at Reims. Next he paid a visit to Canada, at the end of which he presented a report to the government suggesting ways to improve the country's armed forces. In 1911 he went to Germany as guest of the Kaiser to witness maneuvers on the eastern borders of Mecklenburg. There is no record of French's evaluation of the exercises, which were carried out by three leading Army Corps as well as the Guard Cavalry Division. During his stay in Germany he was invested with the Order of the Red Eagle. The emperor also gave French an autographed picture of himself and, as he placed it in his hand, he arrogantly exclaimed; "Remember that Germany never sheathes the sword."[15]

The last decade before 1914 saw international relations marred by a series of crises, mainly arising from national rivalries and antagonisms. Much tension and anxiety resulted. Europeans had no way of knowing whether any current crisis would lead to a general war. What seems comparatively unimportant in retrospect, since major warfare was avoided, seemed highly threatening at the time.

The first Moroccan crisis of 1905–6, in which Germany's crude bullying and hints of war created a decidedly unfavorable impression, made the Entente Cordiale a far stronger bond than it had been in the beginning. Under Sir Edward Grey, British foreign secretary, military conversations were opened with the French in order to arrange common action if the two powers were together involved in a war against Germany. The discussions were informal and not binding on either government. They continued in somewhat desultory form for several years and they did not receive any sharp impetus until 1910, when Henry Wilson became director of military operations at the War Office. Wilson was a passionate francophile and because of his close friendship with and admiration for Ferdinand Foch, then commandant at the Ecole de Guerre Supérieure, he became indoctrinated with the conviction that Germany was bent on war. By March 1911 he had formulated detailed plans for the mobilization of the British Expeditionary Force in the event of war. He also made arrangements to concentrate the entire BEF on the left of the French army in a war with Germany. Although the British government made no formal commitment of any kind, some degree of moral obligation was certainly incurred.

It was largely as a result of these conversations that R. B. Haldane, secretary for war, initiated a far-reaching modernization of the British army. He created a general staff and formed an expeditionary force, small but highly trained and ready for immediate service overseas. He set up an adequate reserve and, for home defense, a Territorial Force that comprised all existing militia units. Finally he established the Officers' Training Corps in the universities and most public schools, an act that was to prove its worth during the Great War. All of Haldane's reforms were achieved in close cooperation with the British military hierarchy, especially French and

Major-General Haig, who served at the War Office, first as director of military training and then as director of staff duties.[16]

The second international crisis came in 1908. Austria almost triggered a war with Russia by proclaiming the outright annexation of Bosnia and Herzegovina, the Turkish territory she had been administering since 1878. Britain had little to do with this incident, but the next one, provoked when the Kaiser sent a gunboat to the Moroccan port of Agadir in July 1911, touched her more closely.

Towards the end of the summer, as the situation darkened ominously, the War Office authorities felt compelled to consider a commander for the Expeditionary Force. The obvious candidate was French, who had already been designated to succeed Sir William Nicholson as chief of the Imperial General Staff in the coming spring. French, because of his performance as a tactician in South Africa, was widely reputed to be the best field general in the nation and his enthusiasm for amphibious warfare gave him a measure of interservice appeal. Nevertheless, Nicholson had misgivings about his successor, and there were others in the army who felt the same way about French. The consensus was that French had many fine soldierly qualities but that his intellectual limitations precluded him from becoming an effective commander. Nicholson delayed making a decision as long as he could but, unable to think of a better general with the necessary seniority, reluctantly concluded that French should have the honor of leading the British army in battle.[17] However, in November the crisis ended, with Germany receiving concessions in French Equatorial Africa.

The Agadir crisis and the fears that the incident engendered caused a radical shift of opinion among the military leaders in Britain. Hitherto only a few fanatics like Henry Wilson had acted on the assumption that a major war was likely. The change after Agadir was symbolized by French. When he became CIGS in March 1912 he told the senior staff at the War Office that he meant to get the army ready for a war with Germany, which he regarded as an eventual certainty.[18]

French's conviction in the imminence of a war with Germany contributed to a reversal of his position on conscription, an issue that divided the nation in the pre-1914 period. Traditionalists saw no need to augment the size of the army through compulsory military service. They were content to maintain the primacy of maritime strategy, limiting the functions of the army to small landings and police duties.

Those who favored conscription did so for different reasons. Lord Roberts, who initiated and led the campaign, did not think that the navy could prevent a German invasion. He wanted a conscript army to defend the island, certain that the men to form the necessary reserve would not be forthcoming in sufficient numbers under the current voluntary system.[19] Yet others supported national military service, not for home defense, but for the creation of a mass army for deployment in Europe. These included many notable soldiers such as Henry Wilson, James Grierson, and William Robertson, who wanted to establish for the British army an independent role within Europe that would free it from the domination of the Navy. They understood that if the Continental strategy replaced the traditional strategy, conscription, as practiced on the Continent, must be adopted.[20]

At first French sided with the traditionalists, regarding as absurd Roberts's fears of a sudden invasion. In 1907–8 French, as a member of the CID,[21] had participated in a subcommittee investigation of the invasion question. The subcommittee's conclusion was that, while small raids could not be excluded, an invasion in force was unlikely to escape the Royal Navy's detection.[22]

Within months of arriving at the War Office French had undergone a change of heart and joined the ranks of the conscriptionists.[23] The reason why he switched sides is clear enough. After 1912 Henry Wilson became his most trusted advisor. Throughout their association the intellectually agile Wilson was frequently able to bend Sir John to his will. Thus it was that under Wilson's sustained urgings French became a convert to conscription.

French's acceptance of compulsory military service must not be seen as a sign that he had also become a proponent of the General Staff's Continental policy. French's views on strategy are difficult to determine, owing to conflicting evidence. The official records show only that he was an ardent advocate of operations on the Continent. On the other hand he supposedly told friends of his preference for amphibious undertakings. It is conceivable that Sir John regarded the plan to collaborate with the French as temporary but nevertheless necessary in the short term because of the absence of an amphibious alternative. It may also be that his enthusiasm for combined enterprises had begun to cool. His experience in maneuvres had brought home the difficulties associated with a landing on an enemy coast and so may have served to convince him of the logic of the General Staff's case for fighting alongside the French. The third possibility is that Sir John simply could not make up his mind. I am inclined to support Professor D'Ombrain's thesis that French preferred an amphibious landing but did not rule out sending an army to France or Belgium.[24]

Whatever Sir John's preference, there did not seem to be much doubt after 1911 that the nation would adopt a Continental strategy in the event that it was drawn into a war in support of France.[25] Preoccupied with a host of other matters, French did not devote anywhere near the time that Wilson had to a study of the country over which troops might have to fight. But also unlike Wilson he suspected, as did a number of others in England, that Germany might attempt a wide swing north of the Meuse.[26] If his worst fears proved correct, the BEF would stand in the path of the main onslaught.

Such thinking was anathema to the French, who were irrevocably wedded to a strategy of attack in Alsace-Lorraine and all along their front. The new school of French strategists, replacing a generation that had held the foe in sober respect, went to extremes in advocating an offensive policy based on moral and psychological superiority. The idea was to strike first with the greatest concentration of force without due concern for strategic or tactical principles. That being the case how could they possibly have agreed with someone like French that the main German attack was coming through Belgium? It would have meant adopting a defensive role—a betrayal of Napoleonic tradition.

Wilson never subscribed to the extremist doctrine of the "élan" school, which his good friend Foch had done much to encourage both by his teachings at the Ecole de Guerre and by his book, *The Principles of War*. Still he approved of French offensive policy and to a lesser extent agreed with their reading of German intentions. Wilson rejected the idea of a full-scale German invasion of Belgium on the grounds that the maneuvre would be dangerous and would require more men than the enemy actually possessed. He saw that the Germans might send a few divisions through the southern part of Belgium, in which case they would be opened to sudden and vicious attacks on either flank. Both he and Foch viewed the role of the BEF as an attacking operation in support of a general French advance. Wilson was convinced that, with the approximate equality of Franco-German troops in the Maubeuge-Verdun sector, the six British divisions would exert a decisive impact on the course of events.

Wilson gave an overview of the problems of a Franco-German conflict and of Britain's provisional war plans at a CID meeting on August 23, 1911. During his talk he was frequently interrupted by French and in particular Churchill, who wanted to know what would happen if the Germans crossed above the Meuse and entered France on a front between Lille and Maubeuge.[27] Wilson brushed aside their concerns but he was obviously troubled by them because subsequently he became convinced of the need to "snaffle" Belgium.[28] If the unexpected should occur, he reasoned, the Entente would have a secure base from which to attack the German wing.[29] After French became CIGS Wilson persuaded him that Belgian cooperation was an essential element in successful Anglo-French action south of the Meuse.

In April 1912 Sir John sought through Colonel Tom Bridges, the British military attaché in Brussels, to reopen the negotiations with the Belgians, which had lapsed in 1906. Bridges was instructed to tell the Belgian authorities that when the time came Britain could put 150,000 men in the field but that the Belgians must play their part by further strengthening the fortresses of Liège and Namur and by calling for help as soon as their country was invaded. The military attaché mishandled the talks with the result that the Belgians were even less willing to accept British help than they had seemed at the time of the first approaches six years earlier. Not only would the Belgians not commit themselves but they made it clear that if British troops landed before a German invasion or without a formal request, their army would open fire.[30]

Since diplomacy had failed to draw Belgium into the Entente, Wilson proceeded to tighten and perfect his arrangements with the French. By mid-1914 he had completed the BEF's mobilization plans, assured its transportation across the Channel, and determined its movements and concentration area once in France. The BEF was now ready to move within a minimum space of time from its peace stations in England to its war zone in France.[31]

French's efforts were not only confined to overseeing and helping Wilson with some of his projects. He also paid several visits to France where he watched army exercises, exchanged views with French military leaders, notably Foch, and acquainted himself with the probable field of operations on the northern frontier. His systematic study of deficiencies in Britain's Territorial and Regular forces led to a variety of improvements: essential equipment was purchased, training methods were perfected, new types of ammunition became available, and there were increases in gasoline supplies and the number of horses.

Another step he took to prepare the Expeditionary Force for its projected Continental task was to inaugurate military maneuvres along European lines. One of the notable weaknesses of the British army in the South African War was the inability of its commanders to handle large forces on extended fronts, a failing that was chiefly due to the lack of peacetime maneuvres. It was difficult to find suitable ground of the size required in England and, when found, farmers and landowners were in general opposed to their property being used for training.[32] Only two large-scale maneuvres were held during Sir John's tenure. The first took place in East Anglia in the autumn of 1912 with Haig and Grierson as army commanders. Grierson, with a slightly inferior force, badly outmaneuvred Haig, bringing a premature end to the operations.[33]

The second, held in the Midlands in 1913 between September 22 and 26, ought to be described since it was a near replica of the military events that were to unfold a year later. The bulk of the Expeditionary Force, including the Royal Flying Corps, took part or was represented by token units. The real value of the exercise was to test the working of the higher commands and their staff in an encounter battle. The object was for French, who personally directed a "Brown Force" consisting of two corps and a cavalry division, to dislodge from a fortified position a much smaller "White Force" under Major-General C. C. Monro. Communications were inadequate and Sir John badly mishandled the disposition of his forces, creating a large gap between the two corps. During the exercises French and his chief of staff,

General James Grierson, clashed over his tactical judgment. French never forgave Grierson for proving him wrong and after a suitable interval transferred him to another post.[34]

In June 1913 French was promoted to the rank of field marshal and was thus on the penultimate branch of the tree. Up to now his career had been one of unbroken success. In South Africa he had distinguished himself in the field, when so many established reputations had failed, and at home he had held the chief administrative appointments. The future looked equally bright, for he had been designated by the government to command the British Expeditionary Force in the event of war. However, in the early spring of 1914 the officer corps in the British army was rocked by a tremor that threatened not only to disrupt its discipline but also to bring an abrupt end to French's career.

By the end of August 1913 the Home Rule Bill, a measure providing for a separate parliament at Dublin, had been twice passed by the Commons and twice rejected by the Lords. Under the terms of the Parliament Act it would become law if passed by the Commons once more. The main defect of the bill was its failure to cater to the special problem posed by Ulster where the population, largely of Scottish ancestry, was Protestant and industrial in contrast to the Roman Catholic and agricultural society of southern Ireland. Ulstermen, with the full support of Conservatives in England, were determined to resist by force any settlement that would make them a minority in a Catholic state. Led by Sir Edward Carson, the men of Ulster organized, drilled, and provided themselves with weapons to defy the Home Rule Bill if and when it became law. National volunteers were organized in the south to offset the threat from Ulster. Ireland seemed headed for civil war.

The irresponsibility of the Conservatives was matched by the weakness and indecision of the government. Asquith and the cabinet should have known that Ulster could not be forced to accept Home Rule and they certainly ought to have taken steps to suppress the private armies springing up in Ireland. Instead they adopted a wait-and-see attitude. When the Home Rule Bill was introduced a third time into the Commons in March 1914, it contained a provision that each of the dissenting counties could, at their own wish, opt out of the new Ireland for a period of six years. But the only condition that the opposition would accept was the permanent exclusion of Ulster. This was intolerable to the Nationalists because of the size of the Catholic minorities, which ranged from twenty to nearly fifty percent of the population in the northern counties. Passions on both sides rose to a dangerous level.

If violence did occur, how would the army react? Its officers were predominantly conservative and an extraordinarily high proportion of them were drawn from the ranks of the Protestant Irish gentry. They were horrified over the prospect that military force might be used to coerce

Ulster into accepting government by a Dublin parliament. Henry Wilson was a leading figure in antigovernment circles and, as his own diaries fully reveal, saw nothing incompatible with his duties at the War Office in passing on state secrets to his Conservative friends or in intriguing with the Ulster volunteers. Lord Roberts was another prominent officer who actively campaigned to ensure that the Home Rule Bill was not put on the statute book. As for French his sympathies lay with the Ulstermen, but in the final analysis his soldierly sense of duty prevailed. For a time he was like a ship caught in the storm, flung first one way and then another.

A crisis was foreshadowed when Lord Willoughby de Broke, in order to prevent the coersion of Ulster, put forward the idea that the lords should refuse to pass the annual Army Act, thus depriving the government of any disciplined force after April 30. Given the international situation and the widely held belief that a European war was imminent, it was incredible, indeed nothing short of criminal, that any responsible person should promote a measure designed to wreck the army. Yet the Conservatives, who seemed to have lost all sense of perspective in their fight against Home Rule, leaped at the proposal. Alarmed, the government was at last driven to act while there was still time. On March 14 General Sir Arthur Paget, commanding the forces in Ireland, was instructed to take steps to safeguard stores, arms, and ammunition depots in northern Ireland. On a scene already tense with emotion Winston Churchill, the first lord of the admiralty, delivered a highly belligerent speech warning those who sought to challenge parliamentary institutions by force. If this was done, he concluded, there was only one thing to do: "Let us go forward together and put these grave matters into the proof." Several days later Churchill announced that the "forthcoming practice" of the Third Battle Squadron would take place off the Isle of Arran. To the Conservatives these developments were a clear indication that the government was bent on coercing Ulster, by force if necessary.

Summoned to London, Paget arrived on March 13 and he spent the rest of the day and part of the next closeted with Jack Seely (who had succeeded Haldane as secretary for war in 1912) and French, as well as the leading members of the cabinet. Paget was concerned that the movement of troops in Ulster, although only precautionary, might excite disturbances, even active resistance. He was also anxious lest some of his officers, particularly those of Anglo-Irish origin, refuse to take part in military operations against the Ulster volunteers. In the first matter the government gave Paget full discretionary powers to use his troops in Ireland as he saw fit to protect military installations and to prevent disorderly outbreaks. If necessary he could count on additional troops and the cooperation of the Royal Navy. French felt it was poor strategy to scatter troops all over Ulster "as though it was a Pontypool coal strike," but the politicians overruled his protest. The decision affecting the second point appears to have been taken only by Seely and French. They told Paget that he should be guided by the following principles: first, officers ordered to act in support of civil power should not be permitted to resign their commission but must, if they refused to obey orders, be dismissed from the army; and second, that indulgence might be shown, in cases where it was asked for, to officers who were domiciled in Ulster. The above instructions were given to Paget only in verbal form. By committing nothing to paper the government, in effect, had neatly transferred all responsibility onto Paget's shoulders. The task required courage and tact. Paget fulfilled the first condition but unfortunately not the second.

Early on March 20 Paget, back at his headquarters in Dublin after traveling overnight from London, called a meeting of his senior officers. His best hope of enlisting their support would have been to lay his difficulties before them at the outset and then appeal to their loyalty and sense of duty. As it was he unwisely forfeited their good will by adopting a hectoring tone. He began by describing the precautionary measures he had been charged to carry out, but did so in such an alarmist way that he conveyed the impression that the entire country would be ablaze within twenty-four hours. He indicated that he had obtained a concession for officers whose homes were actually in Ulster but, as for the rest, he wanted to know at once their intentions. Would they obey their orders as yet unspecified, or accept dismissal and forfeiture of pensions? This was a subtle but critical extension of Seely's instructions. The result was that General Hubert Gough, commander of the Third Cavalry Brigade, stationed at the Curragh camp near Dublin, and fifty-seven of his officers, out of a total of seventy, preferred to accept dismissal than be involved in military operations against Ulster.[35]

It was from Wilson that French first learned of what had happened in Ireland. Wilson painted a grim picture of the consequences—mass depletions in the General Staff and regiments and the army reduced to ruin in the face of a hostile Europe. He thought there was still time to resolve the problem if the government reinstated the officers and promised not to employ the army to coerce Ulster into accepting the Home Rule Bill. Wilson, at the request of Sir John and Seely, set down the conditions on paper but these were rejected by the government. Wilson was irritated by Sir John's apparent inaction, which he felt was placing an intolerable strain on the discipline of the army. He wrote in his diary: "I still kept impressing on Sir John the appalling gravity of the situation but I cannot get him to realize, and he acts like a child."[36] Wilson was not the only one dissatisfied with Sir John's behavior.

Lord Roberts knew that no movement of troops could be made without French's approval, yet he could not bring himself to believe that his old comrade was involved in the action being concerted against Ulster. On the day the full story appeared in the newspapers he telephoned Sir John to castigate the politicians whom he held responsible for bringing on the crisis, and to express the hope that the CIGS would refrain from any activities that might help to precipitate a civil war. According to Roberts French replied that he intended to court-martial the mutinous officers.[37] Sir John's account of the telephone conversation is somewhat different. It runs as follows:

> Lord Roberts: "I am speaking from Ascot. What do you think of this terrible state of affairs?"
> Sir J. French: "It is very difficult to speak about such matters on the telephone."
> Lord Roberts: "I hope you are not going to associate yourself with this band of (certain epithets were used which I could hardly catch). If you do you will cover yourself with infamy."
> Sir J. French: "I must do my duty as a soldier like everyone else and put up with whatever consequences may ensue."
> Lord Roberts: "Goodbye."[38]

There is no real evidence that French was determined to punish the officers concerned or, as he was then described by some, "a mere tool of Seely's." French felt strongly that the duty of every officer and soldier was to obey all lawful commands given to them through the proper channel. Although he appreciated the dilemma forced upon Gough and the other officers at the Curragh, he disapproved of their insubordinate behavior. He was horrified over the prospect of a split in the army that would have utterly destroyed everything he had worked for in the past dozen years. To avert such a calamity he earnestly sought whatever reconciliation could be compatible with discipline.

On March 23, a day after arriving in London, Gough met with French and Sir Spencer Ewart, the adjutant-general at the War Office. French's manner was friendly and conciliatory. He insisted that the government had not intended to use the army to coerce Ulster, that the troop movements undertaken and planned were only of a precautionary nature. He said that Paget's ultimatum had been the result of an unfortunate misunderstanding and he urged Gough to return to his command as if nothing had happened. Gough replied that he would be happy to do so if he received a definite assurance that his men would not be used to enforce the Home Rule Bill on Ulster. French offered a verbal guarantee to that effect but Gough observed that there had been so much misunderstanding already that nothing less than a written assurance would satisfy him and his men. French declared that a written guarantee was impossible. Gough, with equal firmness, said that he was very sorry but that he could not take up his command again without a written pledge. French sank into a chair and gave vent to his frustration with a long sigh. A painful silence ensued. At last French said to Ewart: "Well, we can't do anything for him. I have done my best, there is nothing for it but to take him before the Secretary of State."

The three men started down the passage to Seely's room. On the way French made a final effort to change Gough's mind. Taking his arm he exclaimed: "For God's sake go back and don't make any more difficulties, you don't know how serious all this is. If you don't go back, all the War Office will resign. I've done my best for you. If they had attempted to penalize you, I would have resigned myself." Gough replied that he was very grateful but added nothing else.

When they entered the secretary of state's room they found Paget and another officer with Seely. All took a seat around the conference table. Seely's manner, so Gough recalls, was pompous and sententious. He embarked on a long explanation of the relations between the military and the civil power that seemed to Gough to be taken verbatim from the *Manual of Military Law*. The interview then followed the same pattern as with French. Seely said there had been a misunderstanding and explained the reason for the proposed movement of troops in Ireland. He insisted that the government's verbal guarantee ought to be enough and asked Gough to return to his brigade. Gough replied that he would do so if he was given a specific assurance in writing. Seely answered indignantly that no government would submit to such dictation by one of its own servants. Gough avoided being drawn into argument and reiterated his condition. Sir John broke the deadlock and eased the tension when he subtly suggested, "Perhaps General Gough has not made it quite clear that he feels that he will not be able to return to his officers or regain their confidence unless he can show them the authority of the Army Council; and that he feels his own verbal assurances will not be sufficient now that feeling has been so greatly aroused." Gough hastened to thank French and confirmed his observation. "I see," Seely said as he grasped the lifeline with relief. "I think that is only a reasonable request." He added that there would be no difficulty in drawing up a note that would be satisfactory. Gough was directed to return at 4 o'clock that afternoon.

Ewart drafted a statement that was taken to 10 Downing Street for cabinet approval. Seely had an audience with the king and was absent when his colleagues discussed and amended the draft. On his return to Downing Street the cabinet was breaking up for lunch so Asquith handed him the document. Seely stuffed it in his pocked and remained in the cabinet room talking to John Morley. When he got around to reading the note he realized that it did not cover an essential point raised by Gough. Accordingly he added two paragraphs on his own. The first contained nothing of substance but the second gave Gough too much. They read:

> His Majesty's Government must retain their right to use all the forces of the Crown in Ireland, or elsewhere, to maintain law and order and to support the civil power in the ordinary execution of its duty.

But they have no intention whatever of taking advantage of this right to crush political opposition to the policy or principles of the Home Rule Bill.

The amended document arrived at the War Office at 2:30 P.M. whereupon French and Ewart added their initials to it below Seely's. Shortly after 4 o'clock French turned it over to Gough in the presence of the adjutant-general. Gough read it through and asked if he might retire and have fifteen minutes to consider it. French agreed reluctantly, reminding him that the king was waiting to know if all had been settled. In a nearby room Gough found MacEwen and Parker, two colonels who had accompanied him to London, as well as his brother, Johnnie, and Henry Wilson. Together they studied the memorandum. Wilson pointed out that the note, as it now stood, left a loophole for the government. If the Home Rule Bill passed, might not the army be called to enforce it in Ulster under the plea of maintaining law and order? Gough reached for a sheet of War Office paper and wrote down his interpretation of the last paragraph: "I understand the reading of the last paragraph to be that the troops under our command will not be called upon to enforce the present Home Rule Bill on Ulster, and that we can so assure our officers."

Gough then returned to Sir John's room, taking MacEwen and Parker with him as witnesses. He read out his interpretation of the ambiguous phrase to French, who remarked: "That seems all right." French then asked if he could "have a look at that paper." He paced up and down once or twice before sitting at his desk. The day was wearing on, he was tired, exasperated, and eager to tell the king that the crisis was over. Without consulting Seely he scribbled at the foot of Gough's note: "This is how I read it. J.F." With this precious assurance in his pocket, Gough returned triumphantly to the Curragh, where he received an ovation from his officers.[39]

The government was far less satisfied with the agreement, which in effect had severely restricted its freedom of action in Ireland. Asquith wasted no time in repudiating both Seely's added paragraphs and French's special assurance. As head of the army French had given a group of officers a pledge that the government now refused to support. It was an impossible position for him, as it was for Ewart and Seely. Asquith did not wish to lose French. He wrote, "His position is a very difficult one, but he has been so loyal and has behaved so well that I would stretch a great many points to keep him."[40] French consulted with Wilson as to whether he should resign or not. Wilson bluntly told him that he ought to go. For nearly a week French remained on the horns of a dilemma but he finally agreed to do so when he became convinced that the army would not trust a CIGS who retained office under the existing circumstances.[41] And with him went Ewart and Seely. Ironically Wilson, whose head ought to have been the first to roll, escaped punishment.

At the age of sixty-one French became unemployed, though he remained on the active list by virtue of his rank of field marshal. Still fit and full of vigor, he was grief-stricken at the prospect of facing long empty years of retirement and idleness. He was certain that his military career was over, notwithstanding Asquith's promise that he would be recalled, in the event of war, to command the Expeditionary Force. He would soon be out of touch with what was going on at the War Office so that when war came the government would be forced to turn to someone else whether it wanted to or not. If his expectations had proved correct, he would have left a more enduring reputation.

4
BEF to the Continent

Few Englishmen imagined during the summer of 1914 that the nation was about to be dragged into a full-scale European conflict. Indeed the prospect of even a major war on the Continent seemed more remote than it had been for some time. The Balkan wars were over and no fresh crisis had developed. The first half of 1914 was a period of relative calm.

The mood did not change even after the assassination of the Archduke Francis Ferdinand at Sarajevo on June 28, 1914. The consequences of that tragic event evolved slowly at first and rated minimal coverage in the British press. Attention at home was still riveted on the Irish question. Politicians and statesmen were so preoccupied with trying to find a formula acceptable to the conflicting parties that they practically lost sight of the larger international issue. Even French, who had for so long preached the imminence of war and had prepared for it, did not realize that a storm was brewing. It was not until July 30, when Russia defied German demand to demobilize, that he became convinced that war must inevitably follow. On that day French was summoned to the War Office by the new chief of the General Staff, Sir Charles Douglas, and was told privately that he had been selected to command the Expeditionary Force in the event that it should be sent to France.[1] This must have come as a surprise to French, since in recent talks with Churchill he had indicated he no longer expected the command.[2]

On hearing the good news French sought out his old South African chief, Lord Kitchener. French, who was apt to get carried away under the influence of strong emotions, proposed that Kitchener should be appointed to command the BEF with "me as his Chief of Staff."[3] Kitchener would not hear of it. Indeed, it was an absurd suggestion. Sir John had devoted many years organizing and training the BEF and was acquainted with its generals and staffs. He was known to the French, had attended their army maneuvers, and had visited that portion of the Continent where it was expected that British troops might be called upon to fight. Kitchener, on the other hand, had spent most of his military and administrative career in the outer parts of the empire. He had not kept abreast with European tactical principles and knew little about the recent reforms in the British army. Kitchener would have been ill-suited to command the British army in 1914.

On August 1 Germany declared war on Russia, whereupon France began to mobilize. Convinced that France would join the war on Russia's side, Germany demanded passage for her troops through Belgian territory. Belgium, however, faithful to her obligations as a neutral, refused. Thereupon Germany declared war on both France and Belgium and on the 4th her advance units crossed the Belgian frontier. That evening, Britain, as the guarantor of Belgian neutrality, entered the conflict.

On August 5 French established his temporary headquarters at the Hotel Metropole in London. His principal staff officers, selected some time ago while he was still CIGS, consisted of Colonel W. Lambton as military secretary; Brigadier-General G. Macdonogh as director of intelligence; Major-General Sir William Robertson as quartermaster-general; Major-General Nevil Macready as adjutant-general; Brigadier-General Henry Wilson as sub-chief of staff; and General Sir Archibald Murray as chief of staff.[4]

Murray was a reliable and conscientious soldier but his health was not up to the inevitable strain of campaigning. Moreover he did not possess a strong character and it is difficult to resist the conclusion that he never was, or aspired to be, more than an agent for French. His opinions, though respected, made little impact on French and he remained a shadowy figure in the background, signing orders, circulating papers, and tending the machine.

Wilson would have made a better chief of staff than Murray. He liked Sir John because he was a "pure and simple" soldier, but there were times when he wished that his chief had "more brains and knowledge," and concluded regretfully that he "has neither the one nor the other in any real measure."[5] Wilson had not seen any great amount of service commanding troops in action and when given an opportunity in 1916 he showed no distinction. Nevertheless, he was a thoroughly competent staff officer and had a genius for getting things done, whether by skillful maneuvre or intrigue. He knew the French generals personally, spoke their language fluently, and had prepared the BEF for its role in France.

To be sure, French would have preferred Wilson as his chief of staff. He had great faith in Wilson's judgment and enjoyed his lively and stimulating company, which was so different from that of the other soldiers he had met in the course of his professional career. However, Asquith disliked and distrusted Wilson, regarding him as the main cause of the Ulster troubles. He rejected any idea of assigning Wilson to so senior a position. The result was that Wilson became French's right hand man in everything but name.

Sir John's appointment to command the BEF was a foregone conclusion and caused no surprise when it was announced in the press. Indeed it was immensely popular, not only with the public and politicians but also with the French and the rank-and-file in the British army.[6] French's exploits in South Africa, his willingness to accept responsibility, and his work in preparing the army for war had earned him a reputation that was second only to Kitchener's among active soldiers. The general assumption was that the man who had been so successful in directing small operations would repeat his victories on a larger scale.

There were, however, a few army officers who did not share that opinion. Douglas Haig, for one, doubted the suitability of French as commander-in-chief. He was aware of French's strength and limitations, having maintained close ties with him since serving as his chief of staff in South Africa. He knew French to be dedicated and courageous but at the same time felt that his military knowledge was inadequate and his temper too uneven. "In my own heart," Haig wrote in his diary, "I know French is quite unfit for this great command at a time of crisis in our Nation's history."[7] His forecast would prove correct.

Although the army began to mobilize on August 4, no one was certain of how the war was going to be waged. The British, as yet, had not agreed on a plan of action. In the prewar years His Majesty's Government had been concerned with other matters and, without committing itself, had permitted the British General Staff to coordinate plans with the French. Consequently, British military leaders had little choice but to go along with the French strategy. The policy that was worked out in effect made the war contribution of Britain an appendix to the war plan of France.

It was left to the Council of War of August 5 to ratify or overturn the Continental ideas espoused by the General Staff. Asquith was in the chair. Among the others present were Churchill, Haldane and Grey from the cabinet; Battenberg from the navy; Douglas, Cowans, and von Donop from the War Office; Hankey who acted as secretary; and the nation's leading soldiers, past and present—Roberts, Kitchener, French, Haig, Grierson, Wilson, Murray, and Hamilton.

The meeting opened with the general acknowledgment that the country was under a moral, if not legal, obligation to provide as much assistance as possible to France. All looked to the army since the navy offered no projects for amphibious operations. The first question dealt with the composition of the Expeditionary Force—whether to send all six regular divisions abroad or retain one or more until replacements were available. No one considered that the Germans, extended by the unexpected resistance of the Belgian army, would attempt an invasion of the island. The possibility of a raid could not be ruled out but Churchill, speaking on behalf of the admiralty, indicated that the navy was in a state of absolute readiness. He was certain that he could provide for the security of the kingdom and urged that all six divisions be sent out at once.[8] His motion carried.

The assemblage next considered the precise destination of the Expeditionary Force. On this issue there was a considerable diversity of opinion. French began by presenting an outline of the prearranged plan that had been worked out between the British and French general staffs. It was hoped that the Expeditionary Force would mobilize simultaneously with the French army and would be concentrated behind the French left at Maubeuge by the fifteenth day of mobilization. The intention then was to move eastwards towards the Meuse and act on the left of the French against the German right flank. However, the British army had begun to mobilize three days later than the French and therefore the plan would require modification. French now believed that Amiens, seventy miles to the rear of Maubeuge, would be a a safer place to concentrate.

As an afterthought, Sir John wondered if it might not be better to land at Antwerp instead and operate, in conjunction with the Dutch and Belgians, against the flank of the invading German hosts.[9] The suggestion shows that French was not thinking clearly. To discard a plan carefully prepared over a number of years in favor of one that was improvised and ambitious was to ignore the elementary realities of staff work and logistics.

The prospect of a shift to Antwerp terrified Wilson[10] and made Haig shudder.[11] Douglas was equally upset. To their relief the issue was laid to rest when Churchill indicated that he could not guarantee safe passage for the troop ships across the wider part of the North Sea, and by an observation that the approaches to Antwerp lay through Dutch waters and that Holland had not been invaded and was unlikely to depart from neutrality.

Kitchener drew attention to the probability of a wide German sweep through Belgium, in which case the Expeditionary Force would be overwhelmed if it concentrated at Maubeuge. He returned to the idea of a staging at Amiens and received the support of Hamilton, who felt it was urgent for the troops to reach there without delay.

A number of questions were raised by Haig and other officers who had not taken part in prewar talks on grand strategy. If the British Expeditionary Force did not go over at once would the French be beaten? If the French were already in retreat when the Expeditionary Force arrived would its assistance be sufficient to turn the tide of battle? In the event of a French collapse could the Expeditionary Force be extricated? What was the state of the French army and how did it compare in numbers with the Germans? Discussion of these and other questions led to a reexamination of British war strategy and in the end the view prevailed that the French were the best judges to determine at which point the Expeditionary Force should be sent. The decisive factor, Hankey wrote in retrospect, "was that the plan for co-operation by our Expeditionary Force on the left of the

French Army had been worked out by the two Staffs in great detail, and this could not be said of any other plan."[12]

The cabinet on the morning of August 6 sanctioned the proposal to dispatch the Expeditionary Force to the Continent, but owing to an invasion scare that brewed up overnight,[13] it reduced the six divisions to four. In deference to Kitchener's wishes it was provisionally decided that British troops should be concentrated at Amiens. Kitchener did not attend the meeting because he was not yet formally a member of the government. The swearing-in ceremony took place early in the afternoon.

Asquith had been acting secretary for war since March when Jack Seely resigned for mishandling the Curragh incident. In war conditions it was obvious that the War Office would require the undivided energies of a strong man. Asquith's decision to name Kitchener secretary for war was not planned in advance and came only after he had concluded that no current member of the cabinet was suitable. Kitchener was on his way back to Egypt to resume his duties and had boarded a vessel at Dover when he was recalled to London. It was an immensely popular appointment. His impressive record of achievements over the past forty years, aided, it must be noted, by a magnificent physical appearance and proud bearing, had contributed to a seemingly impregnable reputation. Churchill later recalled the mixture of awe, respect, and confidence that he and his colleagues felt for Kitchener, and the belief that he had "plans deeper and wider than any we could see." In the early months of the war he was practically a military dictator; he was never overruled or seriously challenged on any important issue. "All powerful, imperturbable, reserved, he dominated absolutely our counsels at this time," Churchill recorded.[14]

Kitchener was out of his depth among the lawyers and dialecticians who formed so large a part of the Asquith government. By instinct and environment he had acquired the methods of an autocrat and he was incapable of adapting himself to the free and easy ways of a cabinet. Kitchener was a fluent writer but he had difficulty articulating his views orally. He resented the necessity of attending cabinet meetings either during or after a hard day's work at the War Office to engage in swift verbal exchanges for which he was ill-trained. Moreover he disliked having to discuss military secrets with a body of civilians, some of whose names he could not even recall; he suspected that when his colleagues went home at night they revealed everything to their wives. Kitchener sat uneasily in the company of men, belonging to a profession for which he felt the soldier's usual mixture of contempt and apprehension. His main concern at the council table was to tell the politicians only as much as he thought they ought to know and then get back to the War Office as quickly as possible.

To Kitchener's bent for extreme centralization and exaggerated concern for secrecy must be added his unwillingness to accept the need for a strong and independent General Staff. Kitchener's methods had served him well in the past. But he was now sixty-four years old and the problems of modern warfare far transcended previous human experience. His most urgent requirement in these circumstances was an efficient General Staff to deal with army organization and to formulate broad strategic plans. Unfortunately all the trained and qualified soldiers at the War Office had joined the BEF and their places were filled with nonentities. Rather than reconstruct the General Staff, Kitchener pushed it into the background and took on his own shoulders the whole weight of conducting the war. It was a burden that no man, however great his capacity, could properly carry.

Kitchener made a number of mistakes in the opening months of the war but on all the big issues he was right. He correctly predicted the route by which Germany would invade France. He alone foresaw that the war would be long and accordingly set his sights for the creation of an army of millions. All over the country recruiting posters with his imposing features, his finger pointing both accusingly and appealingly, carried the same message: "Your Country Needs You." Before the voluntary system ended in the spring of 1916 no fewer than 2,500,000 men had enlisted—and it was largely Kitchener's prestige and popularity with the nation that pulled them in.

Apart from the ordinary routine of his department Kitchener assumed responsibility for three gigantic tasks. He undertook to raise, train, and equip an army of unprecedented size; supervise the conduct of British military strategy; and mobilize the nation's industries for war. Without his contribution, as Edward Grey pointed out, "the war might have been lost, or victory rendered impossible."[15]

The Council of War reassembled towards the end of the afternoon on August 6. The same persons were in attendance but Kitchener was now secretary for war. Asquith announced that the cabinet had agreed in principle to dispatch the Expeditionary Force. It remained to decide how many divisions would go and where they should concentrate. Kitchener explained that, in view of the prevailing uncertainty, it was not advisable to send more than four divisions to the Continent. The fifth would join the main force as soon as circumstances permitted. The sixth division was to be kept available for any emergency at home and was to form part of the units to follow later.

Attention then turned upon the place to which they should be dispatched. Both Kitchener and French considered that the staging area should be around Amiens. However, there were others who felt that such a move would not only dislocate current arrangements but would prevent the British army from playing a part in the opening stages when its help was likely to be of the most value to the French. The discussion was inconclusive. The general view tended to favor Amiens but a final decision was withheld, pending further consultation with the French General Staff.[16]

Accordingly Kitchener requested through the French Embassy that a specially accredited officer be sent from France to acquaint him with General Joffre's plans and intentions. The French mission, headed by Colonel Huguet, arrived in London on August 12 and held a hurried conference with Sir John and several members of his staff. Huguet dwelt at length on the current dispositions of the French and German armies, after which, aided by Wilson, he converted Sir John into standing firm for Maubeuge as the concentration point.[17] French's change of heart was occasioned, to use his own words, by the following considerations:

> Any alteration in carrying out our concentration, particularly if this meant delay, would have upset the French plan of campaign and created much distrust in the minds of our Allies. Delay or hanging back would not only have looked like hesitation, but might easily have entailed disastrous consequences by permanently separating our already inferior forces.[18]

Later in the day French, Huguet, and Wilson descended upon Kitchener at the War Office. Kitchener, as we have seen, disapproved of the French plan. He had no faith in the offensive doctrine that had recently become current in the French army. Worse still, he distrusted the fighting ability of the French, believing that they would scatter before the Germans "like partridges."[19]

Kitchener listened to the views of his visitors, then stood up and, pointing to a large map on the wall, stressed the dangers of a German enveloping movement. He argued that the Germans would not have dragged Britain into the war by attacking Liège unless they had meant from the first to carry out their main attack through Belgium north of the Meuse River. That being the case, if the BEF were positioned at Maubeuge it would be swamped and forced into a retreat that would be disastrous for its morale. He was adamant that the base should be further back at Amiens to allow freedom of action.

The officers present were just as tenacious in upholding the original plan. They felt that the BEF should be placed in an area that would best harmonize with French strategic dispositions. They expressed the view of the French General Staff that the Germans, faced with the menace of a Russian onslaught, could not provide the required troops for the sweep on the scale that Kitchener anticipated. They assumed that the German advance would come either through Lorraine or possibly through the Ardennes Forest in the extreme south of Belgium. But any German drive was considered to be of only transitory importance. Once the French put Plan XVII (see chapter 5) into effect, the Germans would have to abandon any offensive of their own in favor of countering the French thrust. Thus it was that Joffre wanted the British army to concentrate as far forward as possible in order to protect the French left while the right wing delivered the main blow.

An artist's sketch of the British Expeditionary Force landing in France in August 1914
(Photo courtesy of The Mansell Collection)

Kitchener reiterated that the French plan was dangerous. He indicated that instead of mounting a headlong rush they should wait to counter a German attack. Kitchener was unable to advance conclusive arguments to sustain his case. Although he believed his military instinct and logic to be correct, he had enjoyed little opportunity to study the problem in its complexities and had made no exact calculation either of the strength of the German forces or of their probable distribution. The wrangle continued for three hours until Kitchener, still unconvinced, gave way. In a final gesture and to absolve himself of any responsibility, Kitchener took Sir John along with him and laid the whole issue before the prime minister. Presented with the arguments for both sides, Asquith very naturally declined to overrule the unanimous opinion of the combined General Staffs.[20] The cabinet's provisional decision of August 6 was accordingly set aside.

Kitchener no doubt formed a far more accurate view of the strategy and opening moves of the campaign in the west than did Sir John, Wilson, or for that matter, anybody at Grand Quartier Général (French army headquarters). From the outset he never swerved from the conviction that the war would last at least three years[21] and would require the deployment of several million British troops. He understood that the Expeditionary Force was too small in relation to the two main opposing armies to exercise a decisive influence in the opening battles. What he was determined to avoid was the destruction of the BEF, which would then make it practically impossible to organize the vast resources of the empire into fighting shape.

Both Sir John and Wilson held an exaggerated faith in the infallibility of the French army. They were confident that the French would at once be able to seize the initiative and that the war would be waged in Germany. Again in contrast to Kitchener the two men were unconcerned about long-range needs. They clung to the belief, so firmly expressed by all the leading politicians and soldiers on the Continent, that a prolonged war was impossible under modern economic conditions. The popular concept was that the issue would be settled, one way or the other, within a few months, by a series of bloody battles fought in a war of movement. Since French and Wilson were persuaded that the decisive battles would take place immediately, they felt it was criminal to weaken the Expeditionary Force. They therefore resented Kitchener, not only because he would not allow two divisions to leave the country, but because he held back many regular officers and N.C.O.s to train the new armies.

Kitchener showed much far-sighted wisdom in the instructions he issued to French. But because he wanted so many goals pursued simultaneously, the wording in places was vague and even contradictory. The primary objective of the BEF was to cooperate with the French in preventing or repelling invasion and eventually in restoring the neutrality of Belgium. As the numerical strength of the British force and "its contingent reinforcement" was strictly limited, it would be necessary to exercise the greatest

Sir John French disembarks in France. Colonel Huguet is immediately behind. (Photo courtesy of the Imperial War Museum)

care towards "a minimum of losses and wastage." If asked to participate in any "forward movement" in which the British army might be "unduly exposed to attack," French was to consult the government first. Finally it was understood that Sir John's command was "entirely independent" and that he would "in no case come . . . under the orders of any Allied General."[22] Kitchener's motives in rejecting the principle of unity of command were twofold: to preserve the BEF as a nucleus for the future and to gradually take charge, as Britain's military position grew stronger, of the entire Allied war effort.[23]

Before Kitchener wished Sir John good fortune he reiterated his concerns. He took special pains to warn the commander-in-chief that he was not to allow the British army to be trapped, as the French had been at Sedan, and that if such an event was likely to occur, he was to retire to the coast.[24]

The main body of the BEF began crossing the English Channel on August 12. On each of the next five days an average of thirteen ships left Southampton. There was as yet no danger from German submarines and the Royal Navy, in sealing off the Channel from attack, gave absolute security. The transports crossed at night without escort. All arrangements were carried out with exceptional smoothness and punctuality.[25] The movement was shrouded in such secrecy that the English public knew nothing of what was happening. Even more remarkable is the fact that the Germans did not learn of the BEF's presence in France until an announcement appeared in the Belgian newspapers on August 20.

Much has been written about the British army of 1914 but for the benefit of the reader some points merit repeating. Traditionally Britain had relied on her sea power and maintained an army just large enough to police her colonial empire and protect her shores from invasion. At its fullest extent the army amounted to no more than eleven infantry divisions and three cavalry divisions. The miniature size of the British army gave rise to a serious drawback. Its leaders had never directed mass formations such as were common in the much larger conscript armies of France and Germany. Furthermore, because of pre-war military doctrine and the Treasury's parsimony the British army had insufficient artillery support.

Despite these limitations the BEF was the best army that Britain had ever sent abroad. Its equipment and transport were far above general European standards. The corps commanders, Haig (I Corps) and Grierson (II Corps), were men of high reputation. British regular soldiers were all volunteers serving a term of seven years. They were without a doubt the most professional soldiers in the world. The length of their service as well as the diverse conditions under which they trained and fought had made them tough, disciplined, and adaptable. They were capable of fighting at night, of attacking or retreating, and understood the importance of camouflage and concealment. They wore light khaki uniform, ideal except for the winter season, and carried the excellent Lee Enfield, a clip-fed, bolt-action rifle. In practice they were trained to engage targets at 600 yards and to fire fifteen aimed shots a minute. Altogether the BEF, in terms of personnel, organization, equipment, and training, could bear comparison from top to bottom with any of those armies that entered the conflict in 1914.

French and his staff left Dover on the afternoon of August 14 and spent the night at Amiens. Before taking his place at the head of his army Sir John left for Paris to pay his respects to the president of the Republic, Raymond Poincaré. French wanted his visit kept secret but that proved impossible and an hour before his train reached Paris the big square in front of the Gare du Nord was packed with thousands of people. He was met at the station by Louis Malvy (minister of the interior) representing the French government, Sir Francis Bertie, the British ambassador at Paris, and a number of other distinguished personalities.

As soon as French emerged from the station the waiting crowd broke into an enthusiastic applause. He stood up in his motor car to acknowledge their greetings and at that moment some English volunteers who were present started to sing "God Save the King." The crowd was hushed into sudden silence and listened, the men with their hats off, until the National

Anthem was over. Large crowds had lined Rue Lafayette and as Sir John's car passed slowly he was greeted with cries of "Vive l'Angleterre" and "Vive le Général French."

The field-marshal drove to the British Embassy and, during the few hours he spent there that day, laid the foundations of what was to become a close, lasting friendship with Sir Francis Bertie. After lunch Sir John, accompanied by the British Ambassador, visited President Poincaré at the Elysée. R. Viviani (prime minister), A. Messimy (minister of war), and G. Doumergue (minister of foreign affairs) were also present. French explained that his troops would not be ready to take the field for ten days—that is, until August 24. This meant that the British army would play no part in the crucial opening battles. "How French opinion has been misled," the disgruntled president wrote in his diary. "We thought them ready down to the last button and now they will not be at the rendezvous."[26]

The next day Sir John proceeded by car to General Joffre's headquarters, then located at Vitry-le-François, a sleepy little town on the Marne. The French commander-in-chief was sixty-two-years old, a massive paunchy man with bushy eyebrows and a heavy, nearly white moustache. He was slow of wit, phlegmatic, outwardly calm, and devoted to the pleasures of the table, as good Frenchmen should be. The son of a village cooper he had attended the Ecole Polytéchnique and, despite an undistinguished academic record, had earned a commission in the engineer corps. As a subaltern, Joffre took part in the defense of Paris in 1870–71 and his subsequent rise, via colonial appointments, had been accomplished by easy stages without any remarkable display of brilliance. In 1911 he was appointed chief of the General Staff and it was under the cloak of his authority that the advocates of an all-out offensive strategy gained control of the French military machine and, disregarding rational doctrine, formulated the notorious Plan XVII. Joffre must thus bear at least partial responsibility for the débâcle the French armies suffered in the early days of the war.

If Joffre had intellectual limitations he brought to his task energy, steadfastness, patience, and iron courage. Radiating an air of almost infallible right and might he enjoyed the absolute confidence and loyalty of both officers and soldiers under his command, which accounted for the strong recuperative powers of the French army during the first half of the war. Joffre may not rank among the outstanding military leaders but history would be less than just if it failed to recognize that his actions at a moment of crisis in 1914 undoubtedly saved the Allies from disaster.

At their initial meeting the two Allied commanders formed a high opinion of one another. "He struck me at once," said French, "as a man of strong will and determination, very courteous and considerate, but firm and steadfast of mind and purpose, and not easily turned or persuaded."[27] Joffre, for his part, wrote: "He gave me at once the feeling that he was a loyal comrade-in-arms, firmly attached to his own ideas and, while bringing us full support, anxious not to compromise his Army in any way." Joffre accepted without protest the idea that French's command was to be independent: "I perfectly well understood this point; it was entirely natural that England should not consent to subordinate her troops to any Allied commander. I never had any illusions on this subject, although I realized that the absence of a single authority to direct all the Allied forces composing our left would be a serious cause of weakness." As a pragmatist Joffre knew better than to fret over something that could not be changed, preferring instead to try "to get the best results out of collaboration and mutual confidence."[28]

During the conference Joffre acquainted French with the current military situation, in so far as it was known, and expressed his desire that the BEF should go into action on August 21. French did not think that his troops would be ready to start operations before the 24th but promised to do his best to comply with Joffre's wishes.[29]

French and his party rested at Reims before driving on to Rethel, the headquarters of General Lanrezac, on whose left lay the allotted position of the BEF. Lanrezac, who commanded the Fifth Army, was reputed to be one of the most intelligent and aggressive generals in the French army. Like Joffre he was heavily built but unlike his chief did not convey the impression of solidity and strength. Mistrustful of foreigners, choleric and impatient by nature, his habit of craning his head forward as well as hitching his pince-nez over his right ear, accentuated his "irritatingly pedagogic air."

All along Lanrezac had suspected that the enemy would make a wide sweep through Belgium and it was at his insistence that his army had been permitted to move so far northwest.[30] He was rapidly becoming unnerved by reported enemy movements in front of him and by the indifference of G.Q.G. Nor did he gain much comfort from the arrival of the British army, which he held in low regard, equating it with Territorials, Reservists, and other byproducts of the French military system. Like many of his brother officers he believed that the British were fit only for minor duties or as a reserve force. And so frustrated by Joffre's blindness to the imminent peril on his left and fearful that he would be unable to cope with the job he had been assigned, Lanrezac vented on his newly arrived neighbor the indignation he could not show to his superior.

The pessimism reigning at Fifth Army Headquarters manifested itself the moment French and his party arrived. General Hély d'Oissel, the chief of staff, greeted Huguet with: "At last you're here (meaning the English); it's not a moment too soon. If we are beaten we will owe it all to you."[31] Huguet, newly appointed head of the French Mission at British General Headquarters, was astonished by the remarks, as well he should have been. This was not the spirit with which to receive an ally who had gone out of his way to pay a courtesy call and whose army was being rushed forward ahead of its schedule to accommodate the French High Command. Edward Spears, then liaison officer between the BEF and Lanrezac's army, recorded, "It can only be explained by the fact that the Commander of the Fifth Army was already 'rattled.' "[32] The worst was yet to come, however.

French and Lanrezac, having been introduced, retired together to confer without benefit of interpreters. Their fetish for secrecy overrode common sense. It is difficult to imagine how any useful information could have been exchanged. Lanrezac spoke no English and Sir John, although understanding a little French, did not speak it intelligibly. The linguistic limitations of the two commanders prompted their officers waiting outside to make uneasy jokes about what each was asking the other. At any rate they emerged shortly and, together with their staffs, went into the Operations Room. Lanrezac appeared to be in an unsettled mood. Rather than keeping a difficult conversation going, French stepped up to a map and, placing his finger on a spot where German troops had been located, said to Lanrezac, "Mon Général, est-ce que—." His vocabulary being inadequate he turned to Wilson and asked how to say in French "to cross the river." He was told and then went on, "Est-ce que les Allemands vont traverser la Meuse à—à—." French stumbled over the pronunciation of Huy—a most difficult word for an English tongue since the "u" practically has to be whistled—and finally managed to bring out "Hoy."[33]

"What does he say? What does he say?" demanded Lanrezac impatiently. It was explained that the field marshall wanted to know if he thought the Germans would cross the Meuse at Huy. Lanrezac shrugged his shoulders and replied sarcastically, "Tell the Marshal that in my opinion the Germans have merely gone to the Meuse to fish." Wilson tactfully modified the statement in translation: "He says they're going to cross the river, sir."[34] But the tone and manner of Lanrezac's delivery spoke for themselves. French knew that he had been deliberately insulted and by an officer who was his junior in both rank and experience.

Given the atmosphere of distrust and friction it is not surprising that misunderstandings should have arisen. The most serious one involved the use of the British cavalry. French cavalry units operating on Lanrezac's front had been withdrawn by Joffre to carry out a mission. Lanrezac was desperately in need of information on the German columns and their line of march. Since air reconnaissance had yielded no results owing to the weather he sought to employ the British cavalry. French refused the request. Lanrezac understood him to say that having arrived with only four divisions instead of six, he intended to hold back the cavalry as a reserve and that it would only be used as mounted infantry in the line. In all likelihood French's answer was misinterpreted. He would have been the last person to want to use his cavalry as mounted infantry or prevent it from fulfilling its proper functions. What French probably said was that not having the number of troops originally contemplated, he wished to keep the cavalry as a reserve. If the two commanders had engaged in further talks or maintained personal contact, undoubtedly the matter would have been cleared up. As it was, Lanrezac was left with the impression that French's concept of the use of cavalry was timid and amateurish.

Even more disturbing to Lanrezac was the dispute over the date when the BEF would be ready to move forward. Contrary to what he had told Joffre, French, out of resentment, reverted to the original date of the 24th. When Lanrezac protested that it was too late French added that he wanted another week to allow his men to become acclimatized before sending them into action.[35] To Lanrezac this was the final blow. His face flushed with rage and it required all his self control to keep his temper in check. How could any responsible commander, he told himself, react so casually to the crisis? Did the British field marshal suppose that he could choose his own time to fight? Obviously, as he had known from the start, the British army was a sorry rabble, unreliable and unfit for modern war. The interview closed on a chilly note. It had been a complete fiasco. The effect of the meeting, rather than instilling the desired feelings of unity and confidence, had been to create a gap between the chiefs of the two armies that were to fight side by side. The two men parted, determined to have as little to do with one another as possible. They were to meet only once more and then it was at Joffre's behest and under his eye.

French received a further jolt when he arrived at his headquarters, which was in the process of being set up at Le Cateau. Here he learned that Grierson had died of a heart attack in a train near Amiens. Grierson had been military attaché in Berlin for some years and had an intimate knowledge of the German army. His tactical skill is best illustrated by his easy victory over Haig in the 1912 maneuvres. His untimely death at the age of fifty-five deprived the army of one of its ablest commanders.

To fill the vacancy in the command of II Corps, French importuned Kitchener by telegram and letter to send out Sir Herbert Plumer. But Kitchener, without reference to French, decided to appoint General Horace Smith-Dorrien, an old and loyal friend. Smith-Dorrien was a good strategist, forward-looking and resourceful but, at the same time, not always easy to get on with. Throughout his adult life he suffered from acute headaches and on such occasions he was liable to give vent to fearful explosions of temper, turning on friend and foe alike.[36] Normally, however, he was a humorous and kindly man. Those who knew him recognized that his bursts of rage were out of character and in general he was quite popular in the army. It was Smith-Dorrien's misfortune that French should be one of the few among his contemporaries to dislike him. The two soldiers had once been on cordial terms, having worked together in South Africa. They differed markedly in personal characteristics (the one feature they had in common was a bad temper) so it is very unlikely that they were ever the best of friends. At any rate it was after 1907 that the breach occurred, owing, apparently, to Sir John's professional jealousy.

When Smith-Dorrien succeeded French at Aldershot he wasted no time in putting his own ideas into force. He abolished the "pickets" that had patrolled the streets at night in search of drunken soldiers. He rescinded an order that had forbidden soldiers engaged in maneuvres from entering public houses. He changed the physical appearance of Aldershot by erecting new buildings and recreation facilities for the men and by cutting down the rows of trees between Government House and the edge of the town. In matters of training he insisted that the cavalry learn to fight dismounted.[37]

French could not understand why Smith-Dorrien would want to transform an institution that he had left in good order. He felt that all the changes taking place reflected badly on his tenure at Aldershot. What upset him most was that his pet theories had been discredited by a man who was after all a mere infantry soldier.[38] Sir John's attitude towards his brother officer grew steadily cooler until he came to think of him as an obstinate meddler.

French was not one to hide his feelings and his antagonism towards Smith-Dorrien was evident in a number of ways. During the six years that Smith-Dorrien spent at Aldershot, Sir John never paid the customary social visits except on formal occasions when the king's presence compelled him to do so. The Selection Board, over which French presided as CIGS, had a habit of turning down officers recommended for promotion by Smith-Dorrien. In another instance Sir John denied Smith-Dorrien the opportunity to command an army at the annual maneuvers on what was alleged to be "specious grounds."[39] Naturally Smith-Dorrien resented Sir John's hostility and by the time he left Aldershot their dislike for one another had become well known throughout the army.[40]

Left at home when the army sailed for France in August 1914, Smith-Dorrien was elated when he received a telegram appointing him commander of the II Corps. He arrived at the War Office on August 18 and was quickly ushered into Kitchener's presence. Kitchener's first words were that he had serious misgivings about selecting him to replace Grierson in view of French's personal animosity towards him. Smith-Dorrien replied that for his part he held no such feelings and he felt sure that by loyally serving Sir John he could overcome the latter's dislike of him.[41] On the strength of the interview Kitchener confirmed the appointment.

It was unusual and regarded as bad policy for the secretary of war to deny the supreme field commander's request for the services of an available officer. But Kitchener had not taken such action without reason. If his worst fears were realized, as he expected they would, the first movement of the BEF would be a hurried retreat in which case the commander-in-chief might, in some degree, lose control. He believed it was vital that the new

Douglas Haig
(Photo courtesy of Lord Haig)

Horace Smith-Dorrien
(Photo courtesy of the Hulton Picture Library)

corps commander should be someone who could function effectively in a crisis, someone who would be cool, confident, and completely in charge of himself and his troops.[42] Although Kitchener had a high opinion of Plumer, evidently he placed more trust in Smith-Dorrien.

French would have been less than human if he had not resented Smith-Dorrien's appointment. He knew the senior officers in the army a great deal better than Kitchener and was justified in feeling that his views counted and should have been respected. The least Kitchener should have done was to consult him before taking the decision.

To make matters worse, Smith-Dorrien told Sir John on arriving in France that the king had asked him to report directly on the activities of the II Corps. This meant keeping a special diary for which he required the commander-in-chief's permission. Smith-Dorrien knew that French could withhold his consent only if he was prepared to defy his sovereign.[43] One can only imagine how Sir John must have felt. He not only was saddled with a corps commander he detested but that very person was in a position to criticize him to the king.

It was an unfortunate situation and yet no immediate harm was done. Smith-Dorrien arrived with every intention of rendering loyal service to his chief. French, realizing that he could not change anything, was cordial and civil in his dealings with Smith-Dorrien. All went well at first except for occasional minor differences of opinions.

The BEF left the Maubeuge area on August 17 and headed towards its allotted place in the battle line. As a result of a telephone conversation between G.Q.G. and British General Headquarters, French indicated that if he could not get to the front before the 24th he would throw out small detachments on the 21st to cover the final concentration. French's estimate proved too conservative, for on the 21st the entire BEF was in position and ready to move forward. Neither he nor his principal staff officers, however, anticipated the strength of the army they were about to encounter.

5

The Clash of Battle

The four infantry divisions of the BEF were organized into two corps with Haig in command of the first and Smith-Dorrien in command of the second. A British division numbered about 18,000 men (slightly larger in number than French or German divisions) and was divided into three brigades, each four battalions strong. The BEF also included a 9,000-man cavalry division under General Allenby. On a front where the French had put in sixty-two divisions and the Germans seventy-five, it was hard to imagine that the action of these five divisions could affect the outcome.

While the BEF was moving into position the German army was in the intermediate stage of a gigantic maneuvre. It had taken the German General Staff over fifteen years to prepare the plan. The chief architect was Graf von Schlieffen, a cold, precise, unbending man who fitted almost too perfectly the common perception of a German staff officer. Von Schlieffen believed that Germany's chances of survival in an extended conflict were minimal in view of the superior resources of her probable enemies. Rightly assessing that Russia would be slow to mobilize and deploy, he arranged to leave a single Germany army to contain their advance. The remaining seven German armies were to be concentrated in the west between Aachen and the Swiss frontier. The swift, decisive defeat of France was the key to von Schlieffen's strategy. Convinced that the French would devote their energies to recapturing Alsace-Lorraine, he envisaged a wide sweep to get behind them and bring about another Sedan or Cannae.

Von Schlieffen felt that France's system of fortifications along the frontier, regarded by experts as almost impregnable, could be outflanked through the simple expedient of violating Belgian neutrality. At first he intended to go only through Luxemburg and southern Belgium. But as his plan evolved, he became more ambitious and enlarged the circumference of his wheeling operation, pushing northwards the path of penetration. By 1905 when the scheme was adopted he had chosen Holland as the main avenue of invasion to avoid having the German thrust blunted on the Belgian forts of Liège and Namur. With the Low Countries passed and France invaded, his right wing would complete its scythelike movement by overwhelming Paris from the west and driving the French armies into the arms of the Germans in Lorraine. The plan, named after its creator, was designed to act like a revolving door—the more the French pushed on one side, the more forcefully would the other side swing behind them.

Von Schlieffen was convinced that his maneuvre would succeed only if the German armies on the right were strong enough to quickly overcome all opposition during their sweep towards the heart of France. Accordingly the attacking force, backed by reserve formations (Landwehr and Ersatz) was to consist of five armies, leaving the left wing facing the French frontier with only two armies. Von Schlieffen anticipated the defeat of France within six weeks, whereupon the full strength of Germany would be hurled at Russia.

Von Schlieffen retired as chief of the German General Staff in 1906 and his successor, Helmuth von Moltke, nephew and namesake of the victor of Sedan, modified the war blueprint in essential points. He ruled out the invasion of Holland since he felt confident that the forts of Liège and Namur could be captured. This would leave Germany with one fewer enemy to fight and the use of Dutch ports in case of a British naval blockade. But respect for Holland's neutrality meant that his two large northern armies would be crowded through the fortified bottleneck of Liège. Moreover, von Moltke, worried about the effects of a French offensive towards the Rhine, strengthened the German left wing with new units

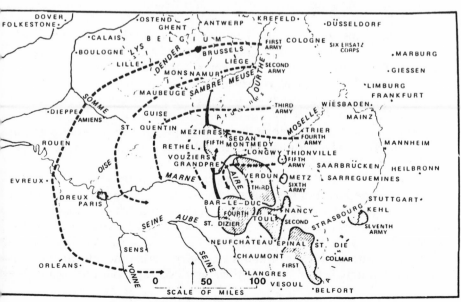

SCHLIEFFEN PLAN – PLAN XVII

formed between 1905 and 1914. By doing so the proportionate weight of the right wing to the left was not as great as originally intended. Many critics believe that von Moltke's alterations doomed German strategy even before the first shot was sounded.[1]

If the German scheme was based on a careful abstract study of war no such statement could be imputed to the French plan. As already noted, the French General Staff had in prewar years developed an almost mystical belief in the virtues of the offensive under all circumstances. However, the introduction of breech-loading artillery, as well as modern infantry weapons such as the machine-gun, had swung the balance decidedly in favor of the defenders by giving them greater stopping power. This could have been deduced from the lessons of various wars, including the American Civil War and the Russo-Japanese War, but the French paid no heed to the signs that contradicted their Clausewitzian beliefs. They were satisfied with Foch's reasoning that "any improvement in firearms is bound to strengthen the offensive." By 1914 their crude doctrines had crystalized into the so-called Plan XVII.

Plan XVII did not dictate a complete pattern of operations but was essential a plan of concentration that enabled Joffre to "advance with all forces united." Five French armies, supported by a cavalry corps and reserve divisions, were massed between Luxemburg and Switzerland. Strong covering forces would fight a defensive action along the northeast frontier until the thirteenth day of mobilization. Then the First and Second armies on the right would deliver a thrust into Lorraine towards the Rhine. The center or Third Army would attack east of Metz. On the left the Fifth Army, facing the Ardennes, would move straight ahead towards Metz or, if the Germans came through Luxemburg and Belgium, strike northwards at their flank. The Fourth Army was held in reserve near the center and reserve divisions were deployed in the rear of both flanks. The BEF, though not officially included in the plan, was to assemble at Maubeuge on the left of the Fifth Army, if Britain entered the war.

Joffre and his staff had convinced themselves that the vigor of the French offensive would catch the German center off balance and throw it into confusion; and that by threatening to break into the Rhineland it would create such panic among the German people that the enemy's right wing, cut off even before it had penetrated France, would be forced into an immediate withdrawal.

As can be seen the French proposed to attack almost exactly where the Germans expected it and so invited the danger of a great envelopment movement around their left. Strangely enough French military leaders had received many warnings about German intentions but had disregarded them. They did not believe that the Germans could muster enough men to penetrate north of the Meuse and they suspected that the information had been deliberately leaked to draw their armies away from the area of the real attack. While the French had accurate knowledge of the strength of the regular German army, they failed to take into account the use of reservists as front-line troops. Because they greatly underestimated the forces at Germany's disposal they assumed that the Germans could not effect such a sweep without weakening their center. If that remote possibility should occur, they saw it as only helping the French offensive and making victory even more certain.[2]

The Germans were first off the mark, pouring into Belgium in accordance with their fast schedule. The two right-wing armies, the First under Alexander von Kluck and the Second under Karl von Bülow, aimed to reduce the ringed fortress of Liège and win admission to the Belgian plain. The city itself fell to the attackers on August 7 but the surrounding forts continued to hold out. On August 12 the Germans brought up their heavy guns, among them the seventeen-inch Skoda howitzers, whose destructive power was greater than anything previously known in the history of warfare. When the last of the Liège forts capitulated on August 16 the vanguard of the German invasion was already pressing the Belgian field army covering Brussels. Rather than risk annihilation the Belgians withdrew northward to the entrenched camp of Antwerp. On the 20th the First German Army entered Brussels while the Second Army began its investment of Namur, the last fortress barring the Meuse route into France.

By then the French plan had been set in motion. To the south the advance of the French First and Second armies into Lorraine gained initial successes, capturing Sarrebourg and threatening Morhange, but counterattacks by the German Sixth and Seventh armies drove them back across the border. While the fighting raged in Lorraine the developments in Belgium compelled Joffre to modify his plan. On August 15 news reached G.Q.G. that the Germans had seized the bridges of the Meuse at Huy, midway between Namur and Liège, and then assailed Lanrezac's I Corps at Dinant, inflicting a thousand casualties before being repelled. The menace on the left could no longer be ignored. Thus Joffre ordered Lanrezac to transfer his army (Fifth) from its concentration area northwards into the angle formed by the Sambre and Meuse rivers. The Fourth Army, which should have been Joffre's strategic reserve, was moved into the line to fill up the ensuing gap. These changes reduced Joffre's forces for the attack in the Ardennes from three armies to two, the Third and Fourth. Pushing blindly in the direction of the German center, supposedly denuded of troops, the two French armies stumbled against the German Fourth and Fifth armies in foggy weather on August 22. The French infantrymen, conspicuous in their brightly colored uniforms, attacked with persistence and reckless valor, suffering appalling losses. Finally after three days of bloody fighting they withdrew to the Meuse.

As regards the French Fifth Army, its mission, once it had reached its newly assigned place on August 20, was to hold in check any German forces advancing from the north and so gain sufficient time to allow the attacks of the Third and Fourth armies to become effective. In no better frame of mind than he was earlier, Lanrezac could not decide what to do. He feared for the safety of his left flank, which would be without support until the BEF came into position. If he advanced across the Sambre as ordered, he believed he would be putting his head into the German noose. Lanrezac did nothing for a day. Then about noon on August 21 he wrote to Joffre, pointing out that if he launched an offensive north of the Sambre he would be forced to give battle alone since the British would not be ready to cooperate with him. If he waited for the two allied armies to act in unison no action could be taken before the 23rd or 24th. Joffre replied: "I leave you absolute judge of the moment when your offensive movement should begin."[3] Meanwhile Lanrezac's corps commanders kept an eye on the Sambre bridges but in the absence of orders did not send troops across to the other side of the river to establish bridgeheads. By the time Lanrezac finally made up his mind to advance it was too late.

Back in London, Kitchener, piecing together what little information was available to the War Office, was convinced that his earlier suspicions had been correct. On August 19 he wired French: "The movement of the German right flank, north of the Meuse—which, if you will remember, I mentioned as likely to happen—seems to be definitely developing. Their Second and Tenth Corps, with three cavalry divisions, are now north of the Meuse, and are possibly being followed by reserve formations."[4] Kitchener reiterated his concern the next day and asked to be kept informed of all developments.[5]

French replied on the evening of the 21st after the BEF had reached the battle zone. He told Kitchener that he did not expect there would be serious fighting on his front before the 24th, adding, "I think I know the situation thoroughly and I regard it as quite favourable to us."[6] Sir John's optimism was reinforced after he consulted with Joffre on the 22d. In his report to Kitchener he estimated the strength of the German turning movement through Belgium, including the troops attacking Namur and others that would be diverted to Antwerp, at six army corps, three cavalry divisions, and two or three reserve divisions—in all seventeen or eighteen divisions. Arrayed against these were the French Fifth Army composed of five army corps (ten divisions), three cavalry divisions, and two reserve corps, as well as the British force of two army corps (four divisions) and one cavalry division. On the basis of this estimate it was observed that after allowing for the German units that would be tied down before Namur and Antwerp, the Allies would enjoy a comfortable numerical superiority, to say nothing of the fact that behind them stood a strong garrison within the Maubeuge fortress and reserve and territorial troops at Valenciennes.[7] As it turned out the force brought by the Germans against the Allied left—the First and Second armies closing in from the north and the Third Army from the east—was not seventeen or eighteen divisions but thirty-four, double the strength that had been supposed.[8]

While French was making arrangements to move forward, as part of Joffre's grand offensive, the long-awaited storm broke over Lanrezac's front. Leading units of von Bülow's Second Army (the main army was engaged in the attack on Namur) descended upon the Sambre on August 21 and forced crossings at two points east of Charleroi. On the 22d the French launched counterattacks with the III and X Corps, hoping to regain the ground lost the previous day. These units were poorly prepared and directed and not only failed but resulted in further retreats. By nightfall Lanrezac's left had been driven back over five miles from the Sambre and an ominous gap had been opened between his army and the British.

Early on the 22d French, accompanied by Wilson, had set out to visit Lanrezac to learn how events were progressing on his front. On the way French spotted Spears's automobile and signaled him to stop. The British party trooped into a small cottage by the roadside and gathered around a table to the left of the door. The lady of the house stared open-mouthed at this intrusion and then, without saying a word, returned to washing her dishes.

A map was spread out and Spears described the situation of the Fifth Army as it was known when he left Lanrezac's headquarters. French inquired about the condition of the X Corps. Spears said that some units had been badly mauled but that the fighting capacity of the corps as a whole remained sound. Sir John hoped that the advance of the Fifth Army, upon which his own plans were based, would take place at the earliest possible moment. Spears was certain that Lanrezac had no intention of attacking even if he were in a position to do so. He added that the information received by the Second (Intelligence) Bureau of the Fifth Army pointed to a German turning movement in Belgium extending far towards the north. Unless the French armies, by a vigorous offensive, disrupted the German maneuvre, the BEF might shortly be facing a grave threat to its left flank.

As the meeting broke up French asked Spears if he knew where Lanrezac could be found. On discovering that Lanrezac was at Mettet he looked at a map and decided that it was too far. Spears was extremely eager for French and Lanrezac to meet again so that their previous misunderstandings could be cleared up. But he could not persuade French to continue his journey.[9] Apparently French felt that he could ill afford to spend time chasing after Lanrezac in view of the high probability that the meeting, like the first one, would be disagreeable and unproductive. In any case French returned to Le Cateau. He may have pondered a while on the information he received from Spears but made no changes either in the disposition of, or in the orders to, his army.

As the day wore on French became increasingly pessimistic. British air and cavalry reconnaissance confirmed and supplemented the evidence collected by the Second Bureau of the Fifth Army. At 11:00 P.M. a French staff officer came to see Sir John. He brought a message from Lanrezac requesting that the British attack the flank of the German formations that were pressing the Fifth Army back from the Sambre. French saw that if he turned to aid Lanrezac the movement would put the enemy on his rear. "In view of the most probable situation of the German Army, as it was known to both of us," French commented subsequently, "and the palpable intention of its commander to effect a great turning movement round my left . . . it is very difficult to realize what was in Lanrezac's mind when he made such a request to me."[10] Sir John could have exercised the option of falling back in order to bring the BEF in line with Lanrezac's left. Instead, with a loyalty that did him credit, he decided to stand his ground for twenty-four hours and await developments. That concession was more than Lanrezac deserved. At the very moment that he was seeking help from French, Lanrezac, in his report to Joffre, wilfully misrepresented the whereabouts of the BEF, placing it "in echelon to the rear of the Fifth Army."[11] It was a clumsy attempt to forestall criticism by shifting the blame on a convenient whipping boy, the British army.

During the night of August 22/23 Lanrezac's position became more critical when Max von Hausen's Third Army, the approach of which had been entirely unsuspected, struck from the east along the Meuse. Bringing four corps and 340 guns into action, von Hausen gained bridgeheads across the river south of Dinant and threatened Lanrezac's rear. The situation was also bleak on nearby fronts. At midday on the 23d came the incredible news that the Belgian Fourth Division was evacuating Namur. On the heels of this Lanrezac learned that the French Fourth Army was not only unsuccessful in the Ardennes but it was being forced into retreat, which would leave his right flank exposed. Adding everything together Lanrezac concluded that his position was untenable and in the evening ordered a general withdrawal. He did not consult with Sir John or even bother to inform him of his intention.

Since early morning the BEF and von Kluck's First Army had been engaged in heavy fighting along the line of the Mons Canal. The British had dug themselves in on either side of the mining town of Mons, just where they had halted at the end of their march forward on the 22d. The II Corps under Smith-Dorrien lined the stretch of the canal from Condé to Mons and occupied the salient formed by a loop in the canal north and east of Mons. Haig's I Corps joined the right of the II Corps four miles southeast of Mons and held the line running across to the left flank of the French Fifth Army. The cavalry division, commanded by General Allenby, was kept in reserve.

The line of the canal was not an easy position to defend. John Terraine in his book *Mons* writes: "The approaches to it from the north were masked by the cluster of hamlets, the rows of houses and factories and the slag heaps which filled the valley. A complex drainage system, varied on the higher ground by woods and spinneys, fringed the Canal, making both movement and vision extremely difficult for the troops stationed along it."[12] The canal itself was seven feet at its maximum depth with an average width of sixty-four feet and, in the course of its sixteen miles in length, was crossed by no fewer than eighteen bridges. It represented practically no obstacle to troops wishing to cross it.

At 5:30 A.M. on the 23d French met his corps commanders in the Chateau of Sars-la-Bruyère (Smith-Dorrien's headquarters) to discuss the day's operations. Sir John later claimed that he told his commanders of the doubts that had arisen in his mind during the past twenty-four hours and impressed on them the necessity of being prepared either to retreat or advance.[13] However, Smith-Dorrien informs us that he got the impression that Sir John was brimming with optimism and that he intended to use the canal position as a jumping-off place for a further advance into Belgium.[14] The field marshal's own action after the meeting would tend to confirm Smith-Dorrien's version. He left for Valenciennes where he conferred with the French commandant and inspected the Nineteenth Brigade (which was completing its detrainment) and did not return to Le Cateau until mid-afternoon, by which time his army had been locked in a duel with the enemy for over six hours. If French, as he asserted, believed that his front might be threatened by a turning movement, how could he, for the sake of secondary matters, have absented himself from his headquarters for so many hours?

The morning of the 23d opened with mist and rain but by 10 A.M. the weather had cleared. The sun was out, the air warm and humid. To the townsfolk of Mons the day seemed much like any other Sunday. Although newspaper reports of battles were eagerly read and frequently discussed, the assumption was that the war would not disturb their placid town, that the great Belgian fortresses would interdict any German movement into Flanders. The trains ran as usual; church bells summoned the faithful to Mass; the streets were filled with children and adults in their best clothes.

The men of the BEF appeared equally unconcerned. They were in good spirits when they arose even though they did show signs of the long, weary marches up from their concentration area. They ate breakfast between 5:30 and 6:00 A.M., after which they occupied themselves in improving their position. They worked at a leisurely pace, pausing now and again to enjoy refreshments and snacks provided by local citizens; to chat and smoke; to gaze at the folk, especially the girls, going off to Mass; or to look skywards as the drowsy hum of an aeroplane propeller sounded over them. Suddenly without warning this comfortable scene changed when three German Corps came up to the Mons Canal on their line of march.

Despite a superiority in aircraft the Germans were as deeply in the fog of war as the British. They knew that the BEF had landed but lacked informa-

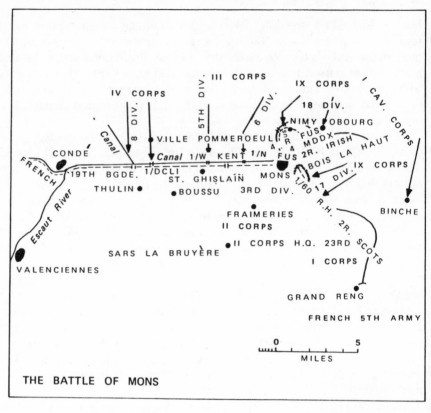

THE BATTLE OF MONS

tion as to its strength and movements. Operating largely in the dark, von
Kluck, whose First Army was wheeling due south from Brussels, was under
the impression that the BEF was detraining at Tournai. He was naturally
surprised when his cavalry reported that the line ahead was strongly held
by British troops. With three army corps at his disposal and another close
behind, von Kluck had more than enough troops to sweep around the
British and it might have spelled ruin for them if he had. However, for
purposes of coordination he had been placed temporarily under the command of von Bülow, who ordered him to stay close. So instead of attempting a decisive maneuvre, von Kluck came at the British like a bull, head
down.

Smith-Dorrien's II Corps (Third and Fifth divisions) had to withstand
the assault of five German divisions. Haig's Corps, almost at right angles to
the front of the II Corps and facing northeast, was only attacked by one
German division and then not heavily.

Before 9:00 A.M. the first shells were bursting on the positions of the
Royal Fusiliers and the Middlesex of the Third Division and soon an infantry division of the German IX Corps was pressing forward against the
curve of the salient between Obourg and Nimy. Gradually the battle spread

westwards along the straight section of the canal as the other two German corps, first the III and then the IV, were brought into action. It was the practice of the Germans at the beginning of the war to attack in dense formation, usually in three double waves. They swarmed forward at Mons, as one soldier said, "like a crowd coming up for Cup Day."

The pattern of fighting was established at the outset. The British soldiers waited in buildings and amongst slag heaps until the oncoming hordes were within range and then broke out with the kind of fire discipline they had learned at Aldershot and Hythe. A British sergeant remembered that the Germans advanced "in solid square blocks, standing out sharply against the skyline, and you couldn't help hitting them." Another soldier reported that the first company of Germans "were simply blasted away to Heaven by a volley at seven hundred yards, and in their insane formation every bullet was almost sure to find two billets." Most of the German attacks were stopped dead and broken up three or four hundred yards short of their objectives, leaving the ground strewn with bodies. The German Official History frankly describes the fighting: "Well-entrenched and completely hidden, the enemy opened a murderous fire . . . the casualties increased . . . the rushes became shorter, and finally the whole advance . . . gradually came to an end." The Germans had never seen fire delivered with such accuracy and rapidity. They believed that they were facing great numbers of machine guns but, in fact, the British, like themselves, had only two per battalion.

In the afternoon the Germans altered their tactics, extending their lines further and preceding their attacks by long artillery bombardments. The British held on stubbornly and kept up a ceaseless fire but the situation was becoming intolerable for the regiments in the salient. Their ground was under good observation from heights north of the canal and German batteries gouged into their hastily dug trenches with deadly results. Having withstood heavy shelling and infantry assaults for six hours the pressure on their dwindling numbers became too intense and around 3:00 p.m. they started to fall back, company by company, to a new position several miles south of Mons. The abandonment of the salient endangered the troops along the straight section of the canal, so these too were now ordered to withdraw. The Germans were in no condition to pursue and on the approach of nightfall they sounded the cease-fire.[15]

Thus ended the battle of Mons. Von Kluck's advance had been held up for one day at the cost of 1,600 casualties, nearly all in the II Corps. German losses are not known but they must have been considerably higher.

As the opening British engagement of the war Mons subsequently developed a peculiar mystique. According to legend the success of the British was due to the intervention of angels. In some romantic British minds the battle was hailed as a great victory and ranked with Hastings and Agincourt. It is true that at Mons the British had fought with courage, skill, discipline, and tenacity. But these qualities were also demonstrated by the Belgians at Haelen, the French at Onhaye, and, of course, the Germans on various occasions. Mons was neither a victory nor a defeat. It is best described as a successful delaying action that had the effect of safeguarding the left flank of the French Fifth Army at a moment of desperate crisis.

Sir John, who was away during the early stages of the battle, does not appear to have exercised much control over it when he returned. Nor did he appreciate the extreme danger in which his army stood even after it had been driven from the line of the canal. Wilson noted in his diary on the 23d: "During the afternoon I made a careful calculation, and I came to the conclusion that we only had one corps and one cavalry division (possibly two corps) opposite to us. I persuaded Murray and Sir John that this was so, with the result that I was allowed to draft orders for an attack tomorrow. . . ."[16] On what information Wilson had based his conclusions and where that information came from is not known. It was not "one" or "possibly two corps" that faced the British but three with another coming down fast on their left wing.

The reports of the Intelligence Department, supplemented by those from the airmen scouting towards Brussels, showed that all roads were thickly covered with masses of German troops marching westwards. Here was conclusive evidence on which all subsequent decisions and news should have been based. But Sir John preferred to rely on the opinions of Wilson, who could not free his mind from the optimistic pronouncements of the French General Staff. Wilson believed that Lanrezac was about to launch an assault as part of a series of French attacks, designed to break the enemy's center. How he gained that impression, in view of the information from Spears on the previous day, is a mystery. Far from preparing a counterstroke, the French were in retreat everywhere.

The danger that the BEF would be overwhelmed in a rash attempt to advance on the following day was averted by a telegram from Joffre saying that there were two-and-a-half corps opposite Smith-Dorrien alone. This half-correct message served its purpose and French canceled his order to attack. He was not yet prepared, however, to fall back. At 8:40 P.M. he sent the following instructions to his corps commanders: "I will stand the attack on the ground now occupied by the troops. You will therefore strengthen your position by every possible means during the night."[17] Three hours later Spears arrived after a hurried drive from Fifth Army headquarters to bring news that Lanrezac had ordered a retreat to begin in the small hours of the 24th.[18] Since this meant that the BEF would be placed in instant peril, Sir John decided that he too must draw back.

In the span of slightly more than twenty-four hours Sir John had changed his mind with a frequency that must have bewildered and perplexed all those who had dealings with him. On the 22d the line was established as a jumping-off place for an advance northward, but in the late evening orders were issued to stand on the defensive. Early next morning it appeared there would be an attack if conditions were favorable; by the end of the afternoon it was definite there would be one; during the evening it was announced that the army would hold its ground; and finally around 11:00 P.M. a decision was taken to withdraw.

6

Retreat

Around 1:00 A.M. on August 24, 1914, Murray summoned the chief staff officers of the I and II Corps, Brigadier-Generals John Gough and George Forestier-Walker, to tell them that Sir John wanted to make a general retreat southwards of some eight miles to a line between La Longueville and La Boiserette. Murray did not lay down the actual order of retirement, as might have been expected, but simply left the Corps Commanders to work out arrangements among themselves.[1] Gough immediately telegraphed a message, which reached Haig at 2:00 A.M. Haig's corps had not been seriously attacked and, having received the orders in good time, was able to get under way before dawn. The II Corps was less fortunate. Smith-Dorrien's headquarters at Sars-La-Bruyère were located on a back country road and had no telephone or telegraphic communication with Le Cateau. Forestier-Walker had to cover thirty-five miles by car over roads now choked with refugees, in addition to the army's own transport, and did not convey the message to Smith-Dorrien until 3:00 A.M.[2] By the time the orders filtered down to the widely scattered units, arrangements made to coordinate the retreat, and roads cleared of transport and other impediments, the Germans returned to the attack.

On the previous night Smith-Dorrien, anticipating another assault at daybreak, had wisely drawn back his corps two or three miles to higher ground. The new depositions proved an advantage when he sought to break contact with the enemy. Once again the rapid and accurate fire of British infantrymen and gunners dominated the battle. While the rear guards kept the Germans at a distance, company by company and battery by battery slipped away. By late afternoon the Germans had suffered so many casualties among their assaulting battalions that they halted for the day, unable to press the pursuit any farther. The men of the II Corps reached the line Bavai-Maubeuge at midnight, tired and hungry but cheerful, because all felt that they had done well. The fighting on the 24th had cost Smith-Dorrien's corps about 2,000 casualties, most of them coming from the Fifth Division.[3]

All things considered, the day had gone astonishingly well. The fighting had been severe and the dangers much greater than at Mons. The slightest miscalculation might have given the enemy a chance to turn the retreat into a rout. But Smith-Dorrien ably conducted the withdrawal, parrying the German envelopment attack and in the process inflicting heavy punishment. During the entire day the average German advance was only three-and-a-half miles. British losses were not severe and no guns were lost, no transport abandoned.

Still there was a sense of disappointment in the British camp. Haig's forces had moved to the front, spent hours in the heat and dust fortifying their position, and now had to turn and march back without having seriously engaged the enemy. The men of the II Corps had hammered the German advance to a standstill and believed that they had won a great victory but, knowing nothing of the superior numbers of the enemy and of the Fifth Army's withdrawal, could not understand the order to retire. "If the Cabinet had sent 6 divisions instead of 4," Wilson confided bitterly to his diary, "this retreat would have been an advance and defeat would have been a victory."[4] But this was wishful thinking. It would have required the cooperation of the French Fifth Army and a great deal more than the additional two divisions to have overcome the enormous strength of the German movement. In fact, by withholding the two divisions at the beginning, Kitchener, however illogical his motives appear, may have rendered the country an inestimable service. The presence of one extra division, let alone two, as John Terraine points out, "might easily have impelled G.H.O. [General Headquarters] into further rashness, which might have smashed up the whole Army."[5]

Wilson was outwardly undismayed. He advised, encouraged, urged, laughed, and for once was an asset rather than a liability. By contrast French plunged into despondency and not even Wilson's ebullience could shake him out of it. The responsibility of command, the sudden collapse of the French plans, and particularly the experience of having been left in the lurch, which had led to the near destruction of the BEF, combined to impose an unendurable strain on Sir John's mercurial temperament. What started off as resentment against Lanrezac turned into outright hostility against the whole French army. As far as he was concerned every Frenchman from Joffre downwards was incompetent and useless. Giving way to the conviction that the campaign was lost, his one idea was to save the BEF, which contained nearly all Britain's trained soldiers. In a note to Kitchener on the 24th he indicated that he was contemplating departure: "I think immediate attention should be directed to the defence of Havre."[6]

Although French retained his main base of operations at Le Cateau he established an advance headquarters at Bavai so that he would be closer to

Henry Wilson
(Photo courtesy of the Hulton Picture Library)

William Robertson
(Photo courtesy of Lord Robertson)

the fighting. Throughout the retreat French spent a good deal of time traveling, on horseback or by car, from one part of the battlefield to another, occasionally stopping to chat with the men or their officers. However valuable this practice was, it kept him away from General Headquarters, where important decisions had to be delayed until his return. The personal approach had worked for French in South Africa but now the circumstances were entirely different. In 1914 his staff was less competent and the problems of control and command were far more complex than had been the case in 1899. It would have been to his advantage if he had emulated Joffre and set up his headquarters at some distance from the front.

The 24th was a hectic day for French. He visited Haig's headquarters, where he was impressed with the orderly withdrawal of the I Corps and then, from different vantage points, watched elements of the II Corps fighting a rear guard action. Leaving the battleline he went to see General Sordet[7] and asked that the French cavalry take a position on the left or outer flank of the BEF in order to delay the enemy's advance. Sordet replied that he could not change locations without instructions from his superior but that he would do whatever he could to help out. Later French traveled to Le Cateau to pick up any messages or news from Joffre or Lanrezac. Here he was heartened by the sight of the advance troops of the Fourth Division, which had recently landed in France. He spoke briefly with their commander, General Snow, before returning to Bavai. In the afternoon Sir John received news to the effect that all three of the French left wing armies (Third, Fourth, and Fifth) were falling back.

French judged from the method and direction of the German attacks that von Kluck was endeavoring to turn the left flank of the BEF and press it back on Maubeuge. He knew that his men could not remain where they were even though they were exhausted and in desperate need of rest. French debated with himself whether or not he should seek shelter in Maubeuge, which was well fortified and provisioned. Two considerations forced themselves on his mind. In the first place he felt certain that this was exactly what the enemy was trying to make him do; and in the second he remembered Hamley's comments about Bazaine immuring his army in Metz in 1870, likening him to a man who, when his ship is sinking, lays hold of the anchor. This settled the matter and French decided to continue the retreat another fifteen miles to a line in the vicinity of Le Cateau.[8]

An awkward problem arose on the 25th when the BEF approached the Forest of Mormal, then thickly wooded, nine miles long and three to four miles wide. Several roads crossed the forest from east to west but none were known to run through it from north to south. To attempt to pass both corps down either side of the forest would have entailed considerable crowding and confusion and also would have required flank marches across the front of an enemy greatly superior in numbers. French therefore decided, quite properly but with considerable trepidation, to divide his army and send I Corps down the east side of the forest and II Corps down the west. Little did French know that the period of their separation would not only be long but packed with great events.[9]

The weather on August 25 was exceedingly hot and proved an additional trial for the troops, half of whom were reservists just called up and not in hardened condition. Under a scorching sun the men, without proper food or sleep, stumbled along, hardly conscious of their surroundings and, when they halted, fell asleep immediately, some standing up. As was the case on the previous day the I Corps was not seriously troubled by the enemy and arrived by separate brigades at its billets and bivouacs in the villages along the banks of the Sambre. The II Corps had a more difficult time since von Kluck inclined his right wing with the view to bring it around the left flank of the BEF. Throughout the day the rear-guard battalions fought a series of small actions and, although there were no striking successes against enemy masses, no units were cut off. The sky darkened around 5:00 P.M. and shortly afterwards a violent thunderstorm broke out. Soaked, exhausted, and famished, the main body of the II Corps staggered into Le Cateau by early evening.

The steadfast attitude and skillful withdrawal of the men of the II Corps enabled them to just pull clear of the enemy's envelopment movement to the east. Nonetheless the Germans continued on their course. Advance elements of von Kluck's III and IV Corps, in marching southeastwards across the rear of the II Corps and through the Forest of Mormal, headed towards the blind flank of Haig's I Corps.

The first sign of trouble occurred at Landrecies, where the rear guard (Fourth Brigade) and the staff of the I Corps had halted for the day. Around 5:30 P.M. there was a panic among the refugees who poured into the little town crying that the enemy were at their heels. Mounted patrols were sent out to reconnoitre but could find no trace of any enemy troops in the immediate vicinity. It seemed to have been a false alarm. However, at 7:30 P.M. a German infantry brigade drove into a picket of Coldstream Guards that were defending the road leading into the town. Less highly trained troops might easily have lost cohesion in the confusion of the night but the Guards, despite their fatigue, rallied with splendid discipline and drove off the Germans.

While this was going on another incident occurred further to the north, at Maroilles. German infantry patrols, belonging to the III Corps, emerged from the forest and captured a bridge over the Sambre that was held by a troop of the Fifteenth Hussars. As the Hussars fell back they were met by a company of the First Royal Berkshires, coming up in relief. The three other companies of Berkshires were delayed as they had to make their way through the transport and refugee congestion in Maroilles itself. By the time they arrived the Germans had barricaded the bridge and put a field

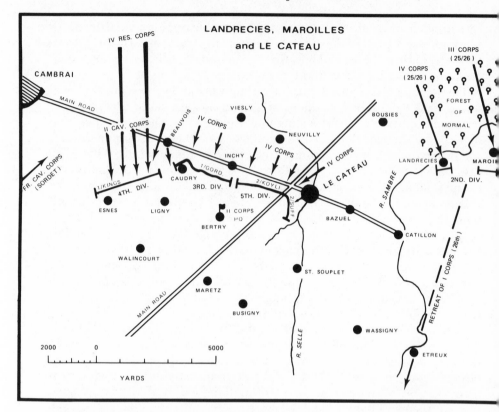

gun into position. The only approach to the bridge was over a long open causeway and the Berkshires lost sixty men in a futile effort to recapture it. The fighting gradually died down after darkness set in.[10]

In Landrecies there was great confusion and reports were circulating that the place was surrounded and the Fourth Brigade cut off from the main body. Haig, possibly because he had not fully recovered from a gastric ailment, was not at his best on this day. Since early morning he had discerned from the distant sound of guns that the enemy was in close touch with the II Corps. He now imagined that the pursuing Germans had achieved their objective and overtaken the entire British force. If retreat were cut off he was determined to make a final stand and force the enemy to pay dearly for his life. "If we are caught, by God, we'll sell our lives dearly," Haig told his staff.[11] Orders were given to organize the town for defense, set up barricades across the roads, and destroy all records that might be of value to the enemy. Next Haig sent a message to General Headquarters saying that he was under heavy attack and requesting reinforcements. French transmitted the appeal to Smith-Dorrien, who was compelled to reply, "Much regret my troops are quite unable to move tonight."[12]

The danger to the I Corps was more imaginary than real. A few shells fell into the town but there was no weight behind the German attack and within a few hours the situation cleared. Haig left Landrecies before the fighting ended. At the time he was firmly convinced that unless extricated immediately the Fourth Brigade was as good as lost. When he rejoined the main body of the corps he issued instructions to the First Division to mount a rescue operation in the morning. At 1:35 A.M. (on the 26th) Haig reported to General Headquarters that the position of the I Corps was "very critical"; and several hours later he suggested that the II Corps, some eight miles away at Le Cateau, should come to his assistance.

Haig's alarming reports created something approaching a panic at General Headquarters, now removed to Saint Quentin. Murray, already suffering from exhaustion, found the additional strain too great.[13] He was sitting at his desk when he was handed a note and moments later an aide noticed that he had slumped forward in a dead faint. French was also shaken and his despondency deepened. Excited cries of help from the normally unflappable Haig could only mean that the I Corps was in the greatest danger. Immediately French conjured up an image of the Germans bringing off an envelopment or, even more serious, of penetrating between the I and II Corps. At this point there is a gap in the records but it appears from what followed that French directed Haig to retreat, not southwest as was originally intended, but south to Saint Quentin or southeast into the area of the French Fifth Army. Lanrezac was warned to expect the arrival of the I Corps and for once agreed to help out.[14] As it happened French protection was not required. When morning came the I Corps, including the Fourth Brigade, was able to pull out in good order. By remaining east of the Sambre Haig followed a line of march that would take him still farther from the rest of the Expeditionary Force.

The threat to the BEF lay not on the right, as French believed, but on the left where the II Corps and the newly arrived Fourth Division under General Snow were billeting in the Le Cateau area. Smith-Dorrien had established his headquarters at Bertry, a village about five miles southwest of Le Cateau. At 10:15 P.M. on the 25th he issued orders for the retreat to resume next day as prescribed by General Headquarters. But as night wore on new developments revealed that this would not be practicable.

At 2:00 A.M. General Allenby, whose cavalry units were covering the flank of the II Corps, arrived at Bertry to consult with Smith-Dorrien. Allenby, after reporting that his brigades were scattered and his men and horses "pretty well played out," asked Smith-Dorrien what he proposed to do. He warned that the Germans were nearby and that unless the II Corps could move at once and get away in the dark it would be forced into battle before it could start the day's march. Smith-Dorrien had no reason to doubt the reliability of this information, for Allenby had been in touch with the enemy all day and he was not a man to exaggerate the difficulties.

Smith-Dorrien then summoned General H. Hamilton, commander of the Third Division, and inquired whether his troops could move off at once. Hamilton replied that his men were still coming in and he could not possibly form up and leave before 9:00 A.M. There was a long silence in the room as Smith-Dorrien reflected upon the situation. The Fifth Division had already reported its arrival but its units were spread over a wide area. The Fourth Division, although not subject to his orders, was still engaged in rear-guard action around Solesmes. It would be left isolated if the II Corps retired. On top of this the roads further rearwards were clogged with transport and refugees; indeed many had been reduced to impassable quagmires by the heavy rainstorm.

Smith-Dorrien was faced with a dilemma: to move at once was impossible; to stand his ground and fight was contrary to his instructions. Since he was not in direct communication with General Headquarters he would have to decide for himself. Turning to Allenby he asked him whether he would serve under his command. Without any hesitation Allenby said he would. There was no doubt that General Snow would do likewise when the request reached him. "Very well, gentlemen, we will fight," Smith-Dorrien announced. At the time Smith-Dorrien was under the impression that the I Corps would be on his right, holding the high ground east of Le Cateau.

After the conference ended Smith-Dorrien had to notify General Headquarters about his change of plans. He set down his reasons in a lengthy memo and sent it off by car to Saint Quentin. It was acknowledged by a reply, which concluded in the following terms:

> If you can hold your ground the situation appears likely to improve. Fourth Division must co-operate. French troops are taking offensive on right of I Corps. Although you are given a free hand as to method this telegram is not intended to convey the impression that I am not as anxious for you to carry out the retirement, and you must make every endeavour to do so.[15]

These words seem to imply that French was in accord with Smith-Dorrien's views. That, however, was not the case. Although French did not feel that he could disregard the judgment of the commander on the spot he rather suspected that the danger was not so great as to require a stand. As far as he could tell it was the I Corps, not the II, that was being hard pressed by the enemy. French's overriding concern was to extricate his army intact from the danger zone so that he could fight another day somewhere else. Now Smith-Dorrien was jeopardizing the entire BEF, indeed the entire Anglo-French army, by not continuing the retreat as he had been instructed.

The messenger carrying the written answer to Smith-Dorrien had no sooner left General Headquarters when someone discovered that a telephone line existed between the local railway station and the station at Bertry. At 6:45 A.M. Smith-Dorrien was summoned to answer a telephone call that he understood to be from Sir John French. Rushing over to the station he was surprised to hear Wilson's familiar voice over the wire. Wilson explained that French wanted him to get on with the retreat as soon as possible. "If you stand and fight," he stated emphatically, "there will be another Sedan." Smith-Dorrien replied that he had no option but to fight; that Allenby's cavalry could not effectively cover his retreat; that his units were scattered and his men too tired to march. He added that in any event it was impossible to break away as the action had already begun and he could hear the guns firing as he spoke. When Wilson asked him what his chances were he replied that he was "fully confident and hopeful" of giving the enemy a smashing blow and then slipping away in the dark. Wilson wished him luck, adding that his was the first cheerful voice he had heard for three days.[16] What Wilson neglected to say was that the I Corps would not be prolonging his right at Le Cateau.

In retrospect it seems incredible that Smith-Dorrien should have been kept in the dark on a matter of such importance. Equally astounding is that General Headquarters, knowing that Smith-Dorrien was about to fight a vastly superior enemy force, not only failed to insist that Haig make every effort to join him, but apparently allowed the I Corps to retreat in a direction away from the II Corps. Haig may be faulted for overreacting to the assault on his rear guard but when he continued his withdrawal on the morning of the 26th he was under the impression that the II Corps was doing the same. At 8:30 P.M. on the same day Haig telegraphed General Headquarters: "No news of II Corps except sound of guns from direction of Le Cateau and Beaumont. Can I Corps be of any assistance?"[17] Haig received no reply. By this hour French and his staff apparently had given up the II Corps as lost. Huguet, who was at General Headquarters, reflected their mood in a telegram to Joffre at 8:00 P.M.: "Battle lost by the English Army which appears to have lost cohesion."[18] At any rate the II Corps was left to work out its own salvation.

A thick mist heralded the dawn of August 26, the anniversary of the Battle of Crécy. The order to stand fast had come so unexpectedly that there was little opportunity to fortify the line or select the best ground to repel an attack. The II Corps occupied a thirteen-mile front, from Le Cateau to Esnes, with the Fourth Division on the left, the Third in the center and the Fifth on the right. Both the Third and the Fifth divisions were very weary and their ranks sadly depleted by the earlier action. The Fourth Division was comparatively fresh but it lacked the very essentials for modern war. The divisional cavalry, the divisional cyclists, the field companies of the Royal Engineers, the heavy artillery, the signal company, and the field ambulances had not yet arrived. In all Smith-Dorrien had 55,000 men and 246 guns.

Once again von Kluck was marching into battle with a complete misconception of the disposition and movement of the British army. He had lost sight of the I Corps, thinking that the entire British force was attempting to retreat in a southwesterly direction. He proposed to catch them in a north-south alignment between Cambre and the Sambre and wipe them out in a Cannae-type battle. His plan was to pin the British with his IV and III cavalry corps while enveloping their right with his III Corps and their left with his II and IV reserve corps. His numerical superiority was overwhelming, no less than 140,000 men, but owing to his faulty leadership his army corps stumbled piecemeal into the British position and the battle ended before his full strength could be brought to bear.

The battle of Le Cateau may be said to have begun on the left, on the Fourth Division's front, the previous night. The rear guards were late coming in and as they did so continued exchanging shots with small enemy patrols. Early in the morning, after a furious bombardment, the Jägers and the dismounted cavalry advanced in masses, firing from the hip. Greeted by a burst of rapid fire they were cut down and brought to a standstill. The Third Division in the center was not under serious German pressure. Until midday the Germans appeared only in small bodies, which were contained without difficulty.

The most serious point of danger was in and around Le Cateau itself, on the extreme right of the Fifth Division's front. Here the Thirteenth and Fourteenth brigades were quite overmatched but their steady and accurate fire, supported by artillery action, threw back one enemy assault after the other. Casualties were heavy, especially in the Fourteenth Brigade, and pressure was extreme, growing steadily from hour to hour. The Germans, having mounted two large guns on a nearby spur, were firing at close range; they were increasing in numbers and gradually inching forward. Although the British were under a searching fire there was no thought of giving way.

Around 1:30 P.M. General Fergusson, commanding the Fifth Division, reported that a German division (the Third) was working around his right, and added that his own troops had been so reduced that he feared they could not hold out much longer. The Germans had already penetrated between the Thirteenth and Fourteenth brigades and their guns were shelling his headquarters from short ranges. Smith-Dorrien had hoped to stand his ground until dusk but he had no reserves left to send Fergusson and no news of the I Corps. As the Fifth Division had reached the limit of human endurance he recognized that retirement could not be delayed if it was to be done in an orderly manner.

Accordingly, the Fifth Division, followed by the Third, disengaged and retreated, but when the moment came for the Fourth to move off it was in danger of being overwhelmed by the newly arrived German IV Reserve

Corps. Fortunately Sordet's cavalry intervened from the west, providing a most opportune diversion and greatly facilitating the departure of the main body of the Fourth Division.[19]

At 6:00 P.M. a drizzling rain set in and the light began to fade. The enemy's pursuit died away. There was considerable confusion and congestion on the roads with infantry, guns, transport, and ambulances converging on them in no particular order. But the men trudged on, wearily and in silence. They resembled, Smith-Dorrien said afterwards, "a crowd coming away from a race meeting."[20] The remainder of the retreat was free from interference except for minor rear-guard actions.

The stand of the Fourth Division and the II Corps in the delaying action at Le Cateau ranks as possibly the most brilliant exploit of the British army during the whole of the war. With both flanks more or less hung in the air the British had hammered an enemy force no less than twice their strength and then had eluded it in broad daylight. While they had paid a heavy price, some 8,000 casualties, they had inflicted upon the Germans losses[21] that are believed to have been out of all proportion to their own. For the second time in four days they had succeeded in holding up an entire German army for a day. By the ferocity of their resistance they had thrown the Germans into confusion, causing von Kluck to overestimate their numbers and to formulate future plans based on this miscalculation.

If ever there was a battle in which leadership counted it was at Le Cateau. On that critical occasion Smith-Dorrien's character and generalship showed themselves to their very best advantage. His decision to stand and fight, which was contrary to the original intention of Sir John French, probably saved the BEF from destruction. As the fierce battle swayed and surged he remained master, both of himself and the situation, and in the end extricated his army from a position that had appeared to be hopeless. His opponent General von Kluck paid him the greatest compliment when he admitted later that he had tried all he knew to outflank him and had failed. He went on to say: "If I had succeeded, the war would have been won."[22]

The British Official Historian applauded the manner in which Smith-Dorrien handled the battle, and after taking everything into account concluded that he was "fully justified" in his decision to fight.[23]

On the other hand French saw the situation differently. It seemed to him, as he explained to Kitchener in a confidential note on August 27, that Smith-Dorrien could have made a greater effort "to get away in the early morning" before the enemy attack developed. By contrast, he added, Haig, although under heavy pressure all night, had "managed to extricate himself sufficiently to carry out the movement assigned to him. . . ."[24] And yet on September 7, when the retreat was over, French made the following comment in his dispatch:

I cannot close . . . without putting on record my deep appreciation of the valuable services rendered by General Sir Horace Smith-Dorrien. I say without hesitation that the saving of the left wing of the Army under my command on the morning of the 26th August could never have been accomplished unless a commander of rare and unusual coolness, intrepidity and determination had been present to personally conduct the operation.[25]

First impressions can be deceiving and a reversal of opinion when all the facts are known is not unusual. In this case French never really altered his view concerning Smith-Dorrien. By praising the commander of the II Corps he hoped to cover the fact that he and his staff had "completely lost their heads"[26] as well as to represent Le Cateau as a great victory.

Five years later, in his book, Sir John excoriated Smith-Dorrien. He claimed that Smith-Dorrien made a serious error by standing his ground; that his men were not really too tired to continue the retreat. He contended that Smith-Dorrien's action unnecessarily cost the British army at least 14,000 officers and men and some 80 guns; and rendered the "subsequent conduct of the retreat more difficult and arduous."

How does French reconcile these statements with what he wrote in his despatch on September 7? He tells us that his despatch was composed, of necessity, very hurriedly. He had not then known of the service rendered by General Sordet, nor how brilliantly the officers and men under Smith-Dorrien had redeemed their leader's mistake.[27]

French, in his eagerness to belittle Smith-Dorrien, did not always confine himself to the facts. He practically doubled the number of British casualties, which, in truth, did not exceed 8,000. Moreover, he had known all along the part played by Sordet's cavalry at Le Cateau. On August 29, 1914, Smith-Dorrien had forwarded to General Headquarters a report of the battle in the course of which he described the excellent work of the French cavalry and asked that the commander-in-chief's thanks might be conveyed to Sordet through Joffre.

Contrary to the impression given by French in his book the II Corps had suffered neither a serious defeat nor lasting damage. It was a force utterly weary and cruelly harassed but still intact and still unbeaten.

The BEF came out of the opening round in better condition than the French, whose attempt to wrest the initiative from the Germans had failed and brought appalling casualties. With Plan XVII in ruins Joffre began to shed some of the delusions that had hitherto gripped French military thinking. At first Joffre attributed the repulse of his armies mainly to "grave shortcomings on the part of the commanders." It cannot be denied that some generals had crumbled under the onerous responsibility of command. During the battle of the Ardennes a divisional commander had lost his nerve, then committed suicide. At Charleroi a general of artillery had been obliged to take over when the commander of the III Corps could not be found during the most critical phase of the battle. But there was more to the French defeat than the failure of a few generals. On August 24 French intelligence discovered that German reserve units were being used in the front line, which explained how the enemy had managed to be equally strong on the right and center at once. Thereupon Joffre conceded that the weight and scope of the German movement was an important element in his misfortunes.

There was also recognition of French tactical mistakes and on the 24th Joffre issued a "Note for All Armies," which emphasized the need for collaboration between infantry and artillery. Field Regulations, it said, had been poorly understood or badly applied. Infantry attacks had been launched at too great a distance and without artillery support, resulting in losses from machine-gun fire that might have been avoided. Henceforth when ground was occupied, entrenchments must be dug and artillery brought up.

In the final analysis Joffre would acknowledge no error of theory or strategy. He ascribed the failure of Plan XVII to a lack of offensive spirit and to poor execution. Although the enemy had been stronger than he had been led to believe, the clear implication was that if the French Third and Fourth armies in the center had fought well, the entire German advance would have collapsed.

If Joffre would not, or could not, recognize that he had made immense miscalculations in the first great collision of the war, it is at least to his credit that he never lost hope that the French armies could recover from their débâcle. With his armies disorganized, decimated, deadly weary, and in full retreat, and with the German right wing advancing on Paris, Joffre maintained an unruffled demeanor and displayed an astonishing calmness. Burning the midnight oil, the French commander spent half the night of August 24–25 endeavoring to formulate a new campaign plan.

Joffre now saw that his most serious problem was to avoid the encirclement of his left flank. Yet he was limited in what he could do, because stationed there were the English to whom he could make only requests, not issue direct orders. It was imperative, therefore, that a new army, directly under his command, be formed on the left of the BEF. On August 25 Joffre drew up a new General Instruction, the second of the war. It was a splendidly succinct document that proposed to allot to the left wing armies their zones for an orderly retreat; and to create in the path of the German right a new army. Called the Sixth Army and commanded by General Maunoury, it was to be constituted by transferring divisions from the French right wing in Alsace, from the center, and from Paris. Together with the BEF and the Fourth and Fifth armies, it would form a mass against the swinging tip of the German movement. While the Sixth Army was forming in the neighborhood of Amiens, the BEF and the two French armies would have to win time by fighting determined delaying actions. Joffre expected the Sixth Army to be in position and ready to join in a renewed offensive by September 2.[28]

If the plan was to have a chance of succeeding it required the cooperation of the British. Therefore Joffre arranged a meeting with French at Saint Quentin for the next day and summoned Lanrezac to be present at it. Unfortunately, the talks (held on the morning of the 26th) were not productive. French, irritated by the presence of Lanrezac and worried about the fate of Smith-Dorrien's force, was in bad temper. Joffre made a few preliminary remarks before inquiring as to the state of the British army. This provoked a tirade from Sir John who said that he had been violently attacked by superior numbers since the commencement of operations and he attributed most of his difficulties to the sudden and headlong retreat of the Fifth Army. Wilson's watered-down translation could not efface the impression his chief's tone had made on the French. Joffre was surprised by the field marshal's excited behavior, since he believed that a commander should always maintain an appearance of calm before his staff. Lanrezac shrugged his shoulders, appearing "to treat the whole affair as quite normal, and merely incidental to the common exigencies of war." His remarks were brief and were neither an answer to the field marshal nor an explanation for the "very unexpected moves he had made." Joffre said nothing but looked hard at his subordinate, evidently dissatisfied with his action and conduct. After a pause Joffre observed that all Allied troops had been pushed hard by the enemy and it should not be supposed that the British army was the only one that had suffered. He expressed the hope that Sir John would conform to the plan contained in the new General Instruction sent out on the previous day.

French had a blank expression on his face. "I know nothing of this order," he exclaimed. All eyes turned on Wilson who explained that the order had been received during the night but had not yet been studied. Joffre appeared disconcerted. He went over the content of his General Instruction but in a dull flat voice that lacked conviction. French raised objections at once, insisting that he must continue his retreat to Saint Quentin. Try as he might, Joffre was unable to shift Sir John from this position. The atmosphere became heavy, almost hostile. Discussion faltered and the pauses grew longer. At last, when the strain seemed intolerable, the meeting broke up.[29]

Since the noon hour was approaching, Sir John invited the French generals to join him at lunch. Lanrezac declined but Joffre accepted. The private and informal talks dissipated much of the tension resulting from the earlier meeting. Joffre understood for the first time the exasperation of Sir John and his staff over the manner in which the BEF had been treated. He realized that they had good grounds for distrusting the French. They had been misled as to the enemy's plans and numbers, thrust into what turned out to be the most dangerous part of the line, and abandoned there by the Fifth Army. Joffre gained French's esteem by conceding that Lanrezac had acted improperly and by frankly admitting that his plans had miscarried. Although the encounter between the two commanders did not produce a definite agreement it did serve one useful purpose. It brought them closer together and led each to understand the other's position better.

Immediately after Joffre left, French set out for Smith-Dorrien's headquarters to find out how the battle was progressing. Beyond the first few miles the roads became more and more congested. Thousands of refugees were fleeing with their belongings while the transports were endeavoring to bring up much-needed food and war matériel to the men at the front. On the way French received a message that Smith-Dorrien had broken off the action and his force was once more on the march. Thereupon he returned to Saint Quentin. In the evening French and his staff moved to Noyon, thirty-five miles further back.[30] No effort was made to notify Smith-Dorrien of this latest development.

It was only after Smith-Dorrien went to Saint Quentin to report to French that he learned of the new location of General Headquarters. He motored on and by the time he reached Noyon it was 1:00 A.M. (on the 27th) and everyone at General Headquarters had gone to bed. Roused from sleep Sir John emerged in his nightshirt. He was relieved to hear that the II Corps was not lost but chided Smith-Dorrien for taking too cheerful a view of the situation.[31] The losses incurred at Le Cateau seemed greater than they were since several thousand missing men, some after many wanderings, eventually rejoined their units. The initial estimate of casualties had the effect of intensifying French's anxiety to bring his army out of danger.

The BEF continued its retirement throughout the hot and oppressive days of August 27th and 28th. Each mile of the retreat was an agony. So great was the fatigue of the troops that they marched in a daze, without any clear notion of where they were or where they were going. Even mounted men slept in their saddles and often crashed to the ground. The ordeal was especially grim for the II Corps, which had fought two general actions and a number of smaller engagements, as well as marched an average of eighteen miles a day since August 24.[32] But if the men of the BEF were desperately weary, footsore, and without sleep they were in no mood to give up. They knew that whatever the reasons for the retreat it was not due to failure on their part to hold their own and so their spirit was very different from that of a routed army. By all accounts they only required rest, food, and replacement of lost equipment before they were ready for battle again.[33]

By this time French and most of his staff had lapsed into a state of mental defeat that was grossly out of proportion to the actual condition of the army. "Sir John and Murray ought to be ashamed of themselves," Wilson wrote in his diary one day when things had gotten out of hand at General Headquarters. "The difficulty is that Sir John had not once taken command."[34]

Sir John felt very deeply the burden of suffering among his soldiers. He did not find it difficult to believe that after days of retreating and intense action they had reached their breaking point. But he failed to realize that the "strict and rigid discipline of Aldershot, Colchester, York, remained instinctive, were never lost and provided an unseen backbone for men who were past endurance."[35] French might have formed a more accurate estimate of the situation had he remained in touch with the army he was supposed to command.

Much of what transpired at General Headquarters can be seen in the reports Huguet forwarded to his chief, which constitute a litany of unrelieved gloom. In them the French liaison officer stated that the British army was beaten and would be unable to take part in the campaign again until after a long rest and complete reorganization; that for three of the five divisions this would require a period not of days but weeks and under conditions that it was not yet possible to determine; that the British government might even "exact that the whole force retire to its base at Le Havre" in order to refit and reorganize.[36] It is true that Huguet was a pessimist by nature and that he never appreciated the dogged endurance and recuperative power of the British soldier. But there can be no doubt that he was reflecting the sentiments of General Headquarters, for Sir John was reporting the same thing in almost the same words to Kitchener.

In order to hasten the retreat General Headquarters ordered that the transport wagons unload all ammunition and other impedimenta not absolutely essential and carry troops instead. This decision virtually ruled out the idea of further action and was bound to have a very dismal effect on morale. The field commanders, none of whom shared the gloomy outlook of General Headquarters, were dismayed when they received the directive. Haig's chief of staff, General Gough, tore it up in anger.[37] Smith-Dorrien countermanded it but his message did not reach General Snow's division until it was too late. Consequently large numbers of men were deprived of equipment, as well as spare clothing and boots, which they were soon to need urgently.

The rapid retreat made further demands on the weary men, who required rest far more than they required additional distance from the enemy. The Germans were not within miles. In fact, after the battle of Le Cateau, von Kluck, again acting on faulty information, swung out (southwest) in a wide loop towards Amiens while the BEF retired due south.

Far from cutting off the British von Kluck brought his army into conflict with the French territorial divisions of General d'Amade and threatened to disrupt Joffre's plan for creating a mass of maneuvre on the left. Nevertheless the swing drew the German First Army away from the Second and exposed its long flank to an attack by the British I Corps and the French Fifth Army. Having perceived the opportunity Haig offered the cooperation of his corps if the French would attack. On the afternoon of the 28th arrangements were concluded for joint action the next day, subject only to the approval of General Headquarters. Early in the evening French informed Haig that he was not to take part in the proposed offensive on the ground that the troops were very tired and required complete rest the following day. Quite apart from the state he imagined the I Corps to be in, Sir John had become thoroughly disillusioned and mistrustful of the French. Since past arrangements had resulted in the English receiving most of the blows, he was not about to risk a repetition of events that might lead to the destruction of the BEF.

Lanrezac, who had a difficult time controlling his temper in the best of circumstances, exploded in anger when he heard that French had forbidden Haig to participate in the planned action. His wrath was fueled by the knowledge that the British were not being pressed by the enemy; that the I Corps was fit and ready and its commander eager to act. "It's a betrayal," he shouted, forgetting his own irresponsible conduct several days before. He added in rapid succession what Spears described as "terrible, unpardonable things about Sir John French and the British Army. . . ."[38]

Initially Lanrezac had been unwilling to carry out the attack and it had required a personal visit from Joffre to bring him to heel. He liked the idea even less now that he would be unsupported but he had no choice in the matter. Next morning Joffre went to Lanrezac's headquarters to superintend the offensive. He sat in silence watching Lanrezac dictate orders and conduct the battle.

What followed was a remarkable feat of arms. As the French Fifth Army attacked von Kluck's columns near Saint Quentin to the northwest, the German Second Army came down unobserved upon its right flank from the direction of Guise to the north. His original plan having miscarried, Lanrezac had to fight facing north if he hoped to save his army. In the confusion of battle Lanrezac, with a coolness and adroitness that he had not shown before, swung his army around and inflicted a sharp check on the German Second Army. Responding to von Bülow's loud cry for help, von Kluck changed his advance to a southeasterly direction and thus away from Maunoury's hastily assembling Sixth Army.

Joffre left Lanrezac's headquarters in the midst of the battle in order to see the British commander, whom he suspected had eyes on the Channel coast. If the British could be persuaded to halt he hoped to stabilize a front on the Aisne along a line Amiens-Reims-Verdun and from there launch a counteroffensive. During the afternoon Joffre arrived at Compiègne where Sir John and his staff were now established. Joffre pleaded with French to remain in contact with his neighbors on each side so as not to create a gap in the line. He was certain that the Russian drive would oblige the Germans to transfer a portion of their forces to the Eastern front, thereby relieving pressure on the Anglo-French army. If the British remained in the battle line until the Sixth Army had been fully assembled, sooner or later circumstances would permit the resumption of a general offensive. Joffre's arguments seemed to produce no effect. He "distinctly saw" Murray tugging at Sir John's tunic as if to forestall him from yielding to persuasion. But Murray's fears were groundless. French made it absolutely clear that in view of his losses his army was in no condition to fight and required forty-eight hours to recuperate. Joffre determined from the field marshal's tone that it was useless to insist. He took his leave and, by his own admission, made no attempt to conceal his disappointment.[39]

While French was adamant in his resolve to continue the retreat he did promise Joffre that he would remain in the line and fill up the gap between the Fifth and Sixth armies.[40] At 9:00 P.M. French heard that the left of the French Fifth Army had been checked in front of Saint Quentin and driven back to the Oise River. The return of the German First Army to the vicinity of the BEF confirmed Sir John's fears and made him more than ever determined to quit the battle line. He was not going to get involved in a French defeat, lose his army, and with it his name and reputation.

With no regard for his ally French alerted Major-General F. S. Robb, the inspector-general of communications, of his aim to make "a definite and prolonged retreat due south, passing Paris to the east or west."[41] In taking this course of action French was disobeying his instructions. Kitchener had laid down that the primary responsibility of the BEF was to support and cooperate with the French against their common foe. Simultaneously he had warned Sir John against participating in forward movements in which large bodies of French troops would not be engaged. Kitchener's emphasis on caution was intended to restrain the aggressive and optimistic British military leaders from risking the destruction of the BEF in some reckless French-sponsored scheme. But in this instance there was no question of a forward movement. Sir John proposed to withdraw altogether from the battle line at the very moment when Joffre was desperately attempting to conduct a general retreat and hold his army together. Kitchener never intended that the BEF should desert the French, least of all when they were on the threshold of defeat.

Strangely enough Sir John made no effort to inform the secretary of war about his change of plans. His telegram on August 30 conveyed the impression that the BEF was in the process of extricating itself from a perilous situation. French was concerned about the casualties but they were not as high as Kitchener feared. Drafts had already been sent over to make good the losses. It seemed also that close cooperation existed between the two armies, by no means a simple accomplishment given the strains inherent in an enforced retirement.

Kitchener had barely laid down what he thought was a reassuring report when he heard from General Robb that French proposed to make a definite and prolonged retreat due south, passing by Paris to the east or west. Robb went against customary military behavior when he informed on French but it was a case of his country's welfare taking precedent over loyalty to his chief. Robb showed great courage for he must have known that he would pay dearly for his action.[42]

Kitchener immediately queried French as to the meaning of Robb's message. Sir John replied that in view of the present condition of his troops he intended to disengage the army and to retire behind the Seine in a south-westerly direction. The retirement would involve a march of about eight days "without fatiguing the troops at a considerable distance from the enemy." He continued by saying that he did "not like General Joffre's plan" and would have preferred a vigorous offensive. "I have no idea of making any definite and prolonged retreat," French concluded.[43]

The contents of the letter were so contradictory that Kitchener must have wondered whether the British commander was in a state of mental collapse. French claimed that the army was too weak to remain in the front line and yet he wanted a vigorous offensive. He planned to retreat independently of his allies for eight days, at a considerable distance from the enemy, but this was not to be regarded as prolonged or definite.

A second note from General Headquarters arrived at the War Office several hours later and, if anything, added to the confusion. It ran as follows:

> I cannot say that I am happy in the outlook as to the further progress of the campaign in France. . . .
> My confidence in the ability of the leaders of the French Army to carry this campaign to a successful conclusion is fast waning, and this is my real reason for the decision I have taken to move the British Forces so far back. . . .
> I feel most strongly the absolute necessity of retaining in my hands complete independence of action and power to retire on my base when circumstances render it necessary.
> I have been pressed very hard to remain, even in my shattered condition, in the fighting line; but I have absolutely refused to do so, and I hope you will approve of the course I have taken. Not only is it in accordance with the spirit and letter of your instructions, but it is dictated by common sense. . . .
> I have tried many times to persuade General Joffre to adopt a stronger and bolder line of action, but without avail. . . .[44]

Kitchener was astonished and horrified by the telegrams from General Headquarters, not only on account of the incoherence in some of the ideas expressed but because of French's declared intention to leave the battle line. Such a move violated the spirit of the Entente and would have a deplorable effect on the French army and nation. Strategically it would permit the Germans to drive a wedge between the BEF and the French army. In these circumstances they would be in a position either to annihilate the British or contain Sir John with a small force while throwing their weight against the French army.[45] Either course would prove disastrous. Kitchener, although alarmed, sent off a restrained telegram to Sir John in the early hours of August 31:

> I am surprised at your decision to retire behind the Seine. Please let me know, if you can, all your reasons for this move. What will be the effect of this course upon your relations with the French Army and on the general military situation? Will your retirement leave a gap in the French line or cause them discouragement, of which the Germans might take advantage to carry out their first programme of first crushing the French and then being free to attack Russia?[46]

Without waiting for a reply Kitchener met that morning with the cabinet, which had been hastily summoned at his request. Like Kitchener, the ministers were mystified and perturbed over the telegrams. What was even more disturbing to them than the state of the army was the revelation that Sir John no longer wished to act in concert with the French.[47] In the end Kitchener demanded and obtained authority to order French to adhere to his original instructions. Accordingly he sent a second message to General Headquarters:

> The Government are exceedingly anxious lest your force, at this stage of the campaign in particular, should, owing to your proposed retirement so far from the line, not be able to co-operate closely with our Allies and render them continual support. They expect that you will as far as possible conform to the plans of General Joffre for the conduct of the campaign.[48]

During the morning and early afternoon of August 31 French was absent from General Headquarters, now relocated at Dammartin, and even his personal staff were ignorant of his whereabouts. When he returned Huguet was waiting to see him with a message from Joffre. The latest tidings had brought the French commander-in-chief some comfort. Intelligence reported that thirty-two trains of German troops had left Berlin and were apparently moving in the direction of Russia. The Russian offensive was beginning to make itself felt on the Western front and German pressure on the Anglo-French forces would inevitably diminish. Joffre also discovered that while Lanrezac's left had been repulsed at Saint Quentin, the other half had won an impressive victory at Guise. Von Bülow's army had been severely mauled and was not pursuing.

Joffre explained in his note that, given the information he had just received, he had given orders to the Fifth and Sixth armies not to yield ground except under severe pressure. As they could not be expected to stand without the British army he begged the field marshal not to withdraw unless the French were themselves compelled to fall back, and he requested that rear guards should at least be maintained so as not to give the enemy the impression that "a distinct movement in retreat is under way and that a gap exists between our Fifth and Sixth Armies."[49]

French felt frustrated and angry while he pondered the note. The next day he called in Major Sidney Clive, liaison officer at G.Q.G., and requested an update on the most recent events. In his diary Clive has noted French's agitation as well as his own concerns:

> He had been very hard pressed from several quarters yesterday to stand or advance. Then he kept on saying: "I should have been *mad* to stop there; they would only have gone back again, leaving my flanks open." I did my best to rub in the necessity for getting a definite statement from the Minister, or from Joffre, as to whether we are playing the game of the Russians in 1812, or merely waiting for a good opportunity to strike.[50]

Trained for the *offensive à outrance,* not for a retreating maneuvre, the French knew little of dismounted action and seemed incapable of standing their ground. Since the High Command's control had practically lapsed, the retreat was being directed by divisional or brigade commanders, each in his own small zone. Thus they were fluid in the extreme, appearing here, there, and everywhere. The impression gained by the British was that they would bolt on very little provocation without due concern for their neighbors. This attitude inevitably led the English to conclude that all plans emanating from G.Q.G. would end in failure. Sir John might have proven more cooperative if he had been taken into Joffre's confidence and made to see the situation as a whole. The British army was an autonomous, not a subordinate force and entitled to know of the French plans in advance.

French told Joffre that while his army could not advance until it had been "reorganized and its ranks filled up," he would stand on the Nanteuil line, providing that the Fifth and Sixth armies remained in their present positions.[51] It was not much of a concession since the Fifth Army was already in full retreat when Sir John's decision was communicated to G.Q.G. Anticipating an unfavorable reply, Joffre had already enlisted the aid of the French government in an effort to keep the British in the front line. Accordingly the French president made an impassioned appeal to the British government for the cooperation of the BEF in maintaining the line between the French Fifth and Sixth armies so as to avert the capture of Paris and the defeat of the Allied army.

Sir John's reply to Kitchener's telegrams arrived at the War Office at midnight. Anxiously awaited by Kitchener it was repeated to him word-by-word as it was deciphered. "If the French go on with their present tactics," the telegram stated, "which are practically to fall back right and left of me, usually without notice, and to abandon all idea of offensive operations, of course, then, the gap in the French line will remain and the consequences must be borne by them." It went on to say that owing to the transfer of many German divisions to the Russian front an offensive movement was open to the French, who "would probably close the gap by uniting their inward flanks. But as they will not take such an opportunity I do not see why I should be called upon again to run the risk of absolute disaster in order a second time to save them." The idea that the French might close the gap by uniting their inward flanks shows that Sir John did not understand the big scheme that Joffre was attempting to bring off or make allowance for his difficulties. Had the BEF withdrawn and the Fifth and Sixth armies closed in to take its place Joffre would have had to abandon his plan and, worst still, would have been outflanked. In the last part of the note French said that he proposed to retire and refit north of Paris since "the shattered condition of the second Army Corps . . . paralyses my power of offense."[52]

The document not only reiterated the reasons for an independent movement from the front but did so in terms that seemed so childish and dangerous that it could only increase Kitchener's anxiety. Kitchener felt that it would be futile to argue further by correspondence. He must cross the Channel at once and do whatever was necessary to avert what might prove an irreparable mistake.

Around 12:30 A.M. on September 1 Kitchener repaired to 10 Downing Street and, much to his annoyance, found the prime minister engrossed in a game of bridge, seemingly unconcerned with the approaching crisis in France. An informal conference was held with such cabinet ministers as could be hastily assembled.[53] After Kitchener gave the gist of French's telegram he explained that retirement behind the Seine might mean the loss of the war. Then the appeal by the French president was read. It profoundly touched everyone in the room. According to a minister who was present, Asquith broke the silence by saying: "If this is done [the withdrawal of the BEF from the line] the French left will be uncovered, Paris will fall, the French Army will be cut off and we shall never be able to hold our heads up in the world again. Better that the British Army should perish than that this shame should fall on us." It was unanimously agreed that Kitchener should leave for France without delay to, as the prime minister noted, "unravel the situation, and if necessary put the fear of God into them all."[54]

Kitchener telegraphed French to expect him and asked him to leave word at the British Embassy in Paris as to where he would find it convenient to meet. A fast cruiser was waiting to convey the secretary of war from

Dover to Le Havre. At 2:30 A.M. on September 1 he departed by special train from Charing Cross and before noon arrived in Paris. There he found that French had chosen the British Embassy as their place of meeting.

Sir John came to the meeting reluctantly, feeling deeply the criticism implied in Kitchener's summons. During the South African War he had served under Kitchener happily and without strain and since then their relationship had been marked by mutual affection and respect. The interview in Paris, however, created a breach that never healed.

The conference lasted three hours and parts of it were attended by Sir Francis Bertie, as well as by Colonel Huguet and several members of the French government. Sir John later expressed indignation at being summoned from his headquarters at a moment when his presence was badly needed. There is no legitimate basis for this complaint. The BEF was managing very well, having fought its last engagements without any coordinating help from General Headquarters. Moreover, there were occasions in the recent past when French would suddenly disappear and even his own staff would be ignorant of his whereabouts.

The first thing that struck French was the sight of Kitchener in a field marshal's uniform and the next was when Kitchener announced his intention of inspecting the troops in the field. Sir John in his book states that what he mainly resented was not Kitchener's visit as secretary of war but the fact that he appeared "in character of a soldier" and assumed the attitude of a superior. There is no substance to the charges that Kitchener was endeavoring to exercise the power and authority of a commander-in-chief in the field. After the opening days of the war Kitchener discarded the frock coat and silk hat for the blue undress uniform of a field marshal. It was thus only natural that he should be in uniform, especially in view of his wish to see for himself the troops of whom he had heard disquieting reports. And if Kitchener used a commanding tone it was not because he desired to exert any control over military operations but to impress upon Sir John his obligation to act in accordance with government policy.

Sir John goes on to say that he felt the arrival within the area of his command of a British field marshal senior to himself and in uniform would undermine his authority with the French as well as with his own troops. Paris was hardly within the purview of his command. But Sir John, sensitive by nature and possessing a strong sense of personal dignity, perceived slights easily, whether they were intended or not. It is quite possible he genuinely believed that the French would gain the impression from Kitchener's appearance that the British government had lost confidence in him or was about to supersede him.

The notion, however, that Kitchener's inspection tour could injure him in the eyes of the BEF is absurd. French's rapport with his own troops was never in question. His tough appearance, frequent visits among the men, and the warmth he radiated made him a much-respected and loved figure in the army. Walking side-by-side with Kitchener, the foremost soldier in the Empire and the man on whom the nation pinned its hope for victory, could only have boosted his stock and done wonders for the morale of the troops who, being outnumbered and outgunned, tended to feel neglected by the people at home. The real reason why French did not want Kitchener to visit the troops had nothing to do with military protocol. He feared that Kitchener would discover what really happened during the retreat. Kitchener would certainly have talked to the two corps commanders, Haig and Smith-Dorrien, and asked for their views on the recent events and on the state of the British army. They could hardly have failed to reply that Sir John had not been at his best, that the dangers to the BEF were more imaginery than real, that the army, although tired and in need of reinforcements, was far from shattered. In these circumstances Kitchener would have had no option but to dismiss French on the spot. But this never came to pass. French, strongly supported by the British ambassador,[55] raised such a furor that Kitchener abandoned his proposed tour of inspection.

On the vital issue of strategy French remained belligerent and noncooperative. He insisted repeatedly that the direction of operations should be left entirely in his hands. Sir John was unable or unwilling to recognize that as commander-in-chief his task was not to determine policy but to execute it. The policy of the government had been defined in his instructions: "To support and cooperate with the French Army."

The French representatives suggested that both Kitchener and Sir John should see Joffre, hoping that such a meeting might lead to a general agreement. But Sir John, convinced that this would be tantamount to admitting that he might be wrong, objected again. During the conversation Huguet noted the contrast in the behavior of the two men:

> The one, Kitchener, calm, balanced, reflective, master of himself, conscious of the great and patriotic task he had come to perform; the other, sour, impetuous, with congested face, sullen and ill-tempered in expression. The difference was striking; the one really looked the man and leader he was, while the other looked on the contrary like nothing but a spoiled child upon whom Fortune had smiled prodigiously but who, the day she left him, seemed abandoned and forlorn.

They seemed to be getting nowhere when Kitchener asked French to retire with him to a private room.[56]

What exactly passed between them will never be known. Since Kitchener left no record we must turn to French's account:

> When we were alone he [Kitchener] commenced by entering a strong objection to the tone I assumed. Upon this I told him all that was in my

mind. I said that the command of the British Forces in France had been entrusted to me by His Majesty's Government; that I alone was responsible to them for whatever happened, and that on French soil my authority as regards the British Army must be supreme until I was legally superseded by the same authority which had put that responsibility upon me . . . I had reminded him of our service in the field together some 13 years before, and told him that I valued highly his advice and assistance, which I would gladly accept as such, but that I would not tolerate any interference with my executive command and authority so long as His Majesty's Government chose to retain me in my present position.

French concludes:

Lord Kitchener came to Paris with no other object than to insist upon my arresting the retreat, although no sign of a halt appeared at any part of the Allied line. . . . It was difficult to resist such pressure. Fortunately I was able to do so.[57]

The last statement was certainly untrue. The results of the interview were expressed in a telegram Kitchener sent from Paris to the cabinet: "French's troops are now engaged in the fighting line where he will remain conforming to the movements of the French Army though at the same time acting with caution to avoid being in any way unsupported on his flanks."[58] Kitchener enclosed a copy to French, adding that he felt sure this represented the agreement they had come to, but that in any case "please consider it an instruction."[59] In acknowledging the letter French wrote: "I fully understand your instructions."[60] It is clear then that it was Sir John who was overruled. No doubt Kitchener, after suffering through French's childish tantrums, made him aware that continued tenure of his command was conditional upon his reversing his decision to leave the battle line.

French returned to General Headquarters in a sulk that grew deeper during the next few days as he continued to brood about the meeting. In a letter to his old friend Winston Churchill he complained bitterly about Kitchener's visit and begged him to do what he could to "*stop this interference* with field operations." He continued: "Kitchener *knows nothing* about European warfare. Of course he's a fine organizer but he never was and never will be a Commander in the field."[61]

With Asquith's blessing, Churchill tried to mediate between the two field marshals. He wrote to Sir John a soothing letter in which he explained, "The Cabinet was bewildered by your telegram proposing to retire from the line, coming on top of . . . your reports as to the good spirits of the troops. We feared that you and Joffre might have quarrelled, or that something had happened to the Army of which we had not been informed. In these circumstances telegraphing was useless, and a personal consultation was indispensable if further misunderstandings were to be avoided."[62]

French replied: "I fear I was a little unreasonable about K. and his visit, but we have been through a hard time and perhaps my temper isn't made any better by it! However, as usual, you have poured balm into my wounds—although they may have been only imaginary—and I am deeply grateful."[63]

The relations between the two field marshals were patched up but only temporarily. Neither would trust the other again. French persisted in the belief that Kitchener had tried to pull rank on him. He realized that he was on probation, that because of his contentiousness Kitchener would not hesitate to remove him from command if he found a pretext. For his part Kitchener, unhappy over the manner in which Sir John had proposed to conduct the retreat of the BEF, concluded in the wake of the Paris interview that he was unsuited for so taxing a command as he now exercised. Thereafter he began to toy with the idea of assuming the post of supreme military commander, in addition to his existing office of secretary of war, in order to formalize his responsibility for the direction of war strategy.

Kitchener's intervention at this juncture in the western campaign was a much greater contribution to the Allied cause than is generally realized. The following week the British army would be called upon to play a part, a highly significant one it turned out, in the crucial battle of the Marne. That it was present at all was due to Kitchener's far-sighted appreciation of the general situation and his courage in overruling the commander in the field.

Kitchener's visit also led to immediate and marked improvements in Anglo-French relations. On September 1, with the I and II Corps finally reunited, Sir John wrote a conciliatory letter to Joffre through the French minister of war. In it he proposed establishing a line of defense along the Marne and offered to hold his current position, providing only that his flanks were secure.[64] Joffre replied that the position of the Fifth Army ruled out a general action on the Marne and he asked that the British cooperate in the defense of Paris.

On August 30 Joffre had abandoned all thoughts of delivering a counterattack under conditions envisaged in his General Instruction No. 2 since he had been compelled to part with the Sixth Army, the nucleus of his striking force, in order to strengthen the Paris garrison. He gave a hint of his future plans in General Instruction No. 4, published on September 1. The retreat was to continue for the Third, Fourth, and Fifth armies and the limit of the movement was fixed along a line behind the Seine and Aube. Once the Fifth Army had "escaped the menace of envelopment," the left-wing armies would resume the offensive. In due course the mobile troops of the fortified camp of Paris as well as portions of the First and Second armies might be called upon to take part in the action.[65] Unlike the previous order (General Instruction No. 2) Joffre did not specify when or where the battle would take place. Evidently this time Joffre had decided not to reveal his real intentions except to a select few. What he had in mind was to strike after he had drawn the advancing German right wing into a pocket between the fortress of Paris and Verdun. In conversation with the former French minister of war (Adolphe Messimy) on September 1, Joffre indicated that he expected to resume the offensive on the 8th and anticipated that it would be called the Battle of Brienne-le-Chateau.[66] The town of Brienne, twenty-five miles behind the Seine, had been the site of one of Napoleon's victories over Blücher.

One of the first steps Joffre took in anticipation of the coming battle was to remove the troublesome General Lanrezac. He stated his reasons as follows: "His [Lanrezac's] physical fatigue had intensified a tendency to criticize, which had always been one of the marked characteristics of his nature. He had become hesitating and timorous. Under the effects of his weakening authority, the staff of the Fifth Army had become profoundly shaken, while his unpleasant personal relations with Sir John French had compromised the co-operation of the British Army with our own."[67] To replace Lanrezac, Joffre selected General Franchet d'Esperey, one of his ablest corps commanders. The change in the leadership of the Fifth Army naturally delighted Sir John and his staff.

In the meantime the Germans made a costly miscalculation. Their intelligence sources indicated that the line of the retreating French Fifth Army did not extend as far west as previously believed. Von Kluck now determined that Lanrezac's flank could be rolled up southeast of Paris, precluding the need of a sweep behind or to the west of the city. In the process of executing the new maneuvre von Kluck recognized that he would be exposing his flank to attack by the forces assembled in the vicinity of the capital. But he considered these to be negligible, confident that only one reserve corps would be enough to leave in front of Paris as a flank guard. The BEF, hitherto the main adversary of the First German Army, was rashly written off after von Kluck learned from a captured letter of Sir John's decision to seek refuge behind the Seine.

Von Kluck made up his mind on the evening of August 30 when he received a message from von Bülow. It requested that the First Army wheel inwardly in order to cut off Lanrezac's forces. Von Kluck was happy to comply since it fitted with what he wanted to do. When contacted, German Supreme Headquarters (OHL) approved of the change in direction. A timid leader, von Moltke was bothered by the gaps that had opened between the three right-wing armies. The number of troops currently employed in the offensive was far below what it had been at the outset. Along the way the Germans had left the III Reserve Corps outside Antwerp to watch the Belgian army; the VII Reserve Corps and one brigade of the VII to besiege the fortress of Maubeuge; a brigade of the IV Reserve Corps to garrison Brussels; the XXIV Reserve Division to reduce Charlemont. More important, two corps, the XI and the Guard Reserve, had been detached from the right-wing armies and sent to East Prussia to help check the Russian advance. Now disposing of only sixty-seven divisions, as against seventy-five in the first week of August, von Moltke did not feel sufficiently strong to adhere to the original plan of sweeping around the far side of Paris. Thus he seized upon von Kluck's move as a fortunate solution.

It was on September 3 that the military governor of Paris, General Galliéni, discovered by means of his aerial observers that von Kluck, instead of following the British rear guards southwards, had changed direction to the southeast. At daybreak on September 4 the cavalry confirmed the air reports. "We must strike," cried the old soldier, and at 9:00 A.M. he sent preliminary orders to Maunoury: "My intention is to send your army forward in liaison with the English forces against the German flank. Make your arrangements at once so that your troops will be ready to march this afternoon as the start of a general movement eastward by the forces of the Paris camp."[68] Then at 9:45 he rang G.Q.G., the first of a series of telephone exchanges. He explained that he proposed to launch the Sixth Army, together with all available forces in the Paris camp, in an attack on von Kluck's flank. The Sixth Army was ready to operate either on the north or the south bank of the Marne River, as circumstances dictated, and he wanted to know which of the options Joffre preferred. Joffre consented to the movement and on the insistence of his chief of staff, General Berthelot, told Galliéni that it should advance along the south bank.[69] By the time Galliéni received the reply he had decided to attack north of the river, which indeed had been his intention all along. Since Joffre's message was a recommendation rather than an order, there would have been no adverse repercussion if a copy had not been sent to General Headquarters, where it led to an unfortunate misunderstanding.

Galliéni believed that the moment had come to end the retreat and he hoped that his own maneuvre would precipitate a general offensive. Concerned only with the defense of Paris, Galliéni had no direct knowledge of the situation of the field armies and so he could not fairly judge the chances of success. But he was convinced the French had no choice since it was unlikely that another such opportunity would present itself.

Joffre had already done much to prepare for an ultimate return to the offensive. Galliéni, however, was precipitating matters. For Joffre the decision of whether to continue the retreat or face the enemy now was not an easy one. He knew that the French army was good for only one more battle. If it failed all was lost. Before reaching a verdict the first requirement was to determine if the French armies could be made ready for battle.

In the afternoon Galliéni drove to General Headquarters at Melun, twenty-five miles to the south of Paris, to explain the latest developments to the British and, if possible, gain their cooperation. On arrival at Melun he learned that both Sir John and Wilson were absent. At length Murray appeared. He explained that the field marshal was away inspecting troops and he had no idea when he would return. Disappointed, Galliéni nonetheless unfolded his plan of attack and tried to show why British help was indispensable. Murray, according to Galliéni, was very "reluctant to share our views" and declared that he could do nothing in the absence of the commander-in-chief. At the end of the discussion Galliéni wrote down a summary of his scheme, which Murray "did not appear to understand very well." Before leaving, the governor of Paris obtained a promise that he would be notified the moment Sir John returned.[70]

Elsewhere another Anglo-French conference was taking place almost at the same time. On the morning of September 4 General Franchet d'Esperey, anxious to repair the frayed relations caused by his predecessor, had expressed a desire to meet Sir John at Bray. But French wanted to visit the I Corps and instead sent Wilson with the head of the intelligence section, General Macdonogh. Arriving at Bray around 4:00 P.M., these officers found out that a quarter of an hour earlier d'Esperey had received an urgent message from Joffre. In it the commander-in-chief considered that a great opportunity for a counterstroke had arisen and he inquired whether the Fifth Army was in a fit state to fight. "I am going to answer that my army is prepared and I hope you will not oblige us to do it alone," Franchet d'Esperey told Wilson. He then outlined a scheme that he had worked out in his head in the brief time since receiving Joffre's message. It was based on the assumption that the BEF would take up a position facing east between the Fifth and Sixth armies. Wilson fully agreed with the plan and indicated he would recommend it most strongly to Sir John.[71]

The plans of Galliéni and Franchet d'Esperey, although containing the same idea of a counterattack against the German right, differed significantly in detail. Galliéni wanted action limited to the two armies in his immediate vicinity, the BEF and the Sixth. Franchet d'Esperey's proposals called for a more ambitious maneuver and involved three armies besides his own.

When French returned to Melun at 7:00 P.M. he was faced with a welter of conflicting proposals. Apart from the plans of Galliéni and Franchet d'Esperey, General Headquarters was in possession of a note from Joffre. It detailed, erroneously as we have just seen,[72] the proposed action of the Sixth Army and requested British assistance on the Seine. Murray, misled by G.Q.G.'s letter, had already issued orders for a further retreat of ten to fifteen miles in order to make room for the Sixth Army on the south bank of the river. Confused, unable to determine which scheme should be given priority, French took no action at all. He allowed Murray's orders to stand and informed Huguet that in view of "constant changes in the situation" he preferred to study it further "before deciding on subsequent operations."[73] In conveying the message to Joffre Huguet observed that "Sir John French, who the day before was anxious to march eastwards, had now changed his mind, under the restraining advice" of General Murray.[74]

At Bar-sur-Aube, where G.Q.G. was installed, Joffre pondered the situation in light of the information that was constantly coming in about the condition of his forces as well as about the enemy's movements. The heat of this September day was overpowering. Joffre went outside his headquarters and sat in the shade of a weeping ash in the courtyard. All through the afternoon he sat there in deep thought, silent and motionless except when an occasional message was handed to him. Then as evening drew near he reached a decision. He got up, lumbered into his headquarters and had an order drafted (General Instruction No. 6) to transform the proposed local action by the Paris garrison into an offensive by the whole Allied left wing. It now remained to convince Sir John to participate in the operations.

Joffre went to bed full of anxiety about British intentions but early in the morning (September 5) his spirits were bolstered by a telephone call from Huguet. The field marshal, Huguet informed him, had studied General Instruction No. 6 and was prepared to carry out the directives laid down. Perhaps because of a recollection of past misunderstandings or a persistence of doubts once deeply felt, Joffre considered it essential to obtain from French personally an unqualified agreement. He sent word to General Headquarters to expect him that very day.

At approximately 10:00 A.M. Joffre set out with his aide, two staff officers, and Major Clive. The party, though delayed by roadblocks and a stop for lunch, covered the 115-mile journey in four hours, arriving at the Chateau of Vaux-le-Pénil, where Sir John was staying. Joffre and his entourage were promptly conducted to a room on the ground floor. Here the field marshal, flanked by Murray and Wilson, was standing at a table waiting for them. Everyone remained standing during the meeting. Joffre placed his cap on the table and, facing Sir John, began to speak.

Usually his voice was low and his delivery slow but on this occasion he poured out an impassioned torrent of words, punctuated by slight gestures of his hands. He explained the recent turn of events and of the necessity of acting rapidly. He described his plan and the part that he intended for the British army. The fate of France and indeed of Europe depended upon the offensive. His own orders were given and whatever happened the French army was committed up to the last man. He could not believe that the British army would refuse to do its share in this hour of supreme crisis. He brought his fist down on the table and cried, *"Monsieur le Maréchal,* the honour of England is at stake."

Sir John needed no interpreter to understand the sense of these words and his strong emotions were touched. With tears rolling down his cheeks he tried to say something in French but gave up. Turning to Major Clive, who stood beside him, he exclaimed: "Damn it, I can't explain. Tell him we will do all we possibly can." Murray, unmoved and unconvinced, observed that the British forces were ten miles further back than the positions called for in the Instruction. They could start only at 9:00 A.M., not at 6:00 A.M. as Joffre requested. "It cannot be helped," Joffre said with a weary shrug.

"Let them start as soon as they can. I have the Field Marshal's word, that is enough."[75]

And so the retreat from the frontiers was over. For the British it had been an especially trying ordeal. They had covered a distance of over 200 miles in thirteen days and that after a strenuous two-day march up to the Mons Canal. The constant marching by day and by night left the men with little time to eat, sleep, wash, or tend to their blistered feet. They fought two engagements against superior numbers, hitting hard and then slipping away unmolested. Throughout the retreat they retained their discipline and morale and at the end they were still an army, and a formidable one. Credit for the successful retreat of the BEF, it may fairly be said, was due less to the generalship of Sir John French than to the skill and coolness of General Smith-Dorrien and, of course, to the courage and endurance of the rank and file.

7

The Counterstroke

When Joffre made up his mind to deliver a counterattack conditions were favorable for its success. Von Moltke's headquarters in Luxemburg were far behind the front with the result that his communications were inadequate to control his armies. The German right-wing armies were exhausted from forced marches and continuous fighting and in some cases had outstripped their supplies. Two German corps had been transferred to the eastern front in anticipation of further Russian successes in East Prussia. Had these corps been available one would have been with von Bülow and might have filled the gap between his army and von Kluck's, while the other would have been attached to von Hausen's command and might have provided the additional strength to overcome the opposing French army (Foch's Ninth). The diversion of German troops came at a moment when the French were increasing their strength by drawing upon their forces in the south. Indeed at the Marne Joffre enjoyed a numerical superiority that he had not been able to achieve in his earlier battles.

Joffre's operational orders directed his two armies in the center, the Fourth and Ninth, to hold while the Third Army on the right and the Fifth, British, and Sixth armies on the left attacked the two flanks of the enemy between Verdun and Paris. Action was to begin on September 6.[1]

But military operations are seldom carried out according to plan. On September 5 elements of Maunoury's Sixth Army unexpectedly ran into von Kluck's rear guard along the Ourcq River. The resulting clash sparked the Battle of the Marne, begun twenty-four hours earlier than Joffre had intended. The crucial factor in the early phase of the battle was the progressive diversion of corps after corps by von Kluck to face Maunoury's army. By doing so he widened enormously an existing gap between himself and von Bülow, a gap that was masked by a screen of two weak cavalry corps and a few Jäger battalions. Into this void marched the BEF and the left of the French Fifth Army.

The BEF was some fifteen miles further back than Joffre intended when it received French's order to turn about and go forward on September 5. As already indicated, Sir John, led to believe that the Sixth Army would be operating south of the Marne, had carried out a rearward march to permit Maunoury to deploy his forces. The consequence of this last withdrawal was to reduce the effectiveness of the BEF in the initial stages of the fighting.

Of the Allied armies at the Marne the BEF was perhaps in the best condition. Although it had suffered about fifteen percent casualties, replacements and reinforcements from home had enabled Sir John to partially refill the ranks and to create a new corps under Sir William Pulteney. Equally important, the rank and file were eager to take the field again. Many units greeted the order to move forward with a spontaneous burst of cheering. Nonetheless the BEF was not without major problems. The delays caused by the transferral of the main base from Le Havre to Saint Nazaire and the congestion of railways around Paris made it impossible to replace much of the lost equipment and guns. The men were still tired after the long, merciless retreat. Finally the losses among the commissioned ranks had been disproportionately heavy, so there was a shortage of experienced officers.

Starting out on the morning of September 6 Sir John slowly felt his way

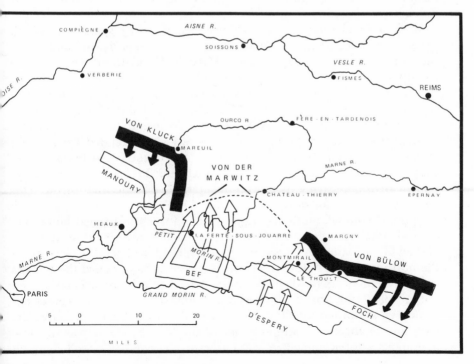

BRITISH ADVANCE AT THE MARNE

as he advanced with the I Corps on the right, the II Corps in the center, and the newly formed III Corps on the left. The ground towards the Marne was difficult, affording plenty of cover to rear guards and intersected by two unfordable rivers, the Grand and Petit Morin. The II and III corps encountered no opposition as they advanced but on the right Haig's leading units ran into von der Marwitz's cavalry east of Rozoy and were driven back. Haig, fearing heavy enemy concentrations in the great forests of Crécy and Malvoisine on his left front, halted his advance and waited for the II Corps to close in on his left. On the approach of Smith-Dorrien's corps the Germans abandoned their positions and by midafternoon Haig had resumed his march. The army as a whole did not make as much progress as had been expected. Only one battalion of the II Corps succeeded in crossing the Grand Morin. The I Corps, in particular, hung back, ending the day eight miles short of its intended destination.

The cavalry was on the move early on September 7 and during the day skirmished with the enemy's rear guards at Moncel, Faujus, and Le Charnois. Behind the cavalry screen the infantry continued its march without serious incident. By nightfall the British stood with their left well beyond the Grand Morin and their right along and behind the river. Although their forward movement on the 7th brought them in line with the French Fifth Army on their right, they did not average more than seven or eight miles.

Sir John accelerated his advance the next day, in response to Joffre's urgent appeal for haste to assist Maunoury's hard-pressed army, and late in the morning reached the Petit Morin. Here the Germans were prepared to put up a more determined resistance. Allenby's cavalry, moving ahead of the I and II corps, tried to get across the river at various points but without success. On the extreme left the III Corps advanced towards La Ferté-sous-Jouarre, located at the junction of the Petit Morin and the Marne. Because of the importance of this crossing the town was defended by a strong German contingent. Aided by the lay of the country and by an ample supply of machine guns the Germans held up the leading units of the Fourth Division, leaving them with no alternative but to wait for the artillery to be brought forward.

In the meantime, on the far right, Haig's attack was pushed home successfully when the Worcestershires carried the bridge near Bécherelle and, backed by two battalions of the guards, compelled the enemy to retire from the northern bank. Before 2:00 P.M. Haig's men had opened the bridges over the Petit Morin to Allenby's cavalry, which quickly crossed and fanned out patrols to the north. The Third and Fifth divisions in the center encountered stiff opposition but they managed to force a passage across the river and by dusk were within a mile of the Marne. The impact of these operations was felt immediately at La Ferté. German fire ceased about an hour after the guns of the Fourth Division had come into action. By night-fall the portion of the town south of the Marne was in British hands.

For most of the army the operations on the 8th came to an end around 6:00 P.M. when a violent thunderstorm made it difficult either to see or move. All in all it had not been a bad day's work. The successful action at the Petit Morin had infused the troops with a new spirit. In their first serious engagement since the start of the counteroffensive they had fought their way over territory that was ideally suited to rear-guard action and overwhelmed a resourceful and gallant enemy. At a cost of 600 killed and wounded they had inflicted at least as many casualties on the Germans and captured 500 prisoners and a dozen machine guns.[2]

The French armies on the right made less satisfactory progress than the British on September 7th and 8th. The Ninth Army under Foch was in deep trouble after being heavily attacked by elements of two German armies. On the next front the Fifth Army advanced cautiously. While Franchet d'Esperey's center and right faced von Bülow's army, his left had a completely open path. Maunoury's Sixth Army, deployed on the left of the BEF, was locked in a fierce struggle and had failed to gain ground. Indeed his center had actually been forced back and he had to be reinforced with two regiments of infantry rushed out from Paris in taxicabs.[3]

There was no longer any hope that Maunoury could drive back or outflank von Kluck's army but only that he would be able to hold his ground. Still an opportunity for a breakthrough existed, for von Kluck, in facing Maunoury, had been obliged to break the continuity of the German front. Having studied the situation Joffre issued General Instruction No. 19 on the evening of the 8th. He observed that the right wing of the German army was broken into two groups, linked only by several cavalry divisions, supported by some mixed formations. Therefore every effort should be made to defeat the German extreme right before it could be reinforced by other detachments released by the fall of Maubeuge. The Sixth Army and the BEF were assigned to carry out this task. The Sixth Army was to tie down the troops opposed to it on the right bank of the Ourcq, while the British force, crossing the Marne between Nogent l'Artaud and La Ferté-sous-Jouarre, was to advance against the left and rear of the enemy on the Ourcq. The Fifth Army was to cover the right flank of the British army by sending a strong detachment to seize Chateau Thierry.[4]

At 5:00 A.M. on September 9 the British army continued to advance northward, the cavalry maintaining touch with the French forces on the right and left. After the difficulties experienced at the Petit Morin British leaders anticipated heavy fighting before securing the line on the Marne. A broad river with few bridges and many houses on its high banks, it offered ideal opportunities to the defenders. But when the British reached the river they found, to their great relief, that most of the bridges were still intact. By 9:00 A.M. the leading troops of the II Corps were four miles beyond the river, well in the rear of von Kluck's left flank on the Ourcq. Had the British been able to press forward immediately along their entire front they might have severed von Kluck's forces from the rest of the German army. Unfortunately the III Corps was checked both by the enemy's stubborn defense and by the destruction of the bridges at La Ferté-sous-Jouarre. And the I Corps, although crossing unopposed at Nogent and Charly, was held up by the threat of a flank attack from Chateau Thierry, which was still in enemy hands. The delay enabled the Germans to scratch together a force to defend the line along the Chateau Thierry-Lizy road, from which they held back the British until nightfall.[5]

The British were disappointed with their progress on the 9th but there is no doubt that their presence north of the Marne exercised a decisive influence on the outcome of the battle. On the 8th von Moltke, frustrated and worried over the vague messages filtering back to him at Supreme Headquarters in Luxemburg, dispatched Lieutenant-Colonel Hentsch, a staff officer, on a tour of the German armies to ascertain what was happening and, apparently, to coordinate a retreat in case of necessity. Hentsch visited the headquarters of the Fifth, Fourth, and Third armies in the afternoon and found they were doing reasonably well. Passing on, he spent the night at Second Army headquarters where the atmosphere was quite different. The sixty-eight-year-old von Bülow seemed to be approaching an emotional collaspe. He was desperately apprehensive about his exposed right and believed that retreat was inevitable. Hentsch agreed with von Bülow and his staff that unless the gap between the First and Second armies could be closed, a task for which the reserves did not exist, the two German armies would have to withdraw. The next morning, while Hentsch discussed the situation with von Kluck's chief of staff, reports of the British advance made it clear that the line of the Marne could not be held. At noon Hentsch used his authority, as von Moltke's envoy, to order the First Army to retreat towards Soissons. Everywhere the German armies began to roll back.[6]

It was around 5:30 P.M. on September 9 before it became evident to the British that the Germans were abandoning the battlefield. The hour was too late to order a general and combined offensive, to say nothing of the fact that both the men and horses in the Anglo-French armies required some rest and refreshment before a further effort could be made. Since the German First Army's line of retreat appeared to lie more or less across the British front, Sir John still had some hopes of intercepting it. Anticipating Joffre's wishes French ordered his troops to continue the pursuit northwards at 5:00 A.M. the next morning. As it happened, von Kluck, foreseeing the danger, escaped from the clutches of his adversaries by beginning his retreat in a northerly direction instead of going straight to Soissons. The successes enjoyed by the BEF at the Marne had not been costly. Between September 6 and 10 the total casualties amounted to 1,701, nearly half of which came from the I Corps.

The battle of the Marne, it has been calculated, pitted some fifty-seven Allied divisions against fifty-three German ones. Tactically its results were disappointing because the Germans had not been defeated. Strategically it was of enormous importance since the battle frustrated Germany's attempt to deliver the quick knockout blow on which she had pinned her hopes for winning the war.

Many British and French writers have severely criticized Sir John's advance from September 6 to 8 as not fully corresponding to the possibilities that lay open to him. They have observed that although the gap was known to be lightly defended, the British infantry marched only eight miles a day when half as much again, about twelve miles, might readily have turned the German position. Yet it seems unlikely that the men could have been driven forward an additional three or four miles a day in view of their previous exertions, the weather, and the difficulties of the ground, which allowed for effective rear-guard action. It should be pointed out that Franchet d'Esperey's left did not advance into the gap any faster than the BEF and, in fact, his cavalry, though virtually unopposed, constantly lagged behind Allenby.

Sir John might have made a greater effort during the early part of the 9th had he been confident that his flanks were secure. But on the left the Sixth Army was very near the limit of its endurance; on his right the Fifth Army was not making much progress; and next to it the Ninth Army was losing ground. For all he knew, "if he pushed forward wildly north of the Marne he might be thrusting his troops into a trap prepared for them."[7]

The battered German armies withdrew from the battlefield of the Marne practically unmolested, in many cases unobserved by their opponents, and they were able to fall back in good order and maintain a relatively even alignment, though the wide gap between von Kluck and von Bülow remained open. By September 13 their right wing had settled on a steep ridge that skirts the north bank of the Aisne River. Here, with admirable foresight, they had already prepared a defensive line in the event of just such a retreat as had occurred. This ridge, along which ran an old road known as the Chemin des Dames, forms one of the finest defensive positions in Europe. It commanded all the crossings of the river and most of the roads on the south bank and threw out such a multitude of curving spurs and shoulders as to inhibit any general attack towards the summit.

In the advance to the Aisne the BEF covered about ten miles a day while, on the right, the French Fifth Army and the Ninth Army could average but six or seven miles a day. The pursuit was hampered by a heavy rainfall that continued for several days with only brief interruptions. Roads became impassable quagmires, the mud resembling liquid glue, and the men, guns, horses, and wheeled transport were repeatedly bogged down. The men of

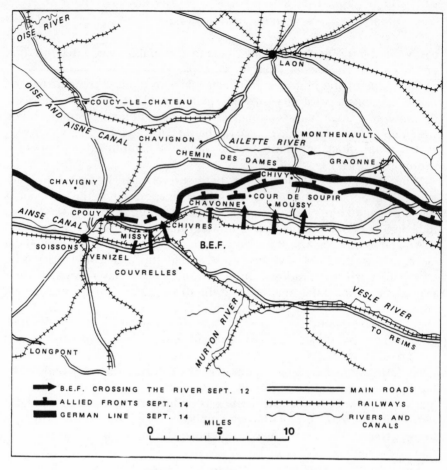

BRITISH ADVANCE AT THE AISNE

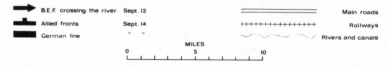

the BEF were ill-equipped for a prolonged downpour since the vast majority had thrown away their greatcoats during the retreat. They protected themselves as best they could, some wore oat sacks found in a granary, while others had to content themselves with skirts picked up in abandoned homes. Drenched to the skin, cold, weary, hungry, and forced to plod through knee-deep slime, it is a wonder they were able to cover the thirty-mile march in three days.

The appalling weather conditions made aerial reconnaissance so difficult that the Royal Flying Corps could furnish no information of value about the enemy's movements. Had Joffre been aware of what the Germans proposed to do and the strength of their position on the Aisne, he probably would have attempted an enveloping movement around their right flank. As things were he decided to launch a frontal attack, the standard procedure against a retreating army that has merely halted to fight a delaying action.

A conference was held on September 13 at Joffre's headquarters now established at Châtillon-sur-Seine to discuss the future plan of campaign. Wilson represented the British High Command. The mood was one of jubilation. The general consensus was that if the Germans made a serious stand in France, it would not be before they reached the Meuse. The Allied leaders talked boldly of continuing the pursuit beyond the Aisne and of driving a wedge in the German front. Various estimates were being tossed about of how long it would take to drive the Germans back across their own frontier. Wilson thought that unless the Allies made a serious blunder they ought to enter Germany in four weeks. Joffre's chief of staff, General Berthelot, predicted three weeks.[8]

The Anglo-French forces, pressing on in pursuit, encountered only token resistance from enemy rear guard units before reaching the line of the Aisne. nearly all the bridges had been destroyed and most possible crossing places were guarded by strong detachments of German infantry with machine guns and batteries. Along a fifteen-mile front the main bodies of the BEF, with the I Corps on the right, the II Corps in the center, and the III Corps on the left, began the passage of the Aisne early on September 13. By means of boats, rafts, pontoons, and, in several cases, the sole remaining girder of a demolished bridge, they made their way across the river, amid a storm of fire from the heights above. Their losses were not excessive and by the end of the day they had forced a passage at most points and established themselves at Venizel, Vailly, Pont Arcy, and Bourg.[9]

The British not only made satisfactory progress on the 13th but maintained close touch with the French on either side. On the extreme left the Sixth Army held a bridgehead north of Soissons. Right of the BEF Franchet d'Esperey's army met with varying fortune. His right wing was held up but the reserve divisions in his center bivouacked three miles north of Berry-au-Bac and the XVIII Corps on his left, after crossing the Aisne, advanced seven miles unopposed to Sissonne. Reviewing the general situation, General Joffre expressed the opinion that the enemy was retreating everywhere without serious resistance. His orders for the 14th called for an energetic pursuit along the entire line with the British advancing northward between Athies and the Oise.

Haig's corps faced the weakest sector in the German defense, the gap between the German First Army and the Second. But with good management and good fortune von Moltke had been able to create a new Seventh Army to fill the void. The advance unit of this reserve force was the VII Reserve Corps, which became available after the capitulation of Maubeuge on September 7. On the 12th the corps commander, General von Zwehl, was directed to march with all speed to Laon, some ten miles north of the Aisne. Von Zwehl made excellent time, halting for only two hours that evening, before pressing on again through the night. At 5:00 A.M. on the 13th the corps bivouacked five miles south of Laon, having covered more than forty miles in 24 hours. Nearly a quarter of the men had fallen out along the way. The rest were back on their feet again at 9:30 A.M. and began moving in a southwesterly direction towards Chavonne.

An hour and a half later von Bülow, anxious and alarmist as ever, ordered the corps to turn to the southeast towards Berry-au-Bac, where his right was threatened. Von Zwehl ignored von Bülow's cry for help, claiming that his men were already committed to their original direction. If he had marched less quickly and if he had adhered to von Bülow's instructions, he would have left the way open for Haig's corps to establish itself on the Chemin des Dames ridge and it is probable that the flank of all the Germans west of Chavonne would have been turned and it is conceivable that the battle would have been decided then and there in favor of the Allies. As it was by 2:00 P.M. on the 13th he had moved his corps into position with the Thirteenth Reserve Division stationed along the Chemin des Dames and the Fourteenth Reserve Division spread out to the east opposite the right wing of the BEF and the left wing of the French Fifth Army. The former division was ready and perfectly placed to hold off Haig's troops when they approached in the afternoon.

The weather broke on the afternoon of the 13th and British aviators were immediately sent out on reconnaissance missions. Their reports revealed only one German cavalry division and about two infantry divisions along the Cerny-Aizy line and another division near Laon. Since there did not appear to be a strong German presence ahead, Sir John felt he was justified in making a great effort to carry out Joffre's instructions.

Accordingly on September 14 an offensive was launched against the German positions along the whole of the British line. The attack broke down almost everywhere. Only on the far right, in Haig's sector, was any part of the objective attained. One brigade of the First Division even reached Cerny and La Bovelle Farm, some distance north of the Chemin des Dames ridge, before enemy resistance stiffened. Had a few reserve units been available to put into the fight the results might have been entirely different for, as is now known, the German First Army was on the verge of withdrawing.

When the fighting died down in the evening the general situation on the British front was far from satisfactory. The I Corps had made some headway but at a cost of 3,500 casualties. British positions were less secure elsewhere and although losses in the Fourth and Fifth Divisions were slight, those in the Third Division numbered almost 1,000. There were two gaps in the line, the first of one-and-a-half miles between the Second and Third divisions and the second, the width of a promontory (Chivres), between the Fourth and Fifth Divisions. It was also apparent that the British forces were too widely extended to allow a strong attack anywhere. There were no reserves left since every battalion was in the firing line.

The French experienced the same difficulties as the English on the 14th and also failed to make significant gains. They found out, as did the British, that the enemy, far from continuing his retreat, was in position, entrenched and backed by artillery, and bent on making every effort to drive his pursuers back over the river. Joffre's note to his commanders and to Sir John early on the 15th pointed out that since the enemy appeared to be willing to accept battle from prepared positions north of the Aisne, it was no longer a question of pursuit but of methodical attack. Each position was to be consolidated as is was gained.[10]

It proved impossible to carry out these intentions. During the next fortnight attacks and counterattacks were made by both sides without any appreciable change in the situation. A deadlock had been reached in this part of the line. As the activity on the Aisne died down, attention concentrated on the open flank to the west and it was there that the next moves in the war would be played out.

8

Deadlock

Before the end of September Sir John suggested to Joffre that the BEF
(now augmented to six divisions[1]) should be transferred from the Aisne
front, where it was awkwardly wedged in between the French armies, to its
former place on the extreme left of the line.[2] The concept originated with
Kitchener, not Wilson, as his biographers have maintained.[3] In the second
week of September Kitchener asked Churchill to explain to Sir John the
advantages of the move.[4] The First Lord crossed over to France on the 17th
and laid Kitchener's case before Sir John and his staff. Yet Wilson, in his
diary, tells us that the idea to bring the BEF northwards hit him on the
24th, at which time he conveyed his views to the commander-in-chief. In
any case French initially opposed the move, remembering only too well the
agony he had experienced at Mons and Le Cateau.[5] But he eventually came
around, no doubt partly influenced by the urgent representations of Winston Churchill, who visited General Headquarters again on the 26th.

For the British there were obvious benefits in resuming their original
position on the left of the line. Their communications would be reduced
and less complicated. Naval assistance would be readily available when
required. Additional British troops were about to land on the coast of
Flanders for a move towards Antwerp, where the Belgian army was still
holding out. It was naturally desirable that all British forces should be
concentrated in one sector of the front. Most important of all was Britain's
concern over the safety of the Channel ports. If the Germans were to seize
Ostend, Calais, and Boulogne, they would be able to threaten the transport
of troops from England to France as well as block the vital avenues of sea-
borne traffic converging on London.[6]

Joffre was unhappy with the proposal and in a note to French pointed
out the disadvantages. He would be compelled to fill a large gap in the line
at a time when his wings were under severe attack. The British march
northward would cut across the French lines of communication, resulting

in the interruption, possibly for as long as ten days, of the transport of French troops to the northern theater of operations. Joffre would have preferred to wait until after things had quieted down along the front. But French was in a hurry so he gave his grudging consent.[7]

The British held a front of twenty-six miles along the Aisne and in some places German lines were less than two hundred yards away. The transferral of so large a body of troops from one part of the field to another, without alerting the enemy, was a task calling for exceptional staff work. It is to the credit of all concerned that this difficult operation was carried out without a hitch. All movement was by night, part being conducted by foot and part by train. During the day the men were confined to their billets so that no sign of their departure could be seen by enemy aircraft. These precautions were successful, for the Germans had no inkling of what was happening until it was too late.

The three corps moved at different dates, beginning with the II Corps (October 2), which detrained at Abbeville and subsequently advanced towards Béthune. The III Corps followed (October 6) and concentrated in the Armentières area. The last troops to withdraw were those of the I Corps who came into the line to the north of Ypres on October 20. Sir John moved his headquarters on October 8 to Abbeville and then on the 13th further forward to Saint Omer.

While the BEF was moving to its new position other British forces were disembarking in northern Belgium with the object of relieving the beleaguered fortress of Antwerp. This contingent, which consisted of the newly formed Seventh Division[8] and Third Cavalry Division, was under the independent command of General Henry Rawlinson. Kitchener felt that Sir John was too busy moving his army from the Aisne and too far away to assume charge of the new operations. Furthermore the British cabinet, wary over the possibility of an invasion, would not allow the Seventh Division to depart "for more than a rapid movement on Antwerp."[9] French was upset with the arrangement and he complained about it to Churchill:

> I am very sorry to have received a wire to-day from the S of S saying, "These troops will not for the present form part of your forces." It annoys me, because *all troops* anywhere in the fighting should be under my command. I am constantly subjected to these pinpricks by the S of S and it makes my very hard and difficult task much harder.[10]

Whether from Churchill or someone else, Kitchener learned of French's feelings and sent a note to General Headquarters explaining the reasons for his action. Sir John's answer implied that he understood and agreed: "I never for a moment supposed you wished to interfere with my operations, and I know perfectly well that I have your confidence. . . . I know perfectly well that the condition of Antwerp came upon you as a bolt from the blue, and was as much a surprise to you as it was to me."[11] But by 1919, when he wrote his book, French had reverted to his previous resentment.[12]

Rawlinson's Seventh Division had scarcely begun to land at Zeebrugge when it became apparent that the expedition to relieve Antwerp could not be carried out. On the night of October 6 the Belgian Council of War decided that the Belgian army should leave the fortress while it still had an escape route and join hands farther down the coast with the relieving forces. Once it became certain that Antwerp would fall, Kitchener directed Rawlinson to place his troops under French's command. The British cabinet had yielded to Kitchener's wish that the Seventh Division should remain in France. On October 9 Rawlinson assembled the Seventh Division and the Third Cavalry Division (which disembarked at Ostend) at Bruges and the combined formation, called the IV Corps, came into the line as the left wing of the BEF.

As Sir John prepared for the next stage in the campaign he was in close touch with General Foch, who now commanded the French armies in the northern sector. French's relations with Foch were marked by sympathy and cordiality. Foch, through Henry Wilson, was well informed about French's state of mind. Thus in conversation with Sir John he was reassuring, tactful, and deferential. However strange and unreasonable Sir John's propositions might be, Foch never countered with a refusal or a criticism. He would begin by outlining the merits of the proposal and then gently bring Sir John around, step by step, often leading him to accept his own views. In difficult times Foch behaved with such authority and conviction that Sir John, troubled and anxious at the start, would leave the interview comforted and confident. This happy relationship was nurtured by Wilson, who served as the intermediary between the two men.

Foch's strong influence over Sir John can be traced to their first meeting on October 8 at Doullens (Foch's headquarters). Foch received French with pomp and ceremony, a move he knew would appeal to the British commander's vanity. The two soldiers then talked about military matters, the gist of which is described below. Sir John was impressed by Foch's warmth, good humor, boundless energy, and above all at what he perceived was his ability to evaluate a military situation quickly and accurately and to deal with it skillfully and promptly. In the evening Sir John penned his feelings and observations in his diary: "It gave me great hope of the future to find him so hopeful and cheery. He is very confident of success."[13]

It was a rare occasion when Sir John departed from a meeting with a French general in better spirits than when he arrived. Since August 23 he had nursed a grievance against the French. This continuing hostility had only very recently erupted into a fresh outpouring of anger as a result of Joffre's action. It seems that Joffre, dissatisfied with the performance of the BEF on the Aisne, had lodged a complaint with the British authorities through the intermediary of the French government. Two days before his visit to Doullens French had vented his feelings on Huguet. "If Joffre had complaints to make," Sir John declared, "they should have been addressed to me alone and he should not involve politicians with military questions which do not concern them and which should never be gone into except between soldiers." He added, "Never have I in the whole course of my career suffered such humiliation. I have had to come to France, to fight for the French, for it to be inflicted. I will never forget it." Huguet reported the incident to Joffre, who did not appear to take it seriously. He drew up a vaguely worded letter and instructed Huguet to take it over to General Headquarters. Sir John was not satisfied with the explanation, telling Huguet that he would not withdraw anything he had said the previous day.[14]

However, French's memory of the quarrel with Joffre began to fade after he met Foch on October 8. Sir John was pleased not only by his reception but by what the French general had to say. Brimming with optimism, Foch asserted that the British could become a decisive factor in the coming victory, that by advancing quickly and resolutely they would outflank the German right wing and compel it to fall back.[15] This was music to Sir John's ears and he decided, without awaiting for the arrival of his I Corps, to take the offensive with the troops he already had.

The plan, hammered out at Foch's headquarters on October 10, called for a combined offensive eastward with the BEF passing to the north of Lille. The movement was to begin on the 13th when the British II and III Corps were expected to be on the scene. "He [French] is," Rawlinson observed, "somewhat optimistic, but that is better than the other extreme."[16]

Sir John held the same mistaken view as Joffre and Foch that a war of movement was still practicable. In fact the situation was no longer fluid. When a stalemate had developed on the Aisne front, both sides engaged in groping efforts to outflank each other in what was called, somewhat erroneously, the "race to the sea." Neither side was able to gain a decided advantage and the result was a series of violent clashes extending successively northward as newly arrived forces collided. In this manner the line extended through Arras and northward again to the Flanders coast.

French was under the impression that he would be opposed by comparatively weak forces and that he would be able to move forward without difficulty. According to G.Q.G. the Germans in this sector were reduced to "a cloud of cavalry." Against this the BEF was a formidable body, four corps and Allenby's cavalry, which now comprised two divisions. Moreover, the left flank of the BEF was protected by the Belgian army (six infantry and two cavalry divisions) that had withdrawn from Antwerp before its surrender.

Having swung back from extreme pessimism to extreme optimism, French was thinking in terms of a Kimberley dash across Flanders. Even after it became apparent that a deadlock had set in Sir John remained convinced that the cavalry was the decisive arm and that without it no

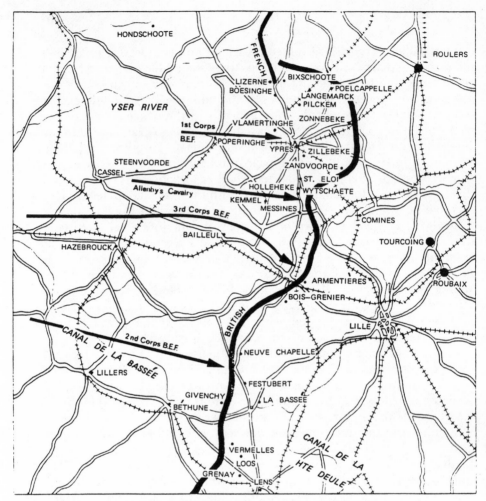

HONDSCHOOTE

ROULERS

FRENCH

LIZERNE BIXSCHOOTE
BÖESINGHE POELCAPPELLE
LANGEMARCK
PILCKEM
YSER RIVER ZONNEBEKE

1st Corps VLAMERTINGHE
B.E.F.
POPERINGHE YPRES ZILLEBEKE
ZANDVOORDE
STEENVOORDE ST. ELOI
CASSEL HOLLEHEKE WYTSCHAETE
Allenby's Cavalry
KEMMEL MESSINES
3rd Corps B.E.F. COMINES

BAILLEUL
TOURCOING
HAZEBROUCK
ARMENTIERES
ROUBAIX
BOIS-GRENIER

BRITISH LILLE

CANAL DE 2nd Corps B.E.F.
LA BASSÉE NEUVE CHAPELLE

LILLERS
FESTUBERT
GIVENCHY LA BASSEE
BÉTHUNE

CANAL DE LA
VERMELLES HTE DEULE
LOOS
GRENAY LENS

THE BATTLEGROUND OF WEST FLANDERS
(OCT.–NOV. 1914)

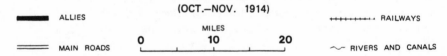

███ ALLIES
+++++++ RAILWAYS

MILES
0   10   20

═══ MAIN ROADS
∼ RIVERS AND CANALS

victory could be consummated. Mobility as an adjunct to fire power had formed the basis of Napoleon's tactics. But the introduction of the machine-gun, especially when its defensive employment was supplemented by barbed-wire obstacles, had ended the cavalry's domination of the battlefield. British cavalrymen were more skilled with the rifle than their European counterparts and could have rendered more effective services during the years of static warfare. The obsession of French, and his successor Haig, in the value of mounted mobility resulted in large numbers of trained men being tied down to a sterile role.

The new German supreme commander, General Erich von Falkenhayn, anticipating an Allied outflanking movement in the northern part of the front, had set out to best them at their own game. His aim was to hold the offensive in check while he swept down the coast and crushed the flank of the attackers. If he could roll up the northern arm of the Allied armies he might still gain that quick decision in the west that had been the central feature of von Schlieffen's strategy. To carry out his plan von Falkenhayn assembled every man he could spare on his right wing. The fall of Antwerp on October 10 had released von Beseler's III Corps for service farther south. In addition von Falkenhayn brought into the line from Germany four new corps of volunteers, many of whom were young boys in their teens, lacking training but fired with ardent patriotism and ready for any sacrifice. The two contingents were united to form a new Fourth Army under Duke Albrecht of Württemberg.

The opening phase of the operations in west Flanders, popularly known as the First Battle of Ypres, lasted from October 13 to November 21.[17] This campaign may be divided into four stages. The British movement into the line (October 12–20); the German attack all along the front (October 21– October 30); the German assault on the salient at Ypres (October 31– November 2); and then, after a brief lull for regrouping and replenishment, the gray tide rolled forward again, the fighting finally ending in the wind and snow.

This narrative, for obvious reasons, must confine itself essentially to the BEF's role in the battle. It should be remembered that the British fought on part of a front that ran from La Bassée to the sea at Nieuport and that both the Belgians and the French were actively and critically engaged as well. Because of the ferocity and length of the battle, because the entire BEF was drawn into the engagement and because of the extraordinarily high casualties it sustained, British historians have tended to ignore or, at best, minimize the contribution made by the other Allied contingents. This has annoyed the French, for as Foch wrote: "On October 31 the French held about 15 miles of the front, the British 12; on November 5, the French held 18 miles and the British 9. It can be seen that the French troops, both as to length of front occupied and numbers engaged, had to sustain the major part of the battle. It would therefore be contrary to the truth to speak of the battle and victory of Ypres as exclusively British."[18] Even allowing for a slight miscalculation in Foch's analysis it is clear that the French were the mainstay of the battle.

Smith-Dorrien's men were the first British troops to arrive from the Aisne, so they were the first committed to the new operations. Sir John had directed the II Corps to march on Lille, where it was to link up with the left of the French Tenth Army, commanded by General de Maud'huy. However, Smith-Dorrien's corps fell far short of its objective. The British encountered strong resistance north of Festubert and Givenchy and on the 14th the Third Division lost its leader, Major-General Hubert Hamilton, who was killed by a shell fragment. The next day the division made a brilliant dash, crossing the dikes with planks and driving the Germans out of one village after another until it had pushed them off the Estaires-La Bassée road. The British pressed on, slowly but steadily, seized Aubers on the 17th and before nightfall that day carried Herlies at the point of the bayonet. From then on they made little headway as the German cavalry units opposing them were relieved by two infantry divisions.

The III Corps, having detrained at Saint Omer on October 11, proceeded at once to concentrate at Hazebrouck. Its commander, Lieutenant-General Pulteney, had instructions to secure the line Armentières-Wytschaete. Pulteney had an abundance of courage, remained imperturbable in the face of crises, and never shrank from a difficult assignment. But he lacked drive and imagination and was too often absorbed in working out details so that he had insufficient time to devote to larger issues.[19]

On the 13th Pulteney moved forward at a cautious pace with cavalry forces operating on both sides of him, Allenby on the left and the French General Conneau on the right. The day was wet and misty, fields were waterlogged, and the countryside was too enclosed to permit the cavalry to render much assistance. The first obstacle was at Meteren, which was defended by a mixed German infantry and cavalry force. The Germans had many machine-guns, were well-entrenched, and the village church tower gave them a splendid view of the British advance. Before they got clean away they inflicted over 700 casualties on the III Corps during a brief but sharp clash.

Once inside the village Pulteney made preparations for an attack on Bailleul, which he believed was strongly held. Next day ground reconnaissance established that the Germans had evacuated Bailleul and had retired behind the Lys. The III Corps entered Bailleul in the evening; on the 16th it occupied Armentières; and by the following day it was three miles south of the Lys. But this represented the high-water mark of the British advance. Pulteney had made fair progress when opposed by inferior forces but he was now, as the II Corps was finding out beyond Aubers and Herlies, against the wall of the main German line.

The IV Corps under Rawlinson, after covering the Belgian retirement from Antwerp, fell back to the east of Ypres. On the night of the 17th a note arrived from Sir John saying he intended to carry out a vigorous attack on the enemy and directing the IV Corps to "move on Menin." As the order did not specify that he was to attack, Rawlinson, bearing in mind that he was not to push too far ahead of the III Corps, moved forward cautiously on the 18th. About midday a liaison officer arrived from General Headquarters to see what progress had been made. He expressed astonishment when told that the men had completed their advance for the day and were now digging trenches. This visit was followed by a second and unmistakable order from Saint Omer that the IV Corps should march on Menin at once. By the time the order arrived and was decoded Rawlinson had information of a considerable concentration of German troops immediately north of Menin. Rawlinson was determined not to be rushed into an attack until he knew more about the strength of the enemy and until he had arranged for cavalry cooperation on each flank. He thus decided to postpone his advance on Menin until next day.

Sir John suspected that Rawlinson had been overawed by local reports of the arrival of large numbers of enemy troops. It was his impression that Rawlinson had acted too cautiously, an impression heightened when he read the IV Corps' summary of operations, which showed that the infantry had not been seriously challenged that day. French had information that the area was lightly defended and it was his opinion that if Rawlinson had attacked on the 18th, as he was supposed to, he probably would have secured Menin and the line of the Lys. Surprisingly Sir John, although cold to Rawlinson at their next meeting, did not officially rebuke him.[20]

When Rawlinson moved out early on the 19th the vanguard of the new formations from Germany had reached the Ypres front. Rawlinson had to operate on a very broad front, supported only by cavalry units on his flanks. All went well at first but late in the morning air reconnaissance revealed strong German forces facing, and approaching the left, of the IV Corps. The Seventh Division had advanced to within three miles of Menin when it fell back at once to avoid utter disaster, entrenching itself east of Gheluvelt. Here, with its flanks secured, it awaited the arrival of the I Corps.

If thus far the British attacks had merely extended the "line of deadlock," Sir John had not abandoned the hope that he might still outflank the Germans. He realized that the task would be more difficult than he had anticipated at the outset but he remained uncertain both about the number of German divisions opposing him and their distribution. He knew von Beseler was operating along the coast route and was concerned whether the much-battered Belgian army, aided by a small detachment of French territorials and cavalry, could stand up against him on the Yser. From British intelligence sources French gathered that the extreme right of the main German armies was anchored in the neighborhood of Courtrai and that von Beseler's was an isolated flanking force. He did not know that von Beseler was actually the cutting edge of a scythelike sweep through Flanders.

Haig visited French's headquarters on the 19th, the day on which his troops were detraining at Saint Omer. He observed that his chief was in a buoyant mood. Haig was instructed to break out towards Thourout and to engage the Germans wherever he met them. Eventually the I Corps was to wheel left or right, as circumstances dictated: either to drive for the coast to cut off von Beseler or to swing in the opposite direction to turn the northern flank of the main German force.

Sir John expected that the I Corps would find the enemy in retreat and that there would be little more than rear-guard fighting. He placed German strength between Menin and Ostend at one corps. Yet his own Intelligence Section had estimated (and as it turned out underestimated) that there were three-and-a-half German corps in the area. As had happened in the past Sir John would not accept any reports that did not fit in exactly with his own views.

The I Corps moved into the battle line on the 20th and on the following day advanced forward with the Second Division between Zonnebeke and Langemarck and the First in rear and to the left of it. Haig did not feel that Sir John's optimism was justified. On the basis of information from neighboring armies as well as his own corps intelligence he came to the conclusion that hard fighting lay ahead. Thus he proceeded cautiously, consolidating each position gained before attempting a further move. The I Corps was only a few miles north of Ypres when it collided head-on with two of the newly formed Reserve Corps of the Fourth German Army. Each army had been uncertain about the movements of the other; each had underestimated or had been ignorant of the strength of the other; and each had been trying to outflank the other. The encounter battle ended in a stalemate, neither side being able to gain the upper hand. At 3:00 P.M. Haig ordered his troops to halt and dig in where they stood. As the left of the I Corps had swung back during the battle the now immortal Ypres salient was formed. Haig's casualties for the day totalled 932, a modest figure considering his two divisions had fought off five enemy divisions.

The presence of growing German power in all likelihood was sufficient to inhibit Sir John's turning movement around Lille. However, at the outset the want of enterprise by local commanders, namely Pulteney and Rawlinson, denied the BEF such advantages as the tide of battle offered. There was indeed justification for Galliéni's remark that the Allies were always twenty-four hours and an army corps behind the enemy.

The general situation on the allied left on the night of the 21st may be summarized as follows: the Belgians, supported by the newly formed and rapidly growing Eighth Army under General d'Urbal, held the front from the sea to the Yser; the I Corps and the IV Corps were deployed between

Bixschoote and Gheluvelt, and Allenby's cavalry positioned beyond Messines; the III Corps, Conneau's cavalry, and the II Corps extended south to La Bassée; and then came de Maud'huy's Tenth Army, which carried the line down to Arras. The Allied front stretched for nearly 100 miles and was manned by inadequate forces.

By now it was clear to Sir John that his men were up against large enemy formations. He wrote:

> On the 21st, all my worst forebodings as to the enemy's increasing strength were realized. Intercepted wireless messages established the certainty that the comparatively small German force which on the night of the 18th we judged to be between Ostend and Menin, was now reinforced by no less than four Corps. . . . Although I looked for a great addition to the enemy's numbers within a few days from the 18th, the strength they actually reached astounded me. This, taken with the speed in which they appeared in the field, came like a veritable bolt from the blue.[21]

Sir John's admission that the sudden appearance and strength of the German reinforcements came to him "like a veritable bolt from the blue" does not speak well for his mental acuity. He had found French Intelligence to be unreliable in the early part of the war and yet accepted as gospel Foch's assurances that the Germans were in no condition to resist a determined advance. In doing so he had closed his eyes to some very obvious probabilities. The one remaining hope of a strategic victory for the Germans lay in seizing the Channel ports and rolling up the Allied line. For this purpose it followed that they would need to concentrate every available man. If the Allies had thinned their line on the Aisne and elsewhere in order to bring troops northwards, what was to prevent the Germans from doing the same thing at the same time? Then too the fall of Antwerp, which was only seventy-five miles from Ypres—four or five days' march—was known to have released large bodies of troops. Was it not reasonable to assume that some of these troops would be shifted to the Ypres front? Sir John's own highly competent chief of intelligence, General Macdonogh, had already warned him of the danger. But Sir John scorned the judgment as the outcome of depression and pessimism. Jack Seely,[22] a frequent visitor at General Headquarters, summed it up perfectly when he told John Charteris (head of I Corps Intelligence Section) that "French will not listen to his Intelligence people, which accounts for that big mistake about the number of divisions we were likely to meet when we advanced on the 20th."[23] It is clear that the blame for the sorry conditions under which the BEF had to fight at Ypres must rest squarely on the shoulders of the commander-in-chief.

French was in an apprehensive mood when Joffre called to see him at Saint Omer on the 21st. After the usual amenities were exchanged Joffre explained that he was transferring his IX Corps to Flanders where it would become part of the Eighth Army. Joffre evidently hoped that the news would spur the British to fresh offensive efforts. But Sir John was unwilling to particpate in any more attacks until the French reinforcements arrived. Joffre, concealing his disappointment, did not pursue the subject. Wilson, who was present at the meeting, recorded what followed:

> All went satisfactorily until Sir John asked for facilities to make a great entrenched camp at Boulogne to take the whole E.F. Joffre's face instantly became quite square and he replied that such a thing could not be allowed for a moment. He would make some works to safeguard against a coup-de-main, but an entrenched camp he would not allow. Sir John was checkmated straight away. . . . So that nightmare is over.[24]

It is dificult to fully understand the workings of Sir John's mind at this point. He appears to have succumbed to conflicting thoughts as he alternated between extremes of exuberance and of depression. During the interview with Joffre he was in low spirits and talking about preparing an entrenched camp on the Channel coast into which he could withdraw if he should be defeated in Belgium. And yet when he reported the day's events to Kitchener, he wrote: "In my opinion the enemy are vigorously playing their last card, and I am confident that they will fail."[25]

Sir John was wrong to think that the Germans were playing their last card. They were merely playing their first one. Starting on October 20 von Falkenhayn launched a series of attacks along a broad front with the aim of breaking through in the Yser-Ypres sector. In the extreme north the Belgians with some French supports were so hard put that they sought to create a water barrier in front of their line by opening the locks at Nieuport. By the 28th the Germans were compelled to halt their advance since an area two miles wide extending from Dixmude to the sea was inundated to a depth of three or four feet.

While the Belgians were engaged in holding the coastal roads the British were fighting desperately to maintain the front between Ypres and La Bassée canal. Because Sir John had not expected to wage a great defensive battle, [26] hardly any preparations had been made to meet the German onslaught. There was no barbed wire or any other obstacle in front of the British positions, no communication trenches, and no secondary line. The hastily constructed trenches were disconnected and at best three feet deep. These were dug where the troops stood and consequently in many places they were below German positions or exposed to enfilading fire.

British carelessness, however, was more than offset by German deficiencies and mismanagement. The German units in this sector were of good fighting material but many had insufficient training and had yet to experience prolonged combat. What was needed was common sense tactics and close supervision. Neither was provided. The men were sent forward in mass formations, to charge straight at machine-guns and volleying rifles. In places where they did get through usually nothing was done to follow up their initial gains or fortify their position against counterattacks. The British Official History makes the following comment:

> Time after time during the battles of Ypres the same phenomenon will be observed: the Germans having come on in overwhelming numbers and succeeded in penetrating our line, sat or stood about helplessly and without precaution. Either they were content to rest after reaching the objective that they had been given, or they did not know what to do next.[27]

The reader will remember that the I Corps had been held up north of Ypres on the 21st by oncoming German hordes. In the evening Sir John had anxious consultations with Haig and Rawlinson. In view of the unexpected strength of the enemy they knew that an advance on Bruges was no longer possible. For the time being the most that the British troops could be expected to do was to hold the ground they occupied.

The attacks on the I Corps began on October 22 and were to last for three weeks with only brief intermissions. Under persistent hammering the British line bent, swayed, cracked, and yielded, but it never broke. The first serious threat occurred on Haig's left. Here the assault was carried out by one of the new corps from Germany, composed largely of *Einjährige,* which corresponded roughly to the British Officers' Training Corps. These fearless youths advanced singing patriotic songs and actually pierced the line north of Pilckem, overwhelming the Cameron Highlanders, one of the finest regiments in the British army. Next day British counterattacks cleared the trenches, capturing 550 Germans and releasing 54 Camerons.

On October 23 the arrival at Ypres of the French IX Corps under General Dubois allowed the British to contract their line, which had been unduly extended. The British First Division was drawn back to Zillebeke so that it might be employed as a compact force in a general attack.

Foch, as offensive-minded as ever, believed that the arrival of French reinforcements would enable him to carry out an enveloping movement that would turn the northern flank of the German Fourth Army. He was eager to strike before the Germans could consolidate their position as they had done a month earlier on the heights along the Aisne. Accordingly he ordered General d'Urbal, commanding the Eighth Army, to launch a three-pronged offensive in the direction of Roulers, Thourout, and Ghistelles. Simultaneously Foch asked the British to support his movement by swinging eastwards. The note did not reach General Headquarters until a few hours before d'Urbal was scheduled to attack. It was not possible for the British to comply with Foch's wishes at such short notice. Since it was too late to arrange for a postponement Sir John tried to cooperate as best he could.

Foch's expectations were unrealistic. He was trying to control the battle from his headquarters at Doullens, more than sixty miles away to the south, and it was not until the 24th that he moved to Cassel, twenty miles west of Ypres, which brought him into closer touch with the situation at front. D'Urbal, far from having sufficient reserves in hand, was slightly outnumbered by the German armies facing him. On top of this the ground over which the advance was to take place was dotted with copses and isolated houses, "admirable for the supporting points and machine-guns nests of the defence." No sooner did d'Urbal get started when he was met with fierce counterattacks.

The next day d'Urbal ordered the IX Corps to "continue to advance." Dubois' men gained over half a mile before they were held up by enemy fire. On the French right Haig's corps, fighting defensively, stopped the Germans in their tracks. These young and unseasoned German troops displayed great courage but they were no match for the British regulars. German records suggest that the new Reserve Corps had suffered such staggering casualties between the 21st and 24th that their offensive power had practically been blunted.

After October 24 the Germans passed temporarily to the defensive, only continuing with their spoiling attacks and counterattacks in the sector where Foch was still seeking his offensive victory. The Allies believed that, while they had large formations in reserve, including the whole of the British First Division, all the German forces available near Ypres had been employed. Sir John met with General d'Urbal on the afternoon of the 24th and concluded arrangements to continue the offensive. He remained very hopeful and in the evening assured the secretary for war that if things continued to go well the battle was "practically won."[28]

There was little justification for such optimism. The Germans, even if no longer attacking, had not lost their determination to win or will to fight. On October 25 the French IX Corps advanced in the direction of Roulers in cooperation with Haig's Second Division. But neither the French nor the English made appreciable progress. Sir John telegraphed London that the "situation is growing more favourable every hour"[29] and ordered the attack renewed. Both Dubois and Haig encountered fierce enemy resistance on the 26th and 27th so that little ground was gained. Although the Allied line had scarcely moved French expressed himself as "confident and very hopeful" and "considered that it was only necessary to press the enemy hard in order to ensure complete success and victory." The Anglo-French attacks were continued on the 28th but again practically no progress was made.

In the meantime the main German attack had shifted to the eastern side of the salient. Here Rawlinson's IV Corps held a front that ran in the shape of a V from near Zonnebeke to Kruiseecke and thence southward to Zandvoorde. The Germans, probing for weaknesses on the Seventh Division's front, exerted enormous pressure, first against Gheluvelt and then against the acute salient at Kruiseecke. On the 26th, by means of a ruse, they succeeded in piercing the sides of this jutting point and annihilating most of the British forces in the village. British counterattacks checked the German advance and by the end of the day the line had been reformed on a blunter curve.

After five days of incessant fighting there were signs that the Seventh Division was approaching exhaustion. Nearly half the officers and more than a third of the men were killed or wounded. The following day Sir John temporarily broke up the IV Corps, assigning the Seventh Division to Haig and the Third Cavalry Division to Allenby. Rawlinson and his staff returned to England to supervise the training of the Eighth Division, which, when sent to France, was to join the Seventh Division in the reconstituted IV Corps.

We must now pass to Allenby's cavalry, which held the front at Messines, between the III and IV Corps. German strength enabled many attacks to be made during the first days of their offensive. These were carried out, usually by small parties, at intervals throughout the day and night. Each one was easily repulsed but the continual strain on the defending troops was never relaxed.

The III Corps, on the right of the cavalry, was deployed along a twelve-mile front in the Armentières area. Pulteney, confronting an enemy force (center of the Sixth Army) more than double his own, had orders to entrench and hold on. This was easy enough for the Fourth Division to do since, apart from enduring occasional shelling and sniping, it was left in comparative peace. The Sixth Division did not fare as well. For a week it withstood frequent attacks, aimed particularly at its right center. Thereafter serious German efforts ceased, although shelling, snipping and petty attacks continued for some time.

At the extreme right of the British line the II Corps was engaged in fighting almost as severe as that at Ypres. The Third Division was on the left of the corps line and linked up with Conneau's cavalry. Opposite the two Allied forces stood four German corps and part of a fifth (left wing of the Sixth Army). The first big attack opened at daybreak on the front of the Third Division. The Germans, easily distinguishable by their gray, spiked helmets, approached in mass formations but British marksmanship prevented them from coming to close quarters. This turn of affairs prompted the Germans to try their luck at night fighting. At dusk they attempted a series of attacks, directed against both ends of the Third Division's line. The fighting dragged on until after midnight when the Germans pulled back, leaving many dead and wounded.

By the 25th the men of the II Corps had been fighting almost continuously for thirteen days and their losses, particularly in officers, had been severe. Near midnight Smith-Dorrien met with Sir John and told him directly that he feared his line might give way during the night. French was "rather short" with Smith-Dorrien, believing him to be too easily dismayed.[30] Yet he could not disregard the warning, for any serious break in the II Corp's front would upset any hopes of a successful offensive further north. The two men discussed prospects and options for about half an hour. Smith-Dorrien returned to his own headquarters no less anxious but he felt better in the morning when the sun came out and the promised assistance began to arrive.

On the 26th nothing serious occurred until midday, when a bitter struggle began for possession of Neuve Chapelle. Under constant shelling the Irish Rifles, which had been attacked twice in the previous twenty-four hours, left their trenches and the Germans passed through, capturing Neuve Chapelle. Over the next three days attacks and counterattacks were launched, but neither side was able to move forward. At the end of the fighting on the 29th the British line ran in a curve around Neuve Chapelle with the Germans only about one hundred yards away. Clearly the German effort against the II Corps had failed. After the 29th the Germans gradually slackened the pressure as they concentrated larger forces further north in a final bid to achieve victory.

By the evening of October 24 Duke Albrecht of Württemberg, commanding the Fourth Army, had realized that he could not effectively breach the French and British front near Ypres with the forces at his disposal. The Sixth Army under Crown Prince Rupprecht of Bavaria had likewise failed to break through the II and III corps. Von Falkenhayn, having finished reviewing the general situation, arranged to bring up a new army under General von Fabeck and insert it like a wedge south of Ypres, between the Fourth and Sixth armies. Drawn mainly from the quiet sectors of the line, von Fabeck's force consisted of six divisions, backed by 257 heavy guns and howitzers. The entry of von Fabeck's group into battle would give the Germans a superiority of two to one in numbers and ten to one in guns. Ironically at this very moment French was assuring Kitchener that the Germans were "quite incapable of making any strong and sustained attack," owing to the tremendous losses they had suffered.[31]

The main attack was to be launched between Zandvoorde and Messines with the object of reaching the Kemmel heights, cutting off the Allied troops north of Ypres and driving them either against the coast or into Holland. Thus the brunt of the assault was to fall on the much-reduced units of the Seventh Division and on the thin chain of three dismounted cavalry divisions. In this sector the Germans had an advantage of six to one.

The German High Command was sparing no pains to force a decision in the West. The news from the Russian front was bad. General von Hindenburg had suffered his first defeat and his subsequent retirement had exposed the eastern provinces of Germany to a Russian invasion. Von

Falkenhayn was anxious to achieve a final victory in France so that he could have the means to reinforce the threatened Eastern front.

Von Fabeck preceded his main offensive, scheduled to take place on the 30th, by launching a preliminary attack on the 29th in order to seize the high ground near Gheluvelt, on the Ypres-Menin road. The direction of the German attack would bring it to the junction of the First and Seventh Divisions, just where the British line formed a salient. Moving through the dense mist of early morning the Germans got to within fifty yards of the British line before they were seen. The fighting was severe and both sides suffered heavy casualties. Several British machine-guns jammed; and at various points along the line wrong-sized cartridges caused a sporadic slackening of rifle fire. Eventually the Germans broke in and secured the crossroads east of Gheluvelt, as well as the area south of the Menin road. Haig rushed up reinforcements to the threatened sector and in the afternoon his counterattacks regained most of the lost ground but not the crossroads. At dusk heavy rain brought the fighting to an end. It had not been a satisfactory day for the British. Haig's reserves had been reduced, his units were mixed up, and he had nothing to show for his losses, which had been considerable. Moreover, the portion of ground that the Germans still held enabled them to conceal their further preparations from the British.

Yet Sir John was satisfied with the results of the fighting on the 29th and issued orders for the attack to continue the next day. He also wired to Kitchener that "if the success can be followed up, it will lead to a decisive result."[32] During the day French had visited Cassel and once again had been infected by Foch's unreasoning optimism.

Haig, at the front with his troops, was more cautious. Notwithstanding his instructions he directed his three divisions to entrench the position that they held, to reorganize their units, and to carry out active reconnaissance. He added that orders for the resumption of the offensive would be issued "when the situation is clearer than at present." Haig's prudence may have saved the day on the 30th.

At 6:30 A.M. (on the 30th) von Fabeck launched his main assault after a one-hour bombardment. The British were prepared to meet that attack since during the night of the 29th they had hastily improved defenses and put up strands of barbed wire. German efforts on the front of the I Corps were costly and unproductive. Their attacks continued in varying strength until noon and, with one or two exceptions, were halted before they reached the wire. Farther south, however, the Seventh Division and Allenby's cavalry suffered heavily from German artillery concentrations and mass attacks. At 8:00 A.M. the Germans forced the cavalry out of Zandvoorde, gravely endangering the right of the Seventh Division immediately to the north. Haig sent two reserve battalions to the scene but the counterattacks failed to recapture Zandvoorde. It was now evident that the

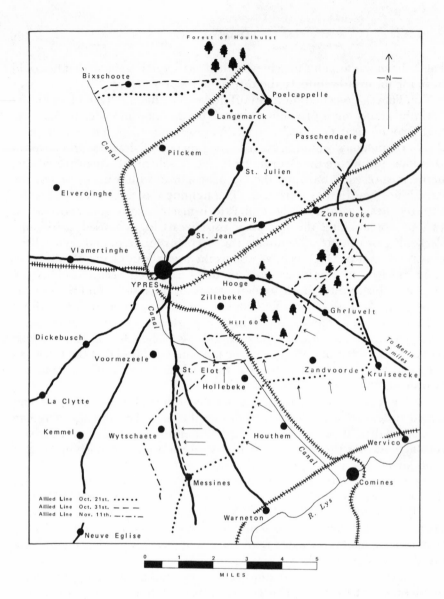

Forest of Houlhulst

Bixschoote

Poelcappelle

Langemarck

Passchendaele

Pilckem

St. Julien

Elveroinghe

Zonnebeke

Frezenberg

St. Jean

Vlamertinghe

YPRES

Hooge

Zillebeke

Gheluvelt

Hill 60

To Menin
3 miles

Dickebusch

Voormezeele

St. Elot

Zandvoorde

Kruiseecke

Hollebeke

La Clytte

Kemmel

Wytschaete

Houthem

Wervico

Messines

Comines

R. Lys

Allied Line Oct. 21st. ● ● ● ● ● ●
Allied Line Oct. 31st. ─ ─ ─
Allied Line Nov. 11th. ─ · ─ · ─

Warneton

Neuve Eglise

0   1   2   3   4   5
MILES

THE FIRST BATTLE OF YPRES

German offensive was being carried out by forces far more numerous than General Headquarters believed was present in the area. The most alarming feature of this realization was the danger of the Germans breaking through south of Ypres, thus cutting off the communication of all Allied troops to the north.

French, who had been disturbed and surprised by the turn of events, stopped briefly to see Allenby before meeting with Haig at Hooge in the afternoon. Told that the situation was serious, French could do nothing to bolster Haig's defenses. His only reserve, the II Corps, was in the process of being relieved in the La Bassée sector by the Indian Corps.

As it turned out Haig managed with what forces he had. He was fortunate that von Fabeck's men did not show the reckless courage of the youthful volunteers who had been repulsed earlier. These Germans appeared to stop as soon as they came under heavy fire, preferring to rely upon their superior artillery and on snipers picking off officers and leaders. Their caution in following up their success enabled Haig to fill in the gaps.

The next day, October 31, was the climax of the German attack. The mist had cleared by 10:00 A.M. and the Germans, able to use observation balloons in directing the fire of their heavy artillery, pounded the British trenches mercilessly. "The worst we ever had," commented a British sergeant. "The ground was literally shaking as if we were in the middle of an earthquake."[33] The main German effort was made between Messines and Wytschaete against Allenby's cavalry. It was undertaken by wily veterans who advanced, not in mass formations as was the normal German practice, but by fire and movement. By using more imaginative tactics and with an enormous advantage in artillery and manpower, the Germans brought such pressure to bear upon Allenby's front that it seemed inconceivable that they should not get through at some point. But the British, reinforced by four French battalions, stood their ground and inflicted heavy punishment until the attacks died down in the evening.

The crisis occurred further north at Gheluvelt, near the junction of Haig's First and Seventh divisions. Lying on a forward spur of a low ridge, Gheluvelt was not only important for observation purposes but it also blocked the approaches to Ypres. The British defenders, numbering about a thousand, consisted of the remnants of five battalions. Against this meager force the Germans launched thirteen battalions, of which at least six were quite fresh. Gheluvelt fell shortly after 11:30 A.M. and, on hearing the news, General Lomax, commander of the First Division, decided to commit his last reserve, the Second Worcestershires.[34] He rode back to the headquarters that he shared with General Monro, commander of the Second Division. He arrived there at 12:45 P.M. and remarked laconically to Monro, "My line is broken." The two generals were in conference with some of their staff when at 1:15 P.M. a shell burst in the room they were in. Lomax was mortally wounded and seven staff officers of the two divisions were killed outright. Monro was fortunate, since he was only badly stunned.

Haig learned of the tragedy at a moment when he was pondering means to hold back the advancing Germans. He assembled his staff officers and traced across a map a line about a mile in front of the walls of Ypres to which his corps, if unable to stand its ground, was to retire and to defend to the last man. The order was being prepared when Sir John appeared at Haig's command post (White Chateau). The roads were so congested with stragglers and transport moving rearward towards Ypres that French had been obliged to walk the last stage of the journey. Haig told French what had occurred and that he proposed to go forward and take personal command of the I Division. Haig wrote in his diary that evening, "Sir John was fully of sympathy and expressed his gratitude for what the Corps, as well as I myself, had done since we landed in France. No one could have been nicer at such a time of crisis."[35] Five years later Sir John recalled his feelings when informed of the desperate state of affairs on the front of the First Division. "Personally I felt as if the last barrier between the Germans and the Channel seaboard was broken down, and I viewed the situation with the utmost gravity. It was a dramatic half hour, the worst I ever spent in a life full of vicissitudes such as mine had been."[36]

Sir John had used all his reserves and his only hope was to obtain help from the French. He hurried off on foot to regain his car and look for Foch. Hardly had he left when an officer galloped up to the White Chateau with the news that the Worcestershires had retaken Gheluvelt and reestablished the line. What had happened was that a force of 350 men under Major Edward Hankey had assaulted and put to rout some 1,200 Germans relaxing after their victory. This may have been the only occasion during the war when the action of a small unit produced such extraordinary results.

Haig's aide-de-camp dashed after French, caught him just as he reached his car, and gave him the good news. French showed no outward sign of relief. The information could not be confirmed and even if true the situation was still exceedingly grave. There remained several hours of daylight that might be utilized by the Germans for a renewal of their attacks. The entire I Corps was utterly exhausted, formations were intermixed, divisional staffs were disorganized by the loss of many senior officers, and of course there were no reserves. French got into his car and drove off towards Cassel. As he passed through the village of Vlamertinghe he was recognized by a French staff officer. His car was stopped and he was told that Foch was conferring with Generals d'Urbal and Dubois in the town hall. He was escorted there and a meeting ensued with the three French generals.

In appealing for help Sir John painted a black picture of the state of the I Corps. He said that his men were exhausted, unable to hold out much

longer, and that unless he could relieve them, or at least send them reinforcements, he would be obliged to retreat.

"Retreat!" Foch interjected. "But the Germans will follow you and throw
you into the sea! Reinforcements, I have no more; the last have just been
given to you by the Commander of the IX Corps. Relieve your I Corps,
impossible! First, I have nothing to replace it with; moreover, if we relieve
it today, everyone else will want to be relieved tomorrow! Let your men
bury themselves; let them be killed where they stand if necessary; but do
not let them retire one inch! Otherwise it will be the beginning of the
débâcle and we will be carried away like straws in the wind. Let them die
where they stand or we are done for!"

French was astonished and momentarily upset at the tone and nature of
Foch's statements. This may account for his melodramatic reply: "Then I
can do no more than die with them."

"No, that won't help matters," exclaimed Foch. "The Germans will pass
over your dead body and will arrive just the same at the coast. In any case if
you go or not, I stand. Are you going to leave me alone?"

Foch told French that he must think of winning, not of dying. He promised to relieve pressure on the British by arranging for counterattacks to be
made on the right and left of the I Corps at daybreak next day. As he
talked Foch scribbled his views down on a piece of paper. He turned to
French and handed him the note, saying, "There, if I were in your shoes,
those are the orders I'd send to Haig." Foch's recommendations ran as
follows:

> It is absolutely essential *not to retreat;* therefore the men must dig in
> wherever they find themselves and hold on to the ground they now
> occupy.
> This does not preclude organizing a position further in rear which
> could join up at Zonnebeke with our IX Corps.
> But any movement to the rear carried out by any considerable body of
> troops would lead to an assault on the part of the enemy and bring
> certain confusion among the troops. Such an idea must be utterly re-
> jected.[37]

French read the note, then sent it to Haig with the following message:

> It is of the *utmost importance* to hold the ground you are on now. It is
> useless for me to say this because I know you will do it if it is humanly
> possible.
> I will see if it is possible to send you any more support myself when I
> reach headquarters. I will then finally arrange with Foch *what* our future
> rôle is to be.[38]

Before the notes arrived at I Corps headquarters Haig had settled on a
new line of resistance. By nightfall German pressure had ceased and the

British front was out of immediate danger. But for next day it was a "question whether the line of battered and ever diminishing British battalions and squadrons, patched in places by French reinforcements,"[39] could withstand the punishment of over 200 heavy guns and at the same time keep back the ever increasing weight of the German infantry.

The fighting was renewed on November 1 but happily for the Allies did not reach the intensity of the previous day. None of the French counterattacks achieved any appreciable progress but their action may have discouraged the enemy from pressing their own assault. The Germans made isolated attacks but they were repulsed everywhere except at Messines, which they captured before noon.

The loss of Messines prompted Foch to summon French to a conference at Vlamertinghe. According to Foch Sir John was in the depths of a depression again, insisting that his men had reached the limit of their endurance. Foch urged him to maintain his position at all costs, repeating the arguments he had employed the day before. As a more practical means of encouragement Foch told French that he would order Conneau's cavalry to reinforce Allenby's front.[40] If, as Foch has observed, French was in an extremely pessimistic mood on his arrival at Vlamertinghe, he was certainly in better spirits after he returned to his headquarters. In summing up the events of November 1 to the War Office, Sir John reported that though Messines had been evacuated he was, "on the whole, much less anxious, as the enemy appeared to be less active along the whole of his front."[41]

Before the autumn sun had cleared the morning mist on November 2 the Germans unleashed a severe artillery bombardment and renewed their attack all along the front. They put in reinforcements and directed their main blow against Wytschaete, capturing the village after heavy fighting. There followed three days of comparative calm in the sense that the battle was confined to desultory shelling and sniping. Von Falkenhayn was biding his time until he could bring up fresh divisions for a renewed effort. Though his previous attacks had not been successful they did have the effect of eroding the fighting capacity of the defenders. His next major thrust, he hoped, would suffice to overwhelm whatever strength remained in the Allied line.

Sir John was now seriously concerned with the condition of the BEF. The British army, as so often happened in the past, had been launched into a great enterprise with wholly insufficient means. Munitions and drafts were not coming over nearly as fast as they were required. Ammunition was in such short supply that some of the field guns were not being used. The losses in manpower had been staggering. The First Division, for example had been reduced to 3,491 men and 92 officers, less than the normal strength of one brigade. Sir John fully realized that he would be held accountable if the British army failed in Flanders. Yet, as he often told his senior staff officers, he did not see how he could continue indefinitely without men and munitions. Before the lull ended French's anxieties were compounded by a disturbing report concerning his own position as commander-in-chief.

On November 1 Kitchener had crossed to Dunkirk for a meeting with President Poincaré, Alexandre Millerand (new minister of war) and Generals Joffre and Foch. In the course of the conversation the French indicated that the British army, and by implication its commander-in-chief, was not sufficiently committed to the defeat of the common enemy. Kitchener replied that if the French were dissatisfied with Sir John he would gladly appoint Ian Hamilton, a highly capable officer, in his place. The French would have welcomed Henry Wilson as a replacement but they were not favorable to a change for an unknown quantity lest they lose whatever influence they exercised over the British command. Joffre turned down the offer on the supposed ground that he worked "well and cordially" with Sir John; and that to make a change in the midst of a campaign would have a deplorable effect on the morale of the men. Kitchener said no more on the subject.[42]

On November 5 Foch indiscreetly informed Wilson of Kitchener's proposal and suggested that French himself ought to be told. Wilson at once carried the story to his chief, who exploded in paroxysms of grief and rage. As soon as he regained his composure French sent his friend and ADC, Captain Freddy Guest, to complain personally to Asquith. Next day Sir John, in company with Wilson, motored to Cassel, where he shook Foch's hand warmly and thanked him for his "comradeship and loyalty."[43]

Foch's disclosure naturally raised his stock at General Headquarters and dissipated any lingering resentment that Sir John may have been nursing over his summary treatment on October 31. It is clear that if Foch has stood against French's recall it was not out of admiration or respect. In the brief time he had known French he found him to be weak, irresolute, unreliable, and often very difficult. Yet he had come to understand him extremely well. For when Huguet mentioned earlier that the field marshal was displeased with him, Foch replied jokingly: "Bah! It is of no importance! You have only to tell him that he has just saved England; that will put him in a good humour again." When Huguet conveyed the core of the message several days later, Sir John, with conviction and candor, replied: "But, my dear fellow, I knew it only too well. I knew it from the beginning."[44]

Captain Guest learned, on his arrival at 10 Downing Street, that the prime minister placed no credit in the report that Kitchener had tried to make a change in the leadership of the British army. Asquith was of the opinion that either the French had misunderstood Kitchener or Wilson had concocted the story to suit his own ends. After Guest left, Asquith sent French a note, arguing that there was not a word of truth "to what has been reported to you," while stressing the government's unqualified trust in its field commander, "who has never been surpassed in the capital qualities of initiative, tenacity, serenity, and resource."[45] Asquith saw Churchill later in the day and asked that he should also try to allay the field marshal's suspicions.[46] Churchill wrote at once, assuring French that the government held him in the highest regard and urging him not to allow mischief-makers to drive a wedge between him and Kitchener.[47]

These letters may have made French feel a bit more secure about his position but did nothing to dissuade him from the belief that the story was true. He was convinced that Kitchener would continue to work for his removal and his hatred for the secretary for war intensified, becoming almost obsessive. For the time being, however, French could not dwell on his personal troubles.

The pause was over on November 6 when the Germans, as a preliminary to their final stroke, renewed pressure on the French on the right of the I Corps. They pierced the French front in three places and pushed to within two miles of Ypres, threatening to cut off the British, who were holding the southern end of the salient. Haig patched the gap in his own sector but the result of the day's fighting failed to remove the dangerous wedge that had been driven in at the junction of the British and French forces. Haig warned Sir John that if the Germans made a further effort there he would have to fall back to a line through Ypres itself. Foch, however, gave assurances that he would regain the lost ground by a counterattack. At 9:30 A.M. on the 7th a message arrived at Haig's headquarters that the French line had been reestablished. But in fact no steps had been taken to accomplish that goal. Foch's men were too weary to respond to orders. When eventually they were driven forward they failed to make any real progress.

On November 8 French and Haig motored to Cassel to attend a conference at Foch's headquarters. Haig expressed grave anxiety about his position and argued in favor of withdrawing to a line along the canal. This would have improved his defense and required fewer troops. Foch, who hoped to use the salient as a springboard for a vast enveloping movement across Flanders, was determined to keep it, regardless of the circumstances. He tried to play down the importance of the fighting in the British sector. He observed that the Germans were in the process of withdrawing troops from the line in order to reinforce the threatened Eastern front. The attacks at Ypres were merely to cover this move and could not succeed in doing much damage. He added that he had given formal orders for the lost ground to be retaken and he seemed to regard it as already done. Foch exuded his usual unbounded optimism and Sir John confessed "to having strongly felt the infection of his hopeful disposition."[48] The upshot was that Haig was left to hold on as best he could.

November 8th, 9th, and 10th passed fairly quietly on the British front and there was nothing to indicate that anything unusual was about to happen. Intelligence service had no information, apart from aviators' reports showing that additional field guns were being moved forward, to suggest that fresh divisions had been put into the line and that preparation for a supreme effort against the British were in progress. The French had reason to believe that the Germans had brought up several fresh corps but they had wrongly concluded that the blow would fall on them, north of Ypres.

At daybreak on November 11, while a thick mist hung over the entire battle area, the Germans opened the heaviest artillery barrage yet experienced by the British army. For the infantry there was nothing to do but lie at the bottom of the trenches, which were shallow and lacked overhead cover. So fierce was the fire that long lengths of trenches were blown in, causing the occupants to run back to less exposed positions in the support line. Around 9:00 A.M. the shelling began to lift and these men, realizing that an assault was coming, doubled forward to whatever remained of their original fire position. Out of the fog came line after line of German soldiers, carrying their rifles at the port and led by officers with drawn swords.

The danger was in the British center, astride the Menin road, where the fiercest onslaught fell. The sector was held by General Wing's division and by the First Guards Brigade, the two formations, including all their reserves, totaling no more than 7,850. Opposed to them were twenty-five battalions—at least 17,500 infantry—of Prussian Guards, considered the finest soldiers in the German army. The Prussian assault south of the road was quickly broken up by the steady fire of Wing's battalions and was never a real threat. To the north the enemy overwhelmed three battalions of the Guards Brigade by sheer weight of numbers, penetrating the British front to a depth of some 600 yards. The British fell back to their "strong points"—heavily wired positions that could be held even if the enemy got in behind them or past a flank—which Haig, on the advice of his chief engineer, had ordered constructed a few days before. Thanks to these strong defensive positions and to the arrival of reserve units, the Germans were halted and eventually driven back from practically all their gains.

At the end of the fighting on November 11th all of Haig's units had suffered heavy casualties and the last reserves had been used. Haig reported to General Headquarters that the enemy was pressing both flanks of the salient and that, unless reinforcements were sent up, both his own and Dubois's corps would be cut off. But with the failure of the Prussian Guards the crisis at Ypres finally passed. For the next several days the Germans made spasmodic attacks, chiefly against Dubois's front, and continued to shell Ypres until its famous Cloth Hall was reduced to a pile of rubble. By mid-November the bitter Flanders winter had set in and the First Battle of Ypres faded away amid the blizzards of the third week. The end of the battle also ended the last phase of open or semi-open warfare. The opposing armies now faced each other along an unbroken line from the Swiss frontier to the sea. With minor fluctuations this line was to remain stabilized for the next three-and-a-half years.

"First Ypres" was a terrible experience for the British army, its dimensions and ferocity far transcending anything known before. What had begun as an envelopment movement in effect turned into a defensive struggle. Lack of major reserves prevented the British from wresting the initiative from the Germans. For the BEF it was a question of holding on until the enemy onslaught spent itself. Sir John had little influence on the battle, the conduct of which was left in the hands of the corps commanders. Fortunately it was on Haig's front that the main German assault fell.

While it cannot be denied that Haig made serious errors as an offensive commander, especially in 1916 and 1917, there has seldom been a finer defensive general in the British army. He had a cool head, the moral courage and ability to make up his own mind and to make his subordinates willingly obey him, and a reasonable degree of comprehension and instinctive skill in higher tactics. By employing his cavalry and by withdrawing units from parts of the front where pressure was less severe he was able to maintain a reserve to fill the breaches or for counterattacks. He was ahead of his British contemporaries in discovering the best use of the scant engineering resources to improve defenses. But in the final analysis it was not on Haig that the result of the battle depended.

Ypres was a soldier's battle, won by the superior musketry, discipline, and dogged courage of the British infantry, rather than by any great tactical brilliance. For over three weeks the BEF, already wearied and bruised by earlier struggles, faced an enemy that was not only brave and formidable but that enjoyed a substantial numerical advantage, in places of up to five and six to one. Surely Britain has never put a finer army in the field.

The cost of Ypres was overwhelming. Over 58,000 British soldiers were killed or wounded (French losses were as great and those of the Germans were put at 134,000), bringing the total casualties since the start of the war to 89,000—more than all the infantry of the first seven regular divisions. The old regular army was shattered, leaving only a framework for the new mass armies that were to come.

The result of the battle was clearly a defeat for the Germans. It is true that the Allies had hoped to envelop or break through the enemy's line, but, while it was desirable for them to do so, it was not essential. That was not the case for the Germans. It was essential for them to get to the Channel ports, destroy the Allied left, and end the war quickly. Time was not on their side.

9

The Close of 1914

Sir John's day began early, before the dawn stand-to, with the reading of the reports of the night's activites. If he had been out during the night he then went to bed for a few hours but otherwise had breakfast at 8:00 A.M. After 9:00 A.M. he saw the various heads of departments and issued orders if any were necessary. He then spent the rest of the daylight hours visiting points of special interest in the line—the corps commanders, men in the trenches, hospitals, or some particular service or department. When he had important visitors he would occasionally take one with him on his travels. If severe fighting was going on Sir John normally conferred with the French generals in his neighborhood, either at their headquarters or his own, while occasionally he motored to Chantilly to see General Joffre. The liaison officers also reported to him regularly, keeping him abreast with what was happening in their sector.

In the evening the heads of services came again with the reports of the day. Before dinner, French took a hot bath and changed into fresh clothes. He dined generally with six or eight members of his staff but now and then one of his old cronies would turn up and join the group. There was no formality; meals were simple and over quickly. So as to give the field marshal's mind a rest it was understood that conversation at the table would not be connected with the war. Afterwards French might spend an hour talking to his staff or a visitor staying in his mess. Then he would return to his office to deal with papers requiring his attention, compile his day's report to Kitchener, and work on his personal correspondence. He went to bed between 11 o'clock and midnight.

Sir John's headquarters at Saint Omer were in an ordinary, unpretentious house that belonged to an attorney. He lived there with a few members of his staff while most of headquarters personnel were lodged in a separate building across the street. French's personal staff consisted of both soldiers and civilians—Lieutenant-Colonel W. Lambton (Military Secretary), Brinsley Fitzgerald (Private Secretary), Colonel Guy Brooke, Major A. F. Watt, and Freddy Guest (ADCs). There was no love lost between the regulars and the irregulars. After a short trial it was found impossible for the two groups to mingle without friction in the social life of the headquarters mess and by an unspoken agreement the staff fell into two separate cliques, only coming together for the purpose of work. The Prince of Wales, who joined Sir John's personal staff in mid-November, stood apart from the rivalry between the two groups.

At the start of the war the twenty-year old Prince Edward had not been permitted to go out with his battalion of Grenadier Guards to France. It was a bitter blow to his pride. Mustering all his resolve he hurried up the vast marble stairs to the War Office and asked if he could see Lord Kitchener. Sitting uncomfortably across from the fierce-looking secretary of war the young prince pleaded his case. "What does it matter if I am killed?" he said in exasperation. "I have four brothers." Without changing expression Kitchener replied, "If I were sure you would be killed, I do not know if I should be right to restrain you. But I cannot take the chance, which always exists until we have a settled line, of the enemy taking you prisoner."[1] Edward walked out of the War Office with no more than a vague promise that there might be a staff job for him in France later on. A month passed and the prince went to the War Office again. But Kitchener remained adamant, saying that only when the line was settled would he be allowed to sail for France. Kitchener kept his word. When German pressure against Ypres began to ease he made arrangements for Edward to join headquarters staff as one of Sir John's ADCs.

Whatever the private wishes of the prince, it was understood that, as the heir-apparent to the throne, no unnecessary risks could be taken with his life. Sir John did his best to keep the young prince occupied with paper work and tasks such as the carrying of dispatches. But Edward was quick to see that the high command was trying to conceal from him his noncombatant role and he frequently complained that his only real job was that of being Prince of Wales. Still he did what he was told to do expeditiously and to the best of his ability. He was punctual in keeping appointments or attending meetings and saluted every senior officer with the precision of a true Grenadier. He was very popular at General Headquarters but, as he would have wanted, was treated like any other subaltern and no one made any fuss about him.

Among the first official duties that Edward was called upon to perform was to march behind the gun carriage bearing Lord Roberts's coffin. On November 11 the old soldier had crossed over to France with his daughter Aileen. He dined with French and afterwards poured avidly over maps of the recent battles. He awoke early next morning, ate breakfast at 8 o'clock, and went straight to visit the Indian troops. At each place soldiers not in the firing line were drawn up for Roberts's inspection and he took delight in talking to them, occasionally meeting one who had fought with him in the frontier wars. The day was wet and stormy and in the evening the veteran came down with a feverish chill. Pneumonia followed and at 8:00 P.M. on November 14th he died peacefully. It was fitting that this beloved soldier should die within the sound of guns and in the midst of the army he had served for sixty-three years.[2]

A stream of privileged civilians now began to reach the front as the fighting became static. One of the first to come was George G. Moore, an American of Irish Protestant ancestry. Moore, who died in 1971 at the age of ninety-six, led a remarkable life. Born in Wyoming, Ontario, he was the youngest in a family of seven sons and three daughters. He graduated from high school at fifteen and through his brother David entered the law office of O'Brien J. Atkinson in Port Huron, Michigan.[3] He was admitted to the Michigan bar at age twenty-one and, though successful from the start, gave up the practice of law after only four years because he deemed the material rewards insufficient.[4] Starting a new career in business, he achieved his first coup when he took over the Michigan United Traction Company and developed it from an 18-mile line to one of 500 miles, among the largest in the nation. Before the age of forty he was an internationally known financier and multimillionaire with varied interests based in Canada throughout the United States to South America and Europe.

Moore was ardently pro-British and he frequently journeyed to England, usually mixing business with pleasure. On one such trip in 1910, aboard the *Mauritania,* he chanced to meet French, who was returning home from a visit to America.[5] The two men had much in common—both were of Irish heritage and both enjoyed good food, high society, and beautiful women. They not only became close friends but in the spring of 1911 leased, and subsequently bought, a large house at 94 Lancaster Gate in London. French had no money and it is doubtful if he contributed much, if anything, to its purchase[6] and maintenance. The house, described by Lady Diana Manners as "ghastly,"[7] overlooked a park and was in a fashionable area of the city. It allowed the two men to live comfortably, hold small parties, and entertain their lady friends.

After the novelty of marriage had worn off, French began pursuing women with the mad passion of a Casanova. Over the years he had a succession of beautiful and well-connected mistresses and was cited as correspondent in at least one divorce action. "The Field Marshall was famous for his love affairs," Moore noted in his memoirs.[8] Elsewhere he wrote, "For several months we spent all our evenings together with feminine friends. . . ."[9] A short, stocky man whose clothes never seemed to fit properly, French bore faint resemblance to the prototype tall, sleek cavalryman. His success with women, therefore, was not due to good looks. Women were attracted to him in some cases because of his professional reputation and position and in others because of his warm personality.

**Winifred Bennett as a young woman. The photo has been retouched.
(Photo courtesy of the Imperial War Museum)**

French's extramarital relations and the attention that some of these affairs received caused his wife much pain and embarrassment. Lady French had ample grounds for a divorce but she acted as if everything were normal, devoting her time to providing a stable home for her children. She tolerated her husband's infidelities partly out of loyalty and affection and partly out of a desire to avoid a scandal.

The large sums French spent on women and other pleasures, estimated by one writer to be "the modern equivalent of about half a million pounds before he was fifty,"[10] kept him deeply in debt. His financial plight was eased somewhat after he moved in with Moore at 94 Lancaster Gate. Moore idolized French and, without expecting to be repaid, lent him much of the money he used to live and entertain in lavish style.

The war altered French's lifestyle but did not prevent him from maintaining his close association with Moore. As soon as it was practical he asked Moore to join him in France. After November Moore became, for all intents and purposes, a full-time resident at General Headquarters.

Another guest, but one whose visits were less prolonged, was Lieutenant-Colonel Repington, military correspondent for *The Times*. He stayed with Sir John, ostensibly not as a correspondent since none was permitted, but as a personal friend. Nevertheless he floated about General Headquarters, gathering scraps of information and rumor that he did not hesitate to use in his publications.

At the end of November the king arrived with his retinue, which included his secretary, Lord Stamfordham. His schedule was heavy and involved a great deal of travel on bad roads in cold, wet weather. Wherever he went he was received by the troops with delight and acclamation. He conferred decorations, gave interviews, and visited hospitals and base establishments. He had long conversations with President Poincaré, General Joffre, and French, and noted in his diary that they were all convinced that victory was in sight. The king did not share their optimism, for he believed Kitchener's prediction that the war would last several years.[11] The Prince of Wales recalled his father's "incredulous expression" when "Sir John assured him the war would be over by Christmas."[12]

The most captivating visitor of all, in Sir John's eyes, was Mrs. Winifred Bennett, who came in search of her lover's grave. She was fortyish, nearly six feet tall, and attractive with an aristocratic bearing. Exquisitely beautiful as a young woman and pampered by her businessman father, she had married Percy Bennett, a British diplomat. Bennett was a cold, self-centered man, so absorbed with his own career that he paid scant attention to his wife's physical and emotional needs.[13] Mrs Bennett loathed her husband, referring to him as "Pompous Percy," and once, in a fit of pique, went through her family album and drew horns on his head.[14] Ultimately she found comfort in the arms of a dashing captain of the Tenth Hussars, Arthur Annesley, who was several years her junior.

**Joffre chatting with French while Haig looks on
(Photo courtesy of "L'Illustration")**

French knew Annesley casually and he had met Mrs. Bennett on one occasion prior to the war. She evidently left a lasting impression on him, for when Annesley was killed outside of Ypres on November 15 he sent her a brief note expressing his condolences.[15] Subsequently she went over to France but it seems improbable that she was able to visit Annesley's grave. The Ypres town cemetery was in an area that, although under British control, was frequently shelled and occasionally infiltrated by German patrols.

French's earlier attraction for Mrs. Bennett was intensified and when he traveled to London at the start of 1915 he arranged to meet her at 94 Lancaster Gate. Thereafter their relationship became intimate. Mrs. Bennett was the last and perhaps greatest love of Sir John's life.

The first year of the affair must have been frustrating for both. They were unable to be together except on his occasional visits to London and therefore had to content themselves with exchanging love letters. There are no records of letters from Mrs. Bennett to French; probably because French destroyed them. But evidence suggests that she wrote almost, but not quite, as frequently as he did. French's letters, each one written over a period of two or three days, are substantial; several are over 800 words long. Of the letters written to her while he was in France most, ninety-two to be exact, have survived. They are filled with passionate endearments and expressions of his love for her that are both engaging and faintly comic. He told her, for example, "With your Gage in my Hand and your love in my heart there is no knightly thing I cannot do."[16] And again: "How you live in my thoughts—my beautiful beloved lady! In my morning visit to you today you were so vivid and real."[17]

Because of his special relationship with Mrs. Bennett, Sir John wrote without inhibition even on subjects about which he should have been more cautious. He laments the death of friends and the frightful losses in battle; makes frequent references, usually unflattering, about the French leaders; complains bitterly about Kitchener and the War Office; and comments about the war, the nature of the fighting, the use of gas and atrocities committed against captured prisoners. French shows the same lack of restraint when treating confidential matters. He discusses, sometimes in surprising detail, his forthcoming plans and preparations for battle; reports on his own movements, troop deployments, and the itineraries of eminent visitors to the front. For the historian these letters contain a wealth of information. They reveal much more than French's own diaries, which were apparently written with eventual publication in mind.

The cynic might wonder how French could satisfactorily prosecute a war while his thoughts were constantly with his mistress back home. In fact his schedule was so crowded that he had little time to think of her except at the end of the day; and his extensive correspondence was both a solace and a relaxation,[18] interfering with his duties no more than would a ride on horseback or late-night conversation. What was more questionable was his practice of divulging military secrets. It is true that the possibility that the enemy might intercept the letters was remote since they were taken personally by officers, often under escort. But if Mrs. Bennett had been indiscreet or misplaced a letter the damage might have been incalculable.

French's love affair with Mrs. Bennett helped to sustain him as he passed through the most difficult phase of his career. The events of the opening months of the war had left their mark on French. Although remarkably fit for a man of sixty-one, he led such a hectic life that he had comparatively little time either to sleep or relax. The responsibility of command, together with his anguish over growing casualty lists, began to tell upon his health. By mid-November he was confined to bed and told to rest after complaining of chest pains. On November 21 French told Haig over lunch that he might have suffered a heart attack.[19] Whatever the nature of his ailment he made a quick recovery and was at work again by the end of the month.

On December 7 Churchill came over to General Headquarters to discuss with the field marshal a project of mutual interest. On the occasion of the first lord's former visit Sir John had broached the idea of a joint military-naval attack along the Belgian sea coast.[20] There was much to recommend it. The scheme would involve shifting the BEF to the extreme end of the line, its left flank resting on the sea and guarded by the Royal Navy. If successful it would not only turn the German flank but also eliminate the dangers of their building submarine bases at Ostend and Zeebrugge. The more Churchill thought about the proposal the more it appealed to him. On December 7 he discussed the matter further with Sir John and before leaving promised to arrange everything with Asquith and Kitchener.[21]

The first lord wasted no time, for by the 8th he had not only met with his colleagues but won their support.[22] Kitchener had always wanted to see the British army operating on the coast, nearest to its home. He felt that this would shorten the supply lines, allow the use of naval power in military operations, and heighten the awareness among the masses that the British army was fighting for Britain. He favored Sir John's scheme on the grounds that it was a limited and local enterprise and yet, if successful, would bring substantial results. He promised the Twenty-seventh Division as reinforcement for the operation.

The transferral of British troops to the left of the line could be accomplished only if they were replaced in their present position by French units. Acting through the British ambassador, Kitchener made a formal request for French assistance to the minister of war.[23] Sir Francis Bertie, when conveying the message, took it upon himself to say (erroneously and what must certainly have been a breach of protocol) that Kitchener had probably acted without consulting French. He added that the secretary for war was behaving improperly and interfering in matters outside his jurisdiction.[24] Millerand did not view the plan with any enthusiasm. Throughout the war it was a settled policy of the French government to avoid having the British occupy a zone next to the sea and to prevent their acquiring a close association with the Belgian forces.[25] Millerand simply replied that he considered the question a military one and would refer it to General Joffre.

As it happened Joffre had his own reasons for opposing the British venture in Flanders. During November and December von Falkenhayn, reacting to von Hindenburg's urgent appeal, transferred no less than eight infantry and five cavalry divisions from France to the Russian front. Joffre felt a responsibility to strike immediately in order to divert the Germans from the great attack on the Russians that they were evidently preparing. In framing an offensive plan Joffre was influenced by the importance of reducing the German salient that bulged forward between the Aisne and the Oise since its apex at Noyon was only fifty-five miles from Paris. The Tenth Army in Artois was to form the left claw of a pincer movement and the Fourth Army in Champagne the right claw. The British, who now occupied a line south of Ypres, between Messines and La Bassée, were well placed to assist in the operation. Sir John had given his word that he would cooperate by attempting to recover the Wytschaete-Messines ridge, but Joffre doubted that the British effort would amount to much unless they could be persuaded to abandon their proposed drive along the Belgian coast.

Sir John discovered, after sounding out a number of his corps commanders and principal staff officers, that they were all equally opposed to the scheme. Wilson expressed himself strongly in his diary on the subject: "The little fool [French] has no sense at all. He told me he could take Ostend and Zeebrugge at once. And how? and if he did? He cannot read a map in scale. It really is hopeless."[26] The general feeling was that Sir John's plan was impractical. It failed to take into consideration the difficulties of campaigning across the waterlogged marshland of Flanders and the fact that the Germans, who were operating along interior lines, could always move reinforcements more quickly than the Allies to any threatened point. By December 11, when Foch came over to General Headquarters for discussions, Sir John had not only made a complete about-face but, as would frequently occur whenever his plans ran into difficulty, placed the blame for his troubles on someone else. There is the following entry in Wilson's diary: "Foch came to see me . . . to tell me that Millerand had sent him a copy of the precious document sent by Winston, K., Grey and Asquith, about our going on the left. . . . Of course, Foch treats it with the greatest contempt. We then went down to see Sir John and the poor little devil was quite apologetic about the left flank scheme and said it was Winston's idea."[27] The rest of the meeting was spent in finalizing plans for the British army's participation in Joffre's offensive, which was set for the 14th.

The British attack was to consist of three successive thrusts, beginning in the north and gradually spreading southwards. Sir John did not feel that the French could inflict a serious defeat upon the enemy or improve their position to any appreciable extent, except locally. Only nine-and-a-half British battalions were committed to the joint operation and no attempt was made at an adquate concentration of artillery to help these units in their tasks. French impressed on "every commander that he was on no account to get ahead of his neighbours in the attack—everybody was to wait for the man on his left."[28] The divisional commanders were far from inspired when they left the conference room and their attitude was reflected in the manner they conducted the operations on their front.

The results of the fighting on December 14 were disappointing. On the left the French XVI Corps was unable to make any progress. The Third Division, next to the French, was charged with capturing Wytschaete and the woods west of it. The men had crossed several hundred yards into No Man's Land when they were halted by machine-gun fire and wire entanglements. Since further action depended on securing the first objectives, no other attack took place that day.

The British operations were continued in a half-hearted way over the next three days. With the ground a hopeless quagmire of mud and the German trenches and wire practically intact, even the most resolute troops would have found it extremely dificult to advance. The absence of a vigorous effort on the part of the British brought Foch to General Headquarters on the 17th. Wilson was hard put to offer an explanation, as the entry in his diary illustrates:

> I made the best case I could about advancing in echelon from the left, and he listened without saying a word. At the end he said, "*Mais mon cher Wilson nous sommes militaries pas avocats.*" That exactly expresses the straits I was pushed to. We discussed everything, and he was as nice as could be; but "*Père Joffre n'est pas commode,*" and it was clear that Sir John would be in a very difficult position if he did not put up some fight.[29]

By now Joffre had made up his mind to discontinue his attacks in the north except on the right of the BEF, near Arras, where the ground was harder. Since he felt he could not rely on effective cooperation from Sir John, his request for help was limited to a demonstration along the British front so as to tie down the Germans and prevent them from reinforcing the sector under attack.[30] Sir John agreed and on the evening of the 17th announced his intention to "attack vigorously all along the front tomorrow with the II, III, IV and Indian Corps." But in the details of the order the II Corps was told merely to resume its attack in conjunction with the French XVI Corps, and the III, IV, and Indian Corps were directed to "demonstrate and seize any favourable opportunity which may offer to capture any enemy's trenches on their front."[31]

The main French thrust near Arras, hampered by fog and rain, ended in a fiasco. The Germans struck the French XVI Corps at Ypres so the British II Corps did not leave the trenches. In the other British sectors the demonstrations ordered resulted in a series of attacks varying in strength. What gains were achieved, in most cases, were quickly relinquished owing to enemy counterattacks or to the impossibility of fortifying the position in the sodden ground. The British operations in Flanders were formally terminated on December 20. Three days later the French operations in the north were also suspended.

While the fighting was going on French decided to replace Murray as his chief of staff. Murray was generally well liked in the army but he was unimaginative, distrustful of the French, and insufficiently robust to stand up to the test of war. He had become touchy and difficult to work with since his breakdown during the retreat from Mons. The experience had shaken his confidence and made him ill at ease with the subordinates who witnessed it.

Sir John knew that Haig, whom he would have preferred as his chief of staff, would not give up his command to accept the post. This narrowed the choice to Wilson or Robertson. The August retreat had permitted Wilson to usurp many of Murray's functions and to gain an increasing ascendancy over Sir John. Irascible, with a subtle mind and ready tongue, Wilson could always be counted on to smooth over the misunderstandings that arose between the French and the British commander. Robertson, as quarter-master-general, had never failed to meet the army's requirements during the retreat as well as in battle. A dour man, respected if not loved by his peers, Robertson had risen from the ranks through sheer hard work and application.

Of the two men French had no doubts that Wilson was better suited for the post. He was not certain, however, if his selection would be acceptable to the home authorities. He sent Lambton to London to find out.

It was no secret in London that the French were dissatisfied with Murray, whom they believed was the main cause of the friction between the two high commands. Kitchener, determined to keep on good terms with his ally, felt that Murray's removal was desirable, though he refrained from suggesting it to Sir John. The French ambassador in London, Paul Cambon, who had spoken to Kitchener about Murray, reported that "Kitchener is aware of Sir A. Murray's shortcomings but as he was French's choice, Kitchener does not like to interfere as he has made it his rule not to do so in such matters."[32]

If French should finally decide to select a new chief of staff Kitchener hoped that he would turn to Robertson. Kitchener disliked and distrusted Wilson through past contact and from reputation. But Kitchener would not have allowed personal bias to color his professional judgment. What he wanted was a chief of staff who would carry out the government's policies

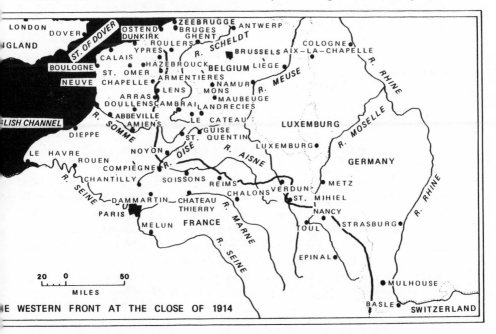

THE WESTERN FRONT AT THE CLOSE OF 1914

rather than his own whimsical designs and who would not subordinate the interests of the British army to those of the French.

From the outset of the war Wilson had been undisguisedly hostile to Kitchener's plans, especially his efforts to multiply the nation's armed forces. He scoffed at Kitchener's "shadow armies," proclaiming to all who would listen that none would be ready for combat for at least two years—by which time he was confident that the war would be over. He considered it a scandal that the BEF should be starved for the sake of Kitchener's "ridiculous and preposterous army," which was "the laughing-stock of every soldier in Europe."[33] His wild and provocative remarks did not fail to reach Kitchener's ears. It is understandable why the secretary for war did not wish to magnify the power at the front of someone who was a known and outspoken opponent of his plans. And yet when Lambton advanced Wilson's name as a replacement for Murray, Kitchener, while showing no enthusiasm for it, indicated that he would not block it. A note to this effect was sent to General Headquarters. French broke the news to Wilson and assured him that the job was his.[34]

In reality the matter was far from settled. On December 20 French sailed for England to consult with the cabinet, which was worried over the military situation on the Continent and the possibility of an invasion by the enemy.[35] Kitchener met him at Folkestone and the two soldiers drove together to the prime minister's weekend retreat. On the way they discussed some of the proposed changes in the headquarters staff. Kitchener expressed misgivings about selecting Wilson as the new chief of staff, citing, as one of the reasons, the resistance that was certain to come from a group of influential army officers who disliked him. At Walmer Castle French received no support from Asquith, who had not forgiven Wilson for his activities during the Curragh crisis. The cabinet, the prime minister declared, considered Wilson dangerous and would not accept him at any price.

Although Kitchener and Asquith may have had just cause to object to Wilson, it is equally clear that the commander-in-chief had the right to select his own principal adviser. If Sir John had pressed for Wilson it is difficult to see how they could have stood in the way. But French, as would appear from his book, was anxious not only about Wilson but also about his own position.

As an alternative to Wilson both Kitchener and the prime minister urged the appointment of Robertson but Sir John claimed that he could not be spared from his current duties. Unable to resolve the impasse, Sir John decided to leave Murray where he was. This was an unfortunate mistake. French desperately needed a competent staff officer to remedy some of the deficiencies at General Headquarters. Because his knowledge of staff work was inadequate he did not appreciate either the extent of Murray's liabilities or how entangled the chain of command had become.

The discussion then turned to matters dealing with military strategy. Kitchener voiced alarm at the reports of large transfers of German troops from the western to the eastern theater of war and at rumors of an ammunition shortage in Russia. A German victory in the east, as seemed likely, would enable them to resume the offensive in Flanders with a substantial numerical superiority. French claimed that Kitchener's fears were not founded upon definite or reliable information. So far as was known the Russians were established in a good position and holding their own well. Even if the Germans succeeded in pushing the Russians beyond the Vistula, which he believed was unlikely, they would never break through the line in the west, regardless of how many troops they brought from the east. According to French the Germans had lost their best troops and their replacements were of such inferior quality that battle police were required to force them into action. On the other hand the British army was stronger and the French army better led than at the outset.[36] Kitchener was not reassured by French's remarks. He directed the commander-in-chief to seek out Joffre after his return and to inquire what he proposed to do in the event of a Russian collapse.

The two field marshals also disagreed on the vital issue of home defense. Kitchener argued that the current lull on the western front would enable the Germans to spare large numbers of troops, perhaps as much as 250,000, for an invasion of England. There were so few trained soldiers left in the country that he doubted whether he could repel it. French, however, was convinced that the Germans did not have the resources for such a venture. He might have added that the superiority of the Royal Navy precluded the dangers of an invasion.

After lunch Kitchener and French left for London by automobile. The journey took them by Broome Park, where Kitchener insisted on stopping to show French around his estate. They remained there an hour, strolling over the grounds and reminiscing about some of the experiences they went through together in South Africa. French later recalled "with deep sorrow" that this was the last day of "happy personal intercourse" with his former military chief before their old friendship finally collapsed.[37] Although outward signs of cordiality were maintained and their correspondence shows that they had reached a good working arrangement, their subsequent relations, until the time of Kitchener's tragic death, were always clouded by a certain mistrust of one another.

The sharp differences between the two men can be partially traced to the arrangement whereby Kitchener was simultaneously a cabinet minister in charge of war strategy and a serving field marshal with greater seniority than that of French. Traditionally the secretary for war was a civilian rather than a soldier and he was not required to have any expert knowledge of the functions of his department. His particular concern, apart from overseeing the War Office establishment, was to manage the finances of the army. The actual task of administering the army and preparing it for war was left to the various military departments while policy was decided by the Army Council. All submissions to the Crown on military matters were made through the secretary for war. In practice he tended to be a representative of the army in the cabinet rather than an agent for cabinet control over the army.

It was natural that Kitchener should treat the office in a very different fashion. Unprepared to wage a great conflict, the nation had called him to the War Office with unanimous acclaim. Regarded as the greatest living soldier in the country, he was expected not to be a mere spokesman for the army, but to apply his expertise in directing the entire war effort. French never realized the immense difference between Kitchener's position and that of a civilian secretary for war.

Still it would be erroneous to blame the existing structure of command as the principal cause of the dispute. The root of the problem appears to lie in the wide temperamental differences between the two field marshals. Sir John was extremely insecure, doubtful of his capacity as a field general and constantly in need of reassurance. The French correctly gauged his character and played upon his weakness when it suited them, but Kitchener was not in the habit of indulging anyone's ego or caprices.

Kitchener was accustomed to doing things in a single-handed way and, working under severe pressure, was apt to impinge on the authority of the commander-in-chief. Sir John, believing that the task for fighting the Germans was his own responsibility and jealous of Kitchener, who had reaped the glory he so badly coveted, came to interpret almost every caution and comment made by the War Office as a criticism of his command. After he heard rumors that Kitchener meant to get rid of him, French grew suspicious and resentful, scenting in every proposal a plot laid for his undoing. A more subtle man would have had no difficulty in handling Kitchener. For example, Haig, after succeeding French, enjoyed a close and happy relationship with Kitchener. But Sir John was not distinguished by a high order of intelligence and he was inclined to strike back, rather than pause to reflect, when he walked into something he did not anticipate.

Another source of friction was their disagreement over almost every key military issue. An especially sore point with General Headquarters was Kitchener's policy of retaining a number of trained officers and NCOs to serve as instructors for the new armies that were being formed. French's optimism forbade him to believe that the war was going to be anything but a campaign of a few months and although by the end of the year he had revised his estimate, he thought it would be over in February or March of 1915. In these circumstances it seemed to him a waste of effort and resources to train new armies that he and his friends predicted would be unable to take the field for at least two years. If Kitchener threw in every available officer and man he was confident that the Germans could be pushed back and the advance resumed.

Events did not bear out French's judgment. Kitchener's appeal drew in volunteers in unprecedented numbers and his methods, despite incredible human and natural obstacles, trained, supplied, equipped, and sent them to the front as first-class fighting units in much less time than French and his staff had ever deemed possible. As the first divisions of the new armies began to land in France in the spring of 1915 Sir John, far from sneering at the impracticability of Kitchener's scheme, was clamoring for more formations and still more.

Finally, no analysis of the Kitchener-French dispute would be complete without reference to the mischievous conduct of Henry Wilson. His relations with Sir John were close and cordial and he was more in the field marshal's confidence than any member of the headquarters staff. Wilson hated Kitchener, having clashed with him on several occasions in the past. He looked on Kitchener as an interfering and ignorant outsider whose evil influence must be checked. In front of even junior officers he poured ridicule on Kitchener, as well as on any of his proposals with which he did not agree, and did his best to poison the mind of the temperamentally suspicious and excitable commander-in-chief.[38]

In London French spent the greater part of the next two days in conference with the cabinet. He repeated to the ministers what he had told Kitchener—that is, he disagreed altogether with their information about the situation on the Russian front and the possibility of a German invasion of the island. In between meetings with the cabinet he met privately with Churchill, who rekindled his interest in the Zeebrugge (Flanders) scheme; talked to old friends; and was received in audience by the king. French returned to Saint Omer on December 23.

The first thing next morning he sent for Wilson. It was a painful interview for both men. Hesitating and frequently groping for words, Sir John praised Wilson's loyalty and services, promising to do everything in his power in the future to assist his career. He could have dispensed with the long preamble since Wilson had already spoken with Lambton and knew what to expect. Eventually French came to the real point, observing that opposition to Wilson at home had proved insurmountable and that he was not going to succeed Murray. Wilson was bitterly disappointed at not getting an appointment that had been definitely promised and that he had worked for and dreamt of for years. Although he made light of the matter in his diary, telling himself that he did not care and that he felt no sorrow at not serving the government or French, the hurt showed through. And the greatest hurt of all was the feeling that his friend had let him down. The fact was not lost on Wilson that if the commander of the BEF had stood firm, the veto placed on him at home would undoubtedly have been withdrawn.[39]

If Sir John was content to wait and play upon events before naming a new chief of staff there was one problem that he found necessary to settle without delay. This involved making changes in the organization of the

BEF. Three new regular divisions, the 27th, 28th, and 29th, had recently been formed in England from units recalled from overseas duty. The Twenty-seventh Division arrived in France on December 23 and the Twenty-eighth was expected early in January. These were to form the V Corps under Lieutenant-General Herbert Plumer. Recognizing that it was too big a task to deal directly with a growing number of corps, Sir John divided the BEF into two armies: the First, commanded by Haig, and the Second by Smith-Dorrien, each consisting of three army corps.[40] Allenby's Cavalry Corps and the Indian Cavalry Corps were kept as a general reserve under the direct orders of French himself.[41]

On December 27 Sir John, accompanied by Wilson, drove to Chantilly to confer with Joffre. He explained the views and fears of the British authorities and, as he had been charged to do, invited Joffre's opinion on the points raised. According to Wilson the French commander was "much amused and said they were *affolés*."[42] His reports indicated that the Russians had inflicted enormous casualties on the Germans in yielding a narrow strip of territory on their front and were now established on a good line. He conceded that the Russians had only about six weeks' supply of ammunition but seemed satisfied that the shortage was merely temporary. In short he professed not to be in the least anxious about the situation on the eastern front. He went on to say that the French General Staff was prepared to meet any eventuality but refused to discuss the consequences of a Russian defeat.

Sir John asked no questions and made no comments, evidently satisfied with Joffre's assessment. He did, however, take the opportunity to resurrect a scheme that the French had rejected several weeks previously. Again he claimed that he could best advance the Allied cause by sweeping along the Belgian coast, in conjunction with the Royal Navy, and he went over all the old arguments. Once more Joffre would not consent to the movement but he gave French reason to hope that it might be undertaken at a later date. In the absence of any support from his own government, Sir John felt it was pointless to pursue the issue.[43]

After the meeting Joffre took French to another part of the room, ostensibly to show him a list of the forthcoming recipients of the Legion of Honour. "*Général Murray va partir?*" Joffre asked casually. When Sir John replied "No," Joffre said, "*Ah, c'est dommage.*"[44]

The French had already heard the news from Wilson. They were disappointed that their good friend had been denied the appointment, apparently on personal and political grounds. They tried to get the ban on Wilson removed, not only by bringing indirect pressure on Sir John, as Joffre had done, but also through diplomatic channels. Cambon sent a note to Kitchener, saying that Joffre was very unhappy with the British effort during the recent operations and blamed their poor performance on the chief of staff. Kitchener showed the letter to Lambton, who was in London on leave, and asked him what it meant. Lambton could offer no explanation but said that he would speak to Sir John about it when he returned to France. Lambton arrived at General Headquarters on the evening of December 29 and went straight to the field marshal's room. At the close of the interview Sir John picked up his pen and wrote the following letter to the War Office:

> Lambton has shown me the "secret" telegram explaining Joffre's views about Murray—I can hardly believe that he ever meant to say that British troops had on any occasion failed to support him but if he really did intend to convey that impression I should be sorry to say what I think of him.
>
> The real truth is that Murray at first allowed himself to speak in very unguarded terms of the conduct of the French in leaving us in the lurch as they certainly did—This became known to them and they have determined to have his blood if they can—
>
> I wish to keep him where he is and I hope you'll support me.[45]

In fact French was much less certain about Murray than he sounded and next day he talked things over with some of his closest associates. Lambton hinted that he shared Kitchener's feelings that Murray's removal would improve the effectiveness of the British army as well as relations with the French. Wilson dwelled on the evils of keeping a man who was considered useless by the headquarters staff, the army, and the French.[46] The growing pressure from the government, the army, and the French led Sir John to conclude that he must make a change when the opportunity arose. The remaining question was whether he should try again to overcome objections to Wilson before offering the post to someone else.

The close of 1914 found Sir John in a hopeful and sanguine frame of mind. The early months of the conflict had seen the British army play a glorious role in resisting the German invasion of France and in successfully withstanding the enemy's most determined efforts to break through to the Channel ports. The Germans had now dug themselves into trenches that stretched from Switzerland to the sea, unable to regain the initiative they had lost. Each passing month would mean a reduction in their strength and a corresponding increase in the fighting power of the Anglo-French armies. Then too the information emanating from the eastern front suggested that the Russian army had shaken off the effects of the disasters of Tannenberg and the Masurian lakes. Sir John was encouraged to believe that the "Russian steamroller" was about to move forward again and he fully expected that once it had gained momentum it would overwhelm all opposition and break through to Berlin. The year 1915 would see the tide of war swing decidedly in favor of the Allies. Or so French thought.

10

The First Attempt at Siege Warfare

The authorities in Whitehall saw no justification for the satisfaction expressed by their high command over the progress of the war. They had entered into the conflict on the understanding that it would be over in a few months and yet, by year's end, the opposing armies lay glaring at each other at close quarters and the likelihood of a decision seemed as remote as ever. The soldiers could offer no way to overcome the deadlock except by frontal assaults that entailed slaughter and sacrifice beyond anything previously contemplated and only terminating when the enemy had been so reduced as to be incapable of further resistance. The politicians refused to accept this grim prospect. The wars in the last half century had not exacted a very heavy toll, so why should the present one prove an exception? If it was not possible to turn the enemy's flank on the main front, why not seek a decisive victory elsewhere? Questioning the wisdom of their military leaders, the politicians took it upon themselves to find a way around the line, to get at the Germans through a back door.

Various projects were aired in the War Council,[1] which had been formed at the end of November 1914 to advise the cabinet on the strategy and direction of the war. Although the papers were written without reference to one another, they had a number of important points in common. They agreed that it was a waste of life and effort to continue to batter away at the enemy's defenses in France and they favored using Britain's strength, particularly sea power, in another and more effective and rewarding field of action. Hankey suggested that, failing the development of new tactics or new weapons, the deadlock in the west could best be broken by an attack on Turkey[2] (which had joined the Central Powers in October). Churchill advanced a plan conceived by Lord Fisher, the first sea lord, for forcing open the Baltic and landing an army on Pomerania, ninety miles north of Berlin.[3] Lloyd George favored attacking Austria from Salonika or Dalmatia with a subsidiary landing on the Syrian coast to cut Turkish communications with Egypt.[4]

All these active-minded Council members, pressing their pet schemes with vigor in discussion, possessed inadequate knowledge of the limitations and requirements of modern warfare. To make matters worse, they did not seek to obtain information and advice from their own naval and military experts. Consequently they ignored such consideration as distances, terrain, climate, and the availability of troops, war materiel, and transport facilities. As A. J. P. Taylor has observed, "The war council cheerfully assumed that great armadas could waft non-existent armies to the ends of the earth in the twinkling of an eye."[5]

This group, which sought to escape from the impasse in Flanders, came to be called "Easterners." They were opposed by "Westerners," who included the leading British soldiers, supported by Joffre and his generals as well as by the French government. Their case was as follows: Germany and her allies occupied a central position on the Continent with secure and comparatively short land communications between them. This meant she could reinforce any front, for offense or defense, with maximum speed and minimum risk. If therefore the Allies mounted a campaign against Austria or Turkey they would increase the advantages the Central Powers already possessed and increase their own disadvantages by prolonging their lines of communication. It was further argued that no victory was possible without the defeat of the principal enemy. Once the Germans were defeated their allies would surrender automatically. But if the Germans won in France, then regardless of what happened on the other fronts, the war would be lost.

Kitchener stood between the two schools of military thought but was appreciably nearer to the "Westerners." As a soldier he knew that the war would be won or lost in the west. Even so he was convinced that no progress would be possible in France until the spring of 1916, when the British armies would be ready to exert their full force. In the interim he favored diversionary attacks with the object of thinning the German line. In the spring and summer of 1915 half a million men would be ready to take the field and, rather than throw them away in an attempt to accomplish an impossible feat, a new and distant theater should be found where the enemy could be struck at his weakest point of resistance.[6]

Kitchener strongly suspected that Sir John would be hostile to any proposal that would divert resources from the main front. Still, before the War Council could decide on a course of action, it would require the views of the commander-in-chief. On the evening of January 2, 1915, Kitchener wrote to French:

> The feeling here is gaining ground that, although it is essential to defend the line we hold, troops over and above what is necessary for that service could be better employed elsewhere. . . . The question of *where* anything effective can be accomplished opens a large field and requires a good deal of study. What are the views of your staff?[7]

The note troubled and angered the field marshal. Wilson recorded his reaction to it:

> Johnnie was very bitter against Asquith and his Cabinet for "saddling him with such a d—— fool as K!" and was violent in language.[8]

French, as a convinced "Westerner," felt that secondary operations would seriously weaken the Entente effort in the decisive theater. He blamed past failures in France on the unavailability of sufficient ammunition. The fighting on the Aisne and at First Ypres during which German artillery had blasted British soldiers from improvished trenches, had led French to conclude that fire power was the key to success. If given enough ammunition he was certain he could achieve a breakthrough. On December 31, 1914, French had wired the War Office, asking that stocks of ammunition be trebled or quadrupled, as well as for large increases in the number of heavy guns.[9]

This was an admission that the high command's exaggerated faith in human will power and cold steel had been misplaced. Prewar military doctrine, as we have seen,[10] assumed that artillery fire would play a subordinate role on the battlefield, merely paving the way for a successful bayonet charge. Sir John had now come to realize that unsupported infantrymen, no matter how determined to advance across open ground to deliver a bayonet charge, were no match for entrenched defenders armed with machine-guns and protected by barbed-wire entanglements.

In reply to Kitchener, Sir John refused to admit that the western front was permanently deadlocked. If attacks fail, "it shows, provided that the work of the infantry and artillery has been properly coordinated, that insufficient ammunition has been expended." With an adequate supply of guns and shells he was convinced that the German line could be broken by direct assault. To conduct operations elsewhere would draw off troops from the vital theater and would play into Germany's hands. If the government insisted on a secondary front he preferred an advance into Serbia from Salonika. He repeated his argument that the best plan of all would be to attack along the coast of Flanders, in conjunction with the fleet, to drive the Germans out of Zeebrugge and Ostend. To enable him to carry out such a campaign he asked for fifty Territorial or New Army battalions, in addition to the reinforcements he had already been promised. He would also require a large supply of heavy guns and artillery shells of all kinds. Sir John concluded by saying that "there are no theatres, other than those in which operations are now in progress, in which decisive results can be attained."[11]

To ensure that his views were properly represented in the War Council Sir John sent copies of his memo directly to Churchill and the prime minister. Wilson felt that Sir John was playing a dangerous game: "I don't know what K. will do but he will seriously consider the possibility of kicking Johnnie out."[12] It was illegal for the commander-in-chief to transmit official matters to other members of the government except through the office of the secretary for war. Apart from bypassing normal channels at least one of the notes had been delivered unsealed. Asquith had the memo printed and circulated to all his cabinet ministers, whose most frequent complaint was that Kitchener kept them too much in the dark. Kitchener was furious with French and rebuked him sharply for his conduct[13]—he might have taken the extreme step had he known that Churchill had also received a copy directly from French.

Sir John offered the following explanation:

Murray did not act in accordance with my instructions which were given verbally to him—but which he seemed to clearly understand—I told him to *hand the document* to you personally telling you that to save time I had sent a copy to the Prime Minister.

I had no idea that you would horribly object to such a course of proceedings as the Prime Minister has been throughout so closely associated with our deliberations—When I came to England the other day you took me to see him immediately—I arrived and you left me alone with him for an hour.

The memorandum was placed in his hands without any comment from me whatever and simply accompanied by a note explaining the reasons. . . .

As to your postscript about the letter not being sealed, of course it should have been and I am sorry it was not. Such details are apt to be overlooked when one's mind is engaged with the command of ¼ million men in war.[14]

Sir John's military appreciation was considered in the War Council on January 7 during a review of strategic options. Kitchener's earlier enthusiasm for the Zeebrugge scheme had been transformed into hostility by French's exorbitant demands. To send out fifty battalions and to maintain them with drafts would dislocate the organization of the New Armies and so weaken the Territorial force as to render it of little value for home defense. Consequently it might necessitate holding back part of the New Armies to defend the shores of the kingdom.

Kitchener wanted his New Armies to take the field complete as large formations with their own divisional, corps, and army organization. French thought it was dangerous to employ them this way since they lacked officers trained in modern warfare. He had urged Kitchener to send them over piecemeal, by battalions or even by brigades, for incorporation into the existing cadres.[15] But Kitchener, placing great faith in the strong esprit de corps of his New Armies, was determined to preserve their unity.

The question of providing the necessary troops was not the only difficulty. As Kitchener explained to his colleagues, Sir John required, in addition, a supply of ammunition equal to fifty rounds per day per gun for a period that might reach ten or twenty days. No one could tell with certainty how long operations might last before the goal was accomplished. It was clear, however, that to break off operations owing to a lack of ammunition might lead to a defeat, even a rout, of the British forces. Every effort was being made to increase the quantities of ammunition but the result was far from sufficient to meet the demand at the front. The current rate of output was about thirteen rounds per gun per day.

Generally the scheme received a chilly reception in the War Council since nearly all the members were becoming dubious about the value of attacks on the western front. Churchill, as the joint author, naturally spoke in favor of it but his arguments were not developed with his usual skill and persuasiveness. His attention, as we shall see, was being drawn elsewhere. After the meeting Kitchener informed French that his scheme had been rejected on the grounds that the advantages would not be commensurate with the heavy losses involved.[16] In a separate note Churchill assured Sir John that "I do not think that anyone could complain of the way in which Kitchener stated your position, though the differences of view were apparent."[17]

Sir John would not accept as final the War Council's decision and, with Asquith's permission, crossed the Channel to argue his case personally. Addressing the War Council on January 13 he touched on all important questions. He observed that while the quantity of gun ammunition received had increased, the army was using less. The savings in the current consumption of ammunition, together with supplies promised from Belgium, would permit him to accumulate all the ammunition that he would need. Given a modest amount of help from the government he claimed that he could carry out the operation at a cost of no more than 8,000 casualties as compared with Kitchener's estimate of 10,000. He was convinced that German reserves of manpower were rapidly being depleted and that by October 1915 they would have to fall back on boys of sixteen to replace their casualties. French's conviction and the force of his personality made such an impression that even Kitchener began to waver. Without departing from the principle of refusing to send out fifty separate battalions, Kitchener declared that by accelerating his program he could have two Territorial divisions ready by the middle of February. To these he could add the Twenty-ninth Division and a Canadian division that had recently arrived. Would four divisions be sufficient? Sir John jumped at the offer. Thereupon the War Council agreed that arrangements should be made for an advance along the coast of Flanders but that a final decision would be postponed until February.[18]

It now remained for French to gain Joffre's acquiescence. But Joffre was not about to consent to any undertaking that did not assist his own plans.

He considered it essential to attack the Germans at the first opportunity, preferably before spring, in order to clear French territory of the invaders as well as relieve pressure on the Russians. For the moment he wanted the British to use their surplus troops to relieve his IX and XX Corps, opposite Ypres, so that he could create a reserve force. Sir John had promised to take over additional lengths of the line but soon thereafter began to waver in his commitment. This change of attitude was no doubt due to Churchill's influence. For example, Churchill wrote on January 11:

> I have received both your letters and have had a talk to [*sic*] Freddie; and in addition a long talk à trois with Gen. Murray and PM. The impression the PM and I formed was I think this:—It is attempting too much to (1) take over the Ypres salient from the French and also (2) to make the coast attack. Either may be possible, but our resources do not cover both. Of these alternatives we were not at all attracted by the first. It is a bleak and dreary rôle for the British Army simply to take over more and more of this trench warfare, so harassing to the troops and so unrelieved by any definite success. The Coast on the other hand offers not only the prospect of a definite success, but relief from a grave danger which threatens our sea-communications, etc. Therefore it seemed to us that in order to make the coast movement you ought either to make Joffre relieve you from taking over the Ypres salient, or, if you take it over, make him relieve you (say) on the point La Bassée-Armentières.[19]

The two Allied commanders met at Saint Omer on the morning of January 17. Sir John severely tried Joffre's patience by evading demands to set a date for the relief of the two French corps. Each time he shifted the conversation to his plan to take Ostend and Zeebrugge. Joffre considered that Sir John was courting disaster by attempting to carry out an extremely risky operation with insufficient forces. Sir John scoffed at the remark. Even if he failed he could not be thrown into the sea because he had command of it. They argued further but neither man would yield an inch. In the end they agreed to meet again after Joffre had put his views in writing.

Two days later Sir John convened his personal staff to discuss his proposed advance along the coast of Flanders. Murray, Wilson, and Robertson all expressed themselves as entirely opposed to the operation. "Sir J. really talked like a child,"[20] Wilson wrote in his diary, "but in the end gave up Ostend." Whatever French said it is almost certain that he had no such intention. If he had truly reversed his position he would have notified Kitchener or at the very least the first lord. No evidence to this effect has yet come to light. More important French told Haig on January 24 that he was concerting plans with the Admiralty to take Ostend and Zeebrugge and that he expected action to begin early in March.[21]

At any rate the War Council shelved the Flanders scheme during the last week in January in favor of an expedition against Turkey. Churchill had fastened on a plan to force the Dardanelles in response to a plea for urgent assistance by the Russians, hard-pressed by the Turks on the Caucasus front. The War Council agreed with the first lord that the capture of the Turkish straits would yield substantial benefits. Apart from relieving pressure on the Russians in the Caucasus it would probably induce Turkey to sue for peace, open a short and secure supply route to Russia, and serve as a stern lesson to pro-German or other wavering elements throughout the Balkans and Near East.

The awaited report from Joffre arrived at General Headquarters on the 19th, the same day that Sir John allegedly abandoned the Flanders project. In it the French commander regarded as possible, even probable, a German offensive in the near future. To prevent the enemy from piercing the line at any point as well as to continue the operations actually in progress it was necessary for him to have large reserves on hand. However, he had practically none since the German onslaught late in 1914 had compelled him to send north, in order to support the British, those army corps that would have formed such reserves. For that reason he counted on Sir John's rapid relief of the French corps around Ypres. He reminded Sir John that the objective was to achieve "a decisive result" and that all "other operations must have a secondary character and must be subordinated to it."[22]

Sir John replied that he found it difficult to understand Joffre's change of attitude regarding the situation on the western front. Three weeks ago when he raised the question, on behalf of the British government, of a possible German attack in the west the French commander had ridiculed the notion. Since then both he and his staff had studied the matter further and had concluded that the Germans did not possess the manpower to make good their losses, much less create new formations. Nonetheless he was anxious to do what he could to help the French. As soon as the reinforcements that he expected arrived from England he would relieve the two corps in question on condition that French troops take over the line now held by his I Corps.[23]

On January 21 Sir John spent the morning at Chantilly in conference with Joffre and Foch. Despite occasional differences of opinion things went smoothly for a change. Three major decisions were taken at the meeting. First, early in March Sir John was to extend his line to Ypres and so free the French IX and XX Corps. In the interim he was to loan Foch some cavalry units, which would permit him to give a portion of the IX Corps a few days' rest. Second, Joffre was to relieve the British I Corps north of La Bassée Canal. Third, the line beyond Ypres to the sea would continue to be occupied by French and Belgian troops.[24]

Sir John had no sooner resolved his differences with the French than he was forced to deal with a long-standing problem at General Headquarters. Murray's health had broken down again and French decided that the time had come to send him home.[25] Murray did not react well to the news. He insisted that with a few days' rest he would be ready to resume his duties.[26] French, however, was adamant, telling Murray that he would have to relinquish his post.[27]

To replace Murray Sir John turned to Robertson, believing that further attempts to secure government approval of Wilson would be futile. Robertson at first declined the job, even though it meant a better position and an increase in pay. Robertson subsequently explained the reasons for his action:

> I had become interested in my work, I knew that the Commander-in-Chief had previously asked for another officer to succeed Murray, which was sufficient proof that I was not his first choice, and although he had appeared quite satisfied with me as Quartermaster-General, there was no certainty that either of us would be equally happy if I became his Chief of the General Staff.[28]

Robertson, however, was circumspect in what he wrote, careful not to offend French, who was still alive when his autobiography was published in 1921. There were more compelling factors. Robertson knew himself to be totally different from the field marshal. He was secure, blunt, inarticulate, inflexible, and understood the army better than anyone else. He held a low opinion of French's professional and personal qualities as commander and doubted whether he could cope with French's shortcomings.[29] He anticipated situations arising repeatedly in which his loyalty to his superior would conflict with his judgment as chief of staff and he shrank from such a prospect.

Sir John asked Robertson to think the matter over for a day or two before rendering a final decision. Robertson changed his mind in the end, deeming it his duty to lay aside his personal fears. He accepted the post on condition that he be allowed to appoint his own men, beginning with the deputy chief of staff. "I can't stand that Henry Wilson," he said pointedly. To which French replied, "Who asked you to stand it? Take who you like!"[30] Robertson chose as his deputy Major-General Perceval, a friend and associate of long standing. Colonel F. Maurice became head of Operations Branch and Macdonogh remained as head of Intelligence. Wilson was posted as principal liaison officer with the French army. As such he remained at General Headquarters and through his personal influence with Sir John retained much of his previous control over military operations—at the expense of Robertson.

The immediate concern at General Headquarters was to devise a policy on how to best utilize the BEF during the coming months. The enemy was within striking distance of the Channel ports, the loss of which would be serious, if not irreparable, to the Allies. In case the Germans should ease up against the Russians in order to concentrate on the western front they would find the British army weak in numbers and woefully short of artillery and ammunition. The need to safeguard the Channel ports, together with the deficiencies in the British army, seemed to indicate that Sir John would have been wise to defer offensive action until such time as his needs were adequately met. Other factors, however, had to be taken into account. In the first place French considered that active operations would do much to bolster the morale of the BEF after its long and trying winter in the trenches. Moreover, the British were not conducting an independent war but fighting as an ally of Russia and France. The Russians were being hammered by the Germans and were crying for relief in the form of energetic action on the western front. A large and valuable part of French territory was in the possession of the enemy and Joffre left no doubt that he proposed to end this outrage whatever the cost. If the BEF had stood tamely on the defensive it would almost certainly have led to a breach with the French. These reasons induced Sir John to adopt an offensive policy even though the BEF was not in a condition to achieve decisive results.

Early in February French called on his army commanders to submit to him suggestions for an attack on their fronts. When the BEF was split in two at the end of 1914 Smith-Dorrien's Second Army took over the northern sector of the new front, from east of Ypres to Bois Grenier. The First Army under Haig continued the line southward from Bois Grenier to Cuinchy–La Bassée Canal, where it joined the left of de Maud'huy's Tenth Army.

Sir John studied the proposals of both Haig and Smith-Dorrien and concluded that an attack by the First Army offered greater advantages. Haig's men occupied trenches in the waterlogged valley of the Lys and the Layes. Immediately in front of them, and approached by a sloping embankment was Aubers Ridge, some twenty miles in length. Between the British line and Aubers Ridge was the village of Neuve Chapelle, strongly held by the Germans, and the Bois du Biez, a thickly forested area. The obstacles were formidable and could not be overcome without considerable losses but they would be counterbalanced by the benefits that a successful action would bring. By capturing Aubers Ridge the army would gain a drier surface, a commanding view of the area, and an admirable jumping-off place for future operations.

Apart from strategical considerations, Sir John was influenced by other motives. He believed that the quality of the troops in the First Army was superior to that of the Second Army, and he had greater confidence in Haig than in Smith-Dorrien.[31] Finally there existed the possibility of French assistance. This hope was strengthened by a note the field marshal received from Joffre on February 16, inviting the British to participate in his projected offensive.

Joffre's aim was to deliver converging blows from Artois and Champagne in order to cut the network of roads and railroads that supplied the German armies in the salient. He wanted the BEF to push towards Aubers Ridge, in cooperation with de Maud'huy's Tenth Army, next in line to the south. Assured that Sir John would consent to the attack, Joffre proposed to modify the arrangement made between them at Chantilly on January 21. He observed that the British I Corps should remain in its position north of the canal. This would simplify matters for the XX Corps, which instead of moving to take over the front of the British I Corps, might remain where it was. But he insisted that Sir John free the French IX Corps near Ypres so that he could reinforce de Maud'huy's front.[32] The request seemed fair since, in addition to the recent growth of the BEF, the First Canadian Division and the Twenty-ninth Division, the last of the regular divisions, were scheduled to disembark in France in February.

Sir John welcomed the proposal to extend the offensive front although he did not feel that he could meet Joffre's demand to relieve the IX Corps. Kitchener had just informed him that the Twenty-ninth Division was no longer available and that, as a substitute, he was sending him the Forty-sixth (North Midland Territorial) Division. Sir John considered that the Territorial troops were of doubtful quality and would require weeks of training before they could be put into the trenches. The other division about to arrive in France, the First Canadian, was due to take over a sector of the First Army's battle-front so as to permit Haig to effectively cooperate with de Maud'huy's army. French was certain that he did not have sufficient troops on hand to simultaneously launch an offensive and prolong his line. Of the two alternatives French chose the former, suggesting to Joffre that the relief of the IX Corps should be delayed until after the combined assault had been carried out.[33]

Joffre explained once more that the support of the IX Corps was essential for the offensive by the Tenth Army. Without the additional troops de Maud'huy's reserves would be inadequate to undertake an "efficacious operation." Joffre made it clear that de Maud'huy's attack was conditional on the British taking over the IX Corps's front-line trenches. He went on to say that the British currently occupied a front of fifty kilometers with about twelve divisions while the French Tenth Army held the same length of front with only eight divisions. Therefore it appeared to him that even without the Twenty-ninth Division the British could do both, i.e., relieve the IX Corps and contribute to his general offensive.[34]

Joffre was not a tactful man and, in proving it again, he only weakened his case by arousing French's anger. "The letter from Joffre was a stupid one," Wilson observed, "inaccurate in some important details and rather hectoring in tone."[35] Sir John's reply on February 23 was equally blunt. He claimed it was on the assumption that the Canadian and the Twenty-ninth Divisions would be available by a certain date that he had consented to take over a sector of the French line. However, the Canadian Division did not arrive until February 19 (ten days late) and the Twenty-ninth Division was diverted elsewhere, a move which he unfairly implied that Joffre had endorsed. Since these conditions had not been fulfilled, "the agreement necessarily falls to the ground, and becomes quite impossible to carry out." French tried to refute Joffre's charges that the British line was overmanned. He contended that of the 350,000 British troops referred to, some 75,000 were either in the base hospital, drafts to replace casualties, or employed on various duties on the lines of communication, and therefore not available for service at the front. He added that the number of troops required to hold a front did not depend solely upon its length but upon other factors such as the character of the ground, the numbers and condition of the enemy, and the amount of artillery ammunition available. He ended by saying that he hoped to take the offensive around March 7 and that if in the meantime Joffre wished to discuss any points further, he would be happy to arrange an interview.[36]

But Joffre was so bitter over French's haggling that he refused to personally pursue the matter. Wilson tried to dissipate the growing tension between the two headquarters lest it lead to an open rupture. He visited Foch and explained what had happened. Foch promised to do what he could to soothe his chief's feelings but wondered if the time had not come to draw the curtain on Sir John's act. Wilson recorded the following in his diary:

> Foch told me de Broqueville[37] had come to see him at 9 A.M. on Sunday to tell him that K. had sent for him and told him that he (K) was sick of sending troops to Sir J., that he never puts up a fight and so mismanaged his troops that he squandered all his reinforcements. De Broqueville went on to Chantilly to tell Joffre. In short—Foch much doubts whether Sir J. is worth keeping, and thinks it quite possible Joffre might say so to his Government. As Foch said: "We have saved him once [but] I doubt if he is worth saving again."[38]

Robertson at first sided with Sir John but, upon examining the available resources, came to believe, as did Wilson, that the withholding of the Twenty-ninth Division by the War Office should not prevent the British from relieving some French troops in the Ypres region. How then does Robertson explain French's refusal to accommodate Joffre? Sir John's attitude, Robertson confided to Hankey, was attributable primarily to remarks made by Churchill during a recent visit to the front. There is the following entry in Hankey's diary:

> Churchill . . . visited French and seems to have told him that Joffre and Millerand were conspiring against him and aimed at having him placed under Joffre's orders. Then the Zeebrugge offensive was thrown out by the War Council, and the 29th Division, which was to have been sent out to render this movement possible, was . . . replaced by the North Midland

Territorial Division. Joffre, hearing of this, pressed French, notwithstanding the abandonment of the Zeebrugge project, to relieve the two French Army Corps in order to render their offensive possible. French, however, declined to do this, partly because he did not know whether he could rely on the North Midland Territorials, but mainly, I gathered, because he was disquieted with what Churchill had told him of Joffre.[39]

Robertson's testimony normally stands up under close scrutiny but when it involves Churchill he is inclined to place the worst possible interpretation on his conduct. Robertson, like nearly all the staff officers at General Headquarters, hated Churchill, partly because of his reputation for thoughtless, precipitate action, and to a greater extent because of his arrogant assumption of military expertise that in fact he lacked. Whether or not one chooses to believe Robertson's charges about Churchill, it does appear he was correct in saying that the failure of certain reinforcements to arrive was not instrumental in Sir John's decision to renege on his agreement with Joffre. If manpower had been the key factor Sir John undoubtedly would have informed Kitchener of the reason why it was so vital to send over the Twenty-ninth Division. He made no attempt to do this.

In fact it was Kitchener who asked French whether the absence of the Twenty-ninth Division was likely to have an appreciable effect on his future plan. Kitchener was under pressure from the War Council to divert the Twenty-ninth Division to the Dardanelles and before making a final decision he wanted additional information on Sir John's forthcoming attack. He wired General Headquarters on February 24:

As the War Council is to discuss the sending of the 29th Division to the Near East on Friday, I think it would be advisable to give me some information of the scope of the joint operations you refer to. Can you give me some details?[40]

Sir John replied immediately:

I hope you and [the] government will not press me for this information. In my opinion any such communication must detract from our object. In the kind of war we are waging arrangements have to be made so long before the actual commencement of operations that it is difficult to keep plans secret. The 29th Division would add materially to [the] degree of success attained.[41]

Because of his strained relations with French Kitchener made no attempt to intervene in the actual planning of the joint offensive. He did, however, hint through de Broqueville that the assault should be launched along a broad front at night and without a preliminary bombardment in order to reduce casualties and achieve surprise. The idea met an icy response in

France. Foch, in an obvious reference to Kitchener's Sudanese campaign, told Wilson: "You would think from Lord K.'s proposal that we were fighting negroes and not Germans." Sir John's reply took on a more personal tone. Wilson recorded the following entry in his diary: "Sir J. was, as usual, loud in his abuse of K.; said he would gladly put him up against a wall and shoot him."[42]

De Brocqueville's mission was not an absolute failure because he did learn of the details of the joint offensive, which he included in a note to Kitchener. The feeling in London was that the Allied attack, like the previous ones, would accomplish little and that it was pointless to pile up reserves in France. On February 27 Kitchener notified Sir John that the Twenty-ninth Division was going to be utilized in the Dardanelles. He added that since the French were also sending a division there it was evident that they considered the home front safe. Unknown to Kitchener the French division destined for the Near East was not a regular one, but rather consisted of troops drawn from the depots in France and North Africa.[43]

Sir John, believing that the French had more reserves than they had acknowledged previously, now indicated that they should reoccupy some trenches that his cavalry had taken over from them several weeks before. Joffre was already bitter towards Sir John and this latest demand threw him into a fit of fury. Sidney Clive was present on one occasion when Joffre vented his spleen against Sir John. He began by saying that he was fed up with French, calling him, among other thing, "*menteur et mauvais camarade.*" Clive's recollection of what transpired continues:

> Evidently the two things which he [Joffre] felt most deeply were a sentence in the last letter from G.H.Q. which said that the non-arrival of the 29th Division was "presumably with his approbation" and the refusal to give his IX Corps a bit of a rest by taking over a bit of the trenches with our cavalry.[44]

Joffre sought Kitchener's intervention in the hope of resolving the temporary crisis in Anglo-French relations. In a note to Millerand he explained that Sir John had refused to relieve the French IX Corps on the grounds that his reinforcements were of inferior quality. He asked Millerand to appeal personally to Kitchener in order to obtain the dispatch of the Twenty-ninth Division to France. Joffre considered that Kitchener's attention should be drawn to the following points: (1) that the French troops being assembled for the Dardanelles had not been removed from the western front; (2) that all his reserves were currently employed in Champagne, where heavy fighting was in progress; (3) that he could not deliver his offensive in the north, the object of which was to support Sir John's operation at La Bassée, unless his IX Corps was relieved.[45]

Millerand forwarded the French commander's note to the War Office, suggesting that Sir John should be placed under Joffre's orders in the interest of achieving unity of direction.[46] Kitchener sent a conciliatory reply, expressing astonishment that any friction should have arisen between Joffre and Sir John. He regretted that he was obliged to divert the Twenty-ninth Division to the Dardanelles but in its place he was sending an equally competent unit, the North Midland Territorials. Kitchener added that Sir John had said nothing to him about the combined offensive beyond mentioning it in one of his dispatches. He went on to describe Sir John's subsequent refusal to supply precise details of the attack, a response that he attributed to advice from Joffre. Kitchener asked to be kept informed of Joffre's future plans so that he would be in a better position to meet his needs.[47]

At the same time Kitchener informed French that he had received from Millerand a letter that contained a number of complaints from Joffre. The secretary for war questioned Sir John's decision not to relieve the French IX Corps in view of the large number of reinforcements that were being sent over to France. He continued:

> The Prime Minister was somewhat astonished after your remarks about the excellence of the Territorial troops at the War Council to read General Joffre's statement giving your opinion of their inferior quality.
> We were both interested to learn that the forthcoming operations are to be at La Bassée and Arras and hope you will do your utmost to make them successful. It is very important of course that your cooperation with Joffre should be as close as possible and that you should do everything in your power to carry out his wishes.[48]

In reply French claimed that the government's decision to send a Territorial division, instead of the Twenty-ninth, had led him to go back on his agreement with Joffre. He felt that it was impossible to carry out with a Territorial division what he had proposed to do with a regular one. He would write to the prime minister to explain why he considered it unsafe to put an untried unit on its first arrival into a very critical and vulnerable part of the line and to assure him that such a decision in no way detracted from his high opinion of the Territorials as expressed in his dispatches. As to his relations with Joffre they had always been most intimate and cordial. There were, of course, occasional differences of opinion but they never quarrelled and French had no idea how it ever came to Millerand that they did.[49]

The field marshal apparently had not appreciated the depth of Joffre's resentment against him. On February 28 Haig, after an interview with de Maud'huy, notified General Headquarters that "our proposed offensive action must be considered an entirely independent operation."[50] This was confirmed by both Clive and Wilson. But Sir John discounted these reports and took it for granted that the Tenth Army would participate in the attack.[51] A letter from the French commander-in-chief on March 7 destroyed his misconceptions. In it Joffre wished Sir John luck in the attack he contemplated on the 10th,[52] but as his IX Corps had not been relieved by the BEF, he could no longer undertake the Arras offensive.[53] Disappointed but not bitter, Sir John told Mrs. Bennett:

> The Frenchmen are gloriously brave and I love them but their leaders try me very hard sometimes. They always look at things from their own point of view and subsequently expect me to do the impossible. . . . They've put me in the cart badly once or twice before and I don't mean to let them do it again.[54]

When Joffre indicated that he could no longer adhere to his side of the arrangement, Sir John, instead of canceling his plans as well, resolved to act independently. His motives were twofold: to show the condescending Frenchmen that the British army was capable of pulling its own weight, and to prove to the skeptical authorities at home that the German army could be beaten. He assured Asquith that he expected to make "good progress"[55] and in letters to Mrs. Bennet expressed himself in similar terms.[56] French saw the assault at Neuve Chapelle as the prelude to a larger battle that would end with the retreat of the German army from France.[57] French had little cause for such optimism. His requests for large guns and lavish supplies of artillery ammunition had only been partially met; in fact he barely had enough shells for one week's heavy fighting.[58] Moreover, the Germans, now that the French had pulled out of the operation, would be able to concentrate all their reserves in the area against Haig's First Army.

The battle of Neuve Chapelle lasted three days, March 10–13, and was the first major British offensive against an organized trench system. Under the direction of Haig and his staff, preparations had started in the last days of February. A number of new techniques were introduced. Models of enemy defenses based on aerial photographs were erected behind the front, enabling the assaulting troops to rehearse the attack in detail. Officers were issued maps showing the German trench network. Each battery was assigned its target and timetable for the battle. Experiments were carried out in rear areas with live shells against specially made entanglements. As the instantaneous fuse had not yet been perfected, the conclusion was that shrapnel was more effective than high-explosive shell in cutting lanes through wire. The duration of the bombardment was fixed at thirty-five minutes, which was considered sufficient to cut wire and destroy trenches.

The methods used to dislodge the Germans at Neuve Chapelle became standard pattern for almost every British attack up to the end of 1916. The idea was to soften up an enemy position for a set length of time, by the end of which it was calculated that the assaulting infantry would have almost reached it. The artillery would then lengthen its range on the next objective and so on. Haig envisaged a battle of three stages, each to succeed the other rapidly but methodically.

Haig had no illusions about achieving a major victory, much less a breakthrough. But tactically he saw that there was a chance of breaking into the German position, widening this gap by vigorous and sustained pressure, and gaining Aubers Ridge. Haig knew that the Germans had reduced their strength in the west in anticipation of their grand offensive against Russia in the late spring. As it turned out, the Germans, perhaps because of a low regard for the offensive abilities of the British army, had denuded their front in that sector to an even greater degree than elsewhere. Only two German divisions lay opposite the six divisions of the First Army on the thirteen-mile frontage from La Bassée Canal to Bois Grenier.

The opening blow was to fall on a slight German salient in front of the ruins of Neuve Chapelle. The assault here was to be carried out on a front of 2,000 yards by two army corps of Haig's First Army, the IV Corps under Rawlinson and the Indian Corps under Willcocks—in all, forty-eight battalions (40,000 men), supported by 372 guns. Close behind was a cavalry corps, ready to exploit any gap in the line. To defend this sector the Germans had only six companies, approximately 1,400 men, with a dozen machine-guns between them. They had begun a secondary defensive line a thousand yards behind the front system but, apart from a few strong points, it was incomplete.[59] British intelligence estimated that the Germans could bring up no more than 4,000 reinforcements within twelve hours and a further 16,000 by the evening of the second day. This forecast proved to be essentially correct.

In view of Haig's enormous superiority in numbers, particularly as Intelligence reports advised him that he could count on a ratio of at least two to one as late as forty-eight hours after the battle commenced, one might question the wisdom of attacking on a front as narrow as that selected. At a conference at Haig's headquarters on February 26 Allenby proposed that the assault should be on a broader front so as to avoid a bottleneck during the follow-through. Haig dismissed his suggestions out of hand, reminding him of his "unfamiliarity with commanding masses of infantry."

At precisely 7:30 A.M. the silence was rent by a roar of over 350 guns.[60] The thirty-five minute bombardment was extremely effective in most places along the German line, blowing entanglements to pieces, leveling trenches beyond recognition, and leaving such defenders as had survived too dazed and unnerved to offer much resistance. At 8:05 A.M., while the artillery lifted 300 yards further, the British infantry clambered out of the trenches and into No Man's Land. Three brigades, one from the Indian

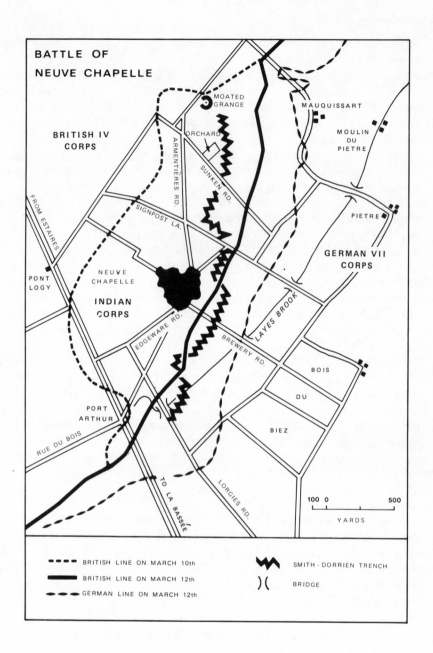

BATTLE OF
NEUVE CHAPELLE

BRITISH IV
CORPS

MOATED
GRANGE

MAUQUISSART

ORCHARD

MOULIN
DU
PIETRE

ARMENTIERES RD.

SUNKEN RD.

SIGNPOST LA.

PIETRE

FROM ESTAIRES

GERMAN VII
CORPS

PONT
LOGY

NEUVE
CHAPELLE

INDIAN
CORPS

LAYES BROOK

EDGEWARE RD.

BREWERY RD.

BOIS

DU

PORT
ARTHUR

BIEZ

RUE DU BOIS

TO LA BASSEE

LORGIES RD.

100 0   500

YARDS

- - - - BRITISH LINE ON MARCH 10th

━━━━ BRITISH LINE ON MARCH 12th

━ ● ━ GERMAN LINE ON MARCH 12th

〰〰 SMITH-DORRIEN TRENCH

)(BRIDGE

Corps and two from the IV Corps, made up the leading wave. They were from right to left, the Garhwal Brigade, the Twenty-fifth Brigade, and the Twenty-third Brigade.

In the center the Twenty-fifth Brigade swept forward practically unopposed, advancing beyond Neuve Chapelle to the so-called Smith-Dorrien trench—a line that the British had built during the fighting in the autumn of 1914. However, on the flanks the assaulting forces encountered difficulties almost immediately. On the extreme right one battalion of the Garhwal Brigade lost direction in the early morning mist and instead of advancing straight to its front bore too far to the south and so came up against a portion of the German defenses that had not been subjected to the preliminary bombardment. At the other end hastily built gun platforms had caused inaccurate fire, leaving German defenses practically intact. Advancing along a 200-yard front, the forward lines of the Second Middlesex were annihilated to a man. Both brigades showed great gallantry in recovering from early setbacks and 1:00 P.M. they had reached their initial objectives.

At this point things began to go wrong. Through inadequate communications, excessive caution, and heightening congestion behind the front, the opportunity to exploit a clear break in the German line was lost. The two corps commanders, unaware that the flanks were secure or that the way ahead was clear, were unwilling to risk a further advance. It was not until 5:30 P.M. that the attack was resumed. British inactivity for nearly five hours gave the Germans time to establish a reserve line and to organize fresh resistance. The British had not gone far when they were held up, forcing them to dig in as night came on.

Haig hoped to push home his attack next day when British artillery could be brought to bear on the new German position. The morning of March 11 broke dull and misty, impeding observation and registration of targets. Gunners were able to lay down only a blind fire with the result that much of the enemy's line escaped untouched. Repeated attacks made in the morning and afternoon were repulsed with heavy losses. The prospects of gaining further ground were negligible. British artillery was no longer effective, the infantry was exhausted, and the enemy, having received substantial reinforcements from adjacent parts of the line, was five times as numerous as on the previous day. Haig, however, was determined to push on to his final objective, Aubers Ridge. Throughout the night of 11th/12th the Germans massed twenty battalions, approximately 16,000 men, and launched a counterattack at dawn. A thick mist effectively covered the advancing German lines from view until they were within sixty yards of the British position. And yet everywhere they were hurled back after leaving hundreds of fallen comrades in front of the British trenches.

The confusion at the front, combined with poor visibility, delayed accurate reports from getting back to First Army Headquarters and prevented

Haig from immediately following up the enemy's repulse. Precious morning hours slipped by before the British attack was actually set in motion. As the mist had nullified the effectiveness of the bombardment, heavy losses were at once incurred and in less than two hours the advance was checked with gains measured literally in yards. During the evening Haig received information that the Germans had constructed a new position east of Neuve Chapelle that they were holding in strength. At 10:40 P.M. he decided to break off the engagement. In all the British had penetrated to a depth of 1,000 yards on a front of a mile and a quarter, barely denting the German line. The casualties were about equal with between 12,000 and 13,000 on both sides.

As the first British attack against a trench system in the war, Neuve Chapelle provided many valuable lessons. It showed that an attack must be made on a front sufficiently wide to prevent the defender's artillery commanding, or his reserves closing, the breach; and that initial successes must be rapidly followed up, that units must not stop if those on their flank are held up. It also demonstrated the limitations imposed on a commander once the battle had gotten under way. The part played by weather conditions, especially by the mist; the difficulties of maintaining communications between headquarters and the front line because of the vulnerability of telephone wires under shell fire; the problems of getting reinforcements to the required place; the danger from machine-gun nests that had escaped the bombardment—all these combined to upset even a well-laid plan.

Officially French gave a different explanation as to why his offensive had failed to break the German line. On March 18 he informed the War Office that:

If the supply of ammunition cannot be maintained on a considerably increased scale it follows that the offensive efforts of the Army must be spasmodic and separated by a considerable interval of time. They cannot, therefore, lead to decisive results.[61]

French's allegation of a shell shortage was a "perfect excuse for failure," enabling him to shift the responsibility from his shoulders onto those of Kitchener and his political colleagues.[62] By arguing that they had denied him the means to do the job he was effectively preempting them from passing judgment on his leadership and claiming that the western front was deadlocked. French recognized that the setback at Neuve Chapelle was due to reasons not related to the supply of ammunition and he admitted as much in private.[63]

Neuve Chapelle convinced French that in addition to an ample provision of shells, the need for accurate registration of enemy positions by the artillery was a vital ingredient if he was to succeed.[64] His new recipe for victory was an improvement over the army's prewar doctrine of attack but it was not a solution to the tactical problems of the western front. To be sure, intensity and accuracy of firepower were essential both to destroy the wire obstacles and the machine-gun posts that formed the backbone of the defense. But battles, even later in the war, were not won by relying upon the use and weight of artillery but upon a host of other considerations as well. Throughout the remainder of 1915 French and Haig clung to the illusion that given a limitless supply of guns and ammunition they could blast a way through the enemy line. This view militated against the study of tactics and turned the war into a contest more of blind military force than astute reasoning.

11

On Trial

If the battle of Neuve Chapelle was not a strategic success it did at least prove that the British army—given the telling results of the preliminary bombardment, the break-in, the spirit and determination of the infantry— could act effectively in offense as well as in defense. Hitherto Joffre and his generals had looked to the British mainly to take over additional lengths of the frontage, thus relieving French troops for offensive action. The role of the British army in attack had been as a secondary and subsidiary part of French activities. After Neuve Chapelle, however, the BEF was seen as an efficient instrument of war and it was asked to take an ever-increasing share in offensive movements.

During the third week of March Joffre was forced to admit that his operations in Champagne had failed, despite the deluge of shelling and the astounding élan of the French infantry. Joffre's confidence was not dimmed, however, and he proposed to try again in that quarter. In a letter sent to General Headquarters dated March 24, he resumed negotiations, abruptly broken off a fortnight before, for an Anglo-French offensive to cut into the great German salient. Joffre concluded from the experience of the recent fighting, both on the French and British fronts, the following:

> In a war such as we are now engaged in, where the enemy occupies defensive positions organized in the strongest manner, and, in addition, has sufficient men and material for an energetic defence, our offensive can only succeed under the following conditions:
>
> (1) The greatest vigour and rapidity of action based on surprise and covering a sufficiently large front.
>
> (2) Possession, on this front, of the necessary numerical superiority.
>
> (3) The possession and full use of all necessary material both for the destruction of supplementary defences and for the "close in" fighting.
>
> (4) The possession of large reserves of ammunition both for field and heavy guns.

Joffre estimated that he would be in a position to fulfill these conditions by the end of April and he asked Sir John to cooperate in his projected offensive. He expected to inflict "such a blow on the enemy that the greatest results may follow and that our movement may be an important step towards the final victory." With a view to free more reserves Joffre requested that the British should relieve the French IX and XX corps north of Ypres as soon as possible.[1]

Sir John delayed sending a reply since he did not wish to make comprehensive commitments until he knew for certain that the necessary resources would be available. Men and munitions were being diverted to the new theater in the Dardanelles and during the month of March only one division had landed in France. Sir John could get no information from London as to when the New Armies would be sent, or even if they were to be sent at all. It seemed to some at General Headquarters that the British government was departing from its original policy, that is, to liberate Belgium and defeat the German army.

The prospect that the main British effort might be shifted to the Mediterranean horrified Sir John. Initially, however, he had approved of the Admiralty's proposal to send ships to force a passage through the Dardanelles. "I hope the Navy will get on quickly with the Dardanelles business," he confided to Winifred Bennett. "It will make an enormous difference and settle old Constantinople for good and all."[2] French's outlook changed abruptly when the naval attack failed and the War Council decided to stage a land invasion. He correctly saw that the new field operations would absorb manpower and material resources that otherwise would be sent to France. He told Mrs. Bennett, "We certainly made a hideous mistake in getting mixed up there at all. I was *dead against it* but they wouldn't listen to me."[3] A month later he was no less emphatic:

> We were absolutely mad to embark on the infernal Dardanelles expedition. It is the very thing the Germans would have wished us to do. Certainly if we win this war it will not be on account of our Great strategic combinations.[4]

During the latter part of March French arranged to meet Kitchener at Dover in the hope of eliciting from him a firm commitment reaffirming the priority of the western front. Kitchener was in a bad mood when he boarded the *Attention* shortly after it docked. He did not think that French had been justified in attacking Aubers Ridge without French support. Apart from the cost in casualties, Haig's offensive had expended 100,000 rounds, or nearly one-sixth of the amount available for the entire BEF.

French discussed the recent battle and placed most of the blame on the corps commanders for the failure to follow up initial successes. He vowed to repair the errors and to do better next time. French also alluded to his strained relations with Joffre. The crux of the problem, he observed, was that the French commander had a tendency to treat him like a corporal.[5]

Kitchener told Sir John that the army's demands for shells were greatly in excess of production and he emphasized the need for stringent economy. He warned that if the BEF continued to expend artillery shells at the current rate he would consider employing the New Armies in a theater of war where the ammunition requirements would not be as great.

Sir John replied that no one at the War Office seemed to appreciate the nature of modern warfare. The current state of deadlock was due, not to a single army or nation, but to the destructive power of modern armaments. The old forms of attack and defense were of the past. The New Armies would encounter the same conditions as presently existed in France, regardless of where they were employed. The only way to rupture the enemy's front was with an unlimited artillery barrage.

Kitchener remained unconvinced but he said no more on the subject. Instead he spoke of an invitation he had received from Joffre to visit him at Chantilly. Kitchener was disinclined to go, but Asquith and Grey were adamant in thinking he should. After some discussion with French, Kitchener decided he should meet Joffre. French inquired if he could be present at the talks. Kitchener replied that it was up to Joffre.[6] When Kitchener left, French started back, reaching Saint Omer at 3:00 A.M. on March 25.

Joffre indicated that Sir John was welcome to attend the Anglo-French conference, which was set for March 29.[7] On the 28th French sent Wilson to G.Q.G. to coach Joffre "in the line he must take if he wants me to carry out the role laid down by his letter of 24th."[8] Joffre was to try to make Kitchener understand the difficulties of waging modern warfare; the danger of becoming seriously involved in secondary theaters of war; the enormous amount of ammunition required in preparing infantry attacks; and the necessity of a prolonged battle to expel the Germans from French and Belgian soil. After Wilson conveyed the message Joffre suddenly announced that in the interest of unity of command, he would propose that the British army be placed under his orders. Wilson observed that if Joffre were in a position to direct the BEF he must also be empowered to remove any subordinate commander he judged to be incompetent. Since the British government was unlikely to sanction such an arrangement Wilson felt that the matter should not even be mentioned. Joffre grudgingly agreed.[9]

The conference opened in mid-morning on the 29th and lasted three hours. Kitchener's immediate concern was to protect Holland against a possible German attack. He stated that he had heard rumors that Germany would soon invade Holland so as to acquire new naval bases and "have more elbow room in Belgium." In such an event he favored sending large detachments to assist the Dutch and using Holland as the main base of operations. Joffre adamantly opposed the suggestion. He insisted that France was the decisive theater and he required every available soldier and round of ammunition. He was convinced that the German line could be broken if the Allies coordinated their efforts properly. He went on to explain the peculiar nature of the present war, observing that massive bombardment was a prerequisite to any successful attack. Kitchener claimed that although he had increased output by three hundred percent he was not able to meet the army's demands for shells. He dwelled on his labor problems that, he stressed, prevented him from providing more ammunition. He said that a sensible system of industrial conscription would have avoided this difficulty.

The date for the next big attack was tentatively set for May 1. Kitchener promised to send two additional Territorial divisions within three weeks. This would enable Sir John to carry out the promised relief of the French IX and XX corps, providing Foch with the needed reserves for the offensive. The meeting ended cordially and the British representatives were invited to stay for lunch.[10]

Before returning to Saint Omer Sir John spoke briefly with Kitchener and it was agreed that they would meet again in London on the 31st to discuss the results of the conference. French was accompanied by Brinsley Fitzgerald when he crossed the Channel on the morning of the 30th. He arrived in London around 1:00 P.M. and spent the rest of the day with "Wendy" (Mrs. Bennett). Next morning he went to York House to keep his appointment with Lord Kitchener.

Kitchener left no doubt that he considered both French and Joffre to be on trial. If within the next month or six weeks they showed that they could make a substantial advance he would support them with all the forces he could collect. If on the other hand they failed, he would look elsewhere to employ the New Armies. "I told him that I thought that he had put the matter very fairly and that I was content to accept what he said,"[11] Sir John wrote in his diary.

The future course of Britain's military policy now rested in French's hands. The operations in the Dardanelles were not going well and Churchill was urging the dispatch of further reinforcements for a greater effort. Lloyd George was still nursing hopes for an expedition to the Balkans. Any diversions to the Near East could only be made at the expense of the army in France. Kitchener was hesitant in shaping a policy, caught as he was between the two schools of military thought. But a real victory in Flanders would settle the much-disputed question in favor of the Westerners. It would also reestablish Sir John's reputation, justify his forecasts and disarm his critics.

From the moment Sir John returned to Saint Omer he devoted himself to preparing for what he called the "big operation." On April 1 he wrote to Joffre, stating that he had ordered an extension of the British line as far north as the Ypres-Poelcappelle road, to be completed no later than April 20. He added that he expected to be in a position to cooperate in the projected combined offensive at the end of April with the whole First Army, which would then have a strength of eight divisions.[12]

The relief of the French troops north of Ypres was carried out without incident by the newly formed British V Corps under General Herbert Plumer. The V Corps, which consisted of the First Canadian Division as well as the Twenty-seventh and Twenty-eighth divisions, held a ten-mile front, from Saint Eloi in the south to the Ypres-Poelcappelle road in the north. On its left stood two French divisions, the Forty-fifth Algerian and the Eighty-seventh Territorial, commanded by General Putz.

On April 14 French troops near Langemarck captured a German prisoner who stated that an attack, arranged for the night of the 15th/16th, would be preceded by asphyxiating gas released from cylinders in the trenches. The prisoner had in his possession one of the crude respirators issued to the German troops. Putz was sceptical about this very circumstantial information, which he nonetheless passed on to British Second Army Headquarters. The next day a squadron of the Royal Flying Corps was ordered over the German lines to verify the presence of any special apparatus or concentration of troops. Its reconnaissance failed to discover anything unusual in the trenches. No attack took place on the night mentioned (April 15 had originally been fixed as the date of the gas attack but it was altered to await a favorable wind). The British at all levels of command were no more inclined to believe the story than Putz, despite a fresh warning from Belgian authorities on April 16. Consequently no precautions against a gas attack were ordered or even suggested.

At 5:00 P.M. on April 22 the Germans opened a sudden and furious bombardment on Ypres and the villages northeast of it.[13] From the German trenches, opposite the French sector, there appeared two wraiths of greenish-yellow fog that spread laterally, joined up, and before a light wind crept forward across No Man's Land. As the deadly fumes reached the Algerians they suddenly clutched their throats and began coughing and vomiting; many fell to the sodden ground, their limbs writhing and features distorted in death. These troops were not of the highest quality and they had no inkling that the enemy might use gas. Horrified by the sight of death and torture in their ranks, those who were not asphyxiated at once turned and fled towards Ypres and the canal, pointing to their throats and uttering the word "gas." They carried the Territorials with them in their panic and by nightfall a four-mile gap had been opened in the line.

If the Germans had pressed their advantage with their usual fanatical ardor they could not have failed to take Ypres and so cut off all the British troops in the salient to the south. But von Falkenhayn merely intended to try the gas as an experiment and no reserves were held ready to exploit success. No special tactics were devised and only limited objectives were set. The attacking troops advanced two miles when they stumbled into their own cloud of gas (many had not bothered to wear their crude respirators)

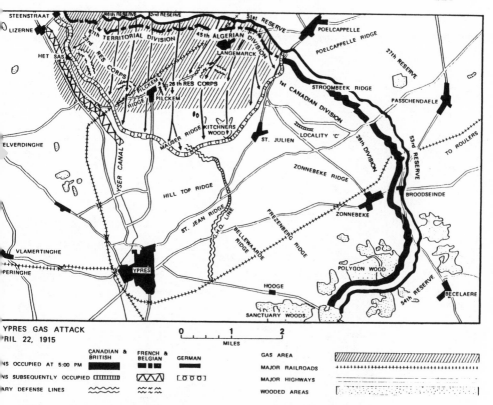

YPRES GAS ATTACK
APRIL 22, 1915

	CANADIAN & BRITISH	FRENCH & BELGIAN	GERMAN		
POSITIONS OCCUPIED AT 5:00 PM	▓	▪▪▪		GAS AREA	▨
POSITIONS SUBSEQUENTLY OCCUPIED	▥	⟋⟍	⟦ōōō⟧	MAJOR RAILROADS	+++++
PRIMARY DEFENSE LINES	∿	∿		MAJOR HIGHWAYS	---
				WOODED AREAS	⟦∴∴⟧

0   1   2
MILES

and cautiously held back. Failure to go beyond allotted objectives prevented the Germans from discovering how completely resistance had disappeared. Over the next few days, while Ypres still lay practically open to them, they were content to move forward only so far as artillery and gas had prepared the way.

The nearest British contingent was the First Canadian Division, which had arrived in France in February. The Canadians had been unaffected by the gas and they had sufficient reserves to extend their line several thousand yards in a southwest direction. When the leading German units brushed against the thin Canadian line they were met with rapid fire and avalanches of shrapnel. The stout resistance offered by the Canadians no doubt was a factor in the German decision to halt and dig in.

Sir John had remained at his command post, anxiously reviewing the piece-meal reports that trickled in during the afternoon and night. Hardly an hour passed when he did not revile the French for having given way. "Although the gas no doubt had something to do with the panic," Sir John later wrote to Lord Kitchener, "this would never have happened if the French had not weakened their line a good deal too much."[14] This time the field marshal's criticism was justified. He had in earlier conversations with

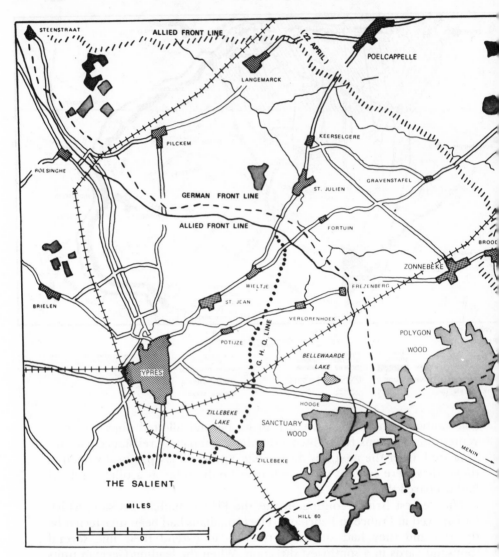

Foch and Joffre expressed misgivings about the quality of the French units that covered the left of the BEF in the salient. The French made no effort to replace or strengthen these second-rate troops, perhaps because they hoped to induce the British to take over that section of the line.

By dawn on April 23 there were bodies of troops amounting to some ten battallions strung out along the gap. But the crisis was not over yet. At 4:00 A.M. on the 24th the Germans, after a violent one-hour artillery cannonade, released chlorine gas against the sharp apex of the Canadian front. Driven by the dawn breeze the gas cloud, fifteen feet high, came on rapidly like a fog bank. The men had no protection but handkerchiefs, towels, and cotton bandoliers soaked with water and urine. Many succumbed to the fumes and fell into the pit of the trench but those that were still able to fight manned the parapet and repeatedly emptied their Ross rifles into the advancing enemy. The Canadians heroically clung to a vital sector of the British front in the face of an almost certain and particularly ugly death. Eventually they were compelled to withdraw the left of their line to less vulnerable positions. But by the time the movement was completed British reinforcements had begun to arrive from further south. Ypres was saved by the desperate efforts of the British and Canadians.

Nevertheless German action on the 24th had reduced the salient to a narrow tongue of land, barely three miles across. French was eager to pull his men back since they provided an easy harvest for the German guns. On the other hand Foch wanted to recapture the lost ground before the Germans could consolidate their position and bring up their artillery. With assurances that large reinforcements were on the way, Foch persuaded the field marshal to cooperate in immediate counterattacks. Foch promised much more than he could deliver. The two French divisions (the Forty-fifth and Eighty-seventh Territorial) were in terrible confusion and had lost many of their officers and nearly all their artillery. Contrary to what Foch implied, there were no reserve units in the immediate vicinity. The result was that General Putz was constantly issuing orders for attacks that either did not take place or were carried out in such a half-hearted fashion that they broke down on meeting the slightest resistance.

Unsupported, French ordered his men to counterattack across open ground against an enemy firmly ensconced in the surrounding heights. A soldier who was present has left us a vivid picture of the fighting: "When dawn broke . . . it was evident enough that we were all in the hallow of a great bowl, with the Germans sitting on the rim and shooting at us." The losses were appalling even by the standards of the Great War. By the evening of the 25th the Canadians alone has lost 200 officers and 5,000 other ranks.

Smith-Dorrien realized that the current policy of fragmentary attacks was both futile and costly. Experience had shown him that nothing but a carefully prepared and vigorous offensive could possibly expel the Germans from the ground they had gained and had been steadily fortifying for several nights. No such effort could be contemplated in his sector. The British and French high commands were organizing a great offensive in Artois and neither Sir John nor Foch was inclined to risk the chances of success by diverting reinforcements for local counterattacks. Yet without additional resources it made no sense even to remain in the salient. The Germans had artillery observation of all the rearward communications and movement in and out of the salient was becoming increasingly dificult, even at night.

During the morning of the 27th Smith-Dorrien communicated to General Headquarters (addressed to Robertson) a note summing up the military situation and recommending a withdrawal from the narrow exposed salient to a straight line covering Ypres and the canal. Towards the end of the afternoon Smith-Dorrien received a reply directing him to hand over to General Plumer forthwith the command of all the troops engaged around Ypres. No reason or explanation was offered. Sir John wrote in his diary on the 27th:

> Smith-Dorrien has, since the commencement of these operations, failed to get a real grip of the situation. He has been very unwise and tactless in his dealings with General Putz. He has acted quite against the instructions I have given him. . . . His messages are all wordy—and unintelligible. His pessimistic attitude has the worst effect on his commanders and their troops, and today he wrote a letter to Robertson which was full of contradictions and altogether bewildering. I have therefore been obliged to take the command of and Ypres operations out of his hands.[15]

These charges have been refuted convincingly by Smith-Dorrien's biographers and do not bear reexamination.[16] The plain truth is that Sir John had never forgiven Smith-Dorrien for his decision to stand and fight at Le Cateau in August 1914. French admitted as much when he told Haig that he regretted not trying Smith-Dorrien by court-martial for having disobeyed his orders.[17] As the months passed French's resentment turned to bitterness and he found fault, as his diary and reports to Kitchener reveal, with nearly everything that Smith-Dorrien did.[18] French's anger erupted into the open upon receipt of Smith-Dorrien's letter on the 27th, but for some time before he had searched for a pretext to sack him. Wilson has the following entry in his diary on April 26: "Sir John asked me how he was to get rid of S. Dorrien. He often asks this and I have no answer."[19]

For his part Smith-Dorrien tried hard to maintain cordial relations with French under circumstances that were at best difficult. He was not one to nurse ill feelings, least of all when there was a great struggle at hand, and his loyalty to Sir John was reflected in the letters he sent to the king. In November 1914 he wrote: "Sir John has been very bold in his handling of us and has earned the complete confidence of everyone . . . I don't believe there is another man in the army who could have steered us as Sir John has done. . . ."[20] Two months later he observed that he would not hesitate to warn "my chief if I think it necessary to save him from a pitfall."[21]

As Sir John's attacks against him became more frequent and intemperate, Smith-Dorrien refrained from making any criticism of his chief either before his subordinates or in public. On one occasion, however, after a diversionary assault by the Second Army had been repulsed, Smith-Dorrien vented his feelings in a note to his wife:

> My attack on Hill 75 failed—and Sir John is furious in consequence—not that that is unusual, for he appears now to live in a state of unreason-

able fury. I don't mind, but it would make things easier if one had not such a wild beast to deal with.

7 p.m. I have seen Sir John again and he had recovered his equilibrium. Fancy if every time an operation did not attain the success I hoped I was to rant and roar at my Generals. In this case I was just as disappointed as Sir J., but I sent a telegram to General and troops thanking them for their efforts and regretting the casualties.[22]

Few senior officers in the British army were the equal of Smith-Dorrien intellectually or could rival his ability in handling large numbers of men with economy and decision. His action and courage in the opening weeks of the war had probably saved the British army from destruction. He was clever, flexible, sensitive, and considerate of his men. He deserved a better fate.

Next morning at 7:50 Sir John instructed Pulmer to prepare for the very withdrawal that Smith-Dorrien had suggested. Three hours later the field marshal called on Foch at Cassel. He said that his troops were extremely tired and could not continue to hold on to a tactically indefensible salient. He did not wish to compromise the coming offensive at Arras by using up his reserves in secondary operations. But Foch rejected any notion of withdrawal, declaring that such a move would be a confession of weakness and would encourage the Germans to make fresh efforts to break through. He emphasized that the lost ground could be recaptured with the troops already available, adding that to win a second battle it was not necessary to lose a first. The outcome was that Sir John agreed to postpone his retirement pending the results of a major counterattack that was to be launched towards Langemarck on the 29th. In reporting the interview Foch told Joffre, "I painted the picture of the consequences of withdrawal darker than they appeared to me."[23]

Crises had the effect of generating in Foch a kind of excitable euphoria. His buoyant assurances or flattering entreaties invariably overwhelmed Sir John who was nervous, indecisive, and subject to pressure. The scenes that followed behind the front could be likened to those of a comic opera if the consequences had not been so tragic. Day after day Sir John would learn of the absence of the much-heralded French offensive and of the continued suffering of his men. On each occasion he would pass from optimism to pessimism, concluding that he must withdraw his troops. During his dark moods the very thought or mention of the French would provoke angry outbursts. Wilson noted in his diary on the 28th that Sir John "had one of the worst explosions against the French I ever heard," saying that he had been "infamously treated" and that "neither Joffre nor Foch knew anything about soldiering."[24] The field marshal's own letters to Mrs. Bennett, especially on the 28th and 29th, are riddled with stinging comments about the French. Take, for example, "Truly I don't want to be allies with the French more than once in a life time. You can't trust them."[25]

No matter how antagonistic Sir John felt towards the French, he would swing the other way the moment he was confronted by Foch, agreeing to wait a little longer before pulling back his men and promising to cooperate in one more counterattack. The carefully weighed words of the Official History regarding this situation are worth quoting:

> For ill now, although for weal in the last year of the war, General Foch was the very spirit of the offensive. Sir John, apart from the desire to conform to his wishes as far as possible, could not fail to be influenced by him; but at heart he was most anxious to withdraw from the impossible position in the Salient and to avoid, if possible, involving the divisions of the New Army in a losing battle as their first experience of war. The struggle at Ypres was therefore continued, and in deference to the French pre-war doctrine of the offensive on all occasions and in all situations, the local commanders, both French and British, were encouraged, nay ordered, to recover by infantry attack the localities they had lost, without even the amount of artillery support which pre-war teaching would have regarded as necessary, let alone what experience had shown to be indispensable.[26]

The French assault on the 29th was postponed until next day because the newly arrived artillery had not had time to register. Sir John consented to keep his troops in their forward position another day. The French movement on the 30th turned out to be a fiasco. In the evening Foch motored to Hazebrouck and persuaded Sir John to delay the British withdrawal for another twenty-four hours. Putz, under pressure from Foch, ordered the attack renewed on May 1 but when the hour came his men refused to leave their trenches. Later in the day Foch visited Sir John but this time he was not seeking a further postponement. He had in his possession a telegram from Joffre, ordering him to act "on the defensive about Ypres" and to conserve all resources for the projected attack on the Arras front. The field marshal welcomed the news and during the night of May 3–4 the British troops were successfully withdrawn to a shorter and more defensible line in front of Ypres.

The most serious phase of the fighting in this Second Battle of Ypres was over. The Germans, relying on superior artillery and the use of gas, had opened a gap in the Allied line. Their attacks never had the weight and quality behind them as had characterized those during the First Battle of Ypres. Thus they made little use of the tremendous advantage they had gained and their delay enabled the Allies to stabilize the situation. While the French, having gone back across the canal, were safe and secure for the moment, the same could not be said of the English in the salient. Surrounded on three sides by German guns the British did not have the means to do much more than exploit a French advance. But Putz's infantry was second class at best and thoroughly demoralized. His reinforcements were not only inadequate but, having some distance to come, were slow in arriving.

Before the weight of fresh French reinforcements could be felt, air reconnaissance on the 26th revealed that the Germans had consolidated their new position. It should have been apparent then that the time for local counterattacks had passed and that only a carefully coordinated plan, requiring many days to mature, had any chance of success. Immediately the British should have retired back to the ramparts of Ypres and the canal to get in line with the French. The salient had no strategic value and by remaining there an additional week thousands of British lives were needlessly sacrificed.

The unexpected German thrust at Ypres had not upset Joffre's original plan to launch a new attack in Artois and Champagne, timed for early May. Sir John, however, became anxious about his assigned part in the forthcoming operations. A feeling that the French had weakened their front too much despite repeated warnings and had retreated too fast when the blow fell revived Sir John's distrust of Foch. He wrote to Kitchener on May 2:

> I was with Foch . . . this morning and I have spoken very seriously to him about recent events and have warned him that if his part of the line to the north of us is in my opinion not left sufficiently strong (with a good deal to spare in view of possible gas annoyances) I shall abandon my support of him in the big business and reinforce my left. I have told him emphatically that I shall do this without a moment hesitation and without any further warning to him if he let me in again.[27]

There were others at General Headquarters who, like Sir John, expressed concern over the Artois offensive, though not always for the same reasons. One such officer was Major-General J. P. Du Cane, the artillery adviser. Before the recent battle he had indicated that even by limiting the field guns to one or two rounds a day he doubted whether the BEF would have sufficient ammunition to attack effectively in Artois. Now with the stocks nearly depleted he was certain that the British army would not be ready for any major action for several months.

Since the beginning of the Battle of the Aisne the BEF's demands for ammunition, especially for heavy and for field artillery, had greatly outstripped production. Bearing in mind that the question of munitions supply was closely tied to the fortunes of the British army and its commander, it seems permissible to disgress in order to explain how the deficiencies arose and why, in spite of the immense resources of the Empire, needs were not fully met.

The supplies and reserves of ammunition for the army were based on the findings of a committee, appointed in 1901, under the chairmanship of Sir Francis Mowatt. The scales laid down were sufficient to maintain a force of seven divisions in a campaign along the lines of the South African War.

The government ordnance factories at Woolwich Arsenal, Waltham Abbey, and Enfield Locke, together with the established commercial munition firms, were deemed sufficient to meet the wants of the army. There was no attempt after 1904 (when the proposals of the Mowatt committee were acted upon) to widen the sources of supply and increase the output despite the lesson of the Russo-Japanese War and the adoption by the British army in 1908 of a quick-firing gun. The General Staff, though under political pressure for caution and economy, does not appear to have felt the need for a change in the existing scales. The leading generals anticipated that if war broke out on the Continent it would only last several months.

Kitchener saw from the beginning that the consumption of munitions was going to be vastly in excess of what the authorities claimed. His calculations were based on the needs of a rapidly expanding army in a war that was to last three to four years. In the early days of August 1914 he summoned the nation's leading munition makers and bluntly told them: "Look here gentlemen, I want you to think this is a very long war. I want you to imagine that the Russians go out and the French go out and that we are left alone to finish the war: and [so] make your preparations accordingly."

Kitchener was reluctant to go outside the circle of established armament manufacturers. He considered that only those with long experience of technical procedure and skilled labor could do a proper job. The initial munition orders placed on the outbreak of the war were intended to meet the requirements of the Expeditionary Force over the next six months. These contracts represented the maximum supply capacity of both the national factories and the old private armament firms in the United Kingdom.

The First World War took on a proportion that no one had believed possible. Field commanders were proved wrong in their forecasts, not only about the duration of the conflict but about the amount of ammunition required. History could offer no precedent of a battle extending along several hundred miles of front and lasting weeks. During the battle of Neuve Chapelle the British shot away nearly as much artillery ammunition as during the whole two-and-three-quarter years of the Boer War. The French and the Germans with armies of sixty to eighty divisions had also underestimated their munition needs but they had been preparing for war for years and had the facilities to meet them. The British, on the other hand, were not organized at the outset of the war to convert and expand their industrial resources. While the French and the Germans merely had to increase the output for their existing armies the British had to augment supplies for the Expeditionary Force and, at the same time, provide on this enlarged scale guns and ammunition for a new army ten times as great as the old.

Most major problems could not be overcome without the collaboration of almost every department of state and the application of controls over labor and capital. The latter condition could not be met as easily as the former. The cabinet, being neither socialist nor protectionist, was opposed to state management of the economy. War-time controls were evolved under pressure of exigencies and not as a result of deliberate policy. The political authorities did not at the outset appreciate the immense changes that the war was to bring to the economic life of the nation. Guided by the belief that the conflict would be over quickly, they clung to the principle of noninterference with the machinery of private enterprise.

To create out of nothing, or next to nothing, the means necessary to supply an immense army was an enormously difficult task. New factories had to be built and old ones expanded. Special apparatus and machines had to be purchased abroad along with much of the raw materials for the manufacture of shells. Getting these commodities to England and distributing them within the country could not be accomplished without substantial delays. For example, the movement of goods between New York and London, which prior to the war took about twenty days, now required two months. Docks and railways were so congested that even transit from London to Liverpool sometimes took five weeks. Under the best of circumstances it would take between six to eight months before a new factory was ready to operate; still longer before it could mass-produce munitions or arms.

Finally, there was a deficiency of workers in essential industries and difficulties with labor. Countless skilled workers had enlisted in the army despite Kitchener's statement on September 8, 1914, that such men were doing their duty by remaining at their trades. There was a lack of facilities to train workers and, on top of this, there was an appalling lack of discipline within the ranks of labor. To a vast segment of the industrial population, which in the past had barely managed to keep above the subsistence level, the wages of full employment and overtime created a wave of drunkenness and absenteeism that impeded the entire war effort.

The shortage of workers meant that the machinery available for the manufacture of munitions was being used only eight hours out of twenty-four. The government tried to augment the supply of labor by calling upon engineering firms not engaged in vital production to release some of their skilled men for work in the armament factories. The appeal had little effect. The workers did not wish to be transferred and the canvassed firms demanded that rather than surrender men they should be allowed to tender for contracts. But the greatest obstacles to increased production were the trade unions, which refused to suspend, even temporarily, the privileges won after many years of hard bargaining. The strict application of trade union rules was disastrous in time of war since they made it impossible to dilute labor by semiskilled men and women. Without sufficient labor, already overextended armament firms were unable to meet their production schedules. War Office pleas for cabinet action were not acted upon until after the Ministry of Munitions was established in June 1915.

Faced with enormous problems and handicapped by the government's refusal to impose controls over the economy, the War Office and the special committees set up to assist it showed commendable industry. Every factory that the authorities felt could be turned to the purpose was utilized; acres of new buildings sprang up all over the country; the best engineering talent in the nation was called upon; officials regularly inspected firms and the quality of production; munitions, materials, and machinery were purchased from neutrals and from the four corners of the Empire.

It would be fatuous to claim that the War Office commited no errors or foresaw everything. In particular Kitchener must be faulted for his early refusal to spread munition orders. But no administration, however capable, can conduct business free of mistakes. Given the nation's unpreparedness in August 1914, only brilliant improvisation and the most prodigious endeavor would have brought the results that were obtained. By May 1915 the War Office had arranged to produce in three days the amount of ammunition usually turned out in one year of peacetime. Nevertheless, demand continued to race ahead of output.

The most critical shortages were not in the supply of conventional artillery ammunition, that is shrapnel, but in the supply of heavy explosive (HE) shells. Much has been written alleging that the British army was denied victory in the spring of 1915 because of the War Office's unjustifiable failure to obtain more heavy explosive shells. As will be shown below, the charge is inaccurate and disproved by the facts.

The British army first used HE shells at Omdurman and again on a larger scale during the South African War. They were not judged to be absolutely successful on account of incomplete detonation and casualties caused through premature explosions. Still their potential value was clear and from 1902 onwards attempts were made to devise a safe fuse that would effectively fragment the shell. Progress was slow. There was no pressure to solve the problem because ordnance experts believed that shrapnel was superior. After the Balkan War of 1912–13, which demonstrated the value of HE shells against fortifications, the British General Staff continued to rely on shrapnel for its field guns instead of following the example of Continental armies. Why? The British General Staff did not anticipate that in a future European war they would be faced by frontier fortresses and massive earthworks that would necessitate the use of high explosive shells.[28] If the prewar military leaders are to be blamed for the decision to exclude HE ammunition from the British arsenal, Sir John, who was CIGS from March 1912 to April 1914, must bear his share of the responsibility.

After the outbreak of war the high command was slow to recognize the limited value of shrapnel. This projectile was deadly against troops in the open and was also effective, if used in great quantities, in cutting up barbed wire. However, it was incapable of destroying field fortifications.

Indeed, it was General von Donop, master-general of the ordnance (at the War Office), who took up the question of providing the British army with heavy explosive ammunition towards the end of August. The MGO had gathered from private sources at the front that the Germans were using HE shells with devastating results. Opinion at General Headquarters was divided but on the whole considered it desirable that some HE ammunition should be provided if this could be done without interfering with the supply of shrapnel. A make-shift method of fusing was devised at Woolwich and found practicable. The main drawback was that the process was complicated and took too long to manufacture. The output reached 2,000 a week and on October 19 the first consignment was dispatched to France for trial.

General Headquarters reported favorably on the shipment of experimental shells and asked that the War Office send out in future, as soon as it was feasible, fifty percent HE and fifty percent shrapnel for the eighteen-pounder and thirteen-pounder guns (November 6). A week later the high command requested that the proportion of HE should be twenty-five percent instead of fifty percent.

About this time MGO's Design Branch submitted a pattern for a new fuse that proved suitable for service. To convert the machinery that was making shrapnel to the manufacture of HE ammunition was out of the question. Such a step would have reduced the supply of the former without producing any of the new shell for at least ten weeks. Additional instead of substituted orders were therefore placed at once in England and the United States, not only with established armament factories but also with firms that had no previous experience in this nature of manufacture.

The question of the relative value of heavy explosive and shrapnel continued to be debated and investigated by the army in France. In January 1915 trials carried out under the direction of Sir John French supported the view that shrapnel produced better results. Shrapnel cut the wire into small pieces, whereas heavy explosives broke it but left it as an entanglement. The Germans, noting the effects of Allied barrages, put up walls in front of their wire to trap shrapnel pellets or sank the wire into shallow pits. The improvement in German defenses led to a fresh demand for an increase in the proportion of heavy explosive ammunition.[29]

Given the uncertainty of the field commander during the first six months of the war it was difficult for the War Office to frame long-term plans. The HE shell involved a highly technical process of manufacture as well as a unique standard of training and skill in workmanship. It would take many months before the output of these projectiles could be substantially multiplied.

Sir John has claimed that as CIGS he strongly advocated the production of heavy explosive shells but that his recommendations were steadily opposed by the government. He contends that during the war he was constantly pressing for greater quantities of all types of ammunition, especially heavy explosive shells, to a War Office seemingly supine or dead to all his demands. He adds that not only was the flow of munitions to France always inadequate but that the War Office was unconcerned about increasing the supply, suggesting instead a reduction in artillery consumption.[30] As so frequently happens in *1914*, Sir John's assertions bear little resemblance to the truth.

No records have been found to suggest that Sir John had done anything to encourage the use of HE ammunition prior to the war. If they had existed it is almost certain that he would have produced excerpts from some in his book. And when the global conflict erupted, as we have seen, the initiative to employ HE ammunition came from von Donop, not General Headquarters.

Nor is French correct in saying that his appeals to the War Office were met with apathy and indifference. Without waiting for a mandate from Sir John and indeed before the British army had even sailed for France in August 1914, Kitchener met with representatives of the nation's leading munition plants and informed them that the government would requisition every round they could turn out.[31] On September 17 Kitchener noted in an address to the House of Lords that "our chief difficulty is one of material rather than of personnel."[32] To Sir John he would write in October 1914: "The supply of ammunition gives me great anxiety. . . . All we can gather is being sent, but at the present rate of expenditure we are certain before long to run short, and then to produce more than a small daily allowance per gun will be impossible."[33]

In short the evidence is abundant that from the very beginning Kitchener was not only aware of but did his best to surmount the munition shortages. If he preached economy, as he did occasionally, it was out of necessity. Shortages developed because of a lack of machinery and materials as well as a failure to organize labor. No belated wartime spurt could immediately overtake the consequences of prewar neglect.

In view of Sir John's frequent complaints about the inadequacy of munitions supply, the War Office questioned the wisdom of mounting an offensive so soon after the Battle of Neuve Chapelle. French assured Kitchener during an interview on April 14 that his stock of shells was sufficient for the projected offensive.[34] Even the furious action in the Ypres area starting on April 22 did not deter French from his goal. On April 29 he telegraphed the War Office that "the expenditure of ammunition is not very excessive . . . here" and "will not hamper future operations."[35] When the fighting subsided French confidently told Kitchener on May 2 that "the ammunition will be all right."[36]

Whatever differences may have existed between Sir John and Foch were resolved during the first week of May. The two soldiers met several times to discuss arrangements for the coming operations.[37] Once again French appears to have had unrealistic expectations about the upcoming battle. As he told Mrs Bennett, "I am just on the eve of commencing what I believe will grow into one of the greatest battles in the history of the world."[38]

Joffre's plan, outlined after the stalemate developed, remained the guiding strategic principle, namely a converging attack on each flank of the intervening bulge of the German front between Reims and Arras. The right thrust would be made by the Fourth Army in Champagne, while the left one in Artois would be carried out by the Tenth Army, now under the command of General d'Urbal. The British attack was allocated to Haig's First Army, which joined d'Urbal's left wing on the Béthune–La Bassée road.[39]

Haig's tactics were not a mere repetition of Neuve Chapelle but included a number of innovations. Special battery units were detailed to be ready to advance at short notice to assist in the exploitation of successful attacks. The Flying Corps provided machines, equipped with wireless telegraphy, for reconnaissance and artillery observation. To enable General Headquarters to closely follow the progress of the attack three airplanes were designated, one always to be in the air, to report when lines were captured.

To avoid some of the problems that had arisen in the previous battle, Haig planned to penetrate the German line at two points north and south of Neuve Chapelle, 6,000 yards apart, followed by a convergent advance. If the operation succeeded it was estimated that six or seven German battalions would be caught in the noose. Haig did not set definite objectives for each day and so he left the course of the battle essentially in the hands of the local commanders. The attacking divisions were ordered to press forward as rapidly as possible from objective to objective to the line of the Haute Deule Canal, six miles beyond Aubers Ridge.

The success of the operation depended in large measure on the artillery's capacity to destroy fortifications and strong points, as well as to prevent the move forward of enemy reinforcements. The preliminary bombardment was limited to forty minutes of which the last ten was to be intense. The brevity of the barrage was dictated as much by a desire to achieve surprise as by a shortage of ammunition.

Haig's First Army consisted of three corps, the First, Indian, and Fourth. Against this force the Germans could muster only three divisions, namely the Thirteenth and Fourteenth of the VII Corps and the Sixth Bavarian. The Germans, however, had learned well the lessons of Neuve Chapelle. Their defensive front was no longer the filmsy structure that had been shattered by artillery eight weeks earlier. It had now been converted into a huge sprawling earthwork with barbed-wire entanglements concealed in ditches, concrete emplacements, machine-guns positioned under their

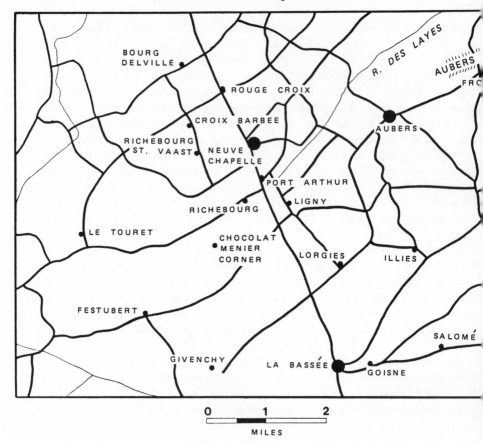

THE BATTLES OF AUBERS RIDGE AND FESTUBERT

parapets and sited to fire just above ground level, underground shelters, switch lines, angular communication trenches, and strong points in the rear to oppose any part of an infantry advance that might succeed in passing the front line.[40]

British leadership at all levels anticipated substantial results from the coming operation. The confident mood was in large part due to the ease with which the German defenses had been overrun in the early stages of the battle of Neuve Chapelle. The view was that the method used last time was essentially correct and only required a few tactical refinements.

Haig's final operation orders were issued on May 6 at 10:00 A.M., fixing the start of the assault for 5:40 on the morning of the 8th. But rain fell all day on on the 6th and next morning there was a dense mist, limiting visibility to fifty yards. These conditions had interfered with artillery observation and air reconnaissance so it was decided to postpone the main attack until the 9th. Sunday morning, May 9, broke fine and clear. The larks could be heard singing and there was a fresh steady breeze from the northeast. At exactly 5:00 A.M. the British artillery barrage opened and reached a crescendo as the time of the infantry assault approached. The defenders were swallowed up in a storm of black and orange smoke, speckled with the white flash from the shrapnel. The bombardment created a spectacle that impressed observers in the British front line but it failed either to cut adequate lines in the wire or neutralize the enemy's fire power. The time allotted for the bombardment was woefully inadequate; marksmanship was poor; the caliber of shells in most cases was too light to affect the massive German earthworks; and many shells failed to explode on impact owing to faulty fuses.

Thus the Germans were back into position behind the parapet when the assaulting infantry went over the top and into No Man's Land. German fire was so accurate and intense that some leading brigades were practically annihilated while others were either forced back into their own trenches or pinned down among the craters that lay between. A second attack was delivered at 8:00 A.M. and a third at 4:00 in the afternoon. By dint of sheer bravery and reckless disregard of life the British captured small stretches of enemy front-line trenches but were driven out by immediate counterattacks. The next morning Haig, after consultations with his corps commanders, decided to postpone further operations. British casualties in what was called the Battle of Aubers Ridge amounted to 458 officers and 11,161 other ranks. In only one day's fighting British losses almost equaled those of the three days of Neuve Chapelle.

The dismay at General Headquarters over the British failure was intensified by the success of the Tenth Army farther south. Following an intense four-hour bombardment, d'Urbal's forces had advanced steadily, if at a heavy cost, and penetrated the German defenses on the Vimy Ridge to a depth of a mile and a half, capturing 2,000 prisoners and 12 guns. One of the objectives of the British attack had been to help the French, but instead the Germans had been able to move reserves from their sector to reinforce Vimy. Partly out of embarrassment and partly out of a desire to assist the French, Sir John yielded to Joffre's entreaties that the First Army should renew its attack.

Before the new assault began, French had persuaded himself that it would succeed. An emotional man, Sir John was deeply troubled by the growing casualty list, which included many friends and even some relatives. To preserve his sanity, or at the very least to be able to live with himself, he had to justify his action, which was certain to commit thousands of young men to suffering and death.

Haig selected to attack in the area of Festubert, a short distance to the south of Neuve Chapelle. On this occasion he revised his tactics. He now proposed to adopt the French method of a prolonged methodical bombardment, followed by an advance with limited objectives. The assault was to be made in two sectors, separated by a gap of 600 yards. The operation would start under cover of darkness with the Second and Meerut divisions breaking out between Chocolat Menier Corner and Port Arthur. At daylight the Seventh Division would strike immediately north of Festubert.

The artillery barrage began on the 13th and by the time it was over 100,000 rounds had been fired. Rain fell on the 13th and on the following day, interfering with accurate artillery registration and also rendering the ground so sodden and sticky that the effect of the burst of the heavy explosive shell was much diminished. The attack, which was to have taken place on the 14th, was therefore postponed for twenty-four hours. This meant that the period of bombardment was extended from thirty-six to sixty hours.

The weather cleared on the 15th so at 11:30 P.M. the Fifth and Sixth brigades (Second Division) and the Garhwal Brigade (Meerut Division), some 10,000 men, advanced on a total frontage of 1,700 yards. Creeping forward in silence with bayonet fixed the Sixth Brigade surprised the Germans in the front-line trenches and put them to flight. However, the Fifth and Garhwal brigades were detected shortly after they rose to advance and were raked from flank to flank.

The dawn attack by the Twenty-second and Twentieth brigades (Seventh Division) was more successful. Starting out at 3:15 A.M. after an intense artillery bombardment, the Twenty-second stormed the German front trenches and reached the support line. On the left the Twentieth went over the parapet at 3:10 A.M. and, hurrying to get across No Man's Land before the end of the bombardment, suffered many casualties from British shelling. The brigade managed to carry the enemy front defenses but was unable to progress any further.

Although the two assaults had made headway, the enemy continued to hold ground dividing the Second and Seventh divisions. On the afternoon of the 16th Haig reviewed the situation with the affected corps and divisional commanders and decided to exploit the partial success in each attack. Haig's movements on the following days were handicapped as much by the intermittent rain and the natural difficulties of the terrain as by the enemy's firepower. British forces bit off small pieces of the German line but were halted far short of any real strategic point. It was not known at the time that the Germans had withdrawn, leaving only small detachments in their former position and taking advantage of the delay that they caused to construct a new line of defense and to bring up reinforcements.

The fighting dragged on until the 25th. With the ammunition stocks nearly depleted and the men completely exhausted French ordered Haig to end all offensive operations. In ten days of fighting, May 15–25, the battle of Festubert had cost the British 710 officers and 16,648 men. During the same period the Germans sustained only about 5,000 casualties.

While the British attack at Festubert did not succeed, it at least compelled the enemy to move up reinforcements that might otherwise have been used in the Vimy Ridge sector. Here the Tenth Army, after a promising start, ran into difficulty. As the fighting continued Joffre repeatedly urged Sir John to make further efforts to draw away German troops from the French front. But the field marshal was unable to meet Joffre's wishes and not only because of insufficient reserves of munitions and manpower. As a means to divert attention from his Aubers Ridge débâcle, he had embarked on a campaign to discredit Kitchener and the Liberal government.

12

The Shells Controversy

French was in excellent spirits when he walked up to a church tower in the early hours of May 9 to witness the start of the British attack at Aubers Ridge. The preliminary barrage was calculated to reduce fortifications and kill or demoralize the defenders so as to prepare the way for the assaulting infantry. As the guns fired at a rate of nearly 1,000 rounds a minute Sir John could see a huge wall of smoke, dust, and splinters rising from the German parapet. Nothing, it seemed, could survive this devastation. But, as already described, the dramatic spectacle was misleading. The bombardment was inadequate, leaving large stretches of wire uncut and machine-gun posts intact. The British assault was quickly brought to a standstill and each subsequent attempt brought losses out of all proportion to the gains.

Since Sir John had expected, indeed predicted, a major victory, the result of the attack naturally deepened his disappointment. He sat in silence as he was being driven back to General Headquarters. There he found a telegram from the War Office, telling him to dispatch 20,000 rounds of eighteen-pounder ammunition to the Dardanelles. The reason for this strange request was that a ship was waiting at Marseilles ready to depart for Mudros. It was imperative that the ammunition should reach Hamilton's[1] hard-pressed forces as quickly as possible. Sending the shells from the reserve stock in France would mean saving time.

Sir John replied that as his attack was in progress and likely to last several days he could not allow the ammunition to leave unless it was replaced immediately from home. Kitchener thereupon sent him a second message: "The state of affairs in the Dardanelles renders it absolutely essential that the ammunition which had been ordered should be sent off at once. I will see that it is replaced."[2] The shells left France on May 10 and within twenty-four hours the amount was made good as Kitchener had promised.

Judging by what happened to the French[3] the loss of these shells probably did not affect the outcome of the battle. In fact even Sir John recognized that the shortage of ammunition was not the only reason for the failure of the attack.[4] Still Kitchener's telegram was ill-timed. French was in a state of mental anguish. He had just seen his men decimated by an enemy whose strength he had underestimated. Added to this was the warning that Kitchener had given him on March 31. He had been on trial and the British defeat would soon be obvious to the home authorities.

French's inner circle rallied around him at this difficult hour. During the recent months, as his fears and suspicions grew, he had become increasingly dependent on the men he trusted, especially Guest and Fitzgerald. Now they did their best to comfort him by arguing that he was not responsible for the British repulse. Sir John was not a man of character and the collapse of his hopes made him only too willing to lay the blame at someone else's doorsteps. Egged on by his civilian entourage he came to believe that Kitchener had denied him the means essential for victory and that, as a result, he should put his grievances before the British nation.

The evidence is not conclusive but would seem to point to Colonel Repington, *The Times* military correspondent, as the chief instigator of the piece. Repington had been an officer of great promise when a love affair with another man's wife forced him to leave the army. Despite his involvement in a marital scandal he enjoyed useful connections, not only in the services but also in politics and society. As a journalist he was very influential, first gaining national recognition for his series of articles on the Russo-Japanese War. But his skill as a military critic was diminished by his penchant for intrigue and by his tendency to allow personal loyalties and prejudice to impede his view of what was happening.

In the early days of the war Kitchener, in order to awaken the nation, gave Repington an interview in which he outlined his plans and predictions. The article appeared in *The Times* on August 15 and provoked loud complaints in the cabinet and "the devil of a fuss" among radical editors, who accused Kitchener of singling out the Northcliffe press for privileged treatment. Annoyed by all this criticism Kitchener refused to see Repington again, leaving him to gather his information from lesser members of the War Office staff. It was a poor substitute since Kitchener's method of doing everything himself made it useless to talk to anyone else.[5] Forced to turn to other sources for his inspiration, Repington eventually drifted to General Headquarters where he impressed French by his wit, charm, and readiness to help. Military correspondents were forbidden to go to the front on security grounds so Repington stayed at General Headquarters as Sir John's personal guest. He was not bothered by restrictions of any kind. He had access to French's plans and thoughts, could visit troops in the field and talk to officers, and see the workings of the General Staff. The special treatment he received bound him to French and thereby placed him in the company of Kitchener's enemies.

Repington's employer, Lord Northcliffe (Alfred Charles Harmsworth), was even more anxious for a change in the management of the War Office. He was the creator of the modern tabloid daily newspaper and he possessed a power such as no press lord has ever wielded before or since. As the wireless had not yet come into existence, the only means of disseminating the news was through the press. Proprietor of the *Evening News* and the *Daily Mail,* in addition to *The Times,* he controlled half the newspaper circulation in London.

For many years Northcliffe had been a fervent admirer of Kitchener and in August 1914 his papers had urged, indeed insisted, that he be appointed secretary for war. But Northcliffe soon became disillusioned with the new War Office chief, partly because of his harsh restrictions on journalists and to a lesser extent because of his firm opposition to conscription. By the spring of 1915 Northcliffe was determined to force Kitchener out of office and he invited Sir John to help him build a case.[6] French disregarded the hint, for he had too much at stake to involve himself in a conspiracy that he felt could not possibly succeed. The First Army's setback at Aubers Ridge, however, changed his perspective.

Repington had witnessed the attack with Sir John on May 9 but what took place immediately after they returned to General Headquarters is unclear. Presumably Repington offered the comforting observation that the field marshal should not reproach himself for the failure, which was due to circumstances beyond his control. The real culprit was Kitchener, who had taken no effective steps to increase the supply of ammunition. French grasped at this explanation as the cause of all the trouble and his disappointment gave way to righteous indignation. He therefore resolved, to use his own words, "on taking the most drastic measures to destroy the apathy of a Government which had brought the Empire to the brink of disaster."[7] These measures involved handing over to Repington a carefully edited mass of correspondence on the subject of munitions that had passed between General Headquarters and the War Office; and of sending his secretary, Brinsley Fitzgerald, and his politically agile ADC Freddy Guest to London to lay the same semidocumented case before Asquith's critics.

Since early spring rumors had been rife in London that the army was being hampered by munition shortages. When they started Asquith consulted Kitchener who replied that he had received assurances from French "that with the present supply of ammunition he will have as much as his troops will be able to use on his next forward movement."[8] On the strength of this statement Asquith delivered a speech at Newcastle on April 20 in which he asserted that the output of ammunition was sufficient to meet the army's wants. Tory frontbenchers and a small segment of the media, with access to reliable sources of information, remained unconvinced.[9]

The disclosures by Guest and Fitzgerald took some by surprise but only confirmed in others better informed what they had already suspected. Arriving in London on May 12 the two men saw a host of prominent politicians, including Bonar Law, the Conservative leader, and Lloyd George, the principal rival to Asquith in the Liberal government.[10]

Repington's first dispatch, which somehow passed the censor, was published in *The Times* of May 14 with a banner headlined, "NEED FOR SHELLS: BRITISH ATTACK CHECKED: LIMITED SUPPLIES THE CAUSE." In the story that followed the war correspondent ascribed the failure of the British offensive against Aubers Ridge to a lack of high explosive shells. The article caused a major political sensation.

The contents showed that the author owed much to official sources and Kitchener at once concluded that French had inspired the story. "Lord K . . . told me Sir J. French certainly had this put in," Margot Asquith, the prime minister's wife, recorded in her diary.[11] On the 14th Kitchener wrote to French in sharp terms: "A good many remarks are being made about *The Times* correspondent who is apparently staying with you and writing to his paper. . . . Until war correspondents are allowed by the Government, I do not think it is right for you to allow Repington to be out with the Army."[12]

French replied the next day. He indicated that Repington was an old friend of ten or twelve years and that he had been staying at General Headquarters as his guest. A government official had recently informed him that a select group of accredited journalists would be arriving in France to cover operations at the front.[13] French went on to say:

They were on their way, I was told, a week ago and in view of the important operations which commenced on the 9th I agreed to let Repington (as he happened to be here) act for *The Times* until Mr. Buchan (*The Times* man) arrived. This has been done—Buchan landed here (I think) on Thursday and from then Repington has done nothing.[14]

The impact of Repington's article had barely begun to be felt when the government suffered a fresh and fatal blow. Lord Fisher, the first sea lord, suddenly resigned, citing as reasons his opposition to the Dardanelles enterprise and his inability to work any longer with Churchill. The news brought to a culmination the Tory party's growing impatience with the conduct of the war. If Fisher was the darling of the Tories, Churchill was their *bête noire*. The crisis at the Admiralty moved them to act. On May 17 Bonar Law informed the prime minister that unless his party were permitted to share responsibility it would assume the role of an active opposition. Asquith yielded to the demand, for the alternative was a Parliamentary debate that might force his resignation and would certainly have an adverse effect on national unity.[15]

From across the Channel French watched the fast-moving events in London with great interest. Acting as though he were an innocent bystander he wrote:

All these government rows at home are most disconcerting to us here. "Whilst they are fiddling Rome is burning." . . . I devoutly wish we could get rid of Kitchener from the War Office. I'm sure nothing will go right whilst he's there. It is so hard to have enemies both in *front* and *behind*.[16]

Although a coalition government was not the result that Sir John had worked for, it might nonetheless serve his purpose if Kitchener were denied the War Office. In an effort to encourage such a move French addressed a long letter to the prime minister on May 20. He began by saying:

You have shown me so much true generous kindness throughout this trying campaign that I venture at this critical juncture to convey to you what is in my innermost thoughts. I am sure in the whole history of war no General in the field has ever been helped in a difficult task by the head of his Government as I have been supported and strengthened by your unfailing sympathy and encouragement. I am sure therefore I may address you privately and informally as a friend.

French went on to complain bitterly about the manner in which the secretary for war treated him. He claimed that Kitchener's attitude had been overbearing and unjust. According to French the crowning blow came when Kitchener sent a personal message through Allenby, saying that the troops under his command were wanting in spirit, that they were improperly led, and that General Headquarters ought to model the performance of its men after that of the British forces in the Dardanelles. French insisted that "so long as I am in command" the presence of Kitchener at the War Office was a serious obstacle to the successful conduct of operations on the western front. He implied that the present impasse could be overcome only by a change in leadership, either at the War Office or at General Headquarters.[17] In attempting to force the prime minister's hand Sir John assumed that his own position was secure. He was encouraged to think along those lines by reports that the activities on his behalf were bearing fruit.

What then were his friends doing in London? Fitzgerald and Guest had passed on to the lesser lights in Parliament, supporting their chief's grievances with copies of appeals for more ammunition that had been sent to the War Office during the past six months. The first thing that Repington did on his return to London was to have a talk with Lloyd George. He turned over to him a hastily drafted paper exposing all the kinds of deficiencies in munitions and guns. Then he visited the Conservative leaders and "told them all I knew, and neither minced my words nor concealed my feelings."[18] George Moore, Sir John's American friend, was equally active. He spent most of his time on Fleet Street trying to persuade newspaper editors to rally behind the anti-Kitchener campaign.[19] And the Northcliffe press continued to publish articles accusing the government, and by implication Kitchener, of dereliction in attending to munition supplies. But Northcliffe overreached himself when he delivered an unprecedented onslaught on Kitchener in the *Daily Mail* on May 21. The story entitled "THE SHELLS SCANDAL: LORD KITCHENER'S TRAGIC BLUNDER" held Kitchener responsible for the shells shortage and stated bluntly that he should go.

Kitchener regarded the sensationalism of the Northcliffe press with a silent contempt. He declined to take the trouble to refute the virulent charges that were being brought against him. He could have retorted, with bitter justification, that if French had any sense he would not have committed himself to an offensive for which he had not the means. Besides, Kitchener had in his possession French's notes of April 29 and May 2 assuring him that the stocks of ammunition were sufficient for the operations. Had he revealed these notes to the public it would have cleared him and made his critics and accusers look extremely foolish. What Kitchener wanted most was to win the war. Until that was achieved there was no time for recriminations. When a delegation of officers at the War Office asked for permission to issue a statement in answer to Northcliffe's accusations, Kitchener replied: "Our job is to get on with the war—it will be quite time enough to answer these when we have won it."[20]

As it turned out Kitchener did not weaken his position by remaining silent. The press campaign, culminating in the vituperative attack by the *Daily Mail* on May 21, set off a reaction in his favor and, if anything, made him more a public hero. The service clubs of Pall Mall banished *The Times* and the *Daily Mail* from their premises; indignant readers canceled their subscriptions; and the circulation of the *Daily Mail* alone fell by 200,000. Three thousand members of the Stock Exchange assembled and, following a bonfire of the Northcliffe papers, gave three cheers for Kitchener. The king showed his unwavering confidence in Kitchener by bestowing upon him the Order of the Garter, the highest honor of knighthood.[21]

The other London dailies were as supportive of Kitchener as they were critical of Northcliffe—their objectivity may have been partially clouded by resentment over the special treatment accorded to Northcliffe's correspondents at General Headquarters. H. A. Gwynne, the editor of the *Morning Post*, wrote of Kitchener on May 22: "He has done more in a shorter time than any other man in his position could have done." The *Globe* of May 22 expressed similar sentiments: "The nation owes to Lord Kitchener a debt of gratitude that it can never repay and it will not be induced to forget it by malicious efforts to belittle his services, impeach his judgment and impugn his professional capacity."

By contrast Northcliffe was depicted as a fiend. "Lord Northcliffe is today the greatest peril which threatens the British Empire, more sinister than even the enemy in the field," fumed the *Daily News* editorial on May 21. The *Daily Chronicle* on May 22 asserted that "if this country were Russia, Germany or Austria . . . Lord Northcliffe would have been taken out into the courtyard and shot within 48 hours."

Northcliffe had thought that he was influential enough to shape public opinion to serve his ends. But he failed to appreciate the hold that Kitchener exercised over the man in the street. In view of public outrage as well as economic consideration, Northcliffe swallowed his pride and gradually called off his crusade.

French had laid himself open to very serious charges by his disloyalty and underhanded methods of intrigue. The *World* of May 25 condemned the field marshal's judgment, not only for his collusion with Northcliffe but for his choice of civilian friends. It described them as mischievous and indiscreet. In particular it cited George Moore, observing that he had no official standing either in the British army or in any of its subsidiary organizations such as the Red Cross Society. The weekly added: "Mr. Moore, in his frequent visits to London, is said to make very outspoken comments on the inner happenings both at home and abroad, and on the face of it it seems extremely undesirable that a private citizen of a neutral country should be afforded such exceptional facilities for knowing the innermost secrets of the campaign." The *New Statesman* went beyond simple criticism of Sir John and, like a number of other journals and newspapers, called for his resignation: "The Commander-in-Chief of our main forces in the field cannot be in the pocket of the proprietor of the 'Daily Mail' and at the same time continue to enjoy the full confidence of the sober public of Great Britain."

In government circles many politicians were demanding that Sir John be dismissed at once; some of them were prepared to let him go quietly while others went so far as to propose that he be required to publicly acknowledge his role in the "Northcliffe plot." Kitchener, who had long held a contemptuous opinion of Sir John, both personally and professionally, also agreed that there should be a change in the high command. He told Asquith that under the circumstances he did not think he could continue to work with French. He reminded the prime minister that in wartime it was absolutely essential for the secretary for war and the commander-in-chief to have implicit faith and trust in each other.

Asquith had been well disposed towards French at least since the days of the Curragh and he put down the constant ill feeling between the two field marshals to a simple incompatibility. He was not impressed by the evidence against French and declined to investigate the matter further. The prime minister could not bring himself to believe that the man who had praised him so lavishly in a recent letter could simultaneously be working behind his back to undermine his government. Moreover he felt that French could not be relieved of command without arousing controversy at home and resentment in the army.

Back at General Headquarters Sir John appeared unconcerned over the domestic furore caused by his activities. However, his professional entourage was certain that he would come to grief unless he disassociated himself from Northcliffe. "Sir John had better walk warily or he will be out," Wilson wrote in his diary after hearing from two of his informants in London. After dinner on May 20 Wilson held a meeting with Lambton and Brooke. He gives the following account in his diary:

> Discussed . . . how we can warn Sir J. but could not think of anything that would not do more harm than good. The silly man sent George Moore over this morning and Brinsley[22] goes tomorrow! The only thing we did was to telephone to Esher to get him over.[23]

Esher had been an intimate friend of Sir John for about ten years, since the days when the two collaborated closely to help improve the army system. A man of acute intelligence, broad interests, and great social gifts, Esher enjoyed considerable political influence through his personal friendship with King Edward VII, King George V, and many leading statesmen, Tory and Liberal. He never held an important political office (he refused the secretaryship for war and the viceroyalty of India) because he had no taste for a life of service in the public eye. Still he regarded himself a loyal servant of the Crown and accepted appointments to a number of committees, including the Committee of Imperial Defence. During the war he served the government as an unofficial observer in Paris and occasionally as an emissary for confidential missions.

Before leaving for France Esher received word that Lord Kitchener wished to see him. Although the new cabinet had not yet been announced[24] Kitchener had reason to believe, correctly as it turned out, that he would remain undisturbed in his office. In view of the prime minister's attitude he had resigned himself to keeping French in command of the British forces. He asked Esher to deliver a personal message to Sir John.

Kitchener explained that he had never sought authority but that he meant to administer the War Office and the army until he was officially dismissed. Although he knew the attacks upon him had been engineered at General Headquarters he bore no malice and had not the slightest intention of punishing Sir John for the imprudences of his friends. "I am out to fight the Germans," he said, "not to fight Sir John French." He wanted Sir John to know that he had no intention of removing or of superseding him. He denied that he had ever entertained the idea of personally taking over command of the armies in the field.

Second, Kitchener was anxious for French to realize that further reinforcements would not be forthcoming until the supply of ammunition was adequate for their needs. When he last saw Sir John and Joffre he said he would despatch the New Armies only if they broke through the German line. There was no evidence that this result would be achieved by the operations now in progress. Yet at the insistence of Sir John he had finally consented to send one division and later a second division, which was absolutely the last that could be equipped for the time being. Since the rest could not be provided with the means to fight, Kitchener saw no logic in simply piling them in France. Besides he thought it prudent to keep an army in reserve in case an emergency should arise, either in a distant theater or in France.

This introduced a third point. Kitchener declared that French could not be fully cognizant of the events that were presently occurring in the Near East and on the Russian front. In war conditions changed rapidly and such changes directly influenced and sometimes rendered nugatory promises made in good faith. For example, after his last conversation with Sir John and Joffre when he expressed the hope of sending part of the New Army, the Russians had suffered a severe defeat in Galicia. The latest information showed that the Germans with slight reinforcements could convert their victory into a decisive one. In the face of a Russian retreat and the consequent possibility of a transfer of German troops to some other place in the widely extended battle line, it followed that there should be some hesitation about committing the last reserve that England possessed.

Last, Kitchener wanted Esher to impress upon Sir John that the task of a field commander was to endeavor to beat the enemy with the troops at his disposal. It was impossible for Sir John, or anyone else in Flanders, to form an accurate judgment of the country's resources or of its obligations in other parts of the world. Just as he did not interfere with the disposition of British troops in France, so too he hoped that Sir John would not interfere with his functions as secretary of war and head of the army. Kitchener added that cooperation should not be difficult since the fields of action were so distinct.[25]

Next morning Esher left Dover and by early afternoon had arrived at General Headquarters in Saint Omer. Brooke and Lambton were there to greet him. They explained that Sir John had been an unwitting tool in the press campaign against Kitchener. The field marshal had first been encouraged to place his case before the public by Repington and then urged on in this course of action by his civilian entourage, in particular Fitzgerald. Their account more or less confirmed what Esher had suspected. He told them that Kitchener was "behaving very well" and that when he saw Sir John he would give him "a d—— good talking."[26]

Esher returned to his car and drove on to Hazebrouck, Sir John's advanced headquarters. He found the field marshal waiting for him in a garden behind the house. After greeting one another in the manner of old friends, the two men sat down and had a long talk.

Esher pointed out that it was extremely dangerous, and yet unproductive, for a soldier to meddle in politics or attempt to manipulate the press for his own ends. Although Esher did not speak ill of the civilians at General Headquarters he hinted in unmistakable terms that they had involved him in considerable difficulty and undermined his position. The entire nation had rallied behind Kitchener, who was now stronger than ever. If Sir John was to give his best it was imperative that he mend his fences with the secretary for war. In the event of difficulties or failures the commander-in-chief would find a friendly Kitchener a bulwark against popular criticism. On the other hand an unfriendly Kitchener could hardly be expected to stand by him.

Sir John's reply, as recorded by Esher, was a distortion of the facts. It may be that Esher softened the entry in his diary but it is more probable that French did not tell the truth. At any rate Esher's account runs as follows:

> From what Sir John said, it became perfectly obvious that he had been a very unwilling participator and had no hand in this newspaper intrigue. That he had been annoyed by Lord K.'s letters and telegrams, and especially by so called messages brought to him by his Generals whom Lord K. had seen, was the root of the whole matter as far as he, Sir John, was concerned. Upon this his friends had reared a superstructure of intrigue; Lord K.'s telegrams, hastily written and his letters not very sympathetically expressed, have made the F.M., highly strung and sensitive as he is, sore and angry. Lord K., himself, irritable and over-worked, has undoubtedly spoken injudiciously to some of his generals who have been over to see him. To Allenby he undoubtedly spoke with unnecessary warmth about the failure of the Army to achieve success in recent operations. Allenby, who is a blunt and not very tactful soldier had the folly to repeat Lord K.'s observations as if they were a deliberate message to Sir John. The combined circumstances produced a frame of mind in him favourable to the foolish activities of his friends.[27]

Esher was of the opinion that when not goaded or exasperated, Sir John rarely allowed personal dislikes, however intense, to warp his perceptions. He knew that the group around Sir John encouraged his weakness and regularly scanned Kitchener's letters and telegrams with an almost perverse desire to find something that could or might be interpreted as an insult. Unfortunately Lambton, whose functions as military secretary had largely been usurped by Fitzgerald, had practically no influence with the field marshal.[28] Esher was convinced that if things were allowed to remain as they were, Sir John would soon find himself in similar difficulties. He turned to Robertson for counsel. That fine soldier suggested going back to the system under which all correspondence between the secretary for war and the commander-in-chief should first be cleared by the respective chiefs of the General Staff. If this were done there would be an opportunity of correcting hasty expressions, of removing possible misunderstandings, and of couching messages in well-considered language. Esher was pleased with the proposal and had no difficulty in convincing Sir John of its merits.

On the evening of the 22nd Esher drafted a letter to Kitchener and next day went over it with Sir John. The note read:

I delivered your messages, as near as I could remember, in your words.

He [French] then said that he commenced the war with a feeling amounting to no less than personal affection for you, whom he considered the greatest soldier he ever met. . . .

He added that, in the face of the enemy, amid so much pain and suffering, with only one objective in view worthy of everybody—the beating of the Germans—no personal feelings, preferences or rivalries should be allowed under any circumstances to prevail.

I have given him most absolute assurances that you have always wished to be loyal to him, and to that his own warm-hearted, impetuous, loyal nature will respond, I feel sure.[29]

At the same time Esher wrote to Lieutenant Colonel Oswald FitzGerald (Kitchener's military secretary): "The little F.M. [French] . . . is secretly ashamed of and annoyed with his gang of mischievous friends. . . . He will never quite recover from the shock to his reputation." Esher, in an attempt to conceal the full extent of French's involvement, went on to say: "And yet I am sure that the whole episode is due to his selection of wrong people and not to personal intrigue or even connivance."[30] In a second letter (May 24) Esher suggested a plan of indirect communication between Kitchener and French as a means of eliminating the personal element from correspondence.[31] Ultimately Kitchener consented to the change in procedure.

Esher's reports minimized Sir John's wrongdoings, criticizing his judgment but absolving him of connivance with the Northcliffe press. Still Esher knew that his efforts would not raise Sir John's standing in London and that the field marshal could not afford another slip. He intimated to Sir John that he should get rid of his meddlesome associates as the surest way of avoiding trouble in the future. Sir John accepted his advice and promptly took action—Repington was told not to set foot at General Headquarters again and in June Moore was put aboard a ship bound for America. Esher also urged that Sir John hold more frequent meetings with Kitchener in the interest of reestablishing mutual trust and confidence. Sir John was full of good intentions and even had some kind words for Kitchener. However, Esher was sufficiently acquainted with French to be accustomed to his mercurial changes of mind and the wild statements he was liable to make in moments of enthusiasm. Before leaving General Headquarters he noted in his diary that French was in a very cheerful disposition, adding, "I only hope that he will remain so."[32] This turned out to be wishful thinking.

13

Last Chance

The experience of the spring offensives convinced General Headquarters that it was following correct methods. Even with small numbers of guns and limited ammunition some units had reached their assigned objectives and compelled the Germans to withdraw from carefully prepared positions. It seemed to those in authority that if they could have pressed home their initial advantage with fresh troops and larger supplies of ammunition the result might have been decisive. Kitchener nursed no such illusion. His views are best expressed in the following sentence (from a paper sent to the CIGS): "The French have an almost unlimited supply of ammunition including H.E. and 14 divisions in reserve so if they cannot get through we may take it as proved that the lines cannot be forced."[1]

Kitchener was not alone in recognizing the futility of hurling human bodies against barbed wire and concrete machine-gun posts. In the aftermath of Arras a wave of dejection and disgust spread across France. The calamitous casualties during 1914 could be accepted as part of the price for halting the German invaders but the continuous and heavy loss of life in pursuit of a strategy that seemed to lead nowhere was more difficult to rationalize. Morale in the army was very low. In fact during the last offensive two battalions had gone over to the enemy singing the "International" and units in at least two corps had refused to leave their trenches. Early in June President Poincaré found that "everyone is complaining about Joffre, and especially about his entourage."[2] Georges Clemenceau led the attack in his newspaper, *L'Homme enchaîné*. He pointed to the high command's mismanagement of the war and stated bluntly that if events were allowed to drift there would be a mutiny in the army. Even the leading generals, including Foch, were opposed to any further attempt to break the German line until the Anglo-French forces were much stronger.

But neither criticism nor failure could shake Joffre's confidence in the viability of his military policy. No sooner had the guns at Arras been stilled than he began to formulate plans for a major offensive in the late summer or autumn. His objective remained the same, that is, to cut off the German salient in the Saint Quentin–La Fère area by converging attacks from Artois and Champagne. Whereas in May, owing to lack of men and matériel, Joffre had been able to apply real pressure only from Artois, he now proposed a large double stroke. The French army was at its peak and he was confident that he could break into the plain of Douai and seize vital German communications, which were only fifteen to twenty miles from the front. Success here would endanger the whole German army north of Verdun.

Joffre's immediate concern was to secure maximum British resources in aid of his offensive. Towards the end of May he sent a message to Kitchener (through General Yarde-Buller[3]), asking that the New Armies be dispatched to France at the earliest possible moment. He also wanted Kitchener to fix a date when they would be ready so that he could formulate his plans.[4] Kitchener's reply, transmitted verbally by Yarde-Buller, was very cautious and he deliberately avoided giving a date when the New Armies would leave for France. He gave the following reasons for wishing to retain the New Armies.

It was understood that the minimum number of rounds per gun, in order to adequately support and protect affiliated infantry units, was seventeen per day. At present the British were able to supply their field guns in France with only ten to eleven rounds a day and it would take at least another month before their output reached the desired number. It followed that if the New Armies were sent out with their proper proportion of artillery the number of rounds per gun per day would be substantially reduced.

Recently Kitchener, against his better judgment, had yielded to the pressing importunities of Sir John and had consented to send out reinforcements before the supply of artillery ammunition had reached the proper scale. As a result he had to endure a very heavy press attack, which had been immensely supported by the army in France. If the government had made a mistake it was not so much due to its failure to produce ammunition in greater quantities as in yielding to demands for the dispatch of additional troops. Kitchener felt it would be a grave mistake for the government to repeat this and he did not wish to send more divisions until the production of artillery ammunition had reached the standard of seventeen rounds per day for the existing force and had expanded sufficiently to enable the same proportion of shells to be supplied to the new troops as they went out.

Apart from the ammunition question there were strategic arguments for keeping the New Armies at home. If these troops were dispatched to Flanders they would be utilized for renewing the offensive. This, Kitchener was convinced, would be playing into the enemy's hands. He agreed with Joffre that the Germans were weaker in France than they had been for some time as their main strength was committed in the east. Yet the latest Anglo-French effort proved almost conclusively that attacks involved colossal losses without corresponding gains. By dissipating their strength the Allies were inviting disaster. The fact that the Russians were in full retreat sharpened Kitchener's fear lest the Germans decide at any moment to break off battle against them and transfer perhaps as many as eight corps to mount a gigantic offensive in the west. In these circumstances the Anglo-French armies would be unable to withstand the enemy's onslaught. It was for such an emergency that Kitchener wished to retain a few divisions in reserve.

In conclusion Kitchener urged Joffre to adopt a defensive strategy, hoping that the Germans would seize the initiative. He was certain that if the Germans hurled their hordes against the Anglo-French line they would not only fail but suffer horrendous losses.[5]

Joffre had made no attempt to inform Sir John of his letter to the secretary for war. Sidney Clive felt compelled to break the news to the field marshal when he learned that Asquith was scheduled to visit General Headquarters at the start of June.[6] Sir John was furious, vowing never to trust Joffre again.[7] Technically Joffre had no right to communicate directly with Kitchener, at least not before obtaining Sir John's approval beforehand. It was not merely the breach in protocol that aroused Sir John's anger but more important the challenge that it represented to his authority.

By June 4 when Joffre forwarded a draft of his scheme to General Headquarters Sir John was in a more settled frame of mind. The French commander asked that the British assist his operation by taking over a stretch of line south of Arras and by attacking in the Lens–La Bassée area alongside the Tenth Army. Sir John agreed in principle to Joffre's proposals and on the 11th notified Kitchener of his decision. He laid it down as imperative that the Anglo-French forces strike before the Germans returned from Galicia and put the whole weight of their shoulder against the western front.[8] Kitchener, as we have seen, preferred a defensive strategy and therefore showed no enthusiasm for the proposed offensive.

Nevertheless Sir John went ahead with his preparations and on the 19th held a meeting with Foch. He indicated he would be ready around July 10 and that the objective of his attack would be the Loos-Hulluch ridge.[9] This conformed with French plans and the next day Haig, whose First Army was to conduct the British operation, was asked to give his views. The sector selected for the attack was dotted by mine pits, slag heaps, quarries, and mining villages, which offered special facilities for the defense. Joffre knew that the ground was unsuitable for an attack but then this was not the first time that he showed a brutal lack of consideration for his ally.

Haig made a personal reconnaissance of the region and took counsel with his Corps Commanders before submitting his report. He concluded:

It would be possible to capture the enemy's first line of trenches (say a length of 1200 yards) opposite Maroc (west of Loos), but it would not be possible to advance beyond, because our own artillery could not support us, as ground immediately in front cannot be seen from any part of our front. On the other hand the enemy has excellent observing stations for his artillery. . . . The enemy's defenses are now so strong that, lacking sufficient ammunition to destroy them, they can only be taken by siege methods—by using bombs, and by hand-to-hand fighting in the trenches—the ground above is so swept by gun and machine-gun and rifle fire that an advance in the open, except by night, is impossible.[10]

Haig's arguments were even sounder than he realized because unknown to him the Germans were in the process of building a second defensive system, two to four miles behind the first. The second line was carefully situated on reverse slopes and so concealed from Allied artillery observation. In front the barbed-wire entanglements, some fifteen feet in breadth, were out of Allied artillery range and made of such strong wire that it could not be severed by hand cutters.[11]

Haig would have preferred no attack until adequate reserves of ammunition had been accumulated but if one had to be made he thought it should be made farther north between Messines and Ypres, a sector held by the Second Army. He still believed that the capture of Aubers Ridge would give the best tactical results.

Sir John went over Haig's memorandum on June 23. He noted in his diary: "I am considering the whole subject very carefully, and am inclined to think we must adhere to our original plans. I think Haig exaggerates the difficulties."[12] Despite Sir John's reservations about Haig's objections to an attack in the Loos-Hulluch sector he transmitted them to Joffre without comment.

Although Sir John saw that a new offensive would have to be undertaken in concert with the French he held the view that it should be put off as long as possible. Recent events had pointed to the desirability of a delay. On June 19th and 20th a conference took place at Boulogne between the French and British munitions ministers and representatives from both G.Q.G. and General Headquarters at which the requirements of trench warfare were realistically assessed. The conclusion arrived at was that an offensive on the western front, if it was to have a reasonable hope of success, would have to extend across a front of twenty-five miles and would require not less than thirty-six divisions, supported by 1,150 heavy guns and howitzers, in addition to the normal complement of field artillery. Since the requisite men, guns, and ammunition could not be provided until the spring of 1916 it was suggested that, until then, an active defensive be maintained in the western theater.

The results pleased Kitchener, who now felt able to meet Hamilton's demands for reinforcements. Towards the end of April 29,000 British troops had landed on six beaches at Gallipoli but found it impossible to drive the Turks from their prepared positions on the dominating slopes. Kitchener hoped that an additional five divisions would permit Hamilton to bring the campaign to a successful conclusion.

On June 26 Kitchener drew up a memorandum that reinforced the findings of the Boulogne conference. It was intended not only for the British cabinet but for G.Q.G. as well. Kitchener observed that he was unimpressed by the arguments for an autumn offensive and that his reasons for remaining on the defensive were based on the unreadiness of the New Armies and the shortage of war matériel. He asserted that the chances of success would be lost if an attack on the main front could not be coordinated with a Russian advance. But until the Russian armies could be provided with much-need guns and ammunition, a synchronized assault was out of the question.[13]

Nothing, however, could shake Joffre from his determination to renew the offensive. The entire male population in France was either in the army or engaged in war-related industries and currently productive trade was at a standstill. This, together with the occupation by the enemy of a large and valuable part of French territory, had a very adverse effect on the morale of the public. Finally as Lord Esher explained:

> There were political reasons . . . which were not put forward, but were of common knowledge in France, that made a successful offensive indispensable to the security of the French Ministry. There had been bitter attacks in the Committee of the Senate upon the conduct of the war, upon General Joffre and M. Millerand, which were not without weight in the decision of the Grand Quartier Général to stick out for the offensive planned by the Staff. From what was said at Chantilly it was clear that the conviction of its necessity was unfaltering.[14]

The pressing need to agree upon a military policy for the western front prompted the British government to request a meeting with the French authorities. Esher told Kitchener that he doubted whether Joffre would or even could agree to complete inaction until the spring of 1916. He claimed that owing to internal factors Joffre was under pressure to try to end the war before winter set in.[15] This fact was confirmed by Sir John, who came over on July 1 to consult with the government about the strategy of the coming months. On July 3 the cabinet met with French and Wilson in attendance. The ministers, having affirmed that the main effort should be in the western theater, concluded that: (1) the French ought to be told what forces would be forthcoming; (2) the British should take over additional lengths of the line, which would free French troops for service elsewhere; (3) pending the development of munitions the Allies should act on the defensive; (4) if the French insisted on delivering an attack it should be a minor one and Sir John "will lend such co-operation with his existing forces as, in his judgment, will be useful for the purpose, and not unduly costly to his army."[16]

While in London Sir John requested an official policy on a line of retreat in case the BEF was driven back.[17] Sir John held that the Channel ports were so vital to England's safety that they must be defended at all costs, even at the risk of losing contact with the French army. Kitchener thought otherwise and presented the following arguments. The loss of the Channel ports would greatly hamper operations but could not decide the issue of the war. The Germans had failed when their army was more efficient than it is now and would assuredly fail again if the Allied armies remained united. On the other hand if the British were to separate and take up a position in front of Calais and Boulogne it would certainly mean defeat in detail, for the Germans could leave a small containing force while falling upon the French in great strength. As Sir John remained unconvinced, the matter was put off until a later date.

Sir John was back at General Headquarters on July 5 but at 6:30 next morning he took the train to Calais to attend the Anglo-French conference. It was not one of Sir John's most memorable trips. There was no official of any kind to greet him when he disembarked on the station platform. He followed in the wake of Joffre and suffered from the dust thrown up by the general's automobile. His annoyance turned to anger when later he learned that Joffre and Kitchener had engaged in private talks in the course of a stroll.[18]

The meeting between Kitchener and Joffre took place just before the conference itself. In the beginning neither man would yield ground but eventually a compromise was reached. If a major assault was deemed necessary it would be undertaken by French forces alone. The English were to extend their front and were to participate only in minor offensive operations. Kitchener promised to send to France during the month of July six new divisions to be followed each succeeding month by six more. As the new troops arriving in France were not properly equipped to fight, he hoped that they would be "put in the trenches rather than called upon for active operations." When the meeting broke up Kitchener was under the impression that he had nearly persuaded Joffre to limit the scope of operations in the west for the remainder of the year.

The first Anglo-French convention of the war got under way at 10:00 A.M. with Asquith in the chair. There was no agenda and no minutes were taken, an unfortunate omission in view of the conflicting testimony and misunderstandings. Kitchener was the only Englishman present who spoke fluent French. "I have never heard so much bad French spoken in my life," Asquith subsequently wrote. "Not one of the French could speak a word of English."

Kitchener dominated the proceedings and enjoyed a great personal triumph. He was calm, frank, and consistent in his arguments and created a tremendous impression on everyone. The French, who hitherto had been prepared to follow Joffre's lead, were won over and agreed to pursue an active defensive strategy in the west. That policy did not preclude local offensives to straighten out awkward salients or to seize important tactical positions.

Joffre appeared to have acquiesced in his government's acceptance of the British view. In reality he had not abandoned his design for a full-scale offensive and continued to make preparations as if nothing new had been decided. When everything was ready he evidently expected to be able to convince both the British and French governments of its necessity.[19]

On July 7 an inter-Allied military conference was held at Chantilly. Besides Joffre the meeting was attended by Sir John and representatives of the Belgian, Serbian, Russian, and Italian armies. Reading from a prepared statement Joffre listed three reasons why a fresh movement in the west was vital: first, to relieve pressure on the faltering Russians; second, to keep up the fighting spirit of the troops; and third, because the Germans were not in great strength along the line. Sir John concurred with Joffre and thought that the attack should take place at the earliest possible moment. The Serbian, Italian, and Belgian delegates indicated that they too would carry out offensive operations in their respective theaters as far as circumstances permitted.[20]

By committing himself to support a major offensive Sir John had acted contrary to the wishes and instructions of the British government. When he returned to General Headquarters the prime minister, who was there as his guest, asked if anything important had taken place at the conference. Sir John replied that nothing definite had been settled.[21] Obviously it was necessary for him to inform subordinates like Haig and Robertson of the decision to participate in the projected offensive. Thus he misled them into believing that the British government had yielded to Joffre's judgment at Calais.[22] In order to achieve his end French was reduced to playing a dangerous double game, deceiving both the British authorities and his subordinates.

During July and August sharp disagreements arose between Sir John and Joffre as to the precise locality of the British attack. On June 20 French had agreed, in spite of strong objections from Haig, to conform to Joffre's wish that the British movement take place south of the La Bassée Canal in close conjunction with d'Urbal's Tenth Army.[23] But by the third week in July Sir John, having made a careful study of the ground and received reports of a second enemy line of defense in the rear, had changed his mind. On July 27 Sir John arranged a meeting with Foch at Frévent in the hope of modifying the original scheme.

Sir John explained that while he had every desire to help the Tenth Army, he would prefer to make his own attack further north against the Wytschaete-Messines and Aubers ridges instead of the sector south of La

Bassée Canal, where the ground was less suitable. Foch maintained that an attack in the Loos-Hulluch area would be of much greater assistance to the Tenth Army in its efforts to capture Vimy Ridge. A subsidiary attack at some distance from the flanks of the main offensive, either north of the La Basée Canal or in the neighborhood of Ypres, could not engage enemy artillery north of the Tenth Army and was not likely to draw off enemy reserves. He conceded that an offensive in the direction of Loos-Hulluch presented considerable difficulties but as far as he could see the German lines were strong everywhere. Therefore an assault on another part of the front would not be much easier and would certainly bring less advantageous results.

Sir John said that before rendering his decision he wished a day or so to consider Foch's arguments.[24] Privately French told Wilson that he had been persuaded and that he intended to attack on the immediate left of the Tenth Army even though he knew that this idea would be vigorously opposed by Haig and Robertson.[25] Sir John's resolve disappeared as soon as he returned to General Headquarters and had to face Robertson. A record of the discussion has not been preserved but at the end Sir John's outlook had changed again. The next day French called in Wilson, whose account of the interview reads as follows:

He . . . horrified me by saying he was not going to attack alongside the French, having told me yesterday he was going to. He went through the usual childish lies, that Joffre never told him anything, that the French could not be trusted, that Foch had changed his plans etc., and that in consequence he would attack elsewhere. He said he wanted to get out of the low ground and would take Messines ridge and Aubers Ridge! The man is really useless and dangerous.[26]

Clive, who was at General Headquarters in the afternoon, noted in his diary that Robertson had no faith in the French scheme. The chief of staff considered that any Allied attack under existing conditions would at best make another dent in the enemy line. He saw no possibility of creating a serious breach in the German front until Allied superiority, both in men and guns, had been greatly increased.[27]

On the 29th Sir John sent letters to both Foch and Joffre. He indicated that he had carefully considered Foch's remarks but could find no cause to alter his expressed opinion, namely that any tactical success south of La Basée Canal was improbable. He disagreed with Foch that the enemy's line was held in anything like the same strength throughout and was convinced that there were several points where an attack offered infinitely greater advantages. He believed that the capture of Aubers and Messines-Wytschaete ridges would deprive the enemy of important facilities for observation, push the British line out of the water-logged valley of the Lys and provide an admirable springboard for offensive operations early in 1916. Sir John admitted that on a former occasion (June 20) he had favored acting in close proximity to the left of the Tenth Army but at that time he did not appreciate the enormous difficulties involved in such an attack. Now that he had stated his views he was quite prepared to assist the general operations in whatever manner and direction which Joffre, as Generalissimo, thought best.[28]

Robertson argued in vain against the inclusion of the last paragraph in the letter, which placed the British army unreservedly in Joffre's hands. He was still angry several hours later when Wilson paid him a visit. Robertson said, according to Wilson, that he was fed up with Sir John, "who chopped and changed every day and was quite hopeless."[29]

Joffre, not surprisingly, dismissed Sir John's concerns and clung to his original suggestion, which he repeated on August 5. He made the absurd and laughable claim that no more favorable ground for an attack could be found than that which extended between Loos and La Bassée.[30] Sir John remained unconvinced but as a means out of the dilemma devised a compromise. He would cooperate at first by artillery fire alone and then wait for the French attack to absorb the enemy's attention before committing his infantry.[31] Wilson got wind of the idea and promptly communicated it to General Pellé, Joffre's new chief of staff.[32] Thereupon Joffre wrote a strongly worded letter to the field marshal, saying that he required a large and powerful attack regardless of conditions.[33] Sir John had no intention of complying with Joffre's demand yet he wished to appear cooperative. He ordered Robertson to draft a reply to the effect that "he would assist according to ammunition."[34] Wilson at once rushed to see Foch and told him what Sir John proposed to do. "Foch . . . was quite open about the deplorable effect if we don't fight," Wilson wrote in his diary. "Sir John had better walk warily."[35] The growing controversy threatened to disrupt Anglo-French relations.

At this point Kitchener, having been invited to inspect the French army and its defenses, crossed the Channel. He was provided with a special train for his personal use and was received, wherever he went, with pomp and ceremony. On August 16 he visited Compiègne, where he saw Joffre and Wilson. During the next two days he had a number of conversations with Wilson and a private conference with Joffre that lasted several hours. Both men used every argument they could think of, whether legitimate or not, to gain Kitchener's support against Sir John.

Kitchener had known for at least three weeks (thanks to Yarde-Buller) that Joffre intended to attack in September and that Sir John had agreed to cooperate.[36] He had no knowledge, however, of the dimensions of the French attack or of the precise nature of the promised British support. Whenever he had asked Sir John for details on these matters he had received vague or dishonest replies.

Since early in the year Kitchener had favored a defensive policy in France until such time as the Allies were ready to strike. Kitchener had placed high hopes in the operations in Italy and Gallipoli as a means to forestall the crisis threatening Russia. But in August, amid reports of fresh disasters on the Russian front, came news of the failure of the Italians on the left bank of the Isonzo and of the collapse of Hamilton's second effort to reach the Narrows. Joffre told Kitchener that unless something was done on the western front it was doubtful whether the Russians could last much longer. Wilson went so far as to hint that Joffre was being held responsible for securing full British assistance and that if he should fail he would be replaced and the politicians would conclude a separate peace. Confronted by all these factors Kitchener relented and agreed to support the French offensive.

In all probability Kitchener would have adopted a different line had he known that Joffre's views were contrary to the declared policy of the French government. Actually Joffre subsequently used Kitchener's assent to persuade the cabinet to sanction his offensive. It was no secret in Paris that the British secretary for war had hitherto favored defensive action and so his change of heart was all the more meaningful.[37]

Sir John had no idea why Kitchener had come to France or that he had conferred with Joffre at Compiègne. The day before the secretary for war was scheduled to visit General Headquarters, French called Haig to his office. There is the following entry in Haig's diary:

French said he had been anxious to warn me not to talk to Lord K. . . . about the forthcoming operations. "If Lord K. were to know," said he, "he would tell the others in the Cabinet, and then all London would know! And the Germans would also get to hear of the proposed attack."[38]

In retrospect it seems amusing that Sir John, while regularly sharing military secrets with his mistress, should have mistrusted Kitchener, of all people. What is equally incongruous is that he should have thought it possible to conceal from the secretary for war the decision to mount the most important Anglo-French offensive that had yet taken place.

Kitchener, accompanied by Wilson, arrived at Hazebrouck at 8:00 A.M. on August 18th. Sir John as usual had not even bothered with the customary observances of military protocol. "Only Billy Lambton at station and no Guard of Honour which is d—— stupid,"[39] Wilson wrote in his diary. Kitchener took no notice of the slight, perhaps because French had treated him with the same neglect on previous occasions.

Kitchener was driven to General Headquarters and after lunch had a prolonged meeting with Sir John. He explained that the Russians had been severely handled and that he was uncertain how much longer they could withstand the German blows. Up to the present he had favored an active-

defensive policy in France but the deteriorating situation on the Russian front had forced him to modify his position. He now felt that the Allies must attack vigorously in order to take some of the pressure off Russia. Therefore he had determined that the British army must act with the utmost energy in helping the French even at the cost of "very heavy losses."[40] Sir John's views are not recorded but he appears to have agreed with the decision. Kitchener's intervention had lifted the burden of responsibility from his shoulders.

Next day Kitchener explained to French why he and the cabinet had not introduced universal military service. He admitted that conscription would bring certain benefits such as reducing the enlistment of key men from essential war industries. On the other hand he was convinced that the liabilities would be far greater. He maintained that there was strong opposition to compulsion among the working classes and that the army had neither the arms, ammunition, nor organization to absorb the number of men who would be called up under compulsory service. He wanted the current voluntary system retained as long as it produced adequate recruits.

French expressed his views on the subject and later, at Kitchener's request, put them down in writing. French observed that while he could not form an accurate judgment on the effect conscription would have on the nation, he thought it would have an adverse impact on the army in the field. In the first place he considered it unwise to start a complex and unproved system in the midst of a great war. Then too he felt that to integrate conscripts with volunteers serving under entirely different terms and conditions would be detrimental to the discipline and spirit of the army.[41] French did not rule out compulsion at a later date and, in fact, toward the end of October, when it was apparent that voluntary recruiting was slackening, he submitted a second note, suggesting that the time had arrived for its adoption "without any delay or hesitation."[42]

Kitchener left General Headquarters on August 20 and returned directly to London. On his arrival he heard of the fall of the fortress of Novo Georgievsk, the last Russian foothold on the Vistula. He telegraphed to French on the following day confirming his instructions and telling him "to take the offensive and act vigorously."[43]

Thereupon Sir John informed Joffre that he would attack south of La Bassée Canal with all the resources at his disposal. Joffre expressed his satisfaction and fixed the date of the Anglo-French offensive for September 8. The French preparations in Champagne, however, proved more difficult than had been anticipated. On August 31 the date of the attack was postponed a week, to September 15, and a few days later it was further delayed until the 25th. By mid-September it was sufficiently clear that the Germans would be unable to drive the Russians out of the war before the onset of winter. The main argument on which Joffre had justified the Allied offensive was therefore no longer valid. But Joffre's real motive was

Field Marshal French makes a wayside inspection of infantry on their way to the trenches.
(Photo courtesy of The Mansell Collection)

Sir John leaving his headquarters in August 1915
(Photo courtesy of Imperial War Musuem)

not to relieve the pressure off the Russians but to redeem his sagging reputation.

On September 14 Joffre gave a final summary of his plans at a conference at Chantilly that was attended by Sir John and three French army group commanders. Joffre considered that the moment was particularly favorable for a general offensive and expressed his confidence in a great and possibly decisive victory. He noted that the Entente partners held a three-to-two advantage in rifles over the Germans, who had now massed one-third of their armed forces against Russia. By weakening certain sectors of the front and concentrating in great strength at the points of attack, the numerical superiority of the Allies would become five or six to one. It was necessary for all attacking troops not only to seize the first enemy trenches but to push on without respite, beyond the second and third lines, to the open country. The cavalry was to exploit the success and capture enemy batteries "a long way in front of the infantry." The scope and strength of the simultaneous attacks were "a certain guarantee of success."

Joffre's original plan of operations had undergone one important change. He had decided to shift his main assault from Artois to Champagne, where there were practically no obstacles or villages in the way of the attackers. This was in sharp contrast to the densely built-up region in which he had asked the British to fight. And by weakening the French stroke in Artois Joffre further damaged the prospects of Haig's attack.

For Sir John the next fornight was a period of acute anxiety. On the whole he was, after nursing momentary doubts, optimistic that the attack would succeed. But he knew that Loos was his last chance personally as well the end of the road in a more permanent way for thousands of his troops. He told Mrs. Bennett on September 18:

Another day of preparation—hard, hard preparation. It is such a big thing Darling and so much, so very much depends upon the next 2 or 3 weeks. I feel here we've left no stone unturned. But, after all, we may fail of real attainment. . . . Whatever may happen I shall have to bear the brunt of it and in cricket language they may "Change the bowler." . . . Darling if it comes to that you won't blame me and that's all I care about in all the world.[44]

In another letter he wrote:

Seriously my darling the "day" is approaching and I am anxiously awaiting it. We shall of course have some terrific losses, but—alas we are getting accustomed to that now. War is a very brutal way of settling differences, and the more I see of it the more I hate it.[45]

To make matters worse Sir John was bothered by a reoccurrence of ill health. The strain of high command continued to take its toll on French's health. Throughout 1915 he was frequently confined to bed, sometimes for a long period, with fever and probably further heart disease.

Sir John's uneasiness over the impending attack, combined with his failing health, appeared to heighten his tendency towards indecisiveness and intemperate outbursts. "Robertson told me this morning that he can't get Sir John to do anything," Wilson wrote in his diary. "He won't even allow instructions to go out."[46] On September 17, when news reached General Headquarters that Kitchener was coming over to confer with Joffre, Sir John erupted into a furious rage. "I saw Brinsley later and he said the explosion was a bad one," Wilson observed in his diary. "Of course Sir J. simply hates K. coming out, and loathes the sight of him and is more jealous than any woman."[47] Kitchener visited General Headquarters on September 20 in order to discuss his meeting with Joffre. As Kitchener was talking, Sir John interrupted with an ill-tempered denunciation of Joffre and the French. Kitchener subsequently commented that Sir John's outburst "had simply knocked him out, he could not understand it" and thought "an open rupture with Joffre quite likely."[48] As might be expected Sir John's behavior contributed to the growing uneasiness among his staff.

On the other hand Haig's outward demeanor, which as usual was calm and self-contained, created a more relaxed atmosphere at First Army Headquarters. Haig's First Army now held a front of some eighteen miles, with its right flank on the Grenay-Lens road, where it joined the left of the French Tenth Army. Its left flank joined the right of Plumer's Second Army at Armentières. The First Army consisted of four corps that were arranged from north to south as follows: the III commanded by Pulteney, the Indian by Sir Charles Anderson, the I by Hubert Gough, and the IV by Rawlinson. The attack was to be carried out by the I and IV corps on a frontage of six miles from Grenay to La Bassée Canal. To oppose this assault force of 75,000 men, only thirteen German battalions, numbering 10,000 to 11,000 troops, were immediately available.

As the day of battle approached a dispute broke out between Haig and French over the disposition of the general reserve, that is, the XI Corps.[49] This corps, under the command of Lieutenant-General R. Haking, consisted of the newly formed but seasoned Guards Division and two New Army divisions (the Twenty-first and Twenty-fourth), which were composed of completely raw soldiers with inexperienced staffs. The Twenty-first and Twenty-fourth divisions had left England on September 9 and August 30 respectively, only several weeks before the final date fixed for the battle. Since the action south of La Bassée Canal was expected to be among the severest of the campaign it is impossible to comprehend why French selected, as a reserve, green divisions when seasoned ones could have been taken from quiet sectors nearby. In January 1915 Sir John, referring to the employment of New Armies in the field, had written: "The experience I have gained during the war leads me to a very decided conclusion that it would not be advisable to organize troops so raised and so trained, and having only such officers and staff as are available, in any higher units than brigades."[50] In other words, he felt that any unit of the New Armies numbering more than 3,000 was likely to fall into chaos during an operation. By September, however, he had decided that it was better to use new, untried troops when the enemy was on the run. These, he contended, had vigor and enthusiasm whereas the more experienced soldiers had acquired the sedentary habits of trench warfare and would be reluctant to push too far forward.

Haig's previous experience had impressed upon him the necessity of keeping fresh divisions forward in order to exploit any initial success. All his available units, including reserves, had been committed to the first assault on the basis that a breakthrough was the essential objective. Haig assumed that the IX Corps would be on hand and at his disposal before the battle actually began.

French, however, had different ideas. He wanted to retain control of the general reserve until, in his judgment, its presence on the battlefield was required. The XI Corps was his only reserve (apart from the Cavalry Corps) and he could not exclude the possibility that the Germans might launch a counterstroke against some other portion of the British front. He aimed to keep the reserves in his own hands until the last possible moment. If the battle opened unfavorably he would not throw them in. On the other hand if all went well he hoped to use them to administer the coup de grâce.

It was during a conference on September 18 that Sir John announced his decision to keep the whole of the general reserve in the neighborhood of Lillers, more than sixteen miles behind the British front. He maintained that the number of troops under Haig's command were sufficient to carry out the initial assault and secure any ground gained. Haig protested, saying that the general reserve was too distant from the battle to take advantage of the first break in the enemy's defenses. He urged that two divisions of the XI Corps be moved forward so that they might be deployed in rear of Vermelles, about 2,000 yards behind the assaulting forces. Sir John dismissed Haig's fears and declared flatly that he would hold back the general reserve until the battle had sufficiently developed to enable him to determine if and when it was needed.

In a formal letter on September 19 Haig renewed his appeal to the commander-in-chief. He observed that the plan of operations of the First Army was based on the assumption that the general reserve would be close at hand and it was essential that the leading units of the XI should be on the line Noeux les Mines–Beuvry (that is, 4,000–5,000 yards behind Vermelles) by daybreak on September 25. Sir John replied in the evening: "Two divisions of the XI Corps will be assembled in the area referred to in your letter by daybreak on the 25th September." But as the reserves would not be arriving in the Lillers area until the 24th it meant that they would have to undergo an exhausting night march in order to be in the position where Haig required them before the battle.

Understandably this did not suit Haig, who wanted the troops placed at his disposal and moved up from their concentration area by the 24th so that they could get a night of complete rest and be available to give the support necessary to carry forward a successful attack. He was worried enough to broach the subject to Kitchener in the course of a conversation on the 20th.[51] Charteris was certain that Kitchener would have overruled French if Haig had asked him to do so.[52] He was wrong. Kitchener would have taken no such action under any circumstances, for it was his policy never to interfere in the actual conduct of field operations.

Haig made one final effort to bring Sir John to a reasonable frame of mind. He sent his chief staff officer to General Headquarters with a plea that the general reserve be on the line previously indicated by the night of the 24th. French gave assurances that before the battle the troops would be where Haig wanted them.

Haig had another major preoccupation. He had decided to use poison gas as a means to compensate for the increased strength of the German defenses and for the British deficiency of artillery and munitions. Much was expected from this new weapon but its use and efficacy depended entirely upon the direction and strength of the wind. Haig wanted a variable date for the assault in case conditions were unfavorable on September 25. The French, however, were not using gas and Joffre insisted that the attack take place as arranged. Haig worked out a compromise that allowed a margin of three days to secure a reliable wind. If the wind did not permit the use of gas on September 25 he would attack that day with only two divisions, waiting until the 26th or 27th to put in his main assault.

Haig spent an uneasy night on August 24–25 in constant consultation with Captain E. Gold, the meteorologist attached to the Royal Flying Corps. Shortly before midnight the wind, hitherto favorable, dropped almost to a calm. Gold, who had access to meteorological reports in both France and England, predicted that just before sunrise a breeze would spring up from the southwest (which was the right direction) and would last several hours. Haig went out with Colonel Fletcher, a staff officer, as soon as it was light. It seemed to him that there was not a breath of wind when he saw the smoke from Fletcher's cigarette drift slowly but surely towards the enemy. At 5:15 A.M. Haig gave the order to "carry on" and then went up to the top of his observation tower.[53]

At 5:30 A.M., as the guns opened fire, the chlorine gas was released from the cylinders in the front trenches of the IV and I corps.[54] The yellowish white fumes built up into a dense cloud, thirty to fifty feet high, which drifted sluggishly across No Man's Land. The progress of the gas varied. In places it reached the German front line; in other sectors it hung about No Man's Land or even drifted back. At 6:30 A.M. the bombardment ceased

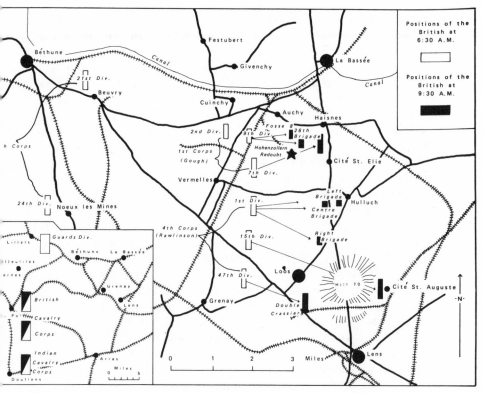

THE BATTLE OF LOOS

and the infantrymen of six divisions, wearing their gas helmets, clambered out of the trenches and advanced through the fog of gas and smoke.

The assault by the I Corps in the northern sector met with varying fortune. The Second Division's advance on the extreme left was held up by gas blowing back and by uncut wire entanglements. On the remainder of the I Corps's front the attack was very successful, overcoming staunch resistance and capturing the enemy's first line.

It was further south on the front of the IV Corps that the deepest penetration was achieved. The First Division on the left swept past the enemy's trenches in the first rush, reaching the outskirts of Hulluch. In the center the Fifteenth Division, whose Highland brigades were urged on by the martial music of bagpipes, rushed straight on through the village of Loos but failed to take the dominant Hill 70 beyond it. The men of the Forty-seventh Division, on the extreme right, had seen action at Aubers Ridge and Festubert and they showed their spirit by kicking a football ahead of them as they crossed No Man's Land. Coming behind a curtain of smoke and gas they stormed through the defenders' front trench and formed a flank covering the right of the Fifteenth Division.

Haig was pleased with what his men had accomplished in the first few hours of fighting. Each division, except the Second, which had encountered adverse conditions, had taken the enemy's first position and advanced beyond it. The Germans were reeling and demoralized and it seemed only to require another vigorous push to clear them from their second line. Haig's corps, in keeping with their instructions, had attacked with their full force and retained no troops as a reserve. They were exhausted after their initial burst of energy and their numbers terribly depleted by casualties. Nothing but fresh troops could carry the attack forward. But those fresh troops did not appear until it was too late. What had been the reason for their absence?

Sir John's final instructions to General Haking were that the Twenty-first and Twenty-fourth divisions were to start moving after 6:00 P.M. on the 24th to the line selected by General Haig, that is, Noeux les Mines–Beuvry. French retained control over the Guards Division, which was to march in rear to the area south of Lillers. Behind the Guards Division stood the cavalry ready, as usual, to push through a breach in the enemy lines.

General Headquarters expected that the Twenty-first and Twenty-fourth divisions could cover the distance—seven to eleven miles—to their final assembly position in three or four hours. This meant that they would arrive by midnight and could get a good night's rest before the battle. However, the march, accompanied by unnecessary hardships and delays, took twice the scheduled time. Nobody, including the staff officers, knew the ground and there had been no time to issue large-scale maps. No marking tapes or other arrangements for directing the men had been provided along the route. The roads were narrow and the marching columns were hampered by the congested traffic, transport vehicles, ambulances, and walking wounded endeavoring to go in all sorts of directions. It was, as the official history caustically described it, "like trying to push the Lord Mayor's procession through the streets of London without clearing the route and holding up the traffic."[55] There were also endless delays at the level crossings to allow side-tracking and passage of supply trains. At Place à Bruay an accident held up the Sixty-fourth Brigade for over an hour and a half. Folly gave way to farce on the outskirts of Béthune, where a military policeman stopped the Seventy-second Brigade because its commander had no pass to enter the area. With no clear direction broken units occasionally lost their way or took wrong turns and then had to struggle back to rejoin their column. Heavy rain added to the difficulties and discomforts of the march.

The two divisions began to arrive in their allotted areas between 1:00 A.M. and 2:00 A.M. on the 25th, the last parties not getting in until after 6:00 A.M. Far from being ready and rested when the attack got under way the men were dead tired, hungry, and soaked to the skin. Sir John should have foreseen the difficulties and delays that invariably occur in moving troops close behind a battle front. War-experienced divisions would have managed to get up more quickly but it is doubtful if even they would have been ready in time. Infantry, unlike cavalry, cannot be moved swiftly from one place to another. At any rate Sir John was obviously at fault for not putting the reserves under Haig in the first instance and, failing to do so, for not ordering the move forward twenty-four hours earlier than he did.

French made another mistake in selecting Chateau Philomel, some three miles south of Lillers, as his forward command post. Here he was conveniently located to command the three reserve divisions but he was not in telephone communication with Haig. For most of the time, therefore, he was out of touch with what was happening at the front.

Around 7:00 A.M. on August 25 Haig, having received the first news of the progress of his two corps, sent a staff officer to inform French of the success of his assault and to urge that the XI Corps be ready to move up at once in support. At 8:45 A.M. an officer arrived from General Headquarters to offer the field marshal's congratulations. Haig sent him back at once to tell Sir John that the reserve brigades of the I and IV corps had reached the German trenches and to beg him to place Haking's corps under his control. French waited until 9:30 A.M. before ordering the advance of the Twenty-first and Twenty-fourth divisions and even then did not put them under Haig. It took an hour for Sir John's orders to reach the two divisions and it was not until 11:15 A.M. that they got under way. Owing to the usual congestion in the battle area it was not until 3:00 P.M. that the leading brigades began to arrive in their new positions about Marzingarbe and Noyelles, still about two-and-a-half miles behind the original British front.

At 11:30 A.M. French visited Haig's headquarters and during the conversation agreed to surrender control of two of Haking's three divisions. Haking informed Haig at 1:20 P.M. that his men were marching to the areas ordered but were experiencing delays on the road. Haig continued to believe that the situation was favorable and that the two reserve divisions would be able to carry forward the attack and break down entirely the tottering German second line of defense. At 2:35 P.M. he directed Haking to make a further advance, to push forward between Hulluch and Cité Saint Auguste and occupy the high ground in the Harnes–Pont à Vendin area. Further delays occurred before these orders were transmitted to the brigades concerned. Consequently by the time they reached the battlefield it was nightfall and they were unable to take part in the fighting on August 25.

Opportunities in battle, once missed, are rarely repeated. Nevertheless Haig decided to continue the attack next day. News had arrived that the Tenth Army's assault had made little progress so that the Germans were still in possession of Vimy Ridge. Success on the British front would undoubtedly ease the way for the French. Then too Haig was under the impression that the Germans were on the verge of defeat, that they had been driven completely from their main defensive position, and that their

German soldiers wiring their "Second Position"
(Photo courtesy of the Imperial War Museum)

Loos in October 1915
(Photo courtesy of the Imperial War Museum)

back line was held by a weak and demoralized force. Because of faulty means of communication Haig was unaware of the tremendous losses suffered by his two corps or of the gaps in the new British front. Still there were two other vital considerations that were known to Haig and to which he failed to give sufficient weight. First, the element of surprise, the key to success on the 25th, was gone. Second, Intelligence had warned First Army headquarters that German local reserves (consisting of five divisions) could begin to reach the threatened sector within twelve hours of the alarm. In fact twenty-two additional battalions were moved into the battle area so that by daylight on the 26th the second position was more strongly held than the first had been at the time of the initial British assault.

The central idea in Haig's plan on August 26 called for the Twenty-first and Twenty-fourth divisions to push through the German second line and take the Haute Deule Canal, five miles further east. The advance was to be supported by the capture of Hill 70 on the right and of Hulluch and Cité Saint Elie on the left. The preliminary bombardment was to open at 5:00 A.M.

When the shelling lifted at 9:00 A.M. on the 26th, the Forty-fifth and Sixty-second brigades (Fifteenth Division) at the southern end charged forward towards the crest of Hill 70. The redoubt had been strengthened during the night but parties of the attacking battalions broke in and in hand-to-hand fighting killed or drove out most of the garrison. Advancing past the flanks of the redoubt the British were cut to pieces by a heavy crossfire from both sides, as well as by artillery fire from Lens and Cité Saint Auguste. After repeated but vain efforts to push the line forward, the survivors withdrew behind the crestline.

At the other end the First Division made an attempt to capture Hulluch, using the Welsh, the Black Watch, and the South Wales Borderers. The Welsh on the right immediately came under fire and lost nearly a hundred men before they reached the Lens-La Bassée road. Here they ran into a party of Germans who, throwing away their arms, ran back as hard as they could and disappeared through the barbed wire into their trenches. The Welsh pressed on, but since they were unsupported on their left, were brought to a halt facing Hulluch. Through a misunderstanding the Black Watch and South Wales Borderers delivered their assault at noon, an hour later than originally scheduled. To reach the western side of Hulluch they had to cross 600 yards of open ground. Before they had covered 100 yards their numbers had been halved and, as there seemed no chance of reaching the village, the attack was broken off. Thus the assault on Hulluch produced no results.

It was now the turn of the Twenty-first and Twenty-fourth divisions. As zero hour approached, the contest for Hill 70 was in doubt and Hulluch was still in enemy hands. The two divisions, exhausted by their night march on the 24th and further tried by a long difficult march through the battle area on the 25th, were in no condition to meet for the first time the full stress and strain of battle. To make matters worse they had to advance over open ground, with insufficient artillery support and with no smoke or gas to cover them, and attack a position strongly manned and protected by a formidable and intact barbed-wire entanglement. It did not require exceptional perspicacity to foresee that an unprepared attack by two inexperienced and exhausted divisions was unlikely to succeed.

At 11:00 A.M. the men of the Twenty-first and Twenty-fourth divisions rose out of the trenches and moved up in close formation across No Man's Land, which was littered with the dead and wounded of the previous day. The Germans watched in silence as the advancing columns drew closer and, when they were at a range of about 1,000 yards, the order to fire was given. The slaughter was fearful. Assailed in front and from both flanks, entire battalions were annihilated. The attack continued and small parties reached the German wire but were unable to penetrate it. Some tried to scramble over it while others ran along its edge, in the hope of finding a gap, until they were cut down. As if things were not difficult enough British artillery shells fell short, causing considerable loss and discouragement in the ranks of the attackers. But the clinching factor was the loss of many front-line officers. The men, having lost all sense of purpose and direction, turned and fled in one huge mass, some going beyond the original trench line and on to the neighborhood of Vermelles and Philosophe before they could be rallied. The Guards Division was rushed up to fill the void. In the late afternoon Haking came down from his headquarters and mingled with some of the survivors of the Twenty-first and Twenty-fourth divisions. To his obvious question he got much the same reply: "We did not understand what it was like; we will do all right next time."

The attack had been a complete failure and by nightfall much of the ground gained in the initial push had been retaken by the Germans. Haig felt frustrated and embittered that the reserve divisions had not reached him in time to reap the fruits of the first success. On September 29 he wrote to Kitchener on the subject:

> You will doubtless recollect how earnestly I pressed you to ensure an adequate reserve being close in rear of my attacking Divisions, and under my orders! It may interest you to know what happened. No reserve was placed under me. My attack, as has been reported, was a complete success. The enemy had no troops in his second line, which some of my plucky fellows reached and entered without opposition. Prisoners state that the enemy was so hard put to it for troops to stem our advance that the officers' servants, fatigue-men, etc., in Lens were pushed forward to hold their 2nd line to the east of Loos and Hill 70.
>
> The two Reserve Divisions (under C-in-C's orders) were directed to join me as soon as the success of the First Army was known at GHQ. They came on as quick as they could, poor fellows, but only crossed our

old trench line with their heads at 6 P.M. We had captured Loos 12 hours previously, and Reserves should have been at hand *then*. This, you will remember, I requested should be arranged by GHQ, and Robertson quite concurred in my views and wished to put the Reserve Divisions under me, but was not allowed.

The final result is that the enemy has been allowed time in which to bring up troops and to strengthen his second line, and *probably* to construct a third line in the direction in which we are heading, viz., Pont à Vendin.

I have now been given some fresh Divisions, and am busy planning an attack to break the enemy's second line. But the element of surprise has gone, and our task will be a difficult one.

I think it right that you should know how the lessons which have been learnt in the war at such cost have been neglected! We *were* in a position to make this the turning point in the war, and I still hope we may do so, but naturally I feel annoyed at the lost opportunity.[56]

Haig deceived himself when he claimed that Sir John's belated release of the reserves had robbed him of a brilliant victory. With an additional two or three divisions he would have advanced further but he would have had to deal with the enemy's reserves, which included the elite Guard Corps. German counterattacks would have hurled back his forward troops and at best he would have gained an awkward salient.

There can be no doubt that Sir John had erred grievously in keeping the reserves too far behind the attacking forces. Still, care must be taken not to overlook Haig's mismanagement of the operations on the 26th. It can be said that he wasted the two new divisions by sending them into battle before securing their flanks, without cover or adequate artillery support, and against a position that he had been warned would be strongly defended. It would have been better to use these troops to reinforce the badly depleted units of the two corps in a carefully prepared attack.

At the desire of Joffre the battle of Loos continued until mid-October, though without tangible gains. The French had also been held up at Artois and Champagne and had suffered nearly 200,000 casualties. The total German losses opposite the French amounted to 130,000. The British lost 50,000 officers and men in the main attacks alone, more than twice the number of casualties they inflicted on the enemy. A large portion of the British casualties occurred after the first failure, when the chance of an important tactical success had vanished. Indeed, in the final attacks on October 13–14 one division suffered almost 3,800 casualties, most of them in the first ten minutes of fighting.

The British leaders were not shaken by the results of the battle, even though they had lost 50,000 men and were no closer to victory than they had been before. If anything, their confidence had increased. They had seen, or knew, that the German front line had been captured, that British infantry had penetrated over two miles in some places, and that localities fortified at leisure with all the skill and experience of the most accomplished German engineers had fallen before them. This surely proved that the German front was not impregnable and that the BEF, given luck, proper leadership, and sufficient ammunition, was capable of achieving a decisive victory. Next time it would be different.

For Sir John, however, time had run out.

14

Recall

All efforts by General Headquarters to depict the action at Loos as successful could not hide the fact that staggering casualties had been incurred to
gain stretches of German line that even on a map of the largest scale,
looked negligible. The meager results gave credibility to Haig's letter of
September 29[1] and once again doubts arose in the cabinet as to Sir John's
fitness for command. But if a replacement was needed for the current
commander there was only one officer of sufficient experience and prestige—Haig. He was not universally admired. Although he had many fine
qualities he was horribly inarticulate and he had not been impressive on the
occasions when he had appeared before the cabinet. Some ministers did
not feel he was likely to succeed where French had failed. In any case, at
this stage the cabinet was not firmly determined to remove French from his
command, but was merely shifting its opinion in that direction.

On October 6 Kitchener asked Sir John for a full report on the actions of
the Twenty-first and Twenty-fourth divisions. The note was tactfully
couched:

> I am very sorry to have to trouble you at this juncture with a request for
> your remarks on the following, but my colleagues are anxious for a
> report from you about the statement made to them that 2 Divisions of
> the New Armies, presumably the 21st and 24th, behaved very badly and
> practically ran away at the first attack. It is also alleged that they had been
> 48 hours without food or water and had been heavily marched before
> being asked to charge a German position on a hill.
>
> I need not say how reluctant I am to have to put these questions to
> you.[2]

French's reply was not as curt as one might have expected, in view of the
implied slight upon his military judgment. He indicated that the two divisions in question had spent the night of September 24th/25th in the vicinity

of Béthune and Noeux les Mines, which he estimated was five miles from the enemy's front line. Circumstances dictated that he maintain a watchful eye on his right flank. Since the French attack was to be in an "eccentric direction," a dangerous gap might be left in the Allied line. As soon as he learned of the First Army's successful attack he visited Haig around 11:00 A.M. on the 25th and placed the two divisions at his disposal. After leaving Haig's headquarters he went to Béthune and Noeux les Mines and personally saw a large part of both divisions as they marched on their way to the front. As each company approached where he was standing it was called to attention and marched past in fine soldiering form. There was no doubt in his mind that the men were highly disciplined and full of spirit and enthusiasm. Moreover Haking, the corps commander, had personally assured him that they were thoroughly rested and fed. French ended by telling Kitchener that he could turn to Robertson if he wished additional information.[3]

Robertson was currently in London acting as a consultant to the General Staff and the government. Kitchener's position as virtual dictator of military strategy was collapsing. The root cause was the persistent ill success that dogged the Allies in every theater of war. The disappointing results of the autumn offensives on the western front had added a quarter of a million men to the heavy toll already taken of the British and French armies. The Italians were attacking spiritedly but ineffectively along the Isonzo River. In the east the Germans had driven the Russians out of Poland and taken over 750,000 prisoners. The operations in the Gallipoli Peninsula had failed and, in the absence of reinforcements, there was a danger that Hamilton's force might be driven into the sea. The succession of Allied defeats had encouraged Bulgaria to join the Central Powers and now Serbia was threatened with immediate disaster. At the eleventh hour the Allies agreed to send an Anglo-French force to Salonika in neutral Greece in order to help Serbia. The Allied response was a desperate expedient, since there was little they could do to avoid a Serbian defeat.

What was as depressing as the military reverses was the faltering leadership, faulty judgment, and lack of unanimity in the highest political circles. With Kitchener's star on the wane there was no one to focus attention on the vital issues and to formulate policies that would command unquestioning respect. Asquith enjoyed considerable prestige because of his air of calm and magisterial wisdom but his dilatory methods were ill-suited for the conduct of a major war. Cabinet discussions on significant military matters were wearisome and usually nonproductive. Members spoke freely and often needlessly, argued back and forth, and settled nothing until events themselves forced some sort of a decision.

Robertson attended several cabinet meetings during the second week of October and discussed the strategy of the war and the future of operations in the Mediterranean. However, he evaded all questions that related to Sir

John's leadership. Understandably he did not wish to appear disloyal to his chief. He showed no such restraint in private conversation with his peers and was, as Wilson put it, "very open in his contempt for Sir J."[4] From the very beginning Robertson had seen his influence with Sir John undermined by Wilson who, as we have noted, devoutly believed in the infallibility of French military judgment. On top of this he found Sir John to be unstable, petty, jealous, unreliable, and professionally incompetent. As he was never sure of what foolishness his chief might commit next, he made it a point to be present whenever Sir John saw the French military leaders or any of his senior commanders.

While in London Robertson received a telephone call from Lord Stamfordham who asked him on behalf of the king whether he did not consider the time had come to replace French. Robertson gave guarded answers both to Stamfordham and later to the king himself during an interview. The king had no executive authority but as sovereign and titular head of the army, he had the right to be kept informed. Still Robertson hesitated to make a definite pronouncement without first knowing if his opinion was shared by Haig. After returning to France Robertson visited First Army Headquarters (on October 17). Haig has preserved a record of their conversation:

> I told him at once that up to date I had been most loyal to French and did my best to stop all criticism of him or his methods. Now at last, in view of what had happened in the recent battle over the reserves, and in view of the seriousness of the general military situation, I had come to the conclusion that it was not fair to the Empire to retain French in command on this main battle front. Moreover, none of my officers commanding Corps had a high opinion of Sir J.'s military ability or military views; in fact, *they had no confidence in him.* Robertson quite agreed, and left me saying "he knew how to act, and would report to Stamfordham." He also told me that the members of the Cabinet who had up to the present been opposed to removing French had come around to the other opinion.[5]

Haig's views on French, as set forth in the foregoing excerpt, had also been communicated to Haldane during an interview several days earlier.[6] Haldane had been charged by the government to make a personal inquiry into the causes of the failure at Loos. It was not a pleasant assignment for Haldane, who was on intimate terms with both Haig and French. Not surprisingly Haig's version of the events conflicted in many places with the one he obtained from General Headquarters.[7] With his lawyer's tact, human understanding, and discretion to balance the evidence, Haldane concluded that no blame could be attached to French.

Neither Asquith nor Kitchener would accept Haldane's report as being definitive. On the contrary, they practically ignored it. The evidence seemed too heavily weighted against Sir John. Asquith told Selborne, "My own view is (I regret to say) that the responsibility rests with Sir J. French and a very serious one it is. K.'s judgment (which of course is much more important) inclines in the same direction but not to the extent of thinking that a case has been made out for removing him from the Command. He seems still . . . to possess the general confidence of his army. I have no doubt myself that before long Haig will have to take his place." Asquith hinted that the change would probably occur after his inquiry had been completed.[8]

The king now took it upon himself to assist in the investigation by interviewing some of the leading soldiers on the spot. The king had nursed doubts about Sir John's suitability as commander-in-chief ever since the retreat from Mons. These doubts were increased by Sir John's behavior in the press campaign against Kitchener and in the matter of the reserves at Loos, as well as by reports from certain soldiers in France.[9] On October 21 His Majesty crossed over to France, ostensibly to visit the British armies in the field. He stayed at the Chateau de la Jumelle in Aire.

In between inspections and official talks the king saw Haking and Gough, Haig, and Robertson. Haking and Gough "pointed out that there was great want of initiative, and fighting spirit, and no proper plans made in high quarters and that everyone had lost confidence in the C. in C."[10] Haig "entirely corroborated what the other two had said, but went much further and said that the C. in C. was a source of great weakness to the army and no one had any confidence in him any more."[11] Robertson indicated that it was "impossible to deal with French, his mind was never the same for two consecutive minutes."[12] The opinions expressed by these soldiers convinced the king that there must be an immediate change in the high command.

Near the end of the visit the king suffered an unfortunate accident. On October 28 while inspecting a unit of the Royal Flying Corps his mare reared in fright at the sudden burst of cheering, slipped on the wet ground, and fell backwards. The king was pinned under the animal and sustained injuries that at first appeared to be more serious than was actually the case. Still, he was badly bruised and in shock and had to be confined to his bed for several days. Sir John urged that the king be removed from the war zone lest the Germans discover his whereabouts. The king's doctors, however, wanted to wait until he had recovered from the shock and until they could ascertain that there were no internal injuries. Unable to persuade the doctors to act, Sir John sent a message directly to the king. The king, who was heavily sedated, replied, "Tell Sir John to go to hell."[13] On November 1 he was taken by ambulance to Boulogne where he was placed on board the hospital ship *Anglia*. To add to his discomfort he became seasick during the crossing so that by the time he reached Buckingham Palace he was utterly exhausted. The king mended slowly and in fact it would be four weeks before he was able to go out in public again.

The king's accident caused great concern at home for reasons that are understandable. Within a few days the country was reassured when it became clear that his injuries were not serious. As the king ceased to dominate the news a serious problem arose. General Monro, who had replaced Hamilton, recommended the evacuation of Gallipoli. The cabinet, buffeted by contradictory opinions, asked Kitchener himself to go out to Gallipoli and report upon the best policy. The government leaders hoped that he could later be persuaded not to return to London but to accept some such post as commander-in-chief of all British forces in the Near East. In this they were unsuccessful. During Kitchener's absence matters were further complicated when a group of influential politicians and soldiers worked to get Robertson appointed chief of the Imperial General Staff. The incumbent, General Archibald Murray, had breathed new life into the Imperial General Staff but he was not strong enough to stand up to so headstrong a secretary of war as Kitchener.

These events coming at the same time or in quick succession fully absorbed the attention of the cabinet. Thus all talk about changes in the high command were forgotten. The campaigning season was over and there was every reason to believe that the status quo would be preserved at least for the time being. Sir John sensed the shift in fortune and promptly took measures to consolidate his position.

On November 2 French's account of the Battle of Loos was published in *The Times* and, not surprisingly, contained many misstatements. In an accompanying article Repington praised Sir John's qualities as a soldier and regretted that the operations at Loos had not been under his direct command. Sir John's crude attempt to blame Haig for the recent setback proved his undoing.

Sir John and Haig, whose friendship dated back two decades, had worked in harmony throughout the first thirteen months of the global conflict. Their first serious dispute occurred over the question of the reserves prior to the Battle of Loos. Relations between the two men were further strained as the fighting died down. On October 3 Haig's weekly report, which covered the first part of the battle, contained a veiled criticism of Sir John's preliminary arrangements. He observed that the leading brigades had swept past the enemy's front line after suffering heavy casualties but, being unsupported by adequate reserves immediately at hand, were later in the day either driven back, killed, or captured. In particular he referred to the Fifteenth Division, which had "entirely broken through the German defences" and faced only scattered bodies of defenders.

Sir John was annoyed by the report and had Robertson draw up a reply to it. The field marshal declared that at dawn on the 25th, the Twenty-first and Twenty-fourth divisions were, as requested, in places about four-and-a-half miles behind the British trenches. He claimed that he had surrendered control of the two divisions at 9:30 A.M. and implied that Haig himself was responsible for the delay in using them. He added that the Third Cavalry Division had been placed at Haig's disposal some days before and he wondered why it was not brought up to support the Fifteenth Division. French then challenged the statement that the Fifteenth Division had only scattered bodies of the enemy in front of it. It seemed to him that in addition to the scattered bodies the enemy had "intact supports and reserves which came up early in the afternoon." The commander-in-chief ridiculed the notion that such gaps as the Fifteenth had made could have been exploited by fresh troops. The futility of pushing reserves through a narrow gap, he asserted, had been demonstrated by what had happened in Champagne on the same day.[14]

Haig's second report enlarged upon previously mentioned statements and answered several points raised by French's note. He argued that the Twenty-first and Twenty-fourth divisions had started out at 10:45 A.M. and 11:00 A.M. respectively and that they did not pass under his command until they had reached the British trenches. Considering the time that must elapse for the movement and deployment of these divisions he doubted whether their leading lines could have passed over the first German line before 2:00 P.M. According to Haig the crucial period was between 9:00 A.M. and 11:00 A.M. If during this period a fresh division had been available he was certain that it could have pushed through with little opposition. To support his claim Haig enclosed statements of divisional commanders as well as a diagram showing the disposition of the German troops opposed to the I and IV corps.

Haig went on to say that he did not feel justified in using the Third Cavalry Division in dismounted work on the morning of the 25th since it appeared that it might be required at any time for mounted action. Besides, the Third Cavalry Division consisted of two brigades, about 1,200 men, and in his opinion was inadequate for the purpose. What was required to support the Fifteenth Division was a considerable infantry force to carry the offensive forward, to prevent the Germans, driven from two prepared positions, from consolidating a third and holding up the advance long enough for their reserves to arrive by train. This the enemy succeeded in doing because there were no fresh troops on the spot to continue the advance when the divisions that had carried the assault were exhausted.

Finally Haig saw no analogy between the situation at Loos and that of the French in Champagne. The First Army, thanks to the use of gas and smoke, had surprised the Germans and pierced their defensive lines. The enemy had neither reserve nor artillery units to stem the British advance. In Champagne, however, Joffre announced his intention by a prolonged opening bombardment. By the time the French broke through the initial defensive system the Germans had moved large numbers of reserves and guns into their second line. In such circumstances troops advancing through a narrow gap were likely to be destroyed.[15]

Here the matter rested until Sir John's dispatch on the battle of Loos appeared in *The Times* on November 2. Haig took strong exception to the following sentences:

> At 9:30 A.M. I placed the 21st and 24th Divisions at the disposal of the GOC First Army, who at once ordered the GOC XI Corps to move them up in support of the attacking troops. . . . At 6 P.M. the Guards Division arrived at Noeux-les-Mines, and on the morning of the 26th I placed them at the disposal of the GOC First Army.[16]

Haig wrote immediately to Sir John, enclosing documentary evidence that these two statements were inaccurate and asking that he make the necessary corrections. He pointed out that the Twenty-first and Twenty-fourth divisions were not entrusted to him until 2:30 P.M. on the 25th and that he did not receive the message informing him that the Guards Division was under his command until 4:15 P.M. on the following day.[17]

Haig was much too clever and had too many influential friends in London to allow himself to be outmaneuvred by French. On November 7 he wrote to General Robb, now Kitchener's assistant military secretary, and, after pointing out the errors in Sir John's dispatch, added:

> I don't know whether you have anything to do with the publication of Despatches, but in any case it is well that someone in the War Office should know the truth. . . .
> I also send you my replies to certain questions which G.H.Q. have sent me regarding my reports in the operations of 25th September. These replies were "to be attached to my report before sending it to War Office" so there seems no reason why you should not be given a copy—I presume a copy did go to War Office. But really after "Ulster" and certain actions in France it is difficult to believe anything that our C.-in-C. says.
> As you can imagine there is a good deal of feeling here as regards the last Despatch—the First Corps which did so splendidly is scarcely mentioned. And the 15th Division (McCracken) is also much upset. From the enclosures I send you will see they went right through the enemy's last line of defences—One man and one only is to blame for the lack of Reserves at the decisive point when wanted. The fact is he does not understand the size or nature of the war in which we are now engaged here in France—Will he learn ever?[18]

On November 8 Sir John forwarded two letters to First Army headquarters. In the first he stated that the passages in question were "substantially correct" and "called for no amendment."[19] In the second he criticized Haig's strategic judgment. He charged that Haig had failed to take into account that considerable time, at least four hours, would be required to bring up, deploy, and advance the reserves into battle. Had he done so he would have kept sufficient reserves on hand to secure important localities gained and to support the assaulting troops, pending the arrival of the General Reserve. French indicated that Haig's weekly report, as well as his subsequent note, would be forwarded with comments to the War Office. He concluded by directing Haig to cease any further argument or correspondence "on a subject which is hereby finally closed."[20]

Haig ignored the order and replied that the disputed statements in the dispatch inferred that the Twenty-first and Twenty-fourth divisions had been at his disposal to use in support of the attacking troops and that the Guards Division had been available on the morning of the 26th. He therefore requested that the actual facts be placed on record.[21] Haig followed up his note by confronting Sir John in his room at General Headquarters. Throughout the meeting the field marshal sat uncomfortably and tried his best to placate Haig. He disclaimed any connection with the recent article by Repington in *The Times*. Moreover, he promised to send all the correspondence on the subject to the War Office and to allow Haig to see his covering letter.[22] This settled the matter finally but did not reestablish their old friendship. Thereafter the two soldiers had as little to do with each other as possible.

With many high-ranking officers returning home on leave or on business and with the almost constant stream of visitors to General Headquarters and First Army headquarters, it rapidly became known in London that harmony had ceased to exist in the military hierarchy in France. This information, together with the countless horror stories told by the wounded arriving from Loos, fueled the movement to replace Sir John as commander-in-chief. Public criticism of Sir John and his staff became more frequent in the press and even spilled onto the floor of the House of Lords. On November 8 Lord Milner hinted that the high command had botched things up and that the battles of Neuve Chapelle and Loos, represented as victories, were in reality defeats. Lord Courteney spoke along the same lines. A week later Lord Saint Davids asked the government: "Is it not about time . . . that a General who is never successful should be removed, and that our men at the Front should be given a fair chance for life and for victory?"[23]

Sir John naturally was upset by mounting criticism of his leadership and by rumors that the government was contemplating his removal. He sent off a telegram to Esher, inviting him to the Chateau de Blendecques, where he was currently staying. French was despondent and in bed with a severe cough when Esher arrived on the evening of the 12th. He asked his old friend if he had any suggestions as to what he might do to forestall any attempt to replace him.[24] The two men had lengthy conversations on the subject before Wilson joined them on the 14th. Wilson did not believe that Sir John could be removed unless it could be proved that the French could no longer work with him or that he had lost the confidence of his troops.

Neither condition existed.[25] The next day they agreed upon a plan, as Wilson's diary shows:

> At 10:30 I went up to Sir John at Blondecque [*sic*]. He was in bed, but better. Esher was in the room. Esher led off by saying that he had been suggesting to Sir John that he should draw up a paper showing that it was the detachments to Gallipoli and Salonika which had ruined our offensive power in the west and that if this drain continued he could not remain responsible for the operations in this theatre. Sir J. and Esher asked my opinion. I said that in the present condition of the Cabinet they would jump at this and ask him to resign, but that, if we could get Joffre to endorse Sir John's views we had got the Cabinet fixed. This was much approved . . . Esher was afraid that if both these letters were fired off, old squiff[26] would connect the larger issue with the personal issue and discount both. We finally settled that Brinsley should go over this afternoon and do the private letter business by word of mouth, while Sir J. settled down to write the big despatch and I said I would take it down to Joffre tomorrow night.[27]

Fitzgerald proceeded at once to Boulogne, where he boarded a steamer for Dover. After arriving in London he talked with Lord Selborne and Walter Long, two of the field marshal's staunchest allies in the cabinet. Selborne indicated that Sir John was in serious difficulty and, although he had not heard anything definite, he rather suspected that a change was imminent. He was much less supportive of Sir John than Fitzgerald had expected. "Argued many points with him and I think did good," Fitzgerald recorded in his diary. Long confirmed Selborne's statement that the cabinet had not discussed replacing Sir John and, from what he had been able to find out, neither had the War Council (now called War Committee). He had made it clear (presumably to Asquith) that if such action were done in haste there would be a row. He promised to get in touch with General Headquarters the instant there was talk of recalling Sir John.[28]

Fitzgerald gained the impression during his brief visit in London that the field marshal was in no immediate danger. He spoke twice to his chief over the telephone, echoing this sentiment on each occasion. In between messages Wilson returned to inform Sir John that Joffre would endorse his letter to the government. Wilson was at General Headquarters when Fitzgerald called the second time. "I told Sir J. . . . that in my opinion he was again safe on his perch,"[29] Wilson wrote in his diary. As it turned out, both Fitzgerald and Wilson were wrong.

At the constant urging of the king, Asquith, who was temporarily in charge of the War Office, decided the time had come to change the commander-in-chief in France. He did not discuss the issue widely, only with those whose opinions counted—Bonar Law, Lloyd George, Grey, and Robertson. All agreed that Sir John had outlived his usefulness. Kitchener was in the Mediterranean theater but it was no secret that he had long been distrustful of French's military competence.

Asquith knew that there were several in the cabinet, notably Long, Selborne, and Curzon, who believed that French, for all his faults, was a better man than Haig. They were apt to be troublesome if given an opportunity and the last thing that his shaky coalition needed was additional pressure. Asquith hoped to induce Sir John to resign without formally being told to do so. He selected as his emissary Lord Esher who recommended himself for this very delicate task, both as a close personal friend of Sir John and as a professional go-between of several decades' standing.

Contacted in Paris, Esher traveled to London where he saw the prime minister at the War Office at 5:00 P.M. on November 23. Asquith told Esher that the government had decided to replace Sir John as commander-in-chief of the BEF. He said that he had given the matter long and patient consideration but had concluded that, in view of the field marshal's deteriorating health and conduct during the recent events, a change was desirable. He expressed warm sentiments for Sir John personally and was anxious to make everything as easy and smooth for him as possible. Asquith wanted Esher to put the decision to French as delicately as he could and to persuade him that, in his own interest, he should take the initiative and resign on grounds of age and fatigue. If French went quietly the prime minister would make him supreme commander of the forces at home, recommend him for a peerage, and ask Parliament to give him a grant at the end of the war.

Esher pointed out that he was being asked to undertake an assignment that he considered very disagreeable. He wanted twenty-four hours to think it over. He returned at 5:00 P.M. on the 24th and before giving his reply put a question to the prime minister. Was his decision final or conditional? Esher had no intention of being used as a tool to maneuvre Sir John out of his command. The prime minister, who was pacing up and down the room, replied, "Yes, you must take it that the decision is final." On receiving that assurance Esher said, "Very well, I will leave for France tomorrow."[30]

Having made the crossing to France, Esher went straight to General Headquarters. The field marshal was away at the front inspecting troops. When he came in at the end of the afternoon Esher told him of his interview with Asquith. Sir John expressed surprise, saying he had not done anything to justify being removed from his command. He admitted that the strain had been great at times but insisted that his health had not interfered with his work, that he was in complete charge and on top of matters. He did not think there was another soldier in the British army who could do any better. Sir John took the news reasonably well in the beginning but after dinner his mood changed. He would fight Asquith and the cabinet, he said, and dare them to turn him out. Esher tried to calm him down, observing that he had nothing to gain and everything to lose by taking on the government.

Next morning Sir John announced that he would leave for London and seek an interview with Asquith. Esher doubted that it would serve any useful purpose but gave up trying to dissuade him. He recommended that the field marshal dispatch a letter to 10 Downing Street, couched in guarded terms but more or less placing himself in the prime minister's hands. French accepted the suggestion and, with Esher's help, drafted the letter. But then he decided to withhold it until after he had consulted with Walter Long in London.[31]

During the day Esher found a moment to write to the prime minister. He described his conversation with the field marshal and ended by saying: "Sir John . . . has written to you himself a letter which I am certain you will consider as only one more proof of that modest, warm hearted and honourable nature which has endeared him ever to his friends, and above all to the officers and men of the army he has loved so well and so gallantly commanded."[32] On Saturday, the 27th, Esher forwarded a second note to the prime minister. In it he said:

The little Field Marshall has just left for London. His letter to you is being taken by him to London and will be sent to you by hand tomorrow morning.

If bad advisers do not get in touch with him before Monday, you will find him ready to admit that the strain of the campaign has told upon him in a degree that makes him incapable of giving his best to the army or to the country in the Field. . . .

I wish I could have prevented him from going to London, but in this I failed.[33]

On arriving in London French, who was with Fitzgerald, learned that Long was spending the weekend in the country. The news further depressed him and he seemed on the verge of giving up. Fitzgerald felt that if he went down by train early next morning he could be back that very evening. With some difficulty he persuaded the field marshal to hold back his letter until he returned.[34]

Fitzgerald joined Long at his retreat on the 28th and the two men spent much of the afternoon discussing the options opened to Sir John. Long was certain that the War Committee had not debated the question of Sir John's removal, much less arrived at a decision. The situation was not hopeless, he declared, and on no account should the field marshal tender his resignation. Long advised that for the present Sir John should write to the prime minister, merely requesting an interview. Fitzgerald agreed with Long's views, as did Sir John when they were communicated to him.[35]

Sir John discarded the old letter and drew up a new one. It ran as follows:

I have seen Esher, who has conveyed to me your kind message. For this and for all your personal kindness to me since I was called upon to command the Army in France I desire to thank you most warmly.

As regards the main subject of our conversation no one knows better than you how grave and important are the issues at stake. My sole desire is to serve my country and the Army to the best of my ability in whatever capacity you and the Government choose to employ me. The strain of the last fifteen months has been a very heavy one, and although I am happy to say I am not conscious that it has had any serious effect upon my mental or physical powers, others may take a different view, and in these circumstances I need not assure you that I shall accept their decision without question.

As I felt able to get away for two or three days I have come over to ask you to be good enough to see me as soon as you conveniently can in order to discuss the whole question, as I think this method is infinitely preferable, in the first instance, to doing so by letter.[36]

Fitzgerald handed the letter personally to the prime minister at 10 Downing Street on the morning of the 29th. After reading the note Asquith set the meeting for 4:00 P.M. At the appointed hour Sir John appeared at 10 Downing Street and was immediately led to the prime minister's room.

Sir John explained that he took Esher's message to mean that the government had reached the conclusion that after fifteen months he could no longer stand up to the strains and responsibility of war and that, in the interest of the country, a younger man should be placed in command of the army. Asquith replied that Sir John had interpreted the message correctly. But he wished to make it clear that the field marshal must make the first step and that, if he decided to retain the command, the government would take no action.

Sir John understood that the prime minister's statement was not to be interpreted literally. It was obvious that if he did not offer to resign on his own the government would insist that he do so when circumstances permitted. Sir John told Asquith that his primary consideration was whether, in his judgment, it was to the advantage of the army that he should relinquish the command to someone else. If he was satisfied that it was, there were two additional conditions that had to be met. First, that he should be consulted as to his successor and second, that he should serve only under a civilian secretary of state. He observed that it would be impossible for him to act as the government's military adviser, which he had been told would be part of his new functions, if a field marshal of greater seniority was secretary for war. Asquith did not comment on these points but instead spoke at length about Sir John's future as commander-in-chief of the Home Forces. It was finally agreed that the field marshal was to write and communicate his decision.[37]

Sir John was in a happy mood when he later met Fitzgerald, declaring that the interview had left him with "a good taste." Long visited French early on the 30th and obtained an account of what had occurred at 10 Downing Street. He then saw the prime minister, who repeated to him essentially what he had said to the field marshal on the previous day. When Long returned on December 1 he indicated the lines along which the field marshal's reply should be written. Fitzgerald drafted the letter and showed it to Sir John. He approved of it, as did Long.[38] On December 2, the day before Sir John and Fitzgerald left for France, the note was delivered to 10 Downing Street. It was to the point:

> In a word I believe that the arrangement which you outlined to me on Monday would have many and great advantages if a successor to myself satisfactory to the army be appointed, and provided that a civilian S of S serve at the War Office.
>
> In my opinion the combination of a soldier of a higher rank as S of S and another soldier as C.-in-C. at home must inevitably produce friction and therefore cannot lead to good administration.
>
> It thus seems to me that before I can take action in the direction you indicated to me on Monday it will be necessary to know what changes if any take place.[39]

The prime minister was determined not to yield to Sir John's demands. His mind was already fixed upon Haig so there was no room to consider French's view about his successor. Moreover Asquith, as much as he wanted to, could not make a change at the War Office. Kitchener was still revered by the masses and to dismiss him would certainly bring down the government.

Spurred on by the king and realizing that the army could not be left indefinitely without an active chief, Asquith decided the time had arrived to convey a blunt message to Sir John.[40] He called in Walter Long and told him he wanted Sir John to submit his resignation at once and without conditions. Although he was personally fond of the field marshal he had carefully evaluated him as a military leader and found him wanting in the qualities that were considered necessary if the war was to be sustained and won. He felt that he had shown him every consideration by the manner in which he had tried, not only to arrange for his resignation but also to provide for his future. On the other hand the field marshal was not treating him with similar regard. He warned that further delay would not improve French's bargaining position and might even jeopardize his future.

By now it was apparent to Long that among his colleagues perhaps only one or two were willing to speak out on behalf of the field marshal. With such meager support Sir John had no chance to dictate the terms of his resignation, let alone retain his command. After leaving 10 Downing Street

Long sent a letter to Sir John, advocating that he resign immediately. He listed no reasons for this but simply stated that the field marshal must trust his judgment.[41]

The letter, described by Fitzgerald as a "bombshell," caused great consternation at General Headquarters. Uncertain of what to do, Sir John consulted with Esher and Fitzgerald and they both agreed that he no longer had any option. Thereupon he wrote out his letter of resignation and recommended Robertson as his successor.[42] In London Robertson's name had occasionally come up when there was talk of finding a replacement for French but neither Asquith nor Kitchener had seriously considered him. Quite apart from being wanted at the War Office, he had never commanded troops in battle.

French's nomination of Robertson, whom he knew was unqualified by experience, no doubt reflected his attitude towards Haig. Sir John maintained, a view that he held until his death, that Haig had deliberately intrigued in order to supplant him. It is true that after Loos, Haig had not hesitated to run down his chief when the opportunity presented itself. He was surely aware that he was a possible successor to French, indeed the most likely one. And yet the evidence suggests that Haig acted less out of personal motives than out of genuine conviction that the retention of French as a commander was a danger to the British army. Still, French could hardly be expected to see the matter in that light.

Sir John's resignation was formally accepted on December 6 and on the 15th the War Office made the following announcement:

> General Sir Douglas Haig has been appointed to succeed Field-Marshal Sir John French in command of the Army in France and Flanders.
>
> Since the commencement of the War, during over sixteen months of severe and incessant strain, Field Marshal Sir John French has most ably commanded our Armies in France and Flanders, and he has now at his own insistence relinquished that command.
>
> His Majesty's Government with full appreciation of and gratitude for the conspicuous services which Sir John French has rendered to the country at the front, have, with the King's approval, requested him to accept the appointment of Field Marshal Commanding-in-Chief the troops stationed in the United Kingdom, and Sir John French has accepted that appointment.
>
> His Majesty the King has been pleased to confer upon Sir John French the dignity of a Viscount of the United Kingdom.[43]

Sir John's pain in giving up the command was acute, an understandable reaction for a soldier who must step down with a great task unaccomplished and a great trust unfulfilled. To the surprise of friends and aides alike, Sir John refrained from unpleasant scenes and bitter recriminations. For once he bore adversity with dignity and composure.

The transferral of command from French to Haig took place on December 18. The meeting was formal and cold, nothing was said except matters of military routine. That same day the field marshal issued a farewell address to the troops and visited friends and comrades with whom he had been closely associated during the sixteen months of his command. He arrived in Paris on the 19th and stayed at the British embassy as a guest of Sir Francis Bertie. While in Paris he had farewell meetings with Foch and Joffre, as well as with the leading members of the French government.[44] The French were not sorry to see him leave,[45] but as a matter of courtesy and protocol presented him with the Croix de Guerre.

On December 21 Sir John, with Bertie, who insisted on seeing him off, traveled to Boulogne. Here the Nineteenth Hussars, his old regiment, formed the guard of honor. Amidst a storm of cheering and applause by the hundreds gathered at the pier, Sir John set sail for England.[46]

Epilogue

The rest of Sir John's career need only be treated briefly since it lies outside the scope of this narrative. French's duties as commander-in-chief of the Home Forces consisted primarily of supervising the training of troops for service abroad and of organizing the defenses of the United Kingdom. Profiting from the experience he had acquired in France, Sir John, or Viscount French of Ypres, as he was known after January 1916, first placed the entire system of military training on a sounder footing. Next he turned to the actual defense of the country against invasion or air raids. Plans were worked out to resist any invading troops on the beaches so as to deny them time or space to deploy. The scheme was never put to the test. Of more immediate concern to French was the protection of Great Britain from air attacks, which were threatening to impede the flow of munitions to the armies overseas. Accordingly he and his staff devised an elaborate system of air defenses under which the movement of German airships and airplanes was followed and reported. By the end of 1917 the German air menace had been effectively checked.

All indications are that French achieved satisfactory results during the twenty-eight months that he served as commander-in-chief of the Home Forces. Although his work was important, no glamor or glory went with it. For sixteen months while he had directed the activities of the BEF in the field he had been, next to Kitchener, the leading figure in the British Empire. Now he occupied a post that many did not even know existed. To someone as status-conscious as French, the demotion must have been particularly painful. On top of this he watched Haig, Allenby, and others who had fought under him reap the glory of final victory. French became convinced that he had been treated unjustly and he nursed this grievance until it developed into an obsession that frequently distorted his perception of what had actually happened. At last when his anger reached the boiling point it spilled over in a book, *1914,* which dealt with the first five months of his command in France.

Few post-World War I books excited more embittered controversy or did more to damage the reputation of the author. Lord French descended to clumsy and ludicrous misstatements, not only to justify his own conduct but to denigrate those he detested, in particular Smith-Dorrien and Kitchener. "The most charitable view is that it is the work of a monomaniac,"[1] commented Sir John Fortescue, then dean of military historians. Even some of French's close friends were distressed over the book. Esher, for example, wrote:

> Looking at the book as dispassionately as I can, it seems to me to damage his personality quite hopelessly.
> The impression left one is that though full of soldierly impulse he was quite unfitted for the task, and never grasped the vastness of the war, or the proper relation of the different parts to the whole.[2]

About a year before the first instalment of *1914* appeared in the columns of the *Daily Telegraph*, French was appointed lord lieutenant of Ireland. Here the situation remained perilously explosive. The Home Rule Bill became law late in the summer of 1914 but its operation had been suspended until the end of the war. John Redmond and his fellow Irish Nationalists strove to rally their people behind the British cause, for they saw that this was the only way of winning self-government for their island without splitting it. But the revolutionary members of Sinn Fein (We ourselves), not content with home rule, wanted complete independence from Britain and the absorption, by force if necessary, of northern Ireland. With the aid of smuggled German arms they staged a rebellion in Dublin during Easter week 1916. The insurgents seized several public buildings and proclaimed a republic but the people of the city did not rise and after fierce fighting they had to yield to British forces. The incident would have quietly faded from the public's mind had not the British executed the ringleaders. As it happened the victims joined the list of Irish martyr-heroes and Irish nationalism was inflamed as never before.

In the aftermath of the Easter rebellion efforts by the British government to reach an accommodation whereby Home Rule would have been implemented at once invariably foundered. Before a solution could be found for this dilemma, the British government compounded its difficulties by extending conscription to Ireland.[3] Outside of Ulster opposition to conscription was universal and culminated in a general strike on April 23, 1918. The Lloyd George[4] cabinet reacted by placing Ireland under military command. Such was the state of affairs in Ireland when French assumed the office of lord lieutenant in succession to Lord Wimborne.

It was hoped that French's Irish blood and his military reputation would command both obedience and respect among the Irish. But the Irish were past the point where they would accept conscription in any form. French made a personal effort to raise 50,000 voluntary recruits but less than 10,000 could be enlisted. The General Election held after the armistice resulted in Nationalist Ireland going over almost wholly to the Sinn Fein camp. Thereafter nothing French did was of any avail and matters went from bad to worse. On December 19, 1919, as the climax of a long series of murders and attempted murders of police officers and other officials by Irish revolutionaries, a daring attempt was made on the life of the lord lieutenant while he motored from Ashtown Station to the Viceregal Lodge. French escaped uninjured and his military escort, firing into the woods whence the shots had come, killed one of the assailants. Facing a growing challenge to its authority, the British government decided to meet force with force.

Throughout 1920 and most of 1921 the campaign conducted by Irish extremists against the forces of the Crown assumed all the features of guerrilla warfare. French complained in April 1920 that the Sinn Fein organization "had grown in strength and could be ousted only by force," and that "the rebels had the advantages of using methods of war . . . denied to us." He called upon the British authorities to admit officially that a state of war existed and to proclaim martial law, which would force armed Irishmen to put on a uniform or else be shot when taken. Lloyd George refused to adopt this measure, saying that "you do not declare war against rebels." Hampered by restrictions of every kind French retained his thankless post until April 30, 1921. As a reward for his services he was created Earl of Ypres in June 1922.

On relinquishing the Viceroyalty French retired into private life, spending much of his time in France, mainly in Paris. In August 1923 he was appointed captain of Deal Castle by Lord Beauchamp, the lord warden of the Cinque Ports. The office carried no special responsibilities but gave the holder the right to reside at the castle. French, who had not had a real home in England for many years, took advantage of the opportunity, moving all his possessions there from Drumdoe, on the southern shore of Lough Arrow in Roscommon. He intended to write his memoirs but had barely begun when ill health forced him to abandon the project.

Near the end of 1924 Lord French began to experience abdominal pain while vacationing in Paris. A French surgeon removed a cancerous growth in what was reported to be a minor operation. There were no complications and French was soon up and about, looking like his old self. Unfortunately there was a recurrence of the problem and a specialist in London advised further surgery. On March 19, 1925, he underwent a severe and prolonged operation in a London nursing home and his progress was apparently satisfactory until disquieting symptoms developed. Then on May 17 French, at his own request, was moved from London to Deal Castle. He stood the journey well but two days later suffered a relapse and sank into semiconsciousness. He died on the evening of May 22.[5]

It is the fate of men in high places to be judged either for what they have done or for what they have left undone. And French, whose long and eventful career as a soldier included the supreme command of the army during one of his country's greatest crises, has attracted both acclaim and condemnation. Critics have traditionally applauded French's achievements up to 1914 while excoriating his leadership as commander-in-chief of the BEF. This narrative does nothing to refute the previously accepted assessment of French's career.

There is no doubt that French's best work had been done before he sailed for France. As a cavalry leader in a colonial war, fought according to rules he understood, he had achieved spectacular results. Back in England his reforms, first at Aldershot and then at the War Office, though not especially imaginative, were nonetheless constructive and helped to transform the British army into a fighting machine second to none. He became the nation's leading cavalryman, perhaps the most distinguished since Cromwell. The great pity is that his career did not end after the Curragh incident when he could have retired, suitably honored and rewarded. He had reached the limits of his ability.

Had the Great War come ten years earlier it is possible that French would have given a better account of himself. As it was he assumed command of the Expeditionary Force when he was perhaps a little too old to adapt himself to conditions that were widely different from those he had experienced in the past.

In fairness to French it should be pointed out that few commanders ever had a greater task to fulfill or a more difficult part to play. For one thing he had to withstand the first onslaught against an enemy that was resourceful, throughly prepared, vastly superior in numbers, and in possession of the initiative. For another the British army was handicapped by acute shortages of material and equipment essential to wage siege warfare such as developed in the winter of 1914. Finally the British army's operational plans were subordinated to those of the French and consequently its commander had little influence in such vital matters as choice of ground and the timing of offensives.

When all these factors are taken into account it need also be said that French was definitely unsuited by experience, knowledge, and temperament to command the BEF. Throughout the sixteen months that he served in France he rarely gave the impression that he was on top of matters. During the intial phase, that is the war of movement, his generalship was marked on some occasions by recklessness, on others by indecisiveness, and on still others by near paralysis produced by fits of deep depression. Particularly at Mons it was only German miscalculation and the clever action of Smith-Dorrien that saved the BEF from destruction; and during the retreat it was the unrivaled discipline of the rank and file that held the army together and Kitchener's intervention that kept French in the battle line.

French's incompetence was no less evident after the deadlock set in. French had been taught to believe that a decisive attack was the solution to all military problems. Only in a decisive attack could decisive results be achieved. Any defensive role was rejected as being damaging to the morale of the men and likely to end in defeat.

French's first major assault against the German line was launched with the expectation that it would lead to a breakthrough. When this did not happen, he mounted a second attack, then a third and a fourth, always with the same presupposition. After each setback the next step was not to question the methods but simply to request more men and artillery. It never occurred to French at some point that he should abandon the brute force of ever heavier and larger bombardments in favor of surprise and tactical finesse. Why did he repeat the same mistakes? The explanation is that he never understood advanced infantry tactics or recognized much need for them. Hence he made no attempt to revise his techniques in the light of battle experience.

French's failure as a commander must also be atributed to certain flaws in his personality. Under the strain of war his volatile temperament swung wildly between excessive optimism and blank despair. He lacked moral courage, seeking to blame others for his own mistakes. Besides this, he was a small-minded man, obsessively jealous of his authority, vindictive towards some of his subordinates, resentful of his superior and incapable of working in harmony with his ally.

By the time the field marshal left France he had lost the respect and confidence of many, if not most, of his senior aides and commanders. Much of this was undoubtedly due to his behavior. By comparison Haig, despite the serious military reverses and the crippling losses incurred by his forces, retained the complete loyalty and trust of his subordinates during the entire period of his tenure as commander-in-chief. His ability to do so sprang chiefly from his integrity, calmness, and self-assurance.

All who knew French or served under him agree that he could inspire the men in the field as few commanders could.[6] That is a valuable asset but by itself does not begin to compensate for his substantial personal and professional weaknesses.

French was a fine cavalry officer, dedicated, brave, and able to elicit the intense devotion of his troops. He was, however, out of his depth in the conditions of 1914–15.

Notes

CHAPTER 1. THE VICTORIAN YEARS

1. Martin J. Blake, "Field Marshal Sir John French," *Journal of the Galway Archaeological and Historical Society* (n.d.): 248–51.

2. Andro Linklater, *An Unhusbanded Life* (London, 1980), 24–25.

3. French began to write his autobiography but he never got beyond the start of his service in the cavalry. Most of what he wrote can be seen in E. G. French, *The Life of Field Marshal Sir John French* (London, 1931), 4–21.

4. Mrs. Charlotte Despard in *T. P.'s Weekly*, September 19, 1914.

5. Winston S. Churchill, *Great Contemporaries* (1937; reprinted ed., Freeport, 1971), 63.

6. Cecil Chisholm, *Sir John French* (New York, 1914), 4–5.

7. Cited in E. G. French, *Sir John French*, 20.

8. Jay Luvaas, *The Education of an Army: British Military Thought, 1815–1940* (Chicago, 1964), 141; Brian Bond, *The Victorian Army and the Staff College, 1854–1914* (London, 1972), 87–88.

9. Lydall often lent French money to pay his debts. When he realized the loans would never be repaid he put a stop to it, telling French never to set foot in his house again.

10. Howard Pease, *The History of the Northumberland (Hussars) Yeomanry, 1819–1919* (London, 1924), 19.

11. Col. John Biddulph, *The Nineteenth and Their Times* (London, 1899), 237–38.

12. Ibid., 249–50.

13. Col. H. E. Colvile, *History of the Sudan Campaign*, Part 2 (London, 1889), 16–20.

14. Sir Charles Wilson *From Korti to Khartum* (London, 1886), 70–77.

15. See, for example, Admiral Lord Charles Beresford, *Memoirs* (Boston, 1914), 2:279–80; Sir Evelyn Wood, *From Midshipman to Field Marshal* (London, 1906), 2:177.

16. Cited in Biddulph, *The Nineteenth and Their Times*, 256.

17. Ibid., 263.

18. Barrow died in 1886 following complications resulting from the opening of an old wound.

19. A regimental commander automatically went on the half-pay list at the termination of his period in command unless he received another post at once.

20. Cited in Walter Jerrold, *Field Marshal Sir John French* (London, 1915), 44–45.

21. A fearless cavalry officer in the Thirteenth Hussars.

22. E. G. French, *Sir John French*, 48.

23. Chisholm, *Sir John French*, 29–30.

CHAPTER 2. WINNING LAURELS IN SOUTH AFRICA

1. E. G. French, *Sir John French,* 52.

2. Gen. Sir James Marshall-Cornwall, *Haig* (New York, 1973), 29–30.

3. Byron Farwell, *The Great Anglo-Boer War* (New York, 1976), 39–44; Rayne Kruger, *Good-bye Dolly Gray* (London, 1959), 3; Julian Symons, *Buller's Campaign* (London, 1963), 93–113.

4. John Selby, *The Boer War* (London, 1969), chap. 3.

5. L. S. Amery, ed., *The Times History of the War in South Africa, 1899–1902* (London, 1902), 2:176–77.

6. Maj.-Gen. Sir Frederick Maurice, *History of the War in South Africa, 1899–1902* (London, 1906) 1:160.

7. Sir Mortimer Durand, *The Life of Field Marshal Sir George White, V. C.* (London, 1915), 2:64.

8. There were some 2,000 European mercenaries fighting for the Boers.

9. Amery, *The Times History,* 2:181–91; Maurice, *The War in South Africa,* 1:162–69; Bennet Burleigh, *The Natal Campaign* (London, 1900), 31–42; G. W. Steevens, *From Capetown to Lady-smith* (New York, 1900), chap. 6; Victor Sampson and Ian Hamilton, *Anti-Commando* (London, 1931), 109–18; Thomas Pakenham, *The Boer War* (New York, 1979), 139–44.

10. See, for example, Erksine Childers, *War and the Arme Blanche* (New York, n.d.), 64–67.

11. Kruger, *Good-Bye Dolly Gray,* 86–87.

12. Durand, *Life of Sir Geroge White,* 2:77–80.

13. Burleigh, *Natal Campaign,* chap. 4; Steevens, *From Capetown to Ladysmith,* chap. 9; Maj.-Gen. Sir Frederick Maurice, *The Life of General Lord Rawlinson of Trent* (London, 1928), 47–48; Amery, *The Times History,* 2:chap. 6; Maurice, *The War in South Africa,* 1:chap. 10.

14. Cited in Duff Cooper, *Haig* (London, 1935), 1:73–74.

15. E. G. French, *Sir John French,* 64.

16. To overcome the shortage of regular cavalry units, the British authorities formed mounted infantry units with officers and men withdrawn from infantry battalions.

17. Amery, *The Times History,* 3:124–44; Maurice, *The War in South Africa,* 1:279–84; Johannes Meintjes, *De la Rey—Lion of the West* (Johannesburg, 1966), chap. 13; Charles Sydney Goldmann, *With General French and the Cavalry in South Africa* (London, 1902), 41–68.

18. Maurice, *The War in South Africa,* 1:411–13; David James, *Lord Roberts* (London, 1954), 280–82.

19. German General Staff, *The War in South Africa,* trans. Col. W. H. H. Waters (London, 1904), 1:139–47; E. G. French, *Sir John French* 70–74; Goldmann, *With General French,* 74–84; Amery, *The Times History,* 3:379–95; Maurice, *The War in South Africa,* 2:17–36.

20. Capt. Cecil Boyle, "The Rush to Kimberley and in Pursuit of Cronje," *Nineteenth Century* 47 (1900): 990.

21. Maurice, *The War in South Africa,* 2:88.

22. Lt.-Col. J. W. Yardley, *With the Inniskilling Dragoons* (London, 1904), 46.

23. George H. Cassar, *Kitchener: Architect of Victory* (London, 1977), 118–21.

24. Goldmann, *With General French,* chap. 5; E. G. French, *Sir John French,* 90–92; Meintjes, *De la Rey,* 157–58; Amery, *The Times History,* 3:553–66; Maurice, *The War in South Africa,* 2:chaps. 12–13.

25. Pakenham, *The Boer War,* 394–95.

26. Maurice, *The War in South Africa,* 2:207.

27. German General Staff, *The War in South Africa,* 2:19.

28. J. G. Maydon, *French's Cavalry Campaign* (London, 1901), 174.

29. Amery, *The Times History,* 3:569.

30. Kruger, *Good-Bye Dolly Gray,* 265; Farwell, *The Great Anglo-Boer War,* 236.

31. Kruger *Good-Bye Dolly Gray,* 267.

32. Goldmann, *With General French,* chap. 7.

33. E. G. French, *Sir John French*, pp. 100–102.

34. Pakenham, *The Boer War*, 449–52.

35. J. C. Smuts, *Jan Christian Smuts* (New York, 1952), 46–47.

36. German General Staff, *The War in South Africa*, 2:305.

37. Maurice, *The War in South Africa*, 3:chap. 8.

38. Farwell, *The Great Anglo-Boer War*, 308–9.

39. Goldmann, *With General French*, chap. 16; E. G. French, *Sir John French*, chap. 18; Amery, *The Times History*, vol. 4; Maurice, *The War in South Africa*, 3:414–18.

40. Cassar, *Kitchener*, 126–31.

41. For more detail see Smuts, *Jan Christian Smuts*, chap. 7; W. K. Hancock, *Smuts: The Sanguine Years, 1870–1919* (London, 1962), 1:chap. 8; Farwell, *The Great Anglo-Boer War*, chap. 36; Pakenham, *The Boer War*, 550–57, 564–65.

CHAPTER 3. BETWEEN TWO WARS

1. Buller had resumed command at Aldershot after his return from South Africa in November 1900.

2. E. G. French, *Sir John French*, 129.

3. Sir George Arthur, *Life of Lord Kitchener* (London, 1920), 3:24.

4. E. G. French, *Sir John French*, 129.

5. T. H. E. Travers, "The Offensive and the Problem of Innovation in British Military Thought, 1870–1915," *Journal of Contemporary History* 13 (1978): 531–39; idem, "Technology, Tactics and Morale; Jean de Bloch, the Boer War and British Military Thought, 1900–1914," *Journal of Modern History* 51 (1979):264–86.

6. For a fuller examination of the controversy see Brian Bond, "Doctrine and Training in the British Cavalry, 1870–1914," in Michael Howard, ed., *The Theory and Practice of War* (London, 1965); Edward M. Spiers, "The British Cavalry, 1902–1914," *Journal of the Society for Army Historical Research* 57 (1979):71–79.

7. The term means white weapon or cold steel.

8. Great Britain, *Royal Commission on the War in South Africa* (London, 1903), 2:306.

9. Jay Luvaas, *The Military Legacy of the Civil War* (Chicago, 1959), 196–97.

10. Nicholas J. d'Ombrain, *War Machinery and High Policy* (London, 1973), 145–47.

11. E. G. French, *Sir John French*, 138–39; see also the letters on the subject exchanged between French and Esher in E. G. French, ed., *Some War Diaries, Addresses, and Correspondence of Field Marshal the Right Honourable the Earl of Ypres* (London, 1937).

12. The advantages of a Staff College education are described in Sir William Robertson, *From Private to Field Marshal* (Boston, 1921), 88–89.

13. For example, see Sir John French, introduction to Gen. F. von Bernhardi, *Cavalry in Future Wars* (London, 1906), and preface to von Bernhardi, *Cavalry in War and peace* (London, 1910).

14. The Army Council determined all questions of military policy. It was composed of the secretary for war, the parliamentary under-secretary, the financial secretary, and the heads of the four military departments—the AG, QMG, MGO, and CIGS.

15. E. G. French, *Sir John French*, 182.

16. Viscount R. B. Haldane, *Before the War* (New York, 1920), 48.

17. Basil Collier, *Brasshat: A Biography of Field Marshal Sir Henry Wilson* (London, 1961), 121.

18. Maj. Gen. Sir C. E. Callwell, *Field Marshal Sir Henry Wilson* (London, 1927), 1:112; Wilson diary, March 16, 1912, Henry Wilson papers, Imperial War Museum, London.

19. James, *Lord Roberts*, chap. 14.

20. D'Ombrain, *War Machinery*, 141–47.

21. The Committee of Imperial Defence provided a centralized machinery to study the strategic needs of the Empire.

22. Lord Hankey, *The Supreme Command, 1914–1918* (London, 1961), 1:67–68.

23. Callwell, *Sir Henry Wilson*, 1:119.

24. D'Ombrain, *War Machinery*, 145.

25. Hankey, *The Supreme Command*, 1:82.

26. CID minutes, August 23, 1911; CAB 2/2, Cabinet papers.

27. Ibid.

28. Bernard Ash, *The Lost Dictator* (London, 1968), 72, 83, 90; Collier, *Brasshat*, 119–20.

29. John Gooch, *The Plans of War* (New York, 1974), 292.

30. Ibid., 292–93; Samuel R. Williamson, *The Politics of Grand Strategy* (Cambridge, Mass., 1969), 215–17; Lt.-Gen. Sir Tom Bridges, *Alarms and Excursions* (London, 1938), 62–63.

31. Callwell, *Sir Henry Wilson*, 1:149–50.

32. Robertson, *From Private to Field Marshal*, 162–63.

33. Edmonds's unpublished autobiography, chap. 22, p. 12.

34. Collier, *Brasshat*, 136–37.

35. Sir James Fergusson, *The Curragh Incident* (London, 1964), chaps. 1–6; Robert Blake, *The Unknown Prime Minister* (London, 1955), 183–91; A. P. Ryan, *Mutiny at the Curragh* (London, 1956), chaps. 1–10; George Dangerfield, *The Damnable Question* (Boston, 1976), chaps. 4–7.

36. Wilson diary, March 21, 1914, Henry Wilson papers.

37. Roberts described the part he played in this affair in a privately printed pamphlet entitled *Ulster and the Army*. A copy can be found among Wilson's papers.

38. Cited in Fergusson, *Curragh Incident*, 126.

39. Gen. Sir Hubert Gough, *Soldiering On* (London, 1954), 105–9; E. G. French, *Sir John French*, 193–95; Bernard Ash, *The Lost Dictator*, 125–27; Anthony Farrar-Hockley, *Goughie* (London, 1975), 104–11; The Rt. Hon. J. E. B. Seely, *Adventure* (New York, 1930), 167–70; Collier, *Brasshat*, 152–53; Ryan, *Mutiny*, chap. 11.

40. Roy Jenkins, *Asquith* (New York, 1964), 313.

41. Wilson diary, March 24–30, 1914, Henry Wilson papers.

CHAPTER 4. BEF TO THE CONTINENT

1. Viscount French of Ypres, *1914* (London, 1919), 2.

2. Churchill, *Great Contemporaries*, 67.

3. French, *1914*, 333–34n.

4. E. G. French, *Sir John French*, 203.

5. Williamson, *Politics of Grand Strategy*, 301.

6. *The Times* August 3, 1914; Général Huguet, *L'intervention militaire britannique en 1914* (Paris, 1928), 61.

7. Haig dairy, August 11, 1915, Douglas Haig papers, National Library of Scotland, Edinburgh. See also Brig.-Gen. John Charteris, *At G.H.Q.* (London, 1931), 10–11.

8. Winston S. Churchill, *The World Crisis* (New York, 1951), 1:249.

9. Council of War minutes, August 5, 1914; CAB 22/1, Cabinet papers; Hankey to Churchill, October 13, 1933; 5/1, M. P. Hankey papers, Churchill College Library, Cambridge.

10. Wilson diary, August 5, 1914, Henry Wilson papers.

11. Haig diary, August 5, 1914, Douglas Haig papers.

12. Hankey, *The Supreme Command*, 1:169–72; Viscount Grey of Fallodon, *Twenty-Five Years* (New York, 1925), 2:66–68; Cassar, *Kitchener*, 227–28; Council of War minutes, August 5, 1914; CAB 22/1, Cabinet papers.

13. News of the discussion about the proposed strength of the BEF had leaked out almost immediately. The press, both conservative and liberal, reacted angrily against what it considered was a reckless denuding of the country.

14. Churchill, *The World Crisis*, 2:171–72.

15. Grey, *Twenty-five Years*, 2:246.

16. Council of War minutes, August 6, 1914; CAB 22/1, Cabinet papers; Cassar, *Kitchener*, 228.

17. Wilson diary, August 12, 1914, Henry Wilson papers.

18. French, *1914*, 6–7.

19. Kitchener's low opinion of the martial qualities of Frenchmen was no doubt based on his experiences during the Franco-Prussian War.

20. Cassar, *Kitchener*, 230–31; Huguet, *L'intervention militaire britannique*, 54–55; Wilson diary, August 12, 1914, Henry Wilson papers.

21. Kitchener rejected the popular notion that a long war would impose an intolerable strain upon the economies of the belligerents. Great Britain and Germany would be fighting for their existence, and each was backed by great resources that would take long to develop and still longer to exhaust. Neither would readily admit the possibility of defeat. Kitchener's calculation, therefore, was based on careful study and not, as is often stated, on intuition.

22. The complete list of instructions can be seen in French, *1914*, 13–15, and Brig.-Gen. Sir James E. Edmonds, *Military Operations: France and Belgium, 1914* (London, 1922), 1:499–500.

23. Ian Hamilton in a speech, 39/12/172, Ian Hamilton papers, King's College Library, London.

24. French to Esher, Esher War Journals, August 21, 1914, Viscount Esher papers, Churchill College Library, Cambridge.

25. Sir Julian S. Corbett, *Naval Operations* (London, 1920), 1:chap. 4.

26. Raymond Poincaré, *Au service de la France* (Paris, 1928), 5:103.

27. French, *1914*, 34.

28. Field Marshal Joseph Joffre, *Personal Memoirs*, trans. Col. T. Bentley Mott (London, 1932), 1:161.

29. Ibid, 161–62.

30. Général Lanrezac, *Le plan de campagne français et le premier mois de le guerre* (Paris, 1929), chap. 2.

31. Huguet, *L'intervention militaire britannique*, 66.

32. Maj.-Gen. Sir Edward Spears, *Liaison 1914* (New York, 1968), 76.

33. Ibid., 75.

34. Callwell, *Sir Henry Wilson*, 1:164n.

35. Huguet, *L'intervention militaire britannique*, 66; Spears, *Liaison 1914*, 76–77.

36. A. J. Smithers, *The Man Who Disobeyed* (London, 1970), 132.

37. Gen. Sir Horace Smith-Dorrien, *Memories of Forty-Eight Years' Service* (New York, 1925), 355–59.

38. Brig.-Gen. C. R. Ballard, *Smith-Dorrien* (London, 1931), 127.

39. Smithers, *Man Who Disobeyed*, 132.

40. Maj.-Gen. Sir C. E. Callwell, *Experiences of a Dug-Out* (London, 1920), 57.

41. Smith-Dorrien, "Statement with regard to the first edition of Lord French's book 1914." A copy of the document can be found in the British Museum, No. 52776.

42. Sir George Arthur, *Not Worth Reading* (London, 1938), 213–14.

43. Smithers, *Man Who Disobeyed*, 164.

CHAPTER 5. THE CLASH OF BATTLE

1. Gerhard Ritter, *The Schlieffen Plan* (London, 1958); L. C. F. Turner, "The Significance of the Schlieffen Plan," in *The War Plans of the Great Powers, 1880–1914*, ed. Paul M. Kennedy (London, 1979); B. H. Liddell Hart, *History of the First World War* (London, 1972), 40–42; Barbara W. Tuchman, *The Guns of August* (New York, 1962), chap. 2; Hajo Holborn, "Moltke

and Schlieffen: The Prussian-German School," in *Makers of Modern Strategy*, ed. Edward Earle Meade (Princeton, N.J., 1952); Gordon A. Craig, *The Politics of the Prussian Army, 1640–1945* (Oxford, 1956), chap. 7, parts 3 and 4; Walter Goerlitz, *History of the German General Staff, 1657–1945* (New York, 1956), chaps. 6 and 7.

2. S. R. Williamson, "Joffre Reshapes French Strategy," in *War Plans of the Great Powers;* Tuchman, *Guns of August,* chap. 3; S. Possony and E. Mantoux, "Du Picq and Foch: The French School," in *Makers of Modern Strategy;* Paul Marie de la Gorce, *The French Army*(New York, 1963), chap. 5; B. H. Liddell Hart, *Reputations: Ten Years After* (Freeport, N.Y., 1968), see chapter on Foch.

3. Spears, *Liaison 1914,* 130.

4. Kitchener to French, August 19, 1914; PRO 30/57/49, Lord Kitchener papers, PRO, London.

5. Ibid., August, 20, 1914; PRO 30/57/49.

6. French to Kitchener, August 21, 1914; PRO 30/57/49, Lord Kitchener papers.

7. Ibid., August 22, 1914; PRO 30/57/49.

8. Tuchman, *Guns of August,* 164.

9. Spears, *Liaison 1914,* 136–37.

10. French, *1914,* 58.

11. Spears, *Liaison 1914,* 150.

12. John Terraine, *Mons* (New York, 1960), 86.

13. French, *1914,* 60.

14. Smith-Dorrien, *Memories,* 382.

15. Edmonds, *France and Belgium, 1914,* 1:chap. 3; Terraine, *Mons,* 90–105; Ernest W. Hamilton, *The First Seven Divisions* (London, 1917), chap. 2; A. Corbett-Smith, *The Retreat from Mons* (London, 1916), chap. 6; Smith-Dorrien *Memories,* 382–86; Alexander von Kluck, *The March on Paris and the Battle of the Marne, 1914* (London, 1920), 34–48.

16. Callwell, *Sir Henry Wilson,* 1:167.

17. Edmonds, *France and Belgium, 1914,* 1:93.

18. Spears, *Liaison 1914,* 171.

CHAPTER 6. RETREAT

1. Edmonds, *France and Belgium, 1914,* 1:97.

2. Smith-Dorrien, *Memories,* 387.

3. Terraine, *Mons,* 112–19; Edmonds, *France and Belgium, 1914,* 1:chap. 4.

4. Callwell, *Sir Henry Wilson,* 1:167.

5. Terraine, *Mons,* 107.

6. Arthur, *Life of Lord Kitchener,* 3:35–36.

7. He commanded a cavalry corps at Avesnes.

8. French, *1914,* 70–71.

9. Terraine, *Mons,* 125–26.

10. Edmonds, *France and Belgium, 1914,* 1:132–34.

11. Charteris, *At G.H.Q.,* 18.

12. Edmonds, *France and Belgium, 1914,* 1:135.

13. Maj.-Gen. Sir Wyndam Childs, *Episodes and Reflections* (London, 1930), 124; Gen. Sir Nevil Macready, *Annals of an Active Life* (London, 1924), 1:205–06; Callwell, *Sir Henry Wilson,* 1:170; Huguet, *L'intervention militaire britannique,* 77.

14. Spears, *Liaison 1914,* 222–23.

15. Smith-Dorrien, *Memories,* 403.

16. Ibid., 405; Callwell, *Sir Henry Wilson,* 1:168–69; Brig.-Gen. A. Hildebrand, "Recollec-

tions of Sir Horace Smith-Dorrien at Le Cateau, August, 1914," *Army Quarterly* 21 (1930–31):15–19.

17. Cooper, *Haig,* 1:156.

18. Spears, *Liaison 1914,* 235.

19. Edmonds, *France and Belgium, 1914,* 1:chaps. 7–9; Terraine, *Mons,* 145–54; Hamilton, *The First Seven Divisions,* chap. 5; Smith-Dorrien, *Memories,* 405–9; J. W. Fortescue, "Horace Smith-Dorrien," *Blackwood's Magazine* 229 (1931); Maj.-Gen. Sir Frederick Maurice, "The 'Unnecessary' Battle of Le Cateau," *National Review* 74 (1919–20).

20. Smith-Dorrien, *Memories,* 408.

21. The number of these losses was never revealed.

22. Cited in Smith-Dorrien, *Memories,* 415.

23. Edmonds, *France and Belgium, 1914,* 1:191–93.

24. French to Kitchener, August 27, 1914; PRO 30/57/49, Lord Kitchener papers.

25. Viscount French of Ypres, *The Despatches of Lord French* (London, 1917), 10–11.

26. J. W. Fortescue, "1914", *Quarterly Review* 232 (1919): 356.

27. French, *1914,* 78–80.

28. Joffre, *Personal Memoirs,* 1:182–93.

29. Ibid., 194–96; Spears, *Liaison 1914,* 228–31; French, *1914,* 82–83; Huguet, *L'intervention militaire britannique,* 82–84; Lanrezac, *Plan de campagne français,* 194–96.

30. French, *1914,* 83–84.

31. Smith-Dorrien, *Memories,* 411.

32. For a record of the marches carried out by the five divisions of the BEF see Edmonds, *France and Belgium, 1914,* 1:542.

33. Lt.-Col. Howard Green, *The British Army in the First World War* (London, 1968), 16; Macready, *Annals of an Active Life,* 1:205; Hamilton, *The First Seven Divisions, 81;* Edmonds, *France and Belgium, 1914,* 1:284.

34. Wilson diary, August 29, 1915, Henry Wilson papers.

35. Green, 16.

36. Huguet's memos to Joffre can be seen in the annexes of the multivolume French official history of the Great War—Ministrère de la guerre: Etat-Major de l'armée. Service historique, *Les armées française dans la grande guerre* (Paris).

37. Charteris, *At G.H.Q.,* 21.

38. Spears, *Liaison 1914,* 258; Laurance Lyon, *The Pomp of Power* (New York, 1922), 37n.

39. Joffre, *Personal Memoirs* 1:213–14.

40. French, *1914,* 92–94.

41. Edmonds, *France and Belgium, 1914,* 1:241.

42. On September 20, 1914, Robb was removed from his position for alleged incompetence. Neither Haig nor Robertson apparently believed that the charges were valid.

43. Arthur, *Life of Lord Kitchener,* 3:46–47.

44. French to Kitchener, August 31, 1914; PRO 30/57/49, Lord Kitchener papers.

45. Cassar, *Kitchener,* 235.

46. Arthur, *Life of Lord Kitchener,* 3:51.

47. Hankey, *The Supreme Command,* 1:190; Edward David, ed., *Inside Asquith's Cabinet: From the Diaries of Charles Hobhouse* (London, 1977), 186; Pease Diary, August 31, 1914, J. A. Pease papers, Nuffield College Library, Oxford.

48. Arthur, *Life of Lord Kitchener,* 3:52.

49. Joffre, *Personal Memoirs,* 1:222–23.

50. Clive diary, September 1, 1914, Sidney Clive papers, King's College Library, London.

51. Joffre, *Personal Memoirs,* 1:223.

52. Arthur, *Life of Lord Kitchener,* 3:52–53.

53. Besides Kitchener and Asquith, the group consisted of Churchill, Lloyd George, McKenna, and Pease.

54. Pease Diary, August 31, 1914, J. A. Pease papers; A. G. Gardiner's review of "1914" in the *Daily News*, June 23, 1919; Asquith to Venetia Stanley, September 1, 1914, Venetia Stanley Montagu papers, private possession.

55. Bertie's intervention may well have been decisive. A note written by Col. W. Lambton (French's secretary) to Bertie would seem to indicate this was the case. It ran as follows: "Sir John was most grateful for your intervention at that time, as without it, I am sure K. would have come up, which would have been a great mistake." October 2, 1914; FO 800/166, F. Bertie papers, PRO, London.

56. Huguet, *L'intervention militaire britannique*, 101–2; Bertie to Grey, September 1, 1914; FO 800/166, F. Bertie papers; Terraine, *Mons*, 190–91; Poincaré, *Au service de la France*, 5:229; Cassar, *Kitchener*, 237–39; Bertie to French, May 10, 1919, and June 22, 1919, John French papers.

57. French, *1914*, 100, 112.

58. Kitchener to Grey, September 1, 1914; FO 800/166, F. Bertie papers.

59. Kitchener to French, September 1, 1914; PRO 30/57/49, Lord Kitchener papers.

60. French to Kitchener, September 3, 1914; PRO 30/57/49, Lord Kitchener papers.

61. French to Churchill, September 3, 1914, in Martin Gilbert, ed., *Companion* (London, 1972), 1:79–80. This work contains selected documents from Churchill's papers for the period of 1914–16. It was published in conjunction with Mr. Gilbert's third volume on the life of Winston Churchill.

62. Churchill, *The World Crisis*, 1:300.

63. Ibid., 301.

64. Joffre, *Personal Memoirs*, 1:230.

65. Edmonds, *France and Belgium, 1914*, 1:531–32.

66. Général Adolphe Messimy, *Mes Souvenirs* (Paris, 1937), 379.

67. Joffre, *Personal Memoirs*, 1:236.

68. Général J. Galliéni, *Mémoires: Défense du Paris, 25 août-11 septembre, 1914* (Paris, 1920), 112.

69. Joffre, *Personal Memoirs*, 245.

70. Galliéni, *Mémoires*, 120–23.

71. Spears, *Liaison 1914*, 387–89; Colonel A. Grasset, *La bataille des deux Morins: Franchet d'Esperey à la Marne, 6–9 septembre, 1914* (Paris, 1934), 51–53.

72. See above, 140.

73. Huguet, *L'intervention militaire britannique*, 112.

74. Joffre, *Personal Memoirs*, 1:246.

75. Spears, *Liaison 1914*, 411–18; Joffre, *Personal Memoirs*, 1:253–55; Callwell, *Sir Henry Wilson*, 1:174; Clive diary, September 5, 1914, Sidney Clive papers; Commandant Louis Edouard Muller, *Joffre et la Marne* (Paris, 1931), 106–7 n.

CHAPTER 7. THE COUNTERSTROKE

1. The text of General Order No. 6 can be seen in Henri Isselin, *The Battle of the Marne*, trans. Charles Connell (London), 1965), 124.

2. Edmonds, *France and Belgium, 1914*, 1:chaps. 15–16; A. Corbett-Smith, *The Marne—and After* (London, 1917), chaps. 2–3; Frederick Coleman, *From Mons to Ypres with General French* (New York, 1916), 109–21; Hamilton, *The First Seven Divisions*, 95–104; Von Kluck, *The March on Paris*, 132–34.

3. B. H. Liddell Hart, *Foch: The Man of Orléans* (Boston, 1932), 101–9; Georges Blond, *The Marne*, trans. H. Eaton Hart (London, 1965), chaps. 10–12; George Herbert Perris, *The Battle of the Marne* (London, 1920), chaps. 6–7.

4. Joffre, *Personal Memoirs*, 1:268–69.

5. Edmonds, *France and Belgium, 1914,* 1:chap. 17; Hamilton, *The First Seven Divisions,* 104–5; John Buchan, *History of the Great War* (Boston, 1922), 1:222–25.

6. Goerlitz, *History of the German General Staff,* 161–62; Blond, *The Marne,* chaps. 12–13; Isselin, *Battle of the Marne,* 186–232; Sewell Tyng, *The Campaign of the Marne* (Longmans, 1935), chap. 32.

7. Edmonds, *France and Belgium, 1914* 1:343.

8. Wilson diary, September 13, 1914, Henry Wilson papers.

9. Hamilton, *The First Seven Divisions,* 108–14; Coleman *Mons to Ypres,* 128–48; Corbett-Smith, *The Marne—and After,* chap. 8; Edmonds, *France and Belgium, 1914* 1:chap. 18.

10. Cooper, *Haig,* 1:176–85; Buchan, *History of the Great War,* 1:276–80; Hamilton, *The First Seven Divisions,* 115–37; Corbett-Smith, *The Marne—and After,* chap. 9; Edmonds, *France and Belgium, 1914,* 1:chaps. 19–20; Coleman, *Mons to Ypres,* chap. 6.

CHAPTER 8. DEADLOCK

1. The Sixth Division arrived in France on September 15 and 16.

2. French, *1914,* 164–66.

3. See Callwell, *Sir Henry Wilson,* 1:178–79; Collier, *Brasshat,* 200.

4. Martin Gilbert, *Winston S. Churchill* (London, 1971), 3:81.

5. Callwell, *Sir Henry Wilson,* 1:179.

6. Edmonds, *France and Belgium, 1914,* 1:463.

7. Joffre, *Personal Memoirs,* 1:300–304.

8. It was composed of well-seasoned troops, mainly collected from various garrisons within the Empire.

9. Cassar, *Kitchener,* 245.

10. French to Churchill, October 5, 1914, in Gilbert, ed., *Companion,* 1:168–69.

11. Arthur, *Life of Lord Kitchener,* 3:70.

12. French, *1914,* 177–83.

13. French diary, October 8, 1914, John French papers.

14. Huguet, *L'intervention militaire britannique,* 146–47.

15. Ibid., 152.

16. Maurice, *Life of General Lord Rawlinson,* 109.

17. Unless otherwise indicated, my source for the First Battle of Ypres is Edmonds, *France and Belgium, 1914,* Vol. 2.

18. Maréchal Foch, *Mémoires* (Paris, 1931), 1:241–42.

19. Anthony Farrar-Hockley, *Death of An Army* (London, 1967), 56–61.

20. Maurice, *Life of General Lord Rawlinson,* 112.

21. French, *1914,* 227–28.

22. Seeley had gone to the western front after the outbreak of war in command of the Canadian Cavalry Division.

23. Charteris, *At G.H.Q.,* 50.

24. Callwell, *Sir Henry Wilson,* 1:184.

25. French to Kitchener, October 22, 1914; PRO 30/57/49, Lord Kitchener papers.

26. French, *1914,* 216.

27. Edmonds, *France and Belgium, 1914,* 2:199.

28. French to Kitchener, October 24, 1914; PRO 30/57/49, Lord Kitchener papers.

29. Ibid., Octber 25, 1914.

30. Callwell, *Sir Henry Wilson,* 1:185.

31. French to Kitchener, October 26,1914; PRO 30/57/49, Lord Kitchener papers.

32. Ibid., October 29, 1914.

33. Farrar-Hockley, *Death of An Army,* 151.

34. This unit belonged to the II Division but it had been loaned to Lomax to be used where necessary.

35. Blake, *Private Papers of Douglas Haig*, 76.

36. French, *1914*, 252.

37. Général Dubois, *Deux années de commandement* (Paris, 1921), 2:55; Foch, *Mémoires*, 1:218–19; Huguet, *L'intervention militaire britannique*, 168–69.

38. Edmonds, *France and Belgium, 1914*, 2:342.

39. Ibid., 2:345.

40. Foch, *Memoires*, 1:224.

41. French to Kitchener, November 1, 1914; PRO 30/57/49, Lord Kitchener papers.

42. Cassar, *Kitchener*, 249–50.

43. Callwell, *Sir Henry Wilson*, 1:186–87.

44. Huguet, *L'intervention militaire britannique*, 169–70 n.

45. Asquith to French, November 6, 1914, vol. 46, H. H. Asquith papers.

46. Asquith to Venetia Stanley, November 6, 1914, Venetia Stanley Montagu papers.

47. Churchill to French, November 6, 1914, John French papers.

48. French, *1914*, 274.

CHAPTER 9. THE CLOSE OF 1914

1. Duke of Windsor, *A King's Story* (New York, 1951), 111–12.

2. James, *Lord Roberts*, 478–85.

3. Moore memoirs, George Moore papers, private possession. In later life Moore wrote down his recollections, hoping to use them as a basis for a book. The book never materialized.

4. Interview with Mrs. Blair Sperber, Moore's granddaughter.

5. Moore memoirs, George Moore papers. Moore dates the year as 1911 but that is an error. It was in 1910 that French returned from America.

6. Lady Diana Manners (later Cooper), who knew both men well, writes in her book that Moore had bought the house for the field marshal out of devotion and admiration. See Diana Cooper, *The Rainbow Comes and Goes* (Boston, 1958), 92.

7. Ibid.

8. Moore memoirs, George Moore papers.

9. Ibid.

10. Linklater, *An Unhusbanded Life*, 51.

11. Harold Nicolson, *King George the Fifth* (London, 1952), 259–60.

12. Duke of Windsor, *A King's Story*, 114.

13. Interview with Mrs. Joan Shivarg, Mrs. Bennett's granddaughter.

14. Ibid.

15. French to Mrs. Bennett, November 19, 1914, John French papers.

16. Ibid., February 24, 1915.

17. Ibid., March 7, 1915.

18. French's letters to Mrs. Bennett make this quite clear. Here is a case in point; "Writing to you is a real joy and rest; the only rest I know here" (February 27, 1915).

19. Haig diary, November 21, 1914, Douglas Haig papers.

20. French diary, December 7, 1914, John French papers.

21. French, *1914*, 305.

22. Churchill, *The World Crisis*, 2:39–40.

23. Arthur, *Life of Lord Kitchener*, 3:88–89.

24. Poincaré, *Au service de la France*, 5:497–98.

25. Churchill, *The World Crisis*, 2:39.

26. Wilson diary, December 10, 1914, Henry Wilson papers.

27. Ibid., December 11, 1914.

28. Edmonds, *France and Belgium, 1915,* 1 : 17.

29. Callwell, *Sir Henry Wilson,* 1 : 192–93.

30. Huguet, *L'intervention militaire britannique,* 184–85.

31. Edmonds, *France and Belgium, 1915,* 1 : 19.

32. Sir Francis Bertie, Memorandum, December 26, 1914, FO 800/166, F. Bertie papers.

33. Callwell, *Sir Henry Wilson,* 1 : 178.

34. Ibid., 193.

35. French, *1914,* 329.

36. H. H. Asquith, *Memories and Reflections 1852–1927* (London, 1928), 2 : 49–50.

37. French, *1914,* 333.

38. Cassar, *Kitchener,* 264–65.

39. Callwell, *Sir Henry Wilson,* 1 : 194–95.

40. The First Army consisted of the I, IV, and Indian corps, the Second Army of the II, III, and V corps.

41. Edmonds, *France and Belgium, 1915,* 1 : 22–23.

42. The word means mad or deranged.

43. Wilson diary, December 27, 1914, Henry Wilson papers; John French diary, December 27, 1914; Minutes of the Conference, John French papers; French to Kitchener, December 28, 1914; PRO 30/57/49, Lord Kitchener papers.

44. Wilson diary, December 27, 1914, Henry Wilson papers.

45. French to Kitchener, December 29, 1914; PRO 30/57/49, Lord Kitchener papers.

46. Wilson diary, December 29, 1914, Henry Wilson papers.

CHAPTER 10. THE FIRST ATTEMPT AT SIEGE WARFARE

1. It was a special committee of the cabinet and consisted of Asquith, Kitchener, Lloyd George, Churchill, Crewe, and Haldane. Balfour represented the opposition and Hankey acted as secretary. In addition, the service chiefs, Fisher and Wolfe-Murray, attended regularly. If the occasion demanded, other ministers or experts were called in.

2. Hankey, *The Supreme Command,* 1 : 244–50.

3. Churchill, *The World Crisis,* 2 : 30–31.

4. Lloyd George, *War Memoires* (Boston, 1933), 1 : 322–30.

5. A. J. P. Taylor, *English History, 1914–1945* (Oxford, 1965), 23.

6. Cassar, *Kitchener,* 270.

7. Arthur, *Life of Lord Kitchener,* 3 : 85–86.

8. Wilson diary, January 3, 1915, Henry Wilson papers.

9. French to Brade (secretary of the War Office), December 31, 1914; WO 32/5152, War Office archives.

10. See above, 62.

11. French to Kitchener, January 3, 1915; PRO 30/57/50, Lord Kitchener papers.

12. Wilson diary, January 3, 1915, Henry Wilson papers.

13. Kitchener to French, January 6, 1915: PRO 30/57/50, Lord Kitchener papers.

14. French to Kitchener, January 8, 1915; PRO 30/57/50, Lord Kitchener papers.

15. Lambton to George V, January 13, 1915; GV Q832/218, Royal archives; Esher War Journals, January 5, 1915, Viscount Esher papers.

16. War Council minutes, January 7, 1915; CAB 22/1, Cabinet papers.

17. Churchill to French, January 8, 1915; Gilbert, ed., *Companion,* 1 : 396–97.

18. War Council minutes, January 13, 1915; CAB 22/1, Cabinet papers.

19. Churchill to French, January 11, 1915; Gilbert, ed., *Companion,* 1 : 401.

20. Wilson diary, January 19, 1915, Henry Wilson papers.

21. Haig diary, January 24, 1915, Douglas Haig papers.

22. Joffre to French, January 19, 1915; WO 158/13, War Office archives.

23. Haig diary, January 20, 1915, Douglas Haig papers.

24. Report of the meeting at Chantilly, January 21, 1915; WO 158/13, War Office archives; Wilson diary, January 21, 1915, Henry Wilson papers.

25. French to Murray, January 25, 1915, Archibald Murray papers.

26. Murray to French, January 25, 1915, Archibald Murray papers.

27. French to Murray, January 25, 1915, Archibald Murray papers.

28. Robertson, *From Private to Field Marshal,* 218.

29. See, for example, Wilson diary, January 17, 1915, Henry Wilson papers.

30. Esher War Journals, March 20, 1915, Viscount Esher papers.

31. Haig diary, February 13, 1915, Douglas Haig papers.

32. Joffre to French, February 16, 1915; WO 158/13, War Office archives.

33. French to Joffre, February 18, 1915; WO 158/13, War Office archives.

34. Joffre to French, February 19, 1915; WO 158/13, War Office archives.

35. Wilson diary, February 21, 1915, Henry Wilson papers.

36. French to Joffre, February 23, 1915; WO 158/13, War Office archives.

37. Kitchener occasionally used the good offices of the Belgian prime minister, the Comte de Broqueville, as a go-between with the French.

38. Wilson diary, February 23, 1915, Henry Wilson papers.

39. Hankey diary, April 2, 1915, M. P. Hankey papers.

40. Kitchener to French, February 24, 1915; PRO 30/57/57, Lord Kitchener papers.

41. French to Kitchener, February 24, 1915; PRO 30/57/57, Lord Kitchener papers.

42. Wilson diary, February 28, 1915, Henry Wilson papers.

43. George H. Cassar, *The French and the Dardanelles: A Study in Failure in the Conduct of War* (London, 1971), 73–77.

44. Clive diary, March 6, 1915, Sidney Clive papers; Wilson diary, March 5 and 6, 1915, Henry Wilson papers.

45. Joffre to Millerand, March 1, 1915; PRO 30/57/57, Lord Kitchener papers.

46. Millerand to Kitchener, March 2, 1915; PRO 30/57/57, Lord Kitchener papers.

47. Kitchener to Millerand, March 4, 1915; PRO 30/57/57, Lord Kitchener papers.

48. Kitchener to French, March 4, 1915; PRO 30/57/50, Lord Kitchener papers.

49. French to Kitchener, March 7, 1915; PRO 30/57/50, Lord Kitchener papers.

50. John Terraine, *Douglas Haig: The Educated Soldier* (London, 1963), 137.

51. See, for example, Clive diary, March 7, 1915, Sidney Clive papers.

52. The attack, originally set for March 7, was postponed until the 10th owing to the waterlogged state of the ground.

53. Joffre to French, March 7, 1915; WO 158/13, War Office archives.

54. French to Mrs. Bennett, March 8, 1915, John French papers.

55. French to Asquith, March 7, 1915; vol. 26, H. H. Asquith papers.

56. French to Mrs. Bennett, March 2 and 7, 1915, John French papers.

57. French diary, March 10, 1915, John French papers.

58. David French, "The Military Background to the 'Shell Crisis' of May 1915," *Journal of Strategic Studies* (September 1979): 199.

59. For the German viewpoint I have relied on G. C. Wynne, *If Germany Attacks* (Westport, Conn., 1976), chap. 1.

60. The account of the battle here is based on the following works: Edmonds, *France and Belgium, 1915,* 1: chaps. 6–7; Marshall-Cornwall, *Haig,* 141–45; Alan Clark, *The Donkeys* (New York, 1962), chaps. 3–4; Smyth, *Leadership in Battle, 1914–1918* (New York, 1976), chap. 4; Brig.-Gen. John Charteris, *Field Marshall Earl Haig* (London, 1929), 138–40; Arthur Conan Doyle, *The British Campaign in France and Flanders* (New York, 1917), 2: chap. 2; John Baynes, *Morale: A Study of Men and Courage* (London, 1967), chap. 2; Dominick Graham, "Sans Doctrine: British Army Tactics in the First World War," in *Men at War: Politics, Technology and Innovation*

in the Twentieth Century, ed. T. H. E. Travers and Christon Archer (Chicago, 1982), 79–80.

61. French to Brade, March 18, 1915; WO 32/5152, War Office archives.

62. David French, "Military Background," 200.

63. French to Mrs. Bennett, March 11, 13, and 16, 1915; French diary, March 16 and 17, 1915, John French papers.

64. Edmonds, *France and Belgium, 1915,* 2:13.

CHAPTER 11. ON TRIAL

1. Joffre to French, March 24, 1915; WO 158/13, War Office archives.

2. French to Mrs. Bennett, February 25, 1915, John French papers.

3. Ibid., May 18, 1915. See also Wilson diary, April 7, 1915, Henry Wilson papers.

4. French to Mrs. Bennett, June 10, 1915, John French papers.

5. Cassar, *Kitchener,* 324.

6. French diary, March 24, 1915, John French papers.

7. French to Joffre, March 24, 1915 (copy); PRO 30/57/77, Lord Kitchener papers; Wilson diary, March 24, 1915, Henry Wilson papers; Clive diary, March 25, 1915, Sidney Clive papers.

8. French diary, March 26, 1915, John French papers.

9. Wilson diary, March 28, 1915, Henry Wilson papers.

10. French diary, March 29, 1915, John French papers; Wilson Diary, March 29, 1915, Henry Wilson papers; Cassar, *Kitchener,* 325.

11. French diary, March 31, 1915, John French papers.

12. French to Joffre, April 1, 1915; WO 158/13, War Office archives.

13. My information for the Second Battle of Ypres has been gathered from Edmonds, *France and Belgium, 1915,* 1:chaps. 8–15; Buchan, *History of the Great War,* 2:46–55; Clark, *The Donkeys,* chaps. 5–6; *Les armées françaises dans la grande guerre,* tomes 2–3; B. H. Liddell Hart, *Foch:* chap. 12; Col. G. W. L. Nicholson, *Canadian Expeditionary Force, 1914–1919* (Ottawa, 1962), 61–88; Doyle, *The British Campaign* 2:chap. 3.

14. Arthur, *Life of Lord Kitchener,* 3:233.

15. French diary, April 27, 1915, John French papers.

16. See Ballard, *Smith-Dorrien,* 304–8, and Smithers, *The Man Who Disobeyed,* 254–58.

17. Haig diary, April 30, 1915, Douglas Haig papers.

18. See, for example, French diary, March 3, 14, 25, and 28, 1915, John French papers.

19. Wilson diary, April 26, 1915, Henry Wilson papers.

20. Smith-Dorrien to Wigram (king's assistant private secretary), November 6 and 9, 1914; GV Q 832/338/339, Royal archives.

21. Smith-Dorrien to Wigram, January 18, 1915; GV Q 832/348, Royal archives.

22. Cited in Ballard, *Smith-Dorrien,* 279.

23. *Les armées françaises dans la grande guerre,* tome 2, vol. 2, annexe 1466.

24. Wilson diary, April 28, 1915, Henry Wilson papers.

25. French to Mrs. Bennett, April 28, 1915, John French papers.

26. Edmonds, *France and Belgium, 1915,* 1:271–72.

27. French to Kitchener, May 2, 1915; PRO 30/57/50, Lord Kitchener papers.

28. David French, "Military Background," 196.

29. Great Britain, *History of the Ministry of Munitions* (London, 1922), vol. 1, pt. 1; Edmonds, *France and Belgium, 1915,* 1:chap. 3; Cassar, *Kitchener,* 331–38.

30. See French, *1914,* chap. 18.

31. Cassar, *Kitchener,* 333.

32. *Parliamentary Debates,* House of Lords (1915), 17:738.

33. Arthur, *Life of Lord Kitchener,* 3:74.

34. Kitchener to Asquith, April 14, 1915; vol. 14, H. H. Asquith papers.

35. French to Kitchener, April 29, 1915; WO 32/5155, War Office archives.

36. The letter is produced in its entirety in Arthur, *Life of Lord Kitchener*, 3:235–36.

37. French diary, May 2 and 7, 1915, John French papers.

38. French to Mrs. Bennett, May 8, 1915, John French papers.

39. For the battles of Aubers Ridge and Festubert see Edmonds, *France and Belgium, 1915*, 2:chaps. 1–3; Clark, *The Donkeys*, chaps. 7–8; Cooper, *Haig*, 1:chap. 11; Buchan, *History of the Great War*, 2:78–79; Doyle, *The British Campaign* 2:chap. 5.

40. Wynne, *If Germany Attacks*, 43–46.

CHAPTER 12. THE SHELLS CONTROVERSY

1. Ian Hamilton had been placed in charge of the land operations after the naval assault on March 18 failed.

2. Arthur, *Life of Lord Kitchener*, 3:238.

3. The French expended considerably more ammunition than the British, 176,000 rounds as opposed to 50,000, and did not fare much better in the joint attack.

4. French to Mrs. Bennett, May 9, 1915, John French papers. French noted that "the devils are very strong and their trenches bristle with machine-guns."

5. Lt.-Col. C. à Court Repington, *The First World War, 1914–1918* (New York, 1921), 1:21–22.

6. Northcliffe to French, May 1, 1915, vol. 7, Lord Northcliffe papers.

7. French, *1914*, 357.

8. Kitchener to Asquith, April 14, 1915, vol. 14, H. H. Asquith papers.

9. Stephen Koss, *Asquith* (London, 1976), 181.

10. Lord Beaverbrook, *Politicians and the War, 1914–1916* (London, 1960), 86.

11. Margot Asquith diary, May 19, 1915, Margot Asquith papers, Bodleian Library, Oxford.

12. Kitchener to French, May 14, 1915; PRO 30/57/50, Lord Kitchener papers.

13. In April Asquith, in an effort to put the relationship between the press and the government on a practical working foundation, agreed to allow six accredited correspondents to take up residence at General Headquarters. They crossed over in May but were never officially recognized by Kitchener.

14. French to Kitchener, May 15, 1915; PRO 30/57/50, Lord Kitchener papers.

15. On the May political crisis see Beaverbrook, *Politicans*, chap. 8; Blake, *The Unknown Prime Minister*, 241–57; Trevor Wilson, *The Decline of the Liberal Party, 1914–1935* (London, 1966), 53–64; Jenkins, *Asquith*, 359–66; Koss, *Asquith*, 181–86; as well as the accounts of those who were involved, such as Churchill, Asquith, Lloyd George, and Hankey.

16. French to Mrs. Bennett, May 21, 1915, John French papers.

17. French to Asquith, May 20, 1915, vol. 27, H. H. Asquith papers.

18. Repington, *The First World War*, 1:39.

19. Wigram to Haig, May 26, 1915. The letter is bound in Haig's diary; Selborne to Fitzgerald, May 21, 1915, B. Fitzgerald papers; Moore memoirs, George Moore papers.

20. Leslie Rundle to George Arthur, n.d.; PRO 30/57/93, George Arthur papers.

21. Cassar, *Kitchener*, 356–57.

22. The two men had only recently returned from London.

23. Wilson diary, May 20, 1915, Henry Wilson papers.

24. The coalition government assumed office on May 26. Churchill was ejected from the Admiralty and relegated to the sinecure post of the Duchy of Lancaster. Kitchener remained at the War Office but control of munitions was given to a new ministry under Lloyd George.

The principal Conservatives joined the cabinet with Balfour replacing Churchill as first lord of the Admiralty.

25. Esher War Journals, May 21, 1915, Viscount Esher papers.
26. Wilson diary, May 22, 1915, Henry Wilson papers.
27. Esher War Journals, May 22, 1915, Viscount Esher papers.
28. Ibid., May 14, 1915.
29. Esher to Kitchener, May 23, 1915; PRO 30/57/59, Lord Kitchener papers.
30. Esher to FitzGerald, May 23, 1915; PRO 30/57/59, Lord Kitchener papers.
31. Ibid., May 24, 1915.
32. Esher War Journals, May 25, 1915, Viscount Esher papers.

CHAPTER 13. LAST CHANCE

1. Edmonds, *France and Belgium, 1915,* 2:46.
2. Poincaré, *Au service de la France,* 6:239.
3. He was head of the British mission at G.Q.G.
4. Joffre to Kitchener, May 27, 1915; England, Box 59, *Archives de guerre.*
5. Private note (presumably written by Kitchener's military secretary, Herbert Creedy) to Yarde-Buller, May 29, 1915; Hankey to Asquith, discussing a conversation with Kitchener, May 29, 1915; WO 159/7, War Office archives.
6. Clive diary, May 26, 1915, Sidney Clive papers.
7. Wilson diary, June 2, 1915, Henry Wilson papers.
8. French to Kitchener, June 11, 1915; PRO 30/57/50, Lord Kitchener papers.
9. French to Foch, June 19, 1915; WO 158/26, War Office archives.
10. Cited in Marshall-Cornwall, *Haig,* 154.
11. Wynne, *If Germany Attacks,* 63–64.
12. French diary, June 23, 1915, John French papers.
13. Lord Kitchener, "An appreciation of the military situation in the future," June 26, 1915; CAB 37/130, Cabinet papers.
14. Reginald Viscount Esher, *The Tragedy of Lord Kitchener* (London, 1921), 138–39.
15. Esher War Journals, June 29, 1915, Viscount Esher papers.
16. J. A. Spender and Cyril Asquith, *Life of Herbert Henry Asquith, Lord Oxford and Asquith* (London, 1932), 2:182; Hankey, *The Supreme Command,* 1:343.
17. French diary, July 1, 1915, John French papers; Robertson to Kitchener, July 4, 1915, 1/13, W. Robertson papers; Kitchener to Cowans (Quartermaster-General), July 4, 1915; WO 159/11, War Office archives.
18. Sir Francis Bertie, Memorandum, July 7, 1915; FO 800/167, F. Bertie papers; Hankey diary, July 5, 1915, M.P. Hankey papers; Wilson diary, July 5, 1915, Henry Wilson papers; Esher War Journals, July 15, 1915, Viscount Esher papers.
19. Cassar, *Kitchener,* 380–82.
20. Report of the meeting; WO 159/11, War Office archives; Wilson diary, July 7, 1915, Henry Wilson papers.
21. Lord Stamfordham, Memorandum, July 9, 1915; GV Q 981/3, Royal archives. The memo drawn up for the king described the prime minister's visit to France.
22. See, for example, Haig diary, July 9, 1915, Douglas Haig papers.
23. French to Joffre, June 20, 1915; WO 158/13, War Office archives.
24. Report of the meeting; WO 158/26, War Office archives.
25. Wilson diary, July 27, 1915, Henry Wilson papers.
26. Ibid., July 28, 1915.
27. Clive diary, July 28, 1915, Sidney Clive papers.

28. French to Foch, July 29, 1915; WO 158/26; French to Joffre, July 29, 1915; WO 158/13, War Office archives.

29. Wilson diary, July 29, 1915, Henry Wilson papers.

30. Joffre to French, August 5, 1915; WO 158/13, War Office archives.

31. Haig diary, August 7, 1915, Douglas Haig papers.

32. Wilson diary, August 12, 1915, Henry Wilson papers.

33. Joffre to French, August 12, 1915; WO 158/13, War Office archives.

34. Wilson diary, August 14, 1915, Henry Wilson papers.

35. Ibid.

36. Yarde-Buller to Kitchener, July 24 and August 1, 1915; WO 159/11, War Office archives.

37. Cassar, *The French and the Dardanelles,* 173.

38. Haig diary, August 17, 1915, Douglas Haig papers.

39. Wilson diary, August 18, 1915, Henry Wilson papers.

40. Edmonds, *France and Belgium, 1915,* 2:129.

41. French to Kitchener, August 20, 1915; PRO 30/57/50, Lord Kitchener papers.

42. Ibid., October 26, 1915.

43. Edmonds, *France and Belgium, 1915,* 2:129.

44. French to Mrs. Bennett, September 18, 1915, John French papers.

45. Ibid., September 21, 1915.

46. Wilson diary, September 13, 1915, Henry Wilson papers.

47. Ibid., September 17, 1915; Clive also made note of the incident in his diary on September 20, 1915.

48. Wilson diary, September 20, 1915, Henry Wilson papers.

49. On the question of the general reserve see especially Brig.-Gen. Sir J. E. Edmonds, "The Reserves at Loos," *Journal of the Royal United Service Institution* 81 (1936); G. C. Wynne, "The Affair of the 21st and 24th Divisions at Loos, 26th September 1915," *The Fighting Forces* (1934).

50. Edmonds, *France and Belgium, 1915,* 2:274n.

51. Haig diary, September 20, 1915, Douglas Haig papers.

52. Charteris, *At G.H.Q.,* 113.

53. Haig diary, September 25, 1915, Douglas Haig papers.

54. For the battle of Loos I have used, in addition to Edmonds, *France and Belgium, 1915,* 2:chaps. 10–22, the following sources: Clark, *The Donkeys,* chaps. 11–12, Buchan, *History of The Great War,* 2:chap. 38. I did not find anything relevant in Philip Warner's *The Battle of Loos* (London, 1976). It is not a description of the battle, as the title suggests, but a collection of eyewitness accounts.

55. Edmonds, *France and Belgium, 1915,* 2:278.

56. Haig to Kitchener, September 20, 1915; PRO 30/57/53, Lord Kitchener papers; Blake, *The Private Papers of Douglas Haig,* 105.

CHAPTER 14. RECALL

1. See above, 270–71.

2. Kitchener to French, October 6, 1915; PRO 30/57/50, Lord Kitchener papers.

3. French to Kitchener, October 9, 1915; PRO 30/57/50, Lord Kitchener papers.

4. Wilson diary, September 26, 1915, Henry Wilson papers.

5. Blake, *The Private Papers of Douglas Haig,* 108–9.

6. Ibid., 107.

7. French diary, October 9, 1915, John French papers.

8. Asquith to Selbourne, October 26, 1915; MS. 80, Lord Selborne papers, Bodleian Library, Oxford.

9. The king, through Stamfordham, was in regular contact with such high-ranking officers as Haig, Robertson, and Smith-Dorrien.

10. King diary, October 24, 1915, Royal archives.

11. Ibid.

12. Haig diary, October 24, 1915, Douglas Haig papers. See also Nicolson, *King George,* 267.

13. French to Mrs. Bennett, October 29, 1915, John French papers.

14. Robertson to Haig, October 16, 1915; WO 158/266, War Office archives.

15. Haig to French, October 21, 1915; WO 158/266, War Office archives.

16. *The Times,* November 2, 1915. A copy of the article can also be found in Haig's papers.

17. Haig to French, November 4, 1915; WO 158/267, War Office archives.

18. Haig to Robb, November 7, 1915, F. Robb papers.

19. Robertson to Haig, November 8, 1915; WO 158/267, War Office archives.

20. Ibid., WO 158/236.

21. Haig to French, November 9, 1915; WO 158/267, War Office archives.

22. Blake, *The Private Papers of Douglas Haig,* 112.

23. *Parliamentary Debates,* House of Lords (1915), 2:368.

24. Esher War Journals, November 14, 1915, Viscount Esher papers; Fitzgerald diary, November 11–13, 1915, B. Fitzgerald papers.

25. Wilson diary, November 14, 1915, Henry Wilson papers.

26. Nickname for Asquith.

27. Wilson diary, November 15, 1915, Henry Wilson papers.

28. Fitzgerald diary, November 16–18, 1915, B. Fitzgerald papers.

29. Wilson diary, November 18, 1915, Henry Wilson papers.

30. Esher War Journals, November 23–24, 1915, Viscount Esher papers.

31. Ibid., November 25–26, 1915; Fitzgerald diary, November 25–26, 1915, B. Fitzgerald papers.

32. Esher to Asquith, November 26, 1915, vol. 28, H. H. Asquith papers.

33. Ibid., November 27, 1915.

34. Fitzgerald diary, November 27, 1915, B. Fitzgerald papers.

35. Ibid., November 28, 1915; Wilson diary, December 4, 1915, Henry Wilson papers.

36. French to Asquith, November 29, 1915, vol. 28, H. H. Asquith papers.

37. Fitzgerald diary, November 28, 1915, B. Fitzgerald papers; Esher War Journals, December 3, 1915, Viscount Esher papers.

38. Fitzgerald diary, November 30–December 2, 1915, B. Fitzgerald papers.

39. French to Asquith, December 2, 1915, vol. 28, H. H. Asquith papers.

40. Stamfordham to Asquith, December 2, 1915; Asquith to Stamfordham, December 3, 1915; GV Q 838/47/48, Royal archives.

41. Fitzgerald diary, December 4, 1915, B. Fitzgerald papers.

42. French to Asquith, December 4, 1915, vol. 28, H. H. Asquith papers.

43. Cited in E. G. French, *Sir John French,* 334.

44. French diary, December 19–20, 1915, John French papers.

45. Huguet, *L'intervention militaire britannique,* 180.

46. Fitzgerald diary, December 21, 1915, B. Fitzgerald papers.

EPILOGUE

1. Fortescue, "Horace Smith-Dorien," 857.

2. Esher to Stamfordham, June 28, 1919; GV O 1470/15, Royal archives.

3. Ireland had been exempt from conscription when it was introduced in England in the

first part of 1916. The desperate search for more recruits, as a reaction to the German onslaught in 1918, was a major consideration in extending the system to Ireland.

4. He succeeded Asquith as prime minister in December 1916.

5. E. G. French, *Sir John French*, chap. 53.

6. See for example Repington, *The First World War*, 1:192; Field Marshal Sir William Robertson, *Soldiers and Statesman, 1914–1918* (London, 1926), 1:71; Childs, *Episodes and Reflections*, 135.

Bibliography

1. MANUSCRIPT COLLECTIONS

Archives de guerre, Vincennes, Paris. Most of the military correspondence relating to the English can be found in the England *(Angleterre)* series.

Archives diplomatique, Quai d'Orsay, Paris. Some of the more sensitive documents for the period 1914–15 were removed, presumably by Delcassé. If that is the case, they cannot be found in his own collection, most of which was destroyed prior to his death.

George Arthur papers, Public Record Office, London.

H. H. Asquith (Oxford and Asquith) papers, Bodleian Library, Oxford.

Margot Asquith papers—1914–1915 diary and some correspondence, Bodleian Library, Oxford.

Francis Bertie papers, Public Record Office, London.

Cabinet papers, Public Record Office, London.

Sidney Clive papers, King's College Library, London.

Herbert Creedy papers, Public Record Office, London.

James Edmonds papers, King's College Library, London.

Viscount Esher papers. The papers have been withdrawn from the Churchill College Library, Cambridge, and are now held by Professor Michael Howard, pending completion of his biography on Esher. Professor Howard was kind enough to place the relevant part of the collection at my disposal.

B. Fitzgerald papers, Imperial War Museum, London.

John French papers, Imperial War Museum, London. These include his personal correspondence, his war diaries, as well as his letters to Mrs. Bennett.

D. Lloyd George papers, House of Lords Office, London.

E. Grey papers, Public Record Office, London.

Douglas Haig papers, National Library of Scotland, Edinburgh.

Ian Hamilton papers, King's College Library, London.

M. P. Hankey papers, Churchill College Library, Cambridge.

Lord Kitchener papers, Public Record Office, London.

A. Bonar Law papers, House of Lords Office, London.

Walter Long papers, Wiltshire County Record Office.

Frederick Maurice papers, King's College Library, London.

Venetia Stanley Montagu papers, private possession.

George Moore papers, private possession.

Archibald Murray papers, Imperial War Museum, London.

Lord Northcliffe papers, British Museum, London.

J. A. Pease (Gainford) papers, Nuffield College Library, Oxford.

H. Rawlinson papers, Churchill College Library, Cambridge.

F. Robb papers, private possession.

W. Robertson papers, King's College Library, London.

Royal archives, Windsor Castle.

Lord Selborne papers, Bodleian Library, Oxford.

H. Smith-Dorrien papers, Imperial War Museum, London.

The Times archives, London.

War Office archives, Public Record Office, London.

Henry Wilson papers, Imperial War Museum, London.

The papers of the Duke of Windsor were inaccessible at the time of writing. The papers of Repington, Guy Brooke, and Freddy Guest apparently have not survived. I was unable to determine whether William Lambton left any papers, since the current Lord Lambton would not reply to my queries.

2. PUBLISHED GOVERNMENT SOURCES AND OFFICIAL HISTORIES

Biddulph, Colonel John. *The Nineteenth and Their Times.* London: Murray, 1899.

Colvile, Colonel H. E. *History of the Sudan Campaign.* Part 2. London: HMSO, 1889.

Corbett, Sir Julian S. *Naval Operations.* Vol. 1. London: Longmans and Green, 1920.

Edmonds, Brigadier-General Sir James E. *Military Operations: France and Belgium.* Vols. 1 & 2 for 1914 and 1915. London: Macmillan, 1922–28.

France, Ministère de la guerre, Etat Major de l'armée. Service historique. *Les armées françaises dans la grande guerre.* Tomes 1–3 and accompanying volumes (annexes). Paris: Imprimerie Nationale, 1923–33.

German General Staff. *The War in South Africa.* Translated by Colonel W. H. H. Waters. Vols. 1 & 2. London: Murray, 1904–6.

———. *Ypres, 1914.* London: Constable, 1919.

Great Britain. *Royal Commission on the War in South Africa.* Vols. 1 & 2. London: HMSO, 1903.

Maurice, Major-General Sir Frederick, and Grant, Captain Maurice Harold. *A History of the War in South Africa, 1899–1902.* Vols. 1–4. London: Hurst and Blackett, 1906–10.

Nicholson, Colonel G. W. L. *Canadian Expeditionary Force.* Ottawa: Queen's Printer, 1962.

Parliamentary Debates, House of Commons and House of Lords.

Pease, Howard. *The History of the Northumberland (Hussars) Yeomanry, 1819–1919.* London: Constable, 1924.

Yardley, Lieutenant-Colonel J. W. *With the Inniskilling Dragoons.* London: Longmans and Green, 1904.

3. PRIMARY AND SECONDARY WORKS

Amery, L. S., ed. *The Times History of the War in South Africa, 1899–1902.* Vols. 2–5. London: Low and Marston, 1902–7.

Arthur, Sir George. *Life of Lord Kitchener.* Vol. 3. London: Macmillan, 1920.

———. *Not Worth Reading.* London: Longmans and Green, 1938.

Ash, Bernard. *The Lost Dictator.* London: Cassell, 1968.

Asquith, H. H. *Memories and Reflections, 1852–1927.* Vol. 2. London: Cassell, 1928.

Ballard, Brigadier-General C. R. *Smith-Dorrien.* London: Constable, 1931.

Baynes, John. *Morale: A Study of Men and Courage.* London: Cassell, 1967.

Beaverbrook, Lord. *Politicians and the War, 1914–1916.* London: Oldbourne, 1960.

Belfield, Eversley. *The Boer War.* Hamden: Archon, 1975.

Beresford, Admiral Lord Charles. *Memoirs.* Boston: Little and Brown, 1914.

Blake, Robert, ed. *The Private Papers of Douglas Haig.* London: Eyre and Spottiswoode, 1952.

———. *The Unknown Prime Minister.* London: Eyre and Spottiswoode, 1955.

Blond, Georges. *The Marne.* Translated by H. Eaton Hart. London: Macdonald, 1965.

Bond, Brian. *The Victorian Army and the Staff College, 1854–1914.* London: Eyre Methuen, 1972.

Bonham-Carter, Victor. *Soldier True: The Life and Times of Field Marshal Sir William Robertson.* London: Muller, 1963.

Bridges, General Sir Tom. *Alarms and Excursions.* London: Longmans and Green, 1938.

Buchan, John. *History of the Great War.* Vols. 1–2. Boston: Houghton Mifflin, 1922.

Bülow, Karl von. *Mon Rapport sur la Bataille de la Marne.* Translated by J. Netter. Paris: Payot, 1920.

Burleigh, Bennet. *The Natal Campaign.* London: Chapman and Hall, 1900.

Callwell, Major-General Sir C. E. *Experiences of a Dug-Out, 1914–1918.* London: Constable, 1920.

———. *Field Marshal Sir Henry Wilson.* Vol. 1. London: Cassell, 1927.

Cassar, George H. *The French and the Dardanelles: A Study of Failure in the Conduct of War.* London: Allen and Unwin, 1971.

———. *Kitchener: Architect of Victory.* London: Kimber, 1977.

Charteris, Brigadier-General John. *At G.H.Q.* London: Cassell, 1931.

———. *Field Marshal Earl Haig.* London: Cassell, 1929.

Childers, Erskine. *War and the Arme Blanche.* New York: Longmans and Green, n.d.

Childs, Major-General Sir Wyndam. *Episodes and Reflections*. London: Cassell, 1930.

Chisholm, Cecil. *Sir John French*. New York: Stokes. 1914.

Churchill, Winston S. *Great Contemporaries*. 1937. Reprint. Freeport: Libraries Press, 1971.

————. *The World Crisis*. Vols. 1–2. New York: Scribner, 1951.

Clark, Alan. *The Donkeys*. New York: Morrow, 1962.

Coleman, Frederick. *From Mons to Ypres with General French*. New York: Dodd and Mead, 1916.

Collier, Basil. *Brasshat: A Biography of Field Marshal Sir Henry Wilson*. London: Secker and Warburg, 1961.

Cooper, Diana. *The Rainbow Comes and Goes*. Boston: Houghton Mifflin, 1958.

Cooper, Duff. *Haig*. Vol. 1. London: Faber, 1935.

Corbett-Smith. A. *The Marne—and After*. London: Cassell, 1917.

————. *The Retreat from Mons*. London: Cassell, 1916.

Craig, Gordon A. *The Politics of the Prussian Army, 1640–1945*. Oxford: At the University Press, 1956.

Dangerfield, George. *The Damnable Question*. Boston: Little and Brown, 1976.

David, Edward, ed. *Inside Asquith's Cabinet: From the Diaries of Charles Hobhouse*. London: Murray, 1977.

D'Ombrain, Nicholas J. "The Evolution of British Defence Strategy, 1904–1914." M.A. thesis, McGill University, 1965.

————. *War Machinery and High Policy*. London: Oxford University, 1973.

Doyle, Arthur Conan. *The British Campaign in France and Flanders*. Vols. 1–2. New York: Doran, 1917.

Durand, Sir Mortimer. *The Life of Field Marshal Sir George White, V.C.* Vol. 2. London: Blackwood, 1915.

Earle, Edward Mead, ed. *Makers of Modern Strategy*. Princeton, N.J.: Princeton University Press, 1952.

Esher, Reginald Viscount. *The Tragedy of Lord Kitchener*. London: Murray, 1921.

Farrar-Hockley, Anthony. *Death of An Army*. London: Tinling, 1967.

————. *Goughie*. London: Hart-Davis and MacGibbon, 1975.

Farwell, Byron. *The Great Anglo-Boer War*. New York: Harper and Row, 1976.

Fergusson, Sir James. *The Curragh Incident*. London: Faber, 1964.

Foch, Maréchal. *Mémoires*. Vol. 1. Paris: Plon, 1931.

French E. G. *The Life of Field Marshal Sir John French*. London: Cassell, 1931.

————. *Some War Diaries, Addresses, and Correspondence of Field Marshal the Right Honourable the Earl of Ypres*. London: Jenkins, 1937.

French of Ypres, Viscount. *The Despatches of Lord French*. London: Chapman and Hall, 1917.

————. *1914*. London: Constable, 1919.

Galliéni, Général J. *Mémoires: Défense du Paris, 25 août–11 septembre, 1914*. Paris: Payot, 1920.

Gilbert, Martin. *Winston S. Churchill*. Vol. 3. London: Houghton Mifflin, 1971. Also the *Companion* series to this volume, 1972.

Goldmann, Charles Sydney. *With General French and the Cavalry in South Africa.* London: Macmillan, 1902.

Gooch, John. *The Plans of War.* New York: Wiley, 1974.

Gorce, Paul Marie de la. *The French Army.* New York: Braziller, 1963.

Goerlitz, Walter. *History of the German General Staff 1657–1945.* New York: Praeger, 1956.

Gough, General Sir Hubert. *Soldiering On.* London: Barker, 1954.

Grasset, Colonel A. *La bataille des deux Morins: Franchet d'Esperey à la Marne, 6–9 septembre, 1914.* Paris: Payot, 1934.

Green, Lieutenant-Colonel Howard. *The British Army in the First World War.* London: Clowes, 1968.

Grey of Fallodon, Viscount. *Twenty-Five Years.* Vol. 2. New York: Stokes, 1925.

Haldane, Viscount R. B. *Before the War.* London: Funk and Wagnalls, 1920.

Hamilton, Ernest W. *The First Seven Division.* London: Hurst and Blackett, 1916.

Hancock, W. K. *Smuts: The Sanguine Years, 1870–1919.* Vol. 1. London: Cambridge University Press, 1962.

Hankey, Lord. *The Supreme Command, 1914–1918.* Vol. 1. London: Allen and Unwin, 1961.

Holmes, Richard. *The Little Field Marshal.* London: Cape, 1981.

Huguet, Général. *L'intervention militaire britannique en 1914.* Paris: Berger-Levrault, 1928.

Isselin, Henry. *The Battle of the Marne.* Translated by Charles Connell. London: Elek, 1965.

James, David. *Lord Roberts.* London: Hollis and Carter, 1954.

Jenkins, Roy. *Asquith.* New York: Chilmark, 1964.

Jerrold, Walter. *Field Marshal Sir John French.* London: Hammond, 1915.

Joffre, Field Marshal Joseph. *Personal Memoirs.* Translated by Colonel T. Bentley Mott. Vols. 1–2. London: Harper, 1932.

Kennedy, Paul M., ed. *The War Plans of the Great Powers, 1880–1914.* London: Allen and Unwin, 1979.

Kluck, Alexander von. *The March on Paris and the Battle of the Marne, 1914.* London: Arnold, 1920.

Koss, Stephen. *Asquith.* London: Lane, 1976.

Kruger, Rayne. *Good-bye Dolly Gray.* London: Cassell, 1959.

Lanrezac, Général. *Le plan de campagne français et le premier mois de la guerre.* Paris: Payot, 1929.

L'Etang, Hugh. *The Pathology of Leadership.* London: Heinemann, 1969.

Liddell Hart, B. H. *Foch: The Man of Orléans.* Little and Brown, 1932.

———. *History of the First World War.* London: Pan Books, 1972.

———. *Reputations: Ten Years After.* Freeport, N.Y.: Libraries Press, 1968.

Linklater, Andro. *An Unhusbanded Life.* London: Hutchinson, 1980.

Luvaas, Jay. *The Education of an Army: British Military Thought, 1815–1940.* Chicago: University of Chicago Press, 1964.

———. *The Military Legacy of the Civil War.* Chicago: University of Chicago Press, 1959.

Lyon, Laurance. *The Pomp of Power.* New York: Doran, 1922.

Macready, General Sir Nevil. *Annals of an Active Life.* Vol. 1. London: Hutchinson, 1924.

Marshall-Cornwall, General Sir James. *Foch.* New York: Crane and Russak, 1972.

———. *Haig.* New York: Crane and Russak, 1973.

Maurice, Major-General Sir Frederick. *Forty Days in 1914.* London: Constable, 1919.

———. *The Life of General Lord Rawlinson of Trent.* London: Cassell, 1928.

Maydon, J. G. *French's Cavalry Campaign.* London: Pearson, 1901.

Meintjes, Johannes, *De la Rey—Lion of the West.* Johannesburg: Keartland, 1966.

———. *General Louis Botha.* London: Cassell, 1970.

Messimy, Général Adolphe. *Mes Souveniers.* Paris: Plon, 1937.

Muller, Commandant Louis Edouard. *Joffre et le Marne.* Paris: Crès, 1931.

Nicolson, Harold. *King George the Fifth.* London: Constable, 1952.

Pakenham, Thomas. *The Boer War.* New York: Random House, 1979.

Perris, Charles Herbert. *The Battle of the Marne.* London: Methuen, 1920.

Poincaré, Raymond. *Au service de la France.* Vols. 5–6. Paris: Plon-Nourrit, 1928.

Repington, Lieutenant-Colonel C. à Court. *The First World War.* Vol. 1. New York: Houghton Mifflin, 1921.

Ritter, Gerhard. *The Schlieffen Plan.* London: Wolf, 1958.

Robertson, Field Marshal Sir William. *From Private to Field Marshal.* Boston: Houghton Mifflin, 1921.

———. *Soldiers and Statesmen, 1914–1918.* Vol. 1. London: Cassell, 1926.

Ryan A. P. *Mutiny at the Curragh.* London: Macmillan, 1956.

Sampson, Victor and Hamilton, Ian. *Anti-Commando.* London: Faber, 1931.

Seely, the Rt. Hon. J. E. B. *Adventure.* New York: Stokes, 1930.

Selby, John. *The Boer War.* London: Barker, 1969.

Sixsmith, E. K. G. *Douglas Haig.* London: Weidenfeld and Nicolson, 1976.

Smith-Dorrien, General Sir Horace. *Memories of Forty-Eight Years' Service.* New York: Dutton, 1925.

Smithers, A. J. *The Man Who Disobeyed.* London: Cooper, 1970.

Smuts, J. C. *Jan Christian Smuts.* New York: Morrow, 1952.

Smyth, Sir John. *Leadership in Battle, 1914–1918.* New York: Hippocrene Books, 1976.

Spears, Major-General Sir Edward. *Liaison 1914.* New York: Stein and Day, 1968.

Spender, J. A., and Asquith, Cyril. *Life of Herbert Henry Asquith, Lord Oxford and Asquith.* Vol. 2. London: Hutchinson, 1932.

Steevens, G. W. *From Capetown to Ladysmith.* New York: Dodd and Mead, 1900.

Symons, Julian. *Buller's Campaign.* London: Cresset, 1963.

Taylor, A. J. P. *English History, 1914–1945.* Oxford: At the University Press, 1965.

Terraine, John. *Douglas Haig: The Educated Soldier*. London: Hutchinson, 1963.

———. *Mons*. New York: Macmillan, 1960.

Tuchman, Barbara W. *The Guns of August*. New York: Macmillan, 1962.

Tyler, J. E. *The British Army and the Continent, 1904–1914*. London: Arnold, 1938.

Tyng, Sewell. *The Campaign of the Marne*. New York: Longmans, 1935.

Williamson, Samuel R. *The Politics of Grand Strategy*. Cambridge, Mass.: Harvard University Press, 1969.

Wilson, Sir Charles. *From Korti to Khartum*. London: Blackwood, 1886.

Wilson, Trevor. *The Decline of the Liberal Party, 1914–1935*. London: Collins, 1966.

Windsor, the Duke of. *A King's Story*. New York: Putnam, 1951.

Wood, Sir Evelyn. *From Midshipman to Field Marshal*. Vol. 2. London: Methuen, 1906.

Wynne, G. C. *If Germany Attacks*. Westport, Conn.: Greenwood Press, 1976.

4. SERIAL PUBLICATIONS

Daily Chronicle

Daily Express

Daily Mail

Daily News

Daily Telegraph

Evening Standard

Globe

Morning Post

New Statesman

Observer

Pall Mall Gazette

Spectator

The Times

Westminster Gazette

World

5. ARTICLES AND PREFACES

Battine, Cecil. "1914: Lord French's Narrative." *Fortnightly Review* 112 (1919): 25–35.

Blake, Martin J. "Field Marshal Sir John French." *Journal of the Galway Archaeological and Historical Society* 8 (n.d.).

Bond, Brian. "Doctrine and Training in the British Cavalry." In Michael Howard, ed., *The Theory and Practice of War*. London: Cassell, 1965.

Boyle, Captain Cecil. "The Cavalry Rush to Kimberley and in Pursuit of Cronje." *Nineteenth Century* 47 (1900): 899–915.

Edmonds, Brigadier-General Sir James E. "The Reserves at Loos." *Journal of the Royal United Service Institution* 81 (1936): 33–39.

Fortescue, J. W. "Horace Smith-Dorrien." *Blackwood's Magazine* 229 (1931): 839–63.

———. "1914." *Quarterly Review* 232 (1910): 352–63.

French, David. "The Military Background to the 'Shell Crisis' of May 1915." *Journal of Strategic Studies* 2 (September 1979): 192–205.

French, Sir John. Introduction to General F. von Bernhardi, *Cavalry in Future Wars.* Translated by Charles Sydney Goldmann. London: Murray, 1906.

———. Preface to General F. von Bernhardi, *Cavalry in War and Peace.* Translated by Major G. T. M. Bridges. London: Rees, 1910.

Graham, Dominick. "*Sans Doctrine:* British Army Tactics in the First World War." In *Men at War: Politics, Technology and Innovation in the Twentieth Century.* Edited by T. H. E. Travers and Christon Archer. Chicago: Precedent Press, 1982.

Hildebrand, Brigadier-General A. "Recollections of Sir Horace Smith-Dorrien at Le Cateau, August 1914." *Army Quarterly* 21 (1930–31): 15–19.

Maurice, Major-General Sir Frederick. "The 'Unnecessary' Battle of Le Cateau." *National Review* 74 (1919–20): 324–39.

Miller, Roger. "The Logistics of the British Expeditionary Force, 4 August to 5 September 1914," *Military Affairs,* 43 (1979): 133–37.

Spiers, Edward M. "The British Cavalry, 1902–1914." *Journal of the Society for Army Historical Research* 57 (1979): 71–79.

Travers, T. H. E. "The Offensive and the Problem of Innovation in British Military Thought, 1870–1915," *Journal of Contemporary History* 13 (1978): 531–53.

———. "Technology, Tactics and Morale; Jean de Bloch, the Boer War and British Military Thought, 1900–1914." *Journal of Modern History* 51 (1979): 264–86.

Williams, Valentine. "The General: An Appreciation." Preface in E. G. French *French Replies to Haig.* London: Hutchinson, 1936.

Wynne, G. C. "The Affair of the 21st and 24th Divisions at Loos, 26th September 1915." *The Fighting Forces* 11 (1934): 30–38.

Index